Mediating Misogyny

Jacqueline Ryan Vickery
Tracy Everbach
Editors

Mediating Misogyny

Gender, Technology, and Harassment

Editors
Jacqueline Ryan Vickery
Department of Media Arts
University of North Texas
Denton, TX, USA

Tracy Everbach
Mayborn School of Journalism
University of North Texas
Denton, TX, USA

ISBN 978-3-319-72916-9   ISBN 978-3-319-72917-6   (eBook)
https://doi.org/10.1007/978-3-319-72917-6

Library of Congress Control Number: 2017964596

Cover credit: Andy_Di/iStock/Getty Images Plus
Cover design by Henry Petrides

Printed on acid-free paper

This Palgrave Macmillan imprint is published by Springer Nature
The registered company is Springer International Publishing AG
The registered company address is: Gewerbestrasse 11, 6330 Cham, Switzerland

We dedicate this book to all the Nasty Women who bravely fight for a safe and equitable world

"She was warned.
She was given an explanation.
Nevertheless, she persisted."

Senate Majority Leader Mitch McConnell's
response to Sen. Elizabeth Warren when she refused
to stop addressing the Senate on February 7, 2017

Acknowledgements

We are grateful to the generations of feminists who came before us, setting the stage for today's activism and resistance to misogyny. We encourage our feminist peers and the feminists who follow to continue this work until we finally achieve an equitable society. Women are strong, talented, and powerful and their contributions to society must be acknowledged, cultivated, and supported. We hope our successors will someday live in a world without fear, discrimination, abuse, and harassment.

Jacqueline Ryan Vickery would like to thank her powerful feminist mentors and friends who continue to shape her scholarship, activism, and pedagogy. You provide the much-needed friendship, strength, righteous anger, wisdom, and laughter that we all need to continue the fight for equality: Megan Janicke, Jen Millspaugh Gray, Shaylynn Lynch Lesinski, Hilary Hawkins Clay, Candice Haddad, Samantha Langsdale, Jessalynn Keller, Mary Celeste Kearney, Shani Barrax Moore, Ricky Hill, Meredith Hinton, Joy Denman Baldwin, and many more. She would also like thank her parents, Michael and Deb Vickery, for enabling her to always stand up for what is right. And to her husband, Joshua Vickery, for his continued support of her goals, strength, and convictions.

Tracy Everbach would like to thank her parents, Nancy and George Everbach, for instilling in her the importance of education and of social justice. She also would like to acknowledge all the women (and a few men) who inspired her and supported her careers in two male-dominated industries – journalism and academia. And for his patience, kindness, and love, she thanks her spouse, Jake Batsell, a man who proudly embraces his own feminism.

Contents

Notes on Contributors

Lindsay Blackwell is a PhD candidate at the University of Michigan's School of Information and a former fellow of the Institute for Research on Women and Gender. Blackwell is a member of the university's Social Media Research Lab, where she researches the motivations of users who engage in online harassment. In particular, Blackwell is interested in the use of online harassment to sanction or punish behavior perceived as inappropriate, such as the public shaming of public relations executive Justine Sacco in 2013 or the 2016 doxxing of Roosh V., a notorious men's rights activist. Blackwell draws from theories of social deviance and criminal justice to better understand why every day people participate in harassing behaviors online, and she plays an active role in supporting people who are experiencing online harassment.

Katie Blevins received her PhD from the Pennsylvania State University. Prior to arriving at the University of Idaho, she spent four years as a visiting assistant professor of communications at Trinity University in San Antonio, Texas. Her teaching focuses on media law, issues of gender and representation, and other critical/cultural areas of interest. Her research looks at news coverage of legal issues that impact women, freedom of information, and social media.

Megan Lindsay Brown is currently a postdoctoral fellow advised by Jill Messing at Arizona State University. During her doctoral studies, Brown's research focused on the use of information communication technologies (ICT) and the impact of mediated spaces on human development, specifically young women. Her work has examined young adult dating relationships, online harassment, interventions using ICT, and the ways ICT interaction impacts individuals' perceptions during development. Currently, her research is focused on the ways online safety planning can support women in domestic violence shelters.

Sara Champlin is an assistant professor in the Mayborn School of Journalism at the University of North Texas. She received her PhD in advertising from the University of Texas at Austin. Her research focuses on using strategic communication campaigns to promote beneficial health outcomes. She is specifically interested in health literacy – a person's abilities to find, understand, use, and communicate about health information. Within this context she is interested in the emergence of risky behaviors and ways in which communication around these issues can be promoted. Similarly, she aims to determine the factors that impact health information-seeking.

Gina Masullo Chen is an assistant professor in the School of Journalism and a faculty research associate with the Engaging News Project, both at The University of Texas at Austin. She spent twenty years as a newspaper reporter and editor before becoming an academic. Her research focuses on the online conversation around the news, with a particular interest in both uncivil debate and how gender intersects in this process. She is co-editor of *Scandal in a Digital Age* (Palgrave Macmillan, 2016) and author of *Online Incivility and Public Debate: Nasty Talk* (Palgrave Macmillan, 2017). Her research has been published in academic journals, including *Communication Research, Computers in Human Behavior, Mass Communication and Society, Journalism Practice, New Media & Society, and Newspaper Research Journal.*

William Cox is a doctoral student in the Department of Communication Studies at the University of Texas at Austin. His research focuses on rhetoric and rhetorical criticism.

Karen Desborough is a PhD candidate in the School of Sociology, Politics and International Studies (SPAIS) at the University of Bristol, UK. Her research examines the emergence, development, and impact of the global anti-street harassment movement, focusing on the role of new digital technologies in enabling the movement's formation and expansion. In addition, she investigates the mobilizing motivations of anti-harassment activists, and the challenges and constraints they face and overcome. Finally, her research evaluates the impact of the movement on resisting street harassment and realizing transformations in gender relations.

Amanda Nell Edgar is an assistant professor in the Department of Communication at the University of Memphis. Edgar's research explores the entanglement of sound and identity in popular culture. Specifically, she is interested in how sonic texts meet their audiences to shape both listener identity and the political culture surrounding issues of race and gender. Her work has appeared in *Women's Studies in Communication, Critical Studies in Media Communication, Communication and Critical/Cultural Studies,* and other journals, and has been featured on the National Communication Association's *Communication Currents.*

Tracy Everbach is an associate professor of journalism in the Mayborn School of Journalism at the University of North Texas. She teaches undergraduate and graduate classes on race, gender and media, news reporting, mass communication theories, and qualitative research methods. Her research focuses on women's work and leadership in journalism, and on representations of race and gender in media. Her work has been published in *Journalism & Mass Communication Quarterly, Newspaper Research Journal, Journal of Sports Media, Media Report to Women, Columbia Journalism Review,* and *American Journalism.* She received her PhD in journalism from the University of Missouri-Columbia. She worked as a newspaper reporter for 14 years, including 12 years at *The Dallas Morning News.*

Michelle Ferrier is the founder of Troll-Busters.com: Online Pest Control for Women Writers. She is an entrepreneur, professor, and speaker around media innovation and digital culture. As an associate professor at the E.W. Scripps School of Journalism at Ohio University, Ferrier directs the Media Deserts Project that uses geographic information systems to map the media ecosystem in the United States. With a research focus on media entrepreneurship, digital identity, social media, and online communities, Ferrier has developed experiential learning and curriculum for higher education around media innovation and entrepreneurship.

Maxwell Foxman is a PhD candidate in communications at Columbia University, where he studies the playful experience of early adopters of digital communications technology with a focus on virtual reality developers. Foxman's previous work primarily surrounded the use of games and play in non-game environments, including politics, social media, and, most recently, the news. Before beginning his PhD, Foxman spent five years in secondary school education, where he founded an independent study program.

Mary Anne Franks is a professor of law at the University of Miami School of Law, where she teaches First Amendment law, criminal law and procedure, family law, and a course on law and technology. She is also the vice-president and legislative & tech policy director of the Cyber Civil Rights Initiative, a nonprofit organization dedicated to combating online abuse. She is an expert on the intersection between privacy, civil rights, technology, and constitutional law and frequently advises legislators and technology industry leaders on these issues. She is the author of the forthcoming book *The Constitutional Cult: Extremism in American Law and Politics* (2018), in addition to numerous scholarly and popular press articles. Professor Franks holds a J.D. from Harvard Law School and doctorate and master's degrees from Oxford University, where she studied as a Rhodes Scholar.

Barbara Friedman is an associate professor at the School of Media and Journalism at the University of North Carolina. Her work emphasizes constructions and contestations of gender, race, and class in historical and contemporary mass media. Currently, her work focuses on media and sexual violence. She is co-director of The Irina Project (TIP), which monitors media representations of sex trafficking and advocates for the responsible and accurate reporting of the issue. She earned her PhD from the University of Missouri-Columbia. Before entering academia, Friedman spent 16 years reporting news and features for metro dailies, community weeklies, and magazines.

Nisha Garud-Patkar is an assistant professor at San Jose State University. Her research interests include digital media, conflict and terrorism, and international communication. She has seven years of newspaper experience, working as a reporter, features writer, and an editor at various English dailies in India, including *Daily News and Analysis* and *The Times of India*. She has also worked as a visiting faculty at the Department of Journalism and Mass Communication, University of Pune, India. She holds a Master of Science in journalism and mass communication from E.W. Scripps School of Journalism at Ohio University in Athens, Ohio.

Sheila Gibbons is the editor of *Media Report to Women* (www.mediareporttowomen.com), the quarterly newsletter that publishes research, news, and commentary about gender and media. She is the co-author of *Taking Their Place: A Documentary History of Women and Journalism* and *Exploring Mass Media for a Changing World*. She has been a journalist and public relations executive for several organizations, including Gannett Co., Inc., a member of the journalism faculty at the University of Maryland, and has more recently been active as a freelance writer/editor and a communications consultant.

Tarleton Gillespie is a principal researcher at Microsoft Research, New England, as a member of the Social Media Collective. He is also an affiliated associate professor in the Department of Communication and the Department of Information Science at Cornell University. Gillespie's research focuses on the ongoing controversies surrounding digital media and commercial providers. His work examines the implications of online media platforms as the new distributors of cultural and political discourse, and the mediating role played by algorithms for public knowledge and discourse. His forthcoming book will examine how content guidelines imposed by social media platforms set the terms for what counts as "appropriate" user contributions, and ask how this private governance of cultural values has broader implications for freedom of expression and public discourse. He received his PhD in communication from the University of California, San Diego.

Lucy Hackworth is an emerging feminist scholar in the field of online harassment, with a background in anthropology and queer/feminist community development. She obtained an Erasmus Mundus Master's Degree in Women's and Gender Studies from the Central European University and the University of Utrecht, during which she completed an investigative thesis into the profiles and behavior patterns of users who attack women online. Hackworth has previously published in the area of ICT use and social adaptation to climate change. She has since been involved in an Australian national working group to address online harassment. Hackworth is currently based in Adelaide, where she works in the field of violence prevention.

Dustin Harp is an assistant professor in the Department of Communication and an affiliated faculty member of the Women's and Gender Studies Program at the University of Texas at Arlington. Her research explores intersections between women and marginalized communities, journalism, and mass communication, with a specific interest in new media technologies and social media. From a critical and feminist perspective, she primarily considers how groups are represented in mediated discourses and ways in which they have been situated as producers of news and knowledge, particularly in the digital environment. Her research appears in top mass communication, gender, and media journals. Harp received her doctorate degree from the University of Wisconsin, Madison, School of Mass Communication and her master's degree from the School of Journalism at the University of Texas at Austin.

Melissa Janoske is an assistant professor in the Department of Journalism and Strategic Media at the University of Memphis, where she is Public Relations

Division head and assistant director of Graduate Studies. She teaches and researches in public relations, social media, and crisis communication. Recent publications appear in *Journal of Contingencies and Crisis Management, Public Relations Review,* and *Journal of Communication Management.* Dr. Janoske earned her PhD at the University of Maryland, where her dissertation was funded by the National Consortium for the Study of Terrorism and Responses to Terrorism (START), a Department of Homeland Security Center of Excellence.

Joy Jenkins is a doctoral candidate at the University of Missouri School of Journalism. A former magazine editor, she holds a Master of Science in mass communication and media management from Oklahoma State University and a Bachelor of Arts in journalism from the University of Oklahoma. Jenkins' research focuses on the role of local media in facilitating social change, the changing roles of journalists in newsrooms, and magazine journalism from sociology of news, critical, and feminist perspectives. Her work has been published in *Journalism Studies*; *Journalism: Theory, Practice and Critique*; *Journalism Practice*; and *New Media & Society,* among others.

Jinsook Kim is a PhD candidate in Media Studies in the Department of Radio-Television-Film at the University of Texas at Austin. She earned her MA in Women's Studies from Ewha Womans University in South Korea, and worked as a researcher at the Korean Women's Institute and Korean Women's Development Institute. Her research interests are in feminist perspectives on new media technologies, hate speech, and social movements. Her works have appeared in peer-reviewed journals, including *Feminist Media Studies* and *Communication, Culture & Critique.* She is currently working on a dissertation exploring online misogynistic discourse and anti-hate activism in South Korea.

Victoria LaPoe is an assistant professor of audio, visual, and digital media at Ohio University. She is co-author of the book, *Indian Country: Telling a Story in a Digital Age,* which evaluates how digital media are changing the rich cultural act of storytelling within Native communities. *Indian Country* contains interviews with more than 40 Native journalists around the country to understand how digital media possibly advances the distribution of storytelling within the American-Indian community. She is also co-author of *Oil and Water: Media Lessons from Hurricane Katrina and the Deepwater Horizon Disaster.* *Oil and Water* explores the visuals and narratives associated with both disasters. Victoria is also the American Indian Editor for the Media Diversity Forum. She is a Native American Journalists lifetime member and a current board member for the Native American Journalists Association.

Amanda Mabry-Flynn is an assistant professor in the Charles H. Sandage Department of Advertising at the University of Illinois at Urbana-Champaign. She received a PhD in advertising from the University of Texas at Austin. Her research focuses on exploring the role social and cultural norms play in advertising and marketing with a focus on public health social marketing campaigns. Specifically, she explores how normative influence relates to gender stereotypes, cultural conceptions of masculinity and femininity, and the prevalence of sexual violence.

Stephanie Madden is an assistant professor in the Department of Journalism and Strategic Media at the University of Memphis. Her research explores the intersection between public relations, activism, risk/crisis communication, and social media. She earned her PhD from the University of Maryland. Previously, Madden was a full-time communication researcher at the National Consortium for the Study of Terrorism and Responses to Terrorism (START), a Department of Homeland Security Center of Excellence. Recent publications appear in *Journal of Contingencies and Crisis Management, Communication Teacher, Public Relations Review,* and *Review of Communication.*

Adrienne Massanari is an assistant professor in the Department of Communication at the University of Illinois at Chicago (UIC). Her recent book, *Participatory Culture, Community, and Play: Learning from Reddit* (2015), is an ethnographic exploration of the Reddit platform focused on its culture and politics. Prior to joining UIC, she was at Loyola University Chicago and served as the Director for the School of Communication's Center for Digital Ethics and Policy. She also has more than ten years' experience as a user researcher, information architect, usability specialist, and consultant in both corporate and educational settings.

Jill Theresa Messing is an associate professor in the School of Social Work at Arizona State University. She has published more than fifty articles and book chapters and has been an expert witness in more than twenty domestic violence-related cases. Messing specializes in intimate partner violence risk assessment, and is on a research team that is adapting the Danger Assessment for use with immigrant, refugee, and Native American victims of intimate partner violence. Messing is committed to evidence-based practice and is concerned with the development and testing of innovative interventions for victims of intimate partner violence.

David B. Nieborg is an assistant professor of media studies at the University of Toronto. He holds a PhD in Media Studies from the University of Amsterdam and was affiliated as a postdoctoral research fellow with MIT, the University of Amsterdam, and the Chinese University of Hong Kong. He has published on the political economy of the game industry, the military-entertainment complex, and games journalism. He had a decade-long career in newspaper journalism and his work is published in academic outlets such as *New Media & Society, Social Media + Society, the European Journal for Cultural Studies,* and *Fibreculture Journal.*

Gwendelyn S. Nisbett is an assistant professor in the Mayborn School of Journalism at the University of North Texas. She received her PhD from the University of Oklahoma in social influence and political communication in 2011. Nisbett's research examines the intersection of mediated social influence, political communication, and popular culture. Her research incorporates a multimethod approach to understanding the influence of fandom and celebrity in political and civic engagement.

Candi Carter Olson is an assistant professor at Utah State University. Her research interests focus on women's press clubs as agents of change, newswomen's history, and women's use of social media to build community and organize activist groups. She received a 2012–2013 American Association of University Women American Fellowship, a 2015–2016 Mountain West Center research grant, and the 2016 American Journalism Rising Scholar award. She has published in *Journalism and Mass Communication Quarterly, Journalism History, Feminist Media Studies, Pennsylvania History*, and *Media Report to Women*, and she has an article forthcoming in *American Journalism*. Carter Olson is also the 2017 chair of the Association for Education in Mass Communication and Journalism's Commission on the Status of Women.

Paromita Pain is a doctoral candidate in the School of Journalism at The University of Texas at Austin. She has ten years' experience as a newspaper reporter. Her research focuses on citizen journalism and gender empowerment. Her work has been published in *Journalism & Mass Communication Educator, Journalism Practice*, and *Media Asia*.

Lauren Reed is an assistant professor in the School of Social Work at Arizona State University. Reed conducts research on the use of social media and mobile phones as a context and tool for dating and sexual violence among youth. Her work focuses on the gendered experience and consequences of digital media abuse. Reed has served as a counselor and crisis intervention social worker for survivors of domestic violence and has facilitated several youth-led dating violence prevention programs in schools and community settings. She seeks to bring a youth participatory lens to gendered youth violence.

Kaitlyn Regehr is an ethnographer and documentarian. Her work has appeared in academic and popular print outlets, including *Variety Magazine* and the *Los Angeles Times*. Regehr has created documentary content for networks such as Super Channel (CA), SWR (DE) and ARTE (FR). Often employing film ethnography, her work has explored intersections between gender, performance, and politics in female-driven communities. Her recent research examines global digital feminism and social media campaigns, including those responding to sexual violence. Her book with photographer Matilda Temperley, on one of the first sex worker unions in America, *The League of Exotic Dancers* was released in May of 2017.

Jessica Ringrose is a professor of sociology of gender and education at the University College London Institute of Education. Her work develops innovative feminist approaches to understanding subjectivity, affectivity, and assembled power relations. Recent research explores teen feminism in schools, and young people's networked sexual cultures and uses of social media. Her books include: *Post-Feminist Education?* (2013); *Deleuze and Research Methodologies* (2013); *Children, Sexuality and Sexualisation* (2015); and she is currently working on two new books *Gender, Activism and #FeministGirl* (with Emma Renold), and *Digital Feminist Activism: Girls and Women Fight Back against Rape Culture* (with Kaitlynn Mendes and Jessalynn Keller).

Scott R. Stroud is an associate professor in the Department of Communication Studies at the University of Texas at Austin. He has been a visiting fellow in the Center for the Study of Democratic Politics at Princeton University. His work focuses on the intersection of philosophy, ethics, and rhetoric. He is the author of *John Dewey and the Artful Life* and *Kant and the Promise of Rhetoric*.

Jacqueline Ryan Vickery is an assistant professor in the Department of Media Arts at the University of North Texas; she earned her PhD from the University of Texas at Austin. Vickery conducts qualitative and feminist research on teens' and women's digital media practices. She is the author of *Worried About the Wrong Things: Youth, Risk, & Opportunity in the Digital World* (2017) and co-author of *The Digital Edge: How Black and Hispanic Youth Are Reimagining the Digital Divide* (in press). Her teaching focuses on digital media, media theory, digital activism, and youth media. Additionally, she is the founder and facilitator of a digital storytelling workshop for teens in foster care.

Rowena Briones Winkler is the managing director of the Oral Communication Program in the Department of Communication at the University of Maryland. Her research agenda explores how social media and technology impact these areas in terms of campaign development and relationship building, particularly in the areas of sexual health, crisis communication, and risk communication. Currently, Briones Winkler has been conducting research on the use of digital media for digital activism and social justice. She is developing strategies for using social media in bystander interventions for sexual assault/domestic violence victim outreach and diversity and inclusion initiatives, particularly on college campuses.

David Wolfgang is an assistant professor of Journalism and Media Communication at Colorado State University, where he teaches communication law and media in society. Wolfgang's research focuses on public discourse and media sociology. In particular, he studies the relationship between journalists and online commenters. Wolfgang is a former journalist and holds a law degree and PhD from the University of Missouri. Wolfgang's work has been published in *Journalism, Journalism Studies, Journalism Practice, Digital Journalism*, and the *Journal of Public Deliberation*.

Jinglun Zhang is a third-year undergraduate studying journalism and economics at Tsinghua University in China and was an exchange student in the School of Journalism at the University of Texas at Austin during the fall 2016 semester. She was the editor of the editorial department at *Qingxin Times* student newspaper at Tsinghua University and worked as a general reporter at *The Daily Texan* student newspaper during her semester in Austin. She aspires to pursue a career in journalism, especially using data and digital storytelling.

List of Figures

List of Tables

1

The Persistence of Misogyny: From the Streets, to Our Screens, to the White House

Jacqueline Ryan Vickery and Tracy Everbach

In 1913, the day before U.S. President Woodrow Wilson's inauguration, thousands of long-skirted women ascended upon Washington, D.C. to fight for their right to vote. As organizers Alice Paul, Lucy Burns, Marcy Church Terrell, Ida B. Wells-Barnett, and other members of the National American Woman Suffrage Association and the Delta Sigma Theta sorority demonstrated, male onlookers harassed, jeered, and attacked them physically. Throughout Wilson's presidency, suffragists picketed in front of the White House, where they endured more physical assaults and arrests. It was the women, and not their attackers, who ended up in prison. Alice Paul eventually staged a hunger strike and was sent to an asylum, where she was force-fed (Cott 1987; "Suffragist Alice Paul clashed with Woodrow Wilson" n.d.; "Women of protest" n.d.; Zahniser and Fry 2014). Eventually the women's bravery, perseverance, and activism paid

J. R. Vickery (✉)
Department of Media Arts, University of North Texas, Denton, TX, USA

T. Everbach
Mayborn School of Journalism, Digital/Print Journalism, University of North Texas, Denton, TX, USA

© The Author(s) 2018
J. R. Vickery, T. Everbach (eds.), *Mediating Misogyny*,
https://doi.org/10.1007/978-3-319-72917-6_1

off: The Nineteenth Amendment to the U.S. Constitution, giving women the right to vote, finally passed in 1920. However, the suffragist movement still had a problem: it strategically marginalized women of color in many ways; for example, by privileging white women's rights at the expense of black men's rights. The only African American organization to participate in the march—Delta Sigma Theta—was forced to stand in the back of the demonstration. Up until the 1960s many people of color, particularly in the South, still faced barriers to voting such as paying poll taxes, passing literacy tests, or facing jail time for violating absurd laws intended to keep blacks from voting (Bernard 2013; Fields-White 2011; "Race and Voting in the Segregated South" n.d.) (Figs. 1.1 and 1.2).

A little more than a century later, on November 8, 2016, enthusiastic feminists gathered to watch the U.S. presidential election results. Earlier in the day, some had gone to the polls wearing pantsuits, the signature clothing of Democratic candidate Hillary Clinton. Most polls had shown

Fig. 1.1 1913 Women's Suffrage March, Washington, D.C. (Library of Congress, Prints & Photographs Division, LC-B2-2513-6)

Wells-Barnett marching with other women suffragists in a parade in Washington, D.C., 1913

Fig. 1.2 Ida B. Wells-Barnett and other suffragists march in D.C., 1913 (*Chicago Daily Tribune* photograph, March 5, 1913)

Clinton in the lead over Republican candidate Donald J. Trump, who had run a blatantly sexist campaign highlighted by an *Access Hollywood* tape that featured him bragging about grabbing a woman's genitals. Finally, many women thought, the glass ceiling would be broken and the first woman president would be elected. Clinton even booked the Jacob K. Javits Center in Manhattan, a building with a huge glass ceiling, to make her victory speech (Flegenheimer 2016).

As the election results began to roll in, it slowly became clear that the election was not going to turn out as Clinton supporters expected. Nor did the outcome reflect what most news media outlets, polling organizations, and major newspaper endorsements had predicted. Although Clinton won the U.S. popular vote, the majority of white women helped Trump win the electoral votes to become the 45th president of the United States.

Trump's long history of misogynistic and racist behaviors, which can be documented for at least four decades (Cohen 2017), is undeniably disturbing. But what is perhaps equally concerning is the extent to which he deliberately used media interviews and his personal Twitter account to unapologetically broadcast and draw attention to his atrocious views and behavior. He boasted of entering beauty contest dressing rooms to gaze at partially dressed women and young girls. He told his friend Philip Johnson that, "you have to treat 'em [women] like shit" (Suebsaeng 2015). After Marie Brenner wrote an article about Trump for *Vanity Fair* that he did not like, he boasted of pouring a bottle of wine down her back, then accused her of lying and attempted to discredit her claim by stating she is "extremely unattractive" (Rosenberg 2016). In a 2013 tweet, he blamed female soldiers for their own sexual assaults because the military allows men and women to serve together (Mehta 2016). In 2015, a college student, Lauren Batchelder, asked Trump at a political forum how his policies would affect women and commented that she didn't think he was "a friend to women." The next day Trump tweeted that Batchelder was an "arrogant young woman" who questioned him "in such a nasty fashion." Men then sent her online death and rape threats and sexually harassed her via phone calls; this continued for more than a year. Trump used Twitter to incite attacks against a private citizen, yet he never apologized nor denounced the harassment his supporters propagated (Johnson 2016).

Trump's misogyny was blatant. His comments were highly publicized and could not be written off as occasional remarks that were taken out of context. His election win felt like a slap in the face to feminists who fought for equality and women's rights. The longstanding battle to create and accept women's roles in public places and as figures of authority was reinforced once again. Sexism was out in the open and undeniable, and, appallingly, many white women were embracing it. The struggle for equality seemed to fail once again. Misogyny was alive and well and moving into the White House.

However, feminists continued to fight back. The day after the election they used Facebook to organize the Women's March on Washington. As history could predict, this was an organization initially headed solely by white women; after warranted criticism, however, the planning committee expanded to include several women of color (Bates 2017). The day after Trump's inauguration, half a million people marched in Washington, D.C. The march became a worldwide phenomenon, with 2.6 million people marching against misogyny, racism, and other injustices in all 50 U.S. states and on all 7 continents (Pictures from Women's Marches…

2017; Przybyla and Schouten 2017). Demonstrators held signs endorsing various humanitarian and equal rights causes: "Marching for Rights! Equality! The Planet! The Future!" "All of Us Together. Women Men Black White Gay Straight Disabled Young Old Native Come Here <3." "They Tried to Bury Us. But They Didn't Know We Were Seeds" ("Why we march" 2017). Still, we cannot overlook the ways the movement marginalized women of color, some of whom blamed organizational racism for their decision not to participate; to be intersectional and inclusive Western feminism has to center the voices, experiences, and bodies of women of color (Bates 2017; Mosthof 2017) (Figs. 1.3 and 1.4).

After the march feminists continued to organize further. Concerted efforts to elect women candidates in local, state, and federal elections

Fig. 1.3 Women's March on Washington, D.C., January 21, 2017 (Photo credit: Jacqueline Ryan Vickery)

Fig. 1.4 Women's March on Washington, D.C., January 21, 2017 (Photo credit: Tracy Everbach)

cropped up across the United States. Emily's List, a group that supports and promotes progressive women candidates, reported that after Trump's election the number of women expressing interest in running for office increased more than 1,000%—from about 900 in 2016 to 11,000 from January to April 2017 (O'Keefe and DeBonis 2017).

We want to emphasize that this book is not about Trump. But the election of Trump—and the ways he unapologetically continues to use digital media to humiliate, shame, and mobilize people to harass women—provides an apropos jumping-off point for thinking about and contextualizing contemporary media culture at the intersection of gender, power, and technology. Likewise, the opening examples of feminist activism highlight the ways in which feminism continues to ignore racism in problematic and oppressing ways. Our purpose is to critically analyze the ways media and digital technologies mediate misogyny, gender-based harassment, racism, and violence against women. We also aim to uncover some of the ways feminists are using digital media technologies to fight back against harassment, sexism, and assault. Finally, we posit what we can do to work toward a solution for this pervasive inequality. We look at these problems with an interdisciplinary, intersectional, and multimethod approach rooted in feminist and media theories. It is our intent that this collection of essays expands our theoretical thinking and practical approaches to creating more inclusive and equitable spaces—both online and offline—not just for women, but for all marginalized and targeted communities.

Before the Internet There Was Mediated Misogyny... Or... Why We Can't Just Blame the Internet

Women have long been subjected to and battled misogyny, including problematic sexist and racist media portrayals. Building on the work of communication scholars George Gerbner and Larry Gross (1976), Gaye Tuchman, Arlene Kaplan Daniels, and James Benet (1978) have referred to mass media's marginalization of women as "symbolic annihilation." Despite being more than half the population, women are trivialized, stereotyped, and condemned in mass media portrayals, which contributes to their continued marginalization in society. In a 2013 update to her research, Tuchman noted that the Internet's prevalence has contributed further to women's exclusion, through audience fragmentation and the echo chambers caused by politically polarizing social media. Simply, if women are underrepresented and minimized, then they are accepted as less powerful than men; their status as second-class members of society persists.

Mass media perpetuate these social constructions on a daily basis. Feminist film scholar Laura Mulvey (1975) argues that visual media position spectators from a masculine perspective and frame images of women through a lens of the "male gaze." Women and the world are viewed from a male perspective in which women are presented as objects of heterosexual male pleasure. Consequently, women also learn to view themselves from a heteronormative masculine perspective. The stereotypical, mediated portrayals of women as sexual objects, judged by their appearance, and as passive members of society who lack power, contributes to the normalization of violence, shaming, and abuse against women, including online abuse (Wood 2015).

Although it is far too simple to merely blame mass media for the perpetuation of sexism, racism, and disempowerment of women and people of color, we cannot deny that media shape cultural dialogue, contribute to hegemonic ideologies, and even profit from stereotypical or damaging representations. Media play an integral role in reinforcing and policing patriarchal norms and practices, that is, in mediating misogyny. Long before the widespread adoption of the Internet, other media industries, including journalism, advertising, film, radio, television, and pornography, contributed to the mediated marginalization, stereotyping, and trivialization of women. This was and is accomplished in part by mediated representations and reinforcements of virtually unattainable beauty standards—standards from which media industries profit. As Jean Kilbourne has noted in five decades of studying advertising, women learn through media that the most important thing about them is their appearance, which must adhere to a stringent standard of beauty and femininity—light-skinned, young, flawless, and thin (Kilbourne 2013). As Kilbourne points out, this idealized version of feminine beauty excludes a majority of the population and subjugates women, reducing them to their bodies and denying them intellectual, physical, and sexual power. Within film, Mulvey argues, women are coded with conventions of "to-be-looked-at-ness" while men are positioned as "bearers of the look" who take pleasure in the looking. When mass media trivialize and hypersexualize women, society also adopts and reflects this construction of idealized femininity that is devoid of power, humanity, and agency. As an extension of this, women online are often attacked for not adhering to standards of heteronormative and hegemonic ideals of white femininity.

Globalization and the mass exportation of U.S. media perpetuate the limited Western ideals of beauty and femininity worldwide. Media images of the ideal Western female—and specifically white female—become the mediated norm in other nations and can lead to a devaluing of their own cultural ideals of femininity and beauty. For example, some women in Asia and Africa undergo surgery to try to achieve the look of the idealized Western white woman (Alibhai-Brown 2010; Jones 2010).

In addition to limiting and even damaging representation, men both on-screen and behind screens dominate entertainment and technology industries. A USC Annenberg study showed that in 2016 U.S. movies, women only played 28% of the speaking roles, stripping them of their voices. In network TV shows women represented only 36% of the speaking roles (Smith et al. 2016). Alarmingly, speaking parts for people of color are almost entirely absent in many feature-length popular films. Writer and videomaker Dylan Marron created the popular Tumblr and YouTube channel called "Every Single Word Spoken" (n.d.) which re-edits popular films to only include lines spoken by a person of color. Entire feature-length films are reduced to mere minutes, or even seconds. For example, the entire *Lord of the Rings* trilogy (557 minutes) is reduced to 47 seconds of dialogue by people of color, none of whom are women.

Further, in media representations, male-dominated media industries often reduce women of color to the appearance of their bodies in stereotypical manners that reproduce and uphold dominant ideologies of patriarchy and white supremacy. They are subjected to racialized derision if they do not meet cultural standards of attractiveness. An example cited by Ralina L. Joseph (2011) is supermodel-turned-TV host Tyra Banks. On her show, *America's Next Top Model*, Banks promoted her own idealized and light-skinned version of African-American beauty. In 2007, when she gained weight, tabloid and gossip websites attacked her failure to maintain her nearly impossible appearance, calling her a "loser," along with other "failures" like Oprah Winfrey. Banks responded with a speech on her show that ended with "Kiss my fat ass!" (Joseph 2011). White culture has exploited black women's bodies for centuries and often reproduce sexualized, racialized, and class-driven stereotypes such as the "Jezebel" (alluring), the "Hottentot Venus" (aggressively sexual), the "welfare queen," the "crack mother," the "mammy," or as "bitches and hoes" (Cox 2013; Rose 2011; Walker-Barnes 2014).

Similarly, the industry often casts Hispanic and Latina women as the "fiery" or "hot" señorita. Although Hispanic and Latino communities around the world are diverse, women from this ethnicity often are portrayed as having one identity—brown-skinned, "spicy," highly sexual, and manipulative (Merskin 2011). They are given stereotypical domestic roles such as maids, nannies, and cooks. Asian women also face limited racial stereotypes in advertising and entertainment media, from the passive, subservient "geisha girl" to the "woman warrior" (Wilson et al. 2013). Native American women are rarely seen in any mass media and when they are, they often appear as uncivilized "savages" or as living in poverty and alcoholism (Wilson et al. 2013). Mass media industries—which lack diversity behind the camera and in boardrooms—continue to reproduce and profit from these stereotypes that reinforce the status quo and power order in society. The representations deprive women of agency and authority, and instead reduce them to objects of white male desire and control.

The Internet Will (Not) Save the Day

In the early days of the Internet's widespread adoption, there was hope that the web would eradicate xenophobic attitudes and representations that had always plagued society and media. Mostly male scholars and technology enthusiasts believed that because the web would provide greater opportunities for diverse representations and communication among dispersed populations, then we would use it to gain a better understanding of our differences (Baym 2010). However, digital platforms have become just one more space where hierarchies of gender, race, class, sexuality, and other constructed differences are reproduced. Platforms such as Twitter, Facebook, and Instagram are not the problem—misogyny perpetuates with or without social media—yet the persistent, searchable, and scalable affordances of social media render interactions more visible (boyd 2010), including sexist and racist attitudes. The anonymity and mobility of the Internet have given rise to a resurgence in the ways extremists communicate and mobilize (Daniels 2008). Additionally, web communities and social media facilitate the formation of politically homogenous and polarizing realms that can serve as breeding grounds for sexism, white supremacy, homophobia, transphobia, hate speech, and other extremist factions (Daniels 2008; Yardi and boyd 2010). Within a convergence culture, people use social media platforms as a way to enhance and extend their engagement with traditional media in practices that can lead to harassment and abuse and the perpetuation of misogyny.

As with other forms of media, the Internet is also used to propagate, perpetuate, and profit from misogyny and racism. For example, in 2014, Valentina Shulz participated as a contestant on the Brazilian reality TV show *Masterchef Junior*. After her appearance on the show she was bombarded with sexually explicit messages on Twitter. Shulz was only 12 years old at the time. One user wrote, "If it's consensual, is it pedophilia?"

In response, feminist activist Juliana de Faria launched a campaign using the hashtag #meuprimeiroassadieo (in English: #myfirstharassment) to invite women to use Twitter as a collective space to share their own stories of sexual harassment (see Chap. 17 by Desborough). The immediate popularity of the hashtag revealed the pervasiveness of harassment in Brazil, with many women sharing stories from adolescence (Viola 2016).

In Mexico in 2016, a woman was harassed online after she defended her four-year-old son's right to attend school with long hair. When harassers discovered she was a single lesbian mother, they threatened to "rescue her son." Via the Internet, she received photos of weapons with her name on them, alongside other threats of rape and death. Such threats must be interpreted in the context of the forced disappearances of 43 Ayotzinapa students in Mexico (Navarro 2016). Misogyny as it is expressed online can never be divorced from cultural and historical contexts or the physical threats women endure on a daily basis. Nor can we overlook the ways misogyny and harassment are intensified via the intersection of other social identities such as race, nationality, or sexuality.

The Gendered Nature of Online Harassment

The prevalence of online misogyny is so widespread that one Australian study contended that the harassment of women is "at risk of becoming an established norm in our digital society" ("Norton Study shows..." 2016). Online harassment, in particular, has been described as an "epidemic." Seventy-six percent of Australian women under 30 report having been harassed online (ibid.). In the United States, young women are disproportionately the targets of severe sexual harassment and stalking online (Duggan 2014). In some nations, such as Pakistan, online harassment of women is "generally accepted as a routine part of Pakistani women's daily lives" (Mohsin 2016). The lines between online abuse and other modes of mediated harassment can be difficult to distinguish; traditional media can amplify or even be the catalyst for online harassment. For example, when a reboot of the *Ghostbusters* movie starring an all-female leading cast was released in summer 2016, Leslie Jones, the only leading black cast member, was forced to leave Twitter temporarily after trolls harassed her with pornography, threats, and racist messages (Rogers 2016). While distinctions are blurry, some forms of abuse—although precipitated by offline encounters—are uniquely mediated and expressed via the Internet.

As part of the Women's Media Center Speech Project, Soraya Chemaly and Debjani Roy designed the Online Abuse Wheel (Fig. 1.5) as a way to contextualize and name online abuse. The wheel is an adaptation of the Power and Control Wheel utilized by the National Center on Domestic and Sexual Violence, which shows the relationship of physical abuse to other forms of abuse (Domestic Abuse Intervention Project 2015). Likewise, the Online Abuse Wheel approaches abusive and violent

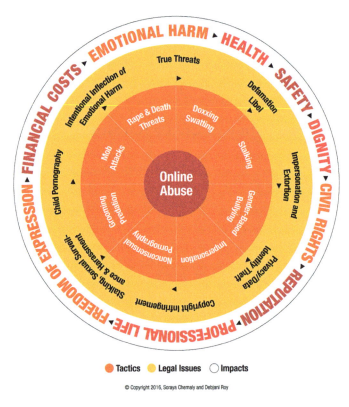

Fig. 1.5 Online Abuse Wheel (Credit: Soraya Chemaly, Debjani Roy & Women's Media Center)

behaviors not as isolated incidents, but as interconnected and ongoing attempts at control. These abuses take many different forms online including: gender-based slurs and harassment, nonconsensual photography (a.k.a. revenge porn), exploitation, doxxing (using the Internet to research and then publish personally identifiable information about an individual or organization with the intent to harass), defamation, death or rape threats, mob attacks, hate speech, stalking, unsolicited (often violent) pornography, online impersonation, spying and sexual surveillance, slut-shaming, swatting (filing false police reports in order to send unnecessary emergency services to someone's home or business), and grief trolling. Chemaly explains, "The purpose of the wheel is not to simplify these acts, but to allow women to put a name to them and access the language needed in order to feel less isolated and address the issue—particularly for women who aren't in the public eye" (Kabas 2016). Although the motivations and effects of different abuse tactics vary, the goal is to "embarrass, humiliate, scare, threaten, silence, extort, or in some instances, encourage mob attacks of malevolent engagements" against women (Women's Media Center 2015).

Karla Mantilla (2015) coined the term "gendertrolling" to describe the specific ways women are targeted online. While men are also harassed online, it is usually their ideas that are under attack. Women, on the other hand, are vilified simply for "assert[ing] their right to voice their opinions in the new public sphere that is the Internet" (p. 28). In other words, men target women precisely because they are women. "Online attacks on women," Mantilla (p. 157) writes, "tend to get lumped together with generic trolling, which covers up the unique characteristics of gendertrolling and obfuscates the fact that this is a pattern that happens to women." Since the 1990s, Emma Alice Jane has been studying hostile misogynistic rhetoric on the Internet—what she refers to as "e-bile." Her extensive research makes clear that "gendered vitriol is proliferating in the cybersphere; so much so that issuing graphic rape and death threats [against women] has become a standard discursive move online, particularly when Internet users wish to register their disagreement with and/or disapproval of women" (2014, p. 558). Misogyny—whether in the form of street harassment, sexual assault, violence, or online abuse—is intended to remind women of their proper patriarchal place, one that is subservient to the interests of men; a place that is not powerful, public, nor political.

Mantilla (2015) identifies seven characteristics or patterns of online attacks against women that distinguish gendertrolling from more generic trolling. Women are attacked because they have asserted an opinion online. The harassment or insults are often graphic, sexualized, and gender-based, including rape and death threats. Attacks are not contained to one platform, but traverse multiple social media accounts. The harassment is intense and frequent to the point of being overwhelming and disruptive to day-to-day activities; it can last for weeks, months, or even years. At times, the attacks are organized in a concerted effort to gang up on the target. She argues that accurately "describing and naming abuse, therefore, is an essential step in attempting to counter it" (p. 155). Jane (2014) notes that the attackers are often anonymous or difficult to identify and that the threats employ explicitly sexual, misogynistic, and/or homophobic rhetoric. Although men also experience trolls and harassment online, research evidences that women are subjected to more severe and sexualized attacks simply for being a woman on the Internet (Duggan 2014).

"You're So Sensitive, Quit Overreacting"

Frequently men tell women that they are overreacting to harassment, online and offline. For example, some men will try to justify catcalling and street harassment as a compliment (Bahadur 2014). Online, the anonymity, the physical distance, and the fact that the attacks aren't physical, tend to lead to misconceptions that women are merely overreacting to verbal banter. Misogynists and racists frequently defend their offenses as "just jokes." Law scholar Danielle Citron (2009, p. 375) notes, "But no matter how serious the harm that cyber gender harassment inflicts, the public tends to trivialize it. Commentators dismiss it as harmless locker room talk, characterizing perpetrators as juvenile pranksters and targeted individuals as overly sensitive complainers." Rather than holding perpetrators responsible or accountable, women are blamed for being offended (or legitimately fearful) in the first place. The refusal to acknowledge the harm, combined with accusations that women are "overly sensitive" and "hysterical," is part of a larger rhetorical and abusive strategy intended to undermine women's autonomy and hold them responsible for their own harassment (Poland 2016). The attitude ignores the fact that many instances of online harassment are not contained to the Internet, but are manifested as actual physical threats and attacks on women, their families and children, their careers, homes, and safety. Such dismissal undermines the emotional toll of harassment and the ways it disrupts women's daily lives, safety, and autonomy.

Another common response is to tell women that if they can't handle the "jokes," then they should just leave. The inflammatory "alt-right" white supremacist website Breitbart suggests that "the solution to online 'harassment' is simple: women should log off [the Internet]" (Yiannopoulos 2016). Such a "solution" intentionally silences women and discourages their participation in the public sphere. Milo Yiannopoulos, who was kicked off Twitter in 2016 for online harassment of *Ghostbusters* actress Leslie Jones, continues, "I, Donald Trump and the rest of the alpha males will continue to dominate the internet without feminist whining. It will be fun!" Perhaps the article could be considered satire (although given his blatant and public statements of misogyny and racism, this is unlikely), yet when women are harassed online they often are told in the same manner that they should quit participating.

As a flagrant example, women's rights activist Kavita Krishnan works to draw attention to and fight against the sexual harassment, abuse, and rape of women in India. Krishnan was one of the leading anti-rape activists who organized protests after a 23-year-old woman was tortured, gang raped, and murdered on a bus in Delhi in 2012. As part of her ongoing advocacy for women's rights in India, Krishnan agreed to participate in a live web chat organized by the Indian news portal, Rediff. During the chat Krishnan received multiple rape threats from a user with the handle "RAPIST." Staff from Rediff eventually asked Krishnan to log off the chat as the threats escalated; she reluctantly complied. The response from the moderators of the platform was not to silence the threats, but to kick off Krishnan for speaking out against assault and violence, thus reifying the notion that it's a woman's responsibility to avoid harassment (Pal 2013).

Anita Sarkeesian, who has publicly criticized the representation of women in video games through her YouTube series *Feminist Frequency* and website of the same name, has received death and rape threats and other harassment for speaking out (Sarkeesian 2016). In 2014, Sarkeesian canceled a talk at Utah State University after three death threats, one of which promised "the deadliest school shooting in American history," and the fact that university officials could not ban firearms from the talk because of state law (Alberty 2014).

Trolls and gender-based harassment take an emotional toll on women and necessitate extra labor to effectively manage. For more than five years feminist writer and activist Lindy West was the target of misogynistic, fat-shaming, and sexist vitriol on Twitter. She repeatedly reported the attacks to Twitter, yet the platform failed to take significant or effective action. On January 3, 2017, West publicly announced that she was leaving Twitter stating, "I have to conclude, after a half a decade of troubleshooting, that it may simply be impossible to make this platform usable for anyone but trolls, robots and dictators" (West 2017).

Time and again women are forced to avoid speaking engagements, close their social media accounts, change email addresses and phone numbers, leave their homes, hide their identities, or even stop participating online altogether because of gender-based harassment. Women must exert intense efforts, extra time, and emotional labor to participate safely in public discussions. When these spaces are deemed unsafe—or when platforms fail to create safe and inclusive environments—women often feel they have little "choice" but to leave. As Jane (2017) points out, if women are coerced into leaving, it's not really a choice. The consequences of harassment are detrimental to individuals who cannot participate, but also for a society that repeatedly fails to value the voices and experiences of women and members of other marginalized communities.

Why This Book and Why Now?

As we address in the next chapter (Vickery, Chap. 2), we know that the online harassment of women, particularly women of color, is a problem as old as the Internet itself. But in recent years the problem appears to be escalating, or, at the very least, women have successfully demanded that society take the issue more seriously. This book includes analyses of politics (Harp, Chap. 10), fandom (Nisbett, Chap. 9), gaming (Nieborg and Foxman, Chap. 6), sports journalism (Everbach, Chap. 7), celebrity and commercial culture (Mabry-Flynn and Champlin, Chap. 12), academia (Carter Olson and LaPoe, Chap. 14), and online message boards (Kim, Chap. 8; and Jenkins and Wolfgang, Chap. 13). We also point out that women are frequently harassed and that they continue to demand change. Feminists are employing digital tools for the purposes of resistance and activism, to organize, and to fight back against inequalities both on and offline (see Stroud and Cox, Chap. 15; Ferrier and Garud-Patkar, Chap. 16; Desborough, Chap. 17; Regehr and Ringrose, Chap. 18; and Masullo Chen, Pain, and Zhang, Chap. 19). The effects of online harassment—or even the fear of potential harassment—have many consequences on marginalized populations. And, of course, the harassment isn't contained to the digital, but also poses physical threats to women's autonomy and safety (see Brown, Reed, and Messing, Chap. 11).

It is tempting to say that the online harassment of women has become worse in recent years as we continue to acknowledge the severity of the problem. The proliferation of digital and mobile media means misogynists can use more channels to find and attack women. Certainly the expansion of digital media and tools make it faster and easier for misogynists and racists to identify each other and then organize concerted attacks against those with whom they disagree. As Jane (2017) reminds us, however, the affordances of the Internet and social media serve to explain the *how* of online harassment, but not the *why*. Which begs the question: why do men attack women online? Simply put, Jane argues, because they can. Men hold the power and any instance in which they feel that "their" territory or power has been threatened or encroached upon becomes justification for attack. In his book aptly titled *Angry White Men*, sociologist Michael Kimmel (2017) argues, "Men's violence toward women does not happen when men's power over women is intact and unthreatened; rather, it happens when men's power breaks down, when his entitlement to that power is threatened and insecure. Violence is restorative, retaliatory [...] when that entitlement is aggrieved, they don't just get mad; they get even"

(p. 183). Although a constant struggle exists and although the gains are slow and gradual, women have progressed toward greater equality in many parts of the world in the workplace, in government, and in media representations. With these strides toward equality comes backlash from men who feel insecure, fearful, and as though they are losing something that they believe is rightfully "theirs" (i.e. power that they should have never initially had). "Fed a steady diet of disinformation and misinformation," Kimmel argues, "America's white men have lashed out at all the wrong targets" (p. 12); specifically, historically marginalized people who continue to fight for and gain greater access to equal rights. The male-dominated spaces of the Internet are merely one landscape in which men aim to reassert their dominance via harassment, violence, and intimidation.

In addition to the simple, yet accurate, explanation that men harass because they can, we add that the Internet provides historically marginalized populations the means to construct their own images and discourses in ways that have not previously been widely accessible or feasible. The increased visibility has many benefits, but also many risks. For example, the often-derided "selfie" (taking and sharing an image of oneself) can be an agentive, transformative, validating, liberating—and, therefore, feminist—practice (Tiidenberg and Cruz 2015). Popular among women and young people, the genre provides marginalized populations the opportunity *to represent themselves*—they are in charge of the lens and therefore the image. This can be used to intentionally counter the problematic stereotypes and limitations of popular mediated images typically produced by white men.

Likewise, popular and seemingly benign social media practices such as "mommy blogging," makeup tutorials, and food and fashion boards, further highlight aspects of the "private" (i.e. feminine) sphere in public spaces. Politically, women are using social media to publicly discuss—and demand attention for—"private" matters such as rape culture, street harassment, and domestic violence, which are symptomatic of structural inequities. Likewise, feminists also organize online to strategize for greater workplace equality. In other words, women use the Internet to amplify the visibility of anti-racist and feminist movements, activism, and solidarity. It is not unusual for online activism campaigns to gain coverage in news journalism or in entertainment media, such as jokes about #NotAllMen and "mansplaining" in the reboot of the popular television series *One Day at a Time*. Or in the news coverage of the #WhyIStayed hashtag, which drew attention to the complexity of intimate partner violence (Grinberg 2014). Women use digital media to increase the visibility of women-produced images, discourse, social issues, experiences, and representation. This expands discourse and leads to opportunities to organize tangible social changes such as greater workplace equality, equal pay, changes to how laws approach domestic violence, revenge porn, or rape, and so forth. Yet the increased visibility of and attention to feminist activism undoubtedly feels threatening to misogynists.

Just as the Internet provides opportunities for activists to organize, so too does it provide the necessary conditions for racists, misogynists, and homophobic people to find each other, to organize, and to attack. Unfortunately, the increased online visibility of feminism and women's capacity to interject our "private" issues in public spaces renders women vulnerable to increased negative attention and backlash. Given the intensity of online harassment—the scope of the problem, the targeted attacks, the potential for escalation—digital platforms, news organizations, and policymakers continue to grapple with the best ways to respond to the crisis.

Aims, Scope, and Limitations

It is our intent that the chapters included in this collection illuminate the severity and scope of the problem at this particular moment in time and from a historical perspective, but also that they provide strategies and resources to organize and fight for a safer world. Grounded in a feminist perspective that values the power of personal and collective storytelling, several authors include personal experiences of harassment. Other contributors rely on qualitative research such as interviews, focus groups, and discourse analysis. And others incorporate quantitative and empirical evidence to make their claims. The interdisciplinary nature of the book—media studies, journalism, communication, advertising, social work, sociology, anthropology, women's and gender studies, and law—highlights the diverse approaches and considerations that represent the multivocality of experiences and approaches. Each chapter uniquely contributes to the broad goals of this book, yet there are underlying facts and arguments that shape and reflect the different perspectives.

1. *Women are disproportionately affected by social, political, and economic inequalities.* Susan Douglas wrote in her 2010 book *The Rise of Enlightened Sexism* that equality for women and girls is a "media illusion" (p. 4). Mass media construct a powerful view of reality that, when compared with fact, is far from the truth. As such, the book aims to highlight the realities of online harassment alongside broader discourses that attempt to deny the severity and specificity of gender-based inequities.

2. *Mediated modes of harassment are an extension of—and not a departure from—cultural and historical roots of discrimination and power imbalances.* Throughout the book we draw connections between online and offline harassment and contextualize misogyny within specific locations, histories, and cultures.

3. *Not all women experience misogyny and harassment in the same ways.* Contributions aim to take an intersectional (Crenshaw 1989) approach that consider the ways gender intersects with race, class, sexuality, ability, geography, age, and religion. Each chapter contextualizes misogyny as part of systemic discriminations against women, but chapters consider different variables that contribute to the perpetuation of or opposition to the harassment of women online.

From the earliest iteration, it was our goal to strive for an intersectional approach that considered the ways in which misogyny was intensified via racism, homophobia, transphobia, ageism, regionalism, ableism, Islamophobia, and fatphobia. Although we are focusing on gender-based harassment, we have tried to resist a homogenizing narrative would erase the diversity of experiences, perspectives, impact, responses, and context. Instead, our goal is to consider how misogyny is influenced by other embodied social identities and experiences. To do this, we solicited chapters from global communities, critical race scholars, queer scholars, media scholars, and women's and gender scholars.

The book offers some diversity of geography, ethnicity, and sexuality; although not as much it could and should. There are likely many reasons for this, one of which might be that those who speak about harassment—even in academic spaces such as this book—risk making themselves a target. We should continue to pay greater attention to who feels safe researching and writing about misogyny and how universities can better protect scholars conducting risky research (a concern Lindsay Blackwell addresses in Chap. 20). Perhaps scholars who fear they may be a target of harassment because they identify as a woman or write about feminist issues are even more concerned if they are also marginalized by other aspects of their identities or scholarship, such as ethnicity or sexuality. We know that one consequence of harassment is the silencing of academics, as Carter Olson and LaPoe address in Chap. 13. In fact, at least one woman of color specifically declined our invitation to contribute to the book precisely because she has been targeted by right-wing websites and was fearful of further harassment. This silencing effect may have influenced the authors who felt comfortable contributing to this book and the topics that get researched.

Despite our best efforts for inclusion, diversity, and intersectionality, any critiques that the book is edited by two white women and consists of many chapters written by white women (and men) are not unwarranted. We need to do more to not only understand misogyny, but also scholarship about misogyny and other areas of research that put scholars and journalists at risk. We intentionally begin the book with critiques of language that focuses on "just gender" (Hackworth, Chap. 3) or discourses that attempt to erroneously dissect gender and race (Madden et al., Chap. 4). We have encouraged our contributors to think about misogyny from an intersectional perspective, something we believe they genuinely tried to do. However, what this collection also highlights is just how hard it is for us—particularly those of us who experience relative privilege—to challenge our own language and biases and to think about intersectionality in ways that are meaningful, complex, and rich. This book contributes to a growing body of work focused on gender and harassment, and we hope it also encourages us to reach further in understanding misogyny at the intersection of other forms of oppression.

In the conclusion, we pose solutions to gender-based online harassment from various perspectives and stakeholders. Ultimately, we cannot eradicate misogyny unless we eradicate the "white supremacist capitalist patriarchy" (hooks 1981). As Paul Batalden specifies, "Every system is exquisitely designed to produce the results it gets. If you want to change the results, you have to change the system" (as quoted by Proctor 2008). Any significant change in cultural values necessitates systemic change. We identified four stakeholders that have the power to at least contribute to creating a safer and more equitable system: digital platforms, news media, law, and universities. This is not intended to be an exhaustive list of influencers and power-holders, but it is an attempt to think about change from an holistic and systemic perspective. Each of these institutions not only has a stake in shaping values and online experiences, but also perpetuates—and even profits from—patriarchy and white supremacy. If we are to create a safer (digital) world—one that is driven by values of equity and protection—then we must consider changing the system. Undoubtedly, we must continue to fight for equity, but we know that misogyny and racism are not individual problems, nor are they really collective problems; rather, they are the outcomes of an intentionally designed white supremacist patriarchal system. We conclude with a series of brief Q&A from scholars, lawyers, and journalists about how we might begin to make changes at structural levels.

References

Alberty, E. (2014, October 16). Anita Sarkeesian explains why she canceled USU lecture. *The Salt Lake Tribune.* http://www.sltrib.com/sltrib/news/58528113-78/sarkeesian-threats-threat-usu.html.csp

Alibhai-Brown, Y. (2010, November 20). Why are Asian women aspiring to western ideals of beauty? *Independent.* http://www.independent.co.uk/lifestyle/fashion/features/why-are-asian-women-aspiring-to-western-ideals-of-beauty-2136868.html

Bahadur, N. (2014). Watch men explain why they harass women on the street. *Huffington Post.* http://www.huffingtonpost.com/2014/11/12/street-harassment-men-catcalling-video_n_6147424.html

Bates, K.G. (2017). Race and feminism: Women's March recalls the touchy history. *NPR.* http://www.npr.org/sections/codeswitch/2017/01/21/510859909/race-and-feminism-womens-march-recalls-the-touchy-history

Baym, N. K. (2010). *Personal connections in the digital age*. Malden: Polity Press.

Bernard, M. (2013). Despite the tremendous risk, African American women marched for suffrage, too. *The Washington Post*. https://www.washingtonpost.com/blogs/she-the-people/wp/2013/03/03/despite-the-tremendous-risk-african-american-women-marched-for-suffrage-too/?utm_term=.16c0d69ad239

boyd, d. (2010). Social network sites as networked publics: Affordances, dynamics, and implications. In Z. Papacharissi (Ed.), *Networked self: Identity, community, and culture on social network sites* (pp. 39–58). New York: Routledge.

Citron, D. K. (2009). Law's expressive value in combating cyber gender harassment. *Michigan Law Review, 108*(3), 373–415.

Cohen, C. (2017, January 20). Donald Trump sexism tracker: Every offensive comment in one place. *The Telegraph*. http://www.telegraph.co.uk/women/politics/donald-trump-sexism-tracker-every-offensive-comment-in-one-place/

Cott, N. (1987). *The grounding of modern feminism*. New Haven/London: Yale University Press.

Cox, K. (2013). Gender and race as meaning systems: Understanding theoretical, historical, and institutional implications of sexualized imagery in rap music. In R. A. Lind (Ed.), *Race/gender/class/media 3.0: Considering diversity across audiences, content, and producers* (3rd ed., pp. 274–279). Pearson: Boston.

Crenshaw, K. (1989). Demarginalizing the intersection of race and sex: A black feminist critique of antidiscrimination doctrine, feminist theory and antiracist politics. U. Chi. Legal F. 139.

Daniels, J. (2008). Race, civil rights, and hate speech in the digital era. In A. Everrett (Ed.), *Learning race and ethnicity: Youth and digital media* (pp. 129–154). Cambridge, MA: The MIT Press.

Domestic Abuse Intervention Project. (2015). http://domesticviolence.org/violence-wheel/

Douglas, S. J. (2010). *The rise of enlightened sexism: How pop culture took us from girl power to girls gone wild*. New York: St. Martin's Griffin.

Duggan, M. (2014). Online harassment. Pew Research Center. http://www.pewinternet.org/2014/10/22/online-harassment/

Every Single Word Spoken. http://everysinglewordspoken.tumblr.com

Fields-White, M. (2011, March 25). The root: How racism tainted woman's suffrage. *NPR*. http://www.npr.org/2011/03/25/134849480/the-root-how-racism-tainted-womens-suffrage

Flegenheimer, M. (2016, October 26). Clinton to ring in election under a real 'glass ceiling': Manhattan's Javits Center. *The New York Times*. http://www.nytimes.com/2016/10/27/us/politics/hillary-clinton-election-night.html?_r=0

Gerbner, G., & Gross, L. (1976). Living with television violence: The violence profile. *Journal of Communication, 26*(2), 172–194.

Grinberg, E. (2014, September 17). Meredith Vieira explains #WhyIStayed. *CNN*. http://www.cnn.com/2014/09/09/living/rice-video-why-i-stayed/index.html

hooks, b. (1981). *Ain't I a woman?: Black women and feminism*. Boston: South End Press.

Jane, E. A. (2014). 'Back to the kitchen, cunt': Speaking the unspeakable about online misogyny. *Continuum: Journal of Media & Cultural Studies, 28*(4), 558–570.

Jane, E. A. (2017). *Misogyny online: A short (and brutish) history*. London: Sage.

Johnson, J. (2016, December 8). This is what happens when Donald Trump attacks a private citizen on Twitter. *The Washington Post*. https://www.washingtonpost.com/politics/this-is-what-happens-when-donald-trump-attacks-a-private-citizen-on-twitter/2016/12/08/a1380ece-bd62-11e6-91ee-1adddfe36cbe_story.html?utm_term=.e252378af9b2

Jones, G. (2010). *Beauty imagined: A history of the global beauty industry*. Oxford: Oxford University Press.

Joseph, R. L. (2011). 'Tyra Banks is fat': Reading (post-)racism and (post-)feminism in the new millennium. In G. Dines & J. M. Humez (Eds.), *Gender, race and class in media: A critical reader* (3rd ed., pp. 519–529). Los Angeles: Sage.

Kabas, M. (2016, February 13). Women's Media Center launches project to document online abuse and harassment. *The Daily Dot*. https://www.dailydot.com/irl/soraya-chemaly-ashley-judd-womens-media-center/

Kilbourne, J. (2013). 'The more you subtract, the more you add': Cutting girls down to size in advertising. In R. A. Lind (Ed.), *Race/gender/class/media 3.0: Considering diversity across audiences, content, and producers* (3rd ed., pp. 179–185). Boston: Pearson.

Kimmel, M. (2017). *Angry white men: American masculinity at the end of an era*. New York: Nation Books.

Mantilla, K. (2015). *Gendertrolling: How misogyny went viral*. Santa Barbara: Praeger.

Mehta, S. (2016, September 7). Trump stands by tweet blaming sexual assaults in military on men and women serving together. *Los Angeles Times.* http://www.latimes.com/nation/politics/trailguide/la-na-trailguide-updates-trump-stands-by-tweet-blaming-military-1473296517-htmlstory.html

Merskin, D. (2011). Three faces of Eva: Perpetuation of the hot-Latina stereotype in *Desperate Housewives.* In G. Dines & J. M. Humez (Eds.), *Gender, race and class in media: A critical reader* (3rd ed., pp. 327–334). Los Angeles: Sage.

Mohsin, M. (2016, April 16). The cyber harassment of women in Pakistan. *The Diplomat.* http://thediplomat.com/2016/04/the-cyber-harassment-of-pakistans-women/

Mosthof, M. (2017, January 30). If you're not talking about the criticism surrounding The Women's March, then you're part of the problem. *Bustle.* https://www.bustle.com/p/if-youre-not-talking-about-the-criticism-surrounding-the-womens-march-then-youre-part-of-the-problem-33491

Mulvey, L. (1975). Visual pleasure and narrative cinema. *Screen, 16*(3), 6–18.

Navarro, C. R. (2016, April 22). Political violence is directly linked to online harassment. *Women's Media Center Speech Project.* http://wmcspeechproject.com/2016/04/22/political-violence-directly-linked-online-harassment-catalina-ruiz-navarro/

Norton study shows online harassment nears epidemic proportions for young Australian women. (2016). Symantec Press Release. https://www.symantec.com/en/au/about/newsroom/press-releases/2016/symantec_0309_01/

O'Keefe, E., & DeBonis, M. (2017, April 21.) Democrats partner with political newcomers aiming to create anti-Trump wave in 2018 midterms. *The Washington Post.* https://www.washingtonpost.com/politics/democrats-partner-with-political-newcomers-hoping-to-create-anti-trump-wave-in-2018-midterms/2017/04/21/91514ec8-2502-11e7-bb9d-8cd6118e1409_story.html?tid=ss_tw&utm_term=.8fc2c84023e0

Pal, D. (2013, August 25). Rape threats on Rediff: Kavita Krishnan speaks out. *First Post.* http://www.firstpost.com/living/rape-threats-on-rediff-kavita-krishnan-speaks-out-727395.html

Pictures from Women's Marches on every continent. (2017, January 23). *New York Times.* https://www.nytimes.com/interactive/2017/01/21/world/womens-march-pictures.html

Poland, B. (2016). *Haters: Harassment, abuse, and violence online.* Lincoln: Potomac Books.

Proctor, L. (2008). Editor's notebook: A quotation with a life of its own. *Patient Safety and Quality Healthcare.* https://www.psqh.com/analysis/editor-s-notebook-a-quotation-with-a-life-of-its-own/

Przybyla, H. M., & Schouten, F. (2017, January 21). At 2.6 million strong, Women's Marches crush expectations. *USA Today.* https://www.usatoday.com/story/news/politics/2017/01/21/womens-march-aims-start-movement-trump-inauguration/96864158/

Race and Voting in the Segregated South. (n.d.) Constitutional Rights Foundation. http://www.crf-usa.org/brown-v-board-50th-anniversary/race-and-voting.html

Rogers, K. (2016, July 19). Leslie Jones, star of "Ghostbusters," becomes a target of online trolls. *The New York Times.* http://www.nytimes.com/2016/07/20/movies/leslie-jones-star-of-ghostbusters-becomes-a-target-of-online-trolls.html

Rose, T. (2011). There are bitches and hoes. In G. Dines & J. M. Humez (Eds.), *Gender, race and class in media: A critical reader* (3rd ed., pp. 321–325). Los Angeles: Sage.

Rosenberg, A. (2016. October 4). "Extremely unattractive": How Donald Trump tries to discredit women based on their looks. *The Washington Post.* https://www.washingtonpost.com/news/act-four/wp/2016/10/14/extremely-unattractive-how-donald-trump-tries-to-discredit-women-based-on-their-looks/?utm_term=.1bfb4bb9e869

Sarkeesian, A. (2016, November 16.) We were planning to celebrate. Now we're planning to act. https://feministfrequency.com/video/we-were-planning-to-celebrate-now-were-planning-to-act/

Smith, S. L., Choueiti, M., & Pieper, K. (2016). Inclusion or invisibility? Comprehensive Annenberg report on diversity in entertainment. http://annenberg.usc.edu/pages/~/media/MDSCI/CARDReport%20FINAL%2022216.ashx

Suebsaeng, A. (2015, August 8). "You have to treat 'em like shit": Before Megyn Kelly, Trump dumped wine on a female reporter. *The Daily Beast.* http://www.thedailybeast.com/articles/2015/08/08/you-have-to-treat-em-like-shit-before-megyn-kelly-trump-dumped-wine-on-a-female-reporter.html

Suffragist Alice Paul clashed with Woodrow Wilson. (n.d.) *PBS.* http://www.pbs.org/wgbh/americanexperience/features/suffragist-alice-paul-clashed-woodrow-wilson/

Tiidenberg, K., & Cruz, E. G. (2015). Selfies, image and the re-making of the body. *Body & Society, 21*(4), 77–102.

Tuchman, G. (1978). Introduction: The symbolic annihilation of women by the mass media. In G. Tuchman, A. K. Daniels, & J. W. Benet (Eds.), *Hearth and home: Images of women in the mass media* (pp. 3–38). New York: Oxford University Press.

Tuchman, G. (2013). Media, gender, niche. In C. L. Armstrong (Ed.), *Media disparity: A gender battleground* (pp. xi–xviii). Lanham: Lexington Books.

Viola, K. (2016, June 3). Women in Brazil stand up to sexual harassment. *The World Post.* http://www.huffingtonpost.com/entry/brazilian-women-stand-up-to-harassment_us_5751d2d5e4b0c3752dcd8d93

Walker-Barnes, C. (2014). *Too heavy a yoke: Black women and the burden of strength.* Eugene: Cascade Books.

West, L. (2017, January 3). I've left Twitter. It is unusable for anyone but trolls, robots and dictators. *The Guardian.* https://www.theguardian.com/commentisfree/2017/jan/03/ive-left-twitter-unusable-anyone-but-trolls-robots-dictators-lindy-west

Wilson, C. C., II, Gutiérrez, F., & Chao, L. M. (2013). *Racism, sexism, and the media: Multicultural issues into the new communications age.* Los Angeles: Sage.

Women of protest: Photographs from the records of the National Woman's Party. (n.d.) https://www.loc.gov/teachers/classroommaterials/connections/women-protest/history3.html

Women's Media Center (2015). Online abuse 101: Speech project. http://wmcspeechproject.com/online-abuse-101/

Wood, J. (2015). *Gendered lives: Communication, gender, & culture* (11th ed.). Stamford: Cengage.

Why we march: Signs of protest and hope. (2017). New York: Artisan.

Yardi, S., & boyd, d. (2010). Dynamic debates: An analysis of group polarization over time on Twitter. *Bulletin of Science, Technology & Society, 30*(5), 316–327.

Yiannopoulos, M. (2016, July 5). The solution to online 'harassment' is simple: Women should log off. *Breitbart.* http://www.breitbart.com/milo/2016/07/05/solution-online-harassment-simple-women-log-off/

Zahniser, J. D., & Fry, A. R. (2014). *Alice Paul: Claiming power.* Oxford: Oxford University Press.

Part I

Feminist Discourses

2

This Isn't New: Gender, Publics, and the Internet

Jacqueline Ryan Vickery

I want to begin with a personal story about an encounter with an online troll. The story will surely anger you, but is unlikely to shock you. It is at once abhorrent, yet familiar. It is alarming, and yet remains all too common and recognizable. Nonetheless, it is precisely because of its status as commonplace, as well-known, and as remarkably *expected* that it demands to be told. Again and again, lest we risk allowing the everyday vitriol and symbolic violence against women to accomplish its goal in silencing us. We know rape—in all its iterations from the corporeal to the symbolic—is a tool intended to discipline women into submission, into silence, to keep us in our appropriate patriarchal spaces and roles (Brownmiller 1975). Thus, while this story is all too commonplace within the spaces of feminist activism, I will share it so that our experiences are not silenced, are not ignored, are not just another statistic. While online gender-based harassments and threats are part of a broader collective social problem, they are simultaneously experienced on an individual affective level.

J. R. Vickery (✉)
Department of Media Arts, University of North Texas, Denton, TX, USA

© The Author(s) 2018
J. R. Vickery, T. Everbach (eds.), *Mediating Misogyny*,
https://doi.org/10.1007/978-3-319-72917-6_2

I teach a course called Digital Literacies and Social Activism. Students use the semester to work in groups on a media advocacy or social justice campaign. During the fall 2015 semester, four female students (three of whom identified as women of color) put together a campaign called *Feel Fearless*, which was intended to draw attention to, problematize, and combat the normalcy of catcalling and street harassment on campus. As a tactic intended to subvert typical rape narratives, the students made flyers that announced the issuance of a male curfew on campus (Fig. 2.1).

The *Feel Fearless* website included an image of the flyer with the text, "Think this is ridiculous? So do we." They explained that it is equally as ridiculous to ask women not to be alone at night when the real problem is not women as potential victims, but men as the most likely perpetrators of crime against women. They included satirical tips for how men could avoid harassing or raping a woman—a twist on the patronizing

Fig. 2.1 Example of the Feel Fearless campaign; the website has been blacked out for privacy concerns (Author photo)

and victim-blaming advice women receive about how "not to be raped" (Culp-Ressler 2014; Maxwell 2012)—and then explained the larger goals of their project. Within three days, the post spread across Tumblr at a rate the young women never expected; it received more than 3,000 notes and re-blogs. Understandably, they were feeling confident about the success of the campaign, but this feeling was short-lived.

The following weekend the four individual students' Twitter accounts, the campaign account, and my Twitter account received a graphically violent image of a beheaded woman being raped. Each image was accompanied by a message of vitriol that was personalized based on things the young women had recently said on Twitter or in their profiles. I am intellectually aware that this level of graphic violence is far too common online. Yet, sitting in my pajamas on a Sunday morning drinking coffee alone in my living room I have to admit that I was shocked. I was shaking. I had a knot in my stomach that I could not quell. From a digital activism perspective, the campaign had been a success: it traversed multiple platforms, generated traffic to the website, and sparked conversation and debate. However, on a personal level, the campaign felt like an utter failure. The campaign's entire message was for women to "feel fearless" in public. Yet on that day, we all felt anything but fearless: the threat of sexual and physical violence successfully instilled fear into women for speaking out about the very topic.

This chapter uses the students' campaign and our experience as a jumping-off point for a larger discussion and contextualization of gender-based and sexual harassment. Through an overview of earlier feminist movements and Internet scholarship, I aim to historicize our contemporary media moment of visible gender-based harassment within a longer history of harassment. Specifically, I focus on scholarship and pop culture writings in the early days of web culture, namely the mid-late 1990s.[1] Gender-based harassment of women has increasingly and recently become a more common topic of discussion and debate within pop culture, activism, legal circles, and scholarship, yet it is important to consider the longer trajectory of such harassment. Unfortunately, yet not surprisingly, this trend is not new. If we are to develop solutions, it is imperative we contextualize our contemporary moment within a larger history and discourse of women at the intersection of power, harassment, and technology.

The Problem: Technology as a Male-Dominated Field

Online gender-based and sexual harassment targeted at women, what Karla Mantilla (2013) refers to as gendertrolling, is a problem as old as the web itself. Early writings about computers and the Internet optimistically believed that we could build a technologically-mediated world that was free of gendered inequities, racism, and other structural differences that lead to discrimination, hate, and xenophobia. These views were proliferated within the tech community, via advertisements, and in journalism. In his 1995 book, *Being Digital*, Nicholas Negroponte wrote that the Internet "has four very powerful qualities that will result in its ultimate triumph: decentralizing, globalizing, harmonizing, and empowering" (p. 229). He continues, "But more than anything, my optimism comes from the empowering nature of being digital. The access, the mobility, and the ability to effect [sic] change are what will make the future so different from the present… We are bound to find new hope and dignity in places where very little existed before" (p. 231). Such a view is inherently technologically deterministic—that is, it presumes that technology can solve problems that larger social and cultural institutions of sexism, racism, and power have created. This "technoevangelism," as Millar writes, "masks the complex social issues of inequality, oppression and the human and ecological costs of technological restrictions. Social change is conflated with technological change, which is viewed as a runaway train inevitably propelling human society 'forward'" (1998, pp. 54–55). While many (male) writers were touting the benefits of the web, feminist scholars and activists were telling a cautionary tale based on personal experiences that were rooted in structural inequalities. Margie Wylie (1995) warns, "far from offering a millennial new world of democracy and equal opportunity, the coming web of information systems could turn the clock back 50 years for women" (p. 3). Let us consider a few of the reasons for her claims.

First, the hope-filled discourse erased the consequences of the "digital divide" and overlooked significant gaps of who had access to computers and the Internet at that time: primarily white, educated, men living in urban areas. Women, people of color, people from lower-income households, people outside of the United States and the West, and/or rural residents typically did not have access to the Internet yet (Zickuhr and Smith 2012). Second, this optimistic belief persisted alongside institutional barriers that excluded women and/or people of color from participating in the design and implementation of computer technologies. This further served to exclude women from the development of social norms and discourses of the web culture (Millar 1998). In 1995, Wylie wrote, "make no mistake about it, the Internet is a male territory" (p. 3). As an early example, on a 1995 listserv discussion about Islamic history, anthropologist Jon Anderson observed someone ask if there were any women in the discussion thread; a woman answered, "'we're here, but not talking' for fear of being shouted down, which she promptly was for making that observation" (p. 14). Dale Spender (1995) notes that due to the web's development in male-dominated spaces—namely, the military and the academy—it has been considered the domain of men.

In the nearly three decades since the web was first developed, more women are participating in online communities and spaces at rates that are similar to or even greater than men (Perrin 2015). Yet, when we look "behind the curtain" if you will, it's evident that the gender gap of technological design and control persists: only 25% of computing jobs are held by women (a percentage that has been declining since 1991) and a whopping 95% of tech start-ups are owned by men (Women Who Tech 2012). Eighty-eight percent of all information technology patents have male-only invention teams. For women of color the numbers are even more dismal: black women hold 3% of computing jobs and Latina women only 1% (Ashcraft et al. 2016). The problem has less to do with an unqualified pipeline and more to do with a toxic and hostile white supremacist patriarchal culture that isolates women within the male-dominated tech industry (ibid.).

Anonymity and the Body

At the same time that Negroponte and other technoevangelists wrote about the "empowering" and "harmonizing" potential of the Internet, women and other members of marginalized communities experienced the ways online communities reproduced—and even intensified—preexisting discourses and tactics of discrimination and harassment. For example, women in positions of authority—such as doctors and professors—were most likely to experience gender-based harassment online (Frank et al. 1998; Ferganchick-Neufang 1998). Much of the cyber-utopian discourse found in science fiction and academia focused on the potentially liberating aspects of anonymity: if we could leave our bodies behind, so the logic went, then we could leave behind racism, sexism, and other power imbalances that are presumed to be connected to our embodied differences (Gibson 1984; Haraway 1991; Lupton 1995). However, as early as 1994, media scholar Anne Balsamo found that:

> New modes of electronic communication, for example, indicate that the anonymity offered by the computer screen empowers antisocial behaviors such as 'flaming' (electronic insults) and borderline illegal behaviors such as trespassing, E-mail snooping, and MUD-rape (unwanted, aggressive, sexual-textual encounter in a multi-user domain). And yet, for all the anonymity they offer, many computer communications reproduce stereotypically gendered patterns of conversation. (p. 139)

Along with many other feminist scholars and activists (Millar 1998; Nakamura 2002; O'Brien 1999), Balsamo's research argues that the "techno-body" is always already gendered and marked by race; her work is significant for drawing attention to this at a time when (predominantly male scholars) were extolling the virtues of anonymity and the potential liberating aspects of the Internet. Writing in the 1990s, Jodi O'Brien (1999) argues that gender can be even more stereotypical and limiting in online spaces than in embodied interactions. The potential to create equitable distributions of power does not rest solely on the technological affordances of the Internet, but rather on the policies, practices, and norms that we as citizens must intentionally harness and create.

Contestations of Space and Power

Historically, patriarchal cultures have tried to contain women to the domestic and private sphere. Men accomplished this by creating laws that prohibited women's participation in public affairs. For example, they created laws that denied women the right to vote, to attain an education, to own land, or to open a bank account, all of which effectively worked to deny women autonomy and a role in public decisions and affairs. Although feminists have worked successfully to abolish many of these discriminatory practices in many nations, the perception that the public sphere "belongs" to men still has many consequences and implications for women today. Further, issues of gender-based inequality often are framed as "women's issues." Patriarchal society contends that issues such as rape, contraception, childbirth, and sexual harassment are not matters of public concern but instead ought to be individualized and contained to the private sphere. Anti-feminists silence or harass women when they bring these privately experienced, yet publicly sanctioned forms of gender-based oppression and inequity into public forums. This happens online—as is the focus of this book—as well as in embodied public spaces, such as when Texas Senator Charles Schwertner used his gavel to break a glass table while trying to silence a woman for testifying against an anti-abortion bill (Zielinski 2017).

Street harassment, more colloquially referred to as catcalling, includes lewd remarks but also more aggressive forms of harassment such as following, blocking a woman's path, and public exposure or masturbation. Street harassment has long been a problem for women, particularly women of color, genderqueer women, people who identify as trans, and/or low-income women (Mirk 2014). Far from being a compliment, as some men have publicly argued (Alter 2014), catcalling is a way for men to objectify women and reassert male dominance and control over women's bodies and movements in public spaces (MacKinnon 1979; Mantilla 2013). Catcalling intimidates women by "reminding her" of her "place," a place that is subservient to men's, one that is not public, not visible, not safe. Fairchild and Rudman (2008) found that women who experience frequent stranger harassment are more likely to fear rape and restrict their freedom of movement in public. Online gender-based sexual harassment functions in a similar manner. Mantilla (2013) explains:

> Gendertrolling has much in common with other offline targeting of women such as sexual harassment in the workplace and street harassment. In those arenas as is the case with gendertrolling, the harassment is about patrolling gender boundaries and using insults, hate, and threats of violence and/or rape to ensure that women and girls are either kept out of, or play subservient roles in, male-dominated arenas... [Gendertrolling] systematically targets women to prevent them from fully occupying public spaces. (pp. 568–569)

Feminist activist projects such as *Take Back the Night* (which holds public events to raise awareness about sexual assault), *Stop Telling Women to Smile* (which is a public art series by Tatyana Fazlalizadeh that addresses gender-based street harassment), and *Holla Back Girl* (which is an international movement to document and stop street harassment via maps and mobile apps and the focus of Chap. 17 in this book), are merely three examples of feminist activism aimed at helping women claim a right to safely be seen and heard in public without intimidation.

The idea that the Internet is a public sphere in some idealized notion of the concept is debatable for reasons linked to conceptualizations of democracy, deliberation, and capitalism (see Dean 2003; Papacharissi 2002). Nonetheless, many online spaces function as public places in the sense that they are accessible spaces where citizens gather to communicate and deliberate and places where strangers interact with those who are different from themselves (Goffman 1971; Sennett 1977). The public aspects of the web can be defined as "networked publics," which, according to danah boyd (2010), "are simultaneously (1) the space[s] constructed through networked technologies and (2) the imagined collective that emerges as a result of the intersection of people, technology, and practice" (2010, p. 39). It is the inherent visibility and participation of women in networked publics that elicits much of the gender-based and sexual harassment targeted at women.

Further, in the early days of the development of the Internet, web culture was primarily a white male-dominated space and "tech culture" was largely constructed as the domain of white men (Borsook 1996; Millar 1998). Jessica Megarry (2014) writes, "Women have never been equal in the online public sphere, and it appears that social media forums remain firmly grounded in the material realties of women's everyday experiences of sexism in patriarchal society" (p. 49). The combination of patriarchal and white supremacist understandings of public spaces—be they physical or virtual—with the male-dominated history of web culture, has undoubtedly contributed to the perception of the web as a white masculine space. Like public streets, public affairs, and other male-dominated spaces and discourses, the history of the web has at least in part produced a culture that perpetually discriminates against and harasses women and other members of communities that social and cultural systems of power continue to marginalize.

Echo Chambers

The affordances of the Internet allow people to form communities based on similar views. From a psychological perspective, humans tend to occupy (and prefer) homophilious networks—that is, networks made up of similar people. This concept is as ancient as humanity itself. Aristotle wrote that people "love those who are like themselves" and Plato observed, "similarity begets friendship" (p. 416; McPherson et al. 2001). The affordances of the Internet allow individuals to find like-minded people and join communities that may not exist within the confines of their geographically and temporally bound day-to-day lives. For example, queer youth integrate digital resources and communities as part of their identity development and as a way to find community, resources, and education that may not otherwise be available to them (Gray 2009; Hillier et al. 2012; MacIntosh and Bryson 2008; Mustanski et al. 2011).

Yet, at the same time, the bringing together of like-minded individuals can also lead to echo chambers. Communication scholars Kathleen Hall Jamieson and Joseph N. Cappella (2008) use the metaphor of an echo chamber to indicate a "bounded, enclosed media space that has the potential to both magnify the messages delivered within it and insulate them from rebuttal" (p. 76). Today, concerns about online echo chambers are well known, yet even back in 1995, Anderson considered how creating networks of like-minded individuals—what he referred to as "cybertribes"—would undermine the optimistic potential of the Internet to dismantle structural power imbalances, such as gender discrimination. He writes:

> Sceptics and critics challenge the utopian vision [of the Internet] with a darker one of 'cybertribes' – bands of like-minded citizens threaded together instantaneously, specifically, globally, sometimes obsessively – eager not just to reinforce each other, but to influence real events, on the one hand, or of profound alienation on the other. (p. 13)

Online communities can, of course, be diverse, but they can also facilitate the creation of homophilious networks that reproduce particular ideas and alienate individuals who try to challenge normative assumptions. Echo chambers tend to cut people off from dissenting opinions and instead have the potential to reinforce extreme ideas. The dark language of "cybertribes" could be used to describe what today we more commonly refer to as communities of organized trolls. There are countless examples of trolls coming together to launch organized attacks on women and feminist activists who call out and challenge the white supremacist patriarchal culture of the Internet, thus reaffirming the Internet is the domain of white straight men.

Speaking Out & Feminist Activism

On a positive note, networked publics and echo chambers also afford women the opportunity to organize, share collective stories, and engage in civic and intellectual debates in highly visible manners. Campaigns such as #YesAllWomen and #MenCallMeThings are two examples of the ways that feminists have used Twitter in particular to help draw attention to gender-based forms of inequity, discrimination, and harassment (Cole 2015). As with earlier sites of public activism, trolls and misogynists often target the women who participate in these campaigns; they are intent on silencing and intimidating women as a way to hinder their efforts.

Since the early days of the web, women have been encouraged to battle online misogyny. Yet, in 1996, Stephanie Brail countered the advice that women should "fight back" against online harassment by drawing attention to the inequity itself.

> Why should we have to fight back as 'the price for admission'? Men don't usually have to jump through a hoop of sexual innuendo and anti-feminist backlash simply to participate [online]. They use their energy posting, while we often use ours wondering if we'll be punished for opening our mouths. And with all our training to be 'nice' are most women even prepared to do such battle? (p. 148)

Going even further back to the early 1900s, suffragists faced harassment, verbal and physical assault, and arrests for asserting their right to protest and vote. As addressed in the Introduction to this book, during the Woman Suffrage Parade of 1913 in Washington D.C., an angry mob hurt more than 300 suffragists. The mistreatment of women at the parade—by spectators and the police—led to Congressional hearings and the firing of the D.C. police superintendent (Harvey 2001). During the Senate hearings, one man unambiguously declared, "There would be nothing like this [rioting] happen if you [women] would stay at home" (ibid.). Anti-suffrage posters and advertisements employed specifically gendered language to intimidate suffragists. The rhetoric is strikingly similar to the language used to harass and intimidate women online today: it focused on women's appearance and/or sexuality, calls to violence, a perceived lack of appropriate femininity, conflated feminism with man-hating, and presumed women lacked the intellectual capacity for public dialogue.[2]

Given this longer misogynistic history, it is unfortunate yet not surprising that women are attacked for speaking out online. Feminist blogger Jessica Valenti summarized her online experience, "I spend the better part of my day fielding tweets and messages about what a slut I am. That I should be 'jizzed on'… that I want to be gangbanged, that I'm worthless" (Cole 2015). In her "What I couldn't say" speech at the *All About*

Women conference in Sydney, feminist media critic Anita Sarkeesian (2015) of *Feminist Frequency* explained, "I rarely feel comfortable speaking spontaneously in public spaces… Over the last several years I've become hyper vigilant… Everyday I see my words scrutinized, twisted and distorted by thousands of men hell bent on destroying and silencing me." At a social justice conference on my own campus, feminist scholar and former television host Melissa Harris-Perry explained that she had not checked the @ replies on her Twitter account in almost six years because she received too much hate speech and death threats as direct result of her anti-racist and anti-sexist views. During an episode of her MSNBC show, she explained:

> I'm at a point where I don't retweet anything that I really like, because I fear that I would send all of my haters and the harassment that comes to me, over to some person who doesn't deserve it. And I keep thinking, I guess [online harassment] is having an effect and quieting whatever little digital voice I might have otherwise had. (Harris-Perry 2014)

These examples reveal the ways in which women who challenge patriarchal norms or draw attention to the ways male behavior contributes to social inequity are likely to be targets of sexual harassment. Online threats of physical and sexual violence have even forced women to cancel public speaking engagements, hire armed bodyguards, and seek covert shelter, all of which effectively silences their voices and erases their bodies from public dialogue and spaces.

Related to the *Feel Fearless* campaign, I have been surprised by the number of people who have asked me, "Well, what did you expect?" when I tell them about the Twitter messages my students and I received in response to the campaign. This somewhat apathetic attitude implies that women who speak out against problematic male behavior should anticipate and expect to be verbally and symbolically abused as a result. One the one hand, advising students that they are likely to receive backlash because of their participation does seem like a responsible and necessary precaution. Yet, this rhetoric falls dangerously close to acceptance: not in the sense that we believe abuse is justified, but that we believe it is inevitable, as though harassment is the tax women must pay for participating in networked publics. As such, I'm uncomfortable with advice that simply tells women to expect harassment and to ignore it.

Frequently, women are told to be quiet, to stop participating, to leave the platform, at least for the time being. This advice—that targets of harassment and violence should exit the dangerous situation—is sadly far too familiar to women. Repeatedly women are told to "just leave" if they are being harassed or threatened. Survivors of rape are advised to skip class to avoid their rapist. Survivors of domestic violence are told they should be the ones to leave their homes to escape violence. In cases of workplace sexual harassment, women are told that if they aren't happy at a job, they should just quit. And in incidents of street harassment, women are frequently expected to exert time and energy to find less convenient routes that (temporarily) allow them to avoid catcalls and harassment. Telling women to exit a space because she is not safe reifies the space as inherently masculine, as "belonging" to men. The rights and entitlements of male students, partners, employees, and citizens are deemed more worthy of protection even at the expense of women's rights to participation.

The students in the *Feel Fearless* campaign chose to remove their names and Twitter handles from the campaign. I understand this response, but I also hate that for them. I want them to receive the credit for their creativity and actions. I want their voices to be heard as women's voices and not just as a generic campaign voice. I want to make it clear that I do not judge a woman for withdrawing from online public spaces in response to harassment. As an individual strategy and practice of self-care and safety, this response is understandable, justifiable, and often necessary. What I am critiquing is the advice that women should be the ones to withdraw from participation in networked publics. The very tactic the *Feel Fearless* campaign employed was to draw attention to the absurdity of responsibilizing women for assault. Though satirical, their suggestion of a male curfew would have undoubtedly reduced the number of threats made and assaults committed against women on campus.

Conclusion: Using the Past to Inform the Future

Via a consideration of the longer history of gender-based harassment of women—both online and offline—it is my hope that we can begin to trace the continuity and evolution of the problem, and ultimately the solutions. In many ways, the harassment of women online parallels a longer trajectory of misogyny and sexism that coalesces around four central patterns: woman become targets when they: (1) occupy positions of power; (2) draw attention to the ways women's "private" experiences are rooted in systematic inequalities of power; (3) call out men, masculinity, and patriarchy for contributing to and benefiting from social injustices and inequities; and/or (4) assert their right to occupy and participate in public spaces. A recognition of this longer history and continuity allows activists and scholars to situate the problem within a broader context of feminist literature and activism. In other words, the problem is not merely the Internet, but systems of gender-based inequities.

I believe that situating online gender-based harassment within a longer history of feminist strategies and activism urges us to analyze the strategies of earlier feminist movements—including our successes and failures—as a way to consider theoretically and pragmatically what has worked in the past and what tactics can work for us now. As in the past, we need to work on intentionally forming allyships, solidarity, consciousness-raising, naming our experiences, speaking truth to power, and fostering collective action through overt political and economic actions. We must also situate our current moment within a larger economic, social, and political context. As women continue to use the Internet as a tool for increasing visibility and as feminists organize and activists fight for greater equity, we know there will be a backlash from men who feel threatened by changes.

Many of the recent prominent online harassment incidents that have garnered the attention of news and entertainment media are a reaction to women gaining access to historically masculine and male-dominated spaces such as politics, Hollywood, sports, video games, and "geek" fandoms (all of which are addressed in various chapters throughout this book). It is not just the formerly male-dominated spaces of the Internet that have evolved, but also other cultural spaces and values. Some men view these changes as threatening to their sense of entitlement and traditional masculine values of power, strength, and dominance. As Michael Kimmel (2017) writes about "angry white men": "The game has changed, but instead of questioning the rules, they want to eliminate the other players" (p. 15). Although feminism benefits men by challenging the limiting and harmful constructions of masculinity, to many men, access to rights continues to be viewed as a zero-sum game: if women gain, then they lose (see Chap. 8). As such, it is important to address the online abuse of women alongside broader historical changes within society, politics, culture, and the economy. Feminist resistance is not merely about fighting back against the harassment of women, be it online or offline, but also about eradicating the hegemonic notions of masculinity that underpin misogyny.

I started this chapter with a personal story because I believe we must continue share our own stories of disempowerment, intimidation, and harassment as a way to collectively connect our individual experiences to systems of power and oppression. Indeed, "the personal *is* political" has become a familiar battle cry of second-wave feminism. As Carol Hanisch (1970) explained in her formative essay about the 1960s Women's Liberation Movement, the coming together of women to share common private experiences allowed them to stop blaming themselves for their own oppression and instead to situate their experiences within larger systems of oppression. She writes, "There are no personal solutions at this time. There is only collective action for a collective solution" (p. 4). Ending gender-based and sexual harassment is not only about individual protection, it is a call to action. It is about charging society with the task and responsibility of taking women seriously, of validating our voices, our experiences, and our very right to participate in public affairs. Ultimately ending gender-based and sexual harassment is about creating spaces in which women are incorporated into public spaces and debates without marginalization, harassment, or intimidation.

Notes

1. Tim Berners-Lee developed the World Wide Web (WWW) in 1989; it became publically available August 6, 1991.
2. For examples, simply search online for images of anti-suffragists posters.

References

Alter, C. (2014, November 3). Watch this guy try to defend catcalling and totally fail. *Time.* Available: http://time.com/3554551/defend-catcalling-steve-santagati-cnn/

Anderson, J. (1995). 'Cybariates', knowledge workers and new creoles on the superhighway. *Anthropology Today, 11*(4), 13–15.

Ashcraft, C., McLain, B., & Eger, E. (2016). Women in tech: The facts. National Center for Women & Information Technology. https://www.ncwit.org/sites/default/files/resources/womenintech_facts_fullreport_05132016.pdf

Balsamo, A. (1994). Feminism for the incurably informed. In M. Dery (Ed.), *Flame wars: The discourse of cyberculture* (pp. 125–156). Durham: Duke University Press.

Borsook, P. (1996). The memoirs of a token: An aging Berkeley feminist examines wired. In L. Cherny & E. R. Weise (Eds.), *Wired_women: Gender and new realities in cyberspace* (pp. 24–41). Seattle: Seal Press.

boyd, d. (2010). Social network sites as networked publics: Affordances, dynamics, and implications. In Z. Papacharissi (Ed.), *Networked self: Identity, community, and culture on social network sites* (pp. 39–58). New York: Routledge.

Brail, S. (1996). The price of admission: Harassment and free speech in the wild, wild west. In L. Cherny & E. R. Weise (Eds.), *Wired_women: Gender and new realities in cyberspace* (pp. 141–157). Seattle: Seal Press.

Brownmiller, S. (1975). *Against our will: Women and rape.* New York: Simon & Schuster.

Cole, K. K. (2015). "It's like she's eager to be verbally abused": Twitter, trolls, and (en)gendering disciplinary rhetoric. *Feminist Media Studies, 15*(2), 356–358.

Culp-Ressler, T. (2014, June 10). All of the things women are supposed to do to prevent rape. *Think Progress.* https://thinkprogress.org/all-of-the-things-women-are-supposed-to-do-to-prevent-rape-b9365bf520c1#.gibhp1ps4

Dean, J. (2003). Why the net is not a public sphere. *Constellations, 10*(1), 95–112.

Fairchild, K., & Rudman, L. A. (2008). Everyday stranger harassment and women's objectification. *Social Justice Research, 21*(3), 338–357.

Ferganchick-Neufang, J. K. (1998). Virtual harassment: Women and online education. *First Monday, 3*(2). Available: http://firstmonday.org/ojs/index.php/fm/article/viewArticle/575

Frank, E., Brogan, D., & Schiffman, M. (1998). Prevalence and correlates of harassment among US women physicians. *Archives of Internal Medicine, 158*(4), 352–358.

Gibson, W. (1984). *Neuromancer.* New York: Ace Books.

Goffman, E. (1971). *Relations in public: Microstudies of the public order.* New York: Basic Books.

Gray, M. L. (2009). *Out in the country: Youth, media, and queer visibility in rural America.* New York: NYU Press.

Hanisch, C. (1970). The personal is political. In *Notes from the second year women's liberation.* New York: Radical Feminism.

Haraway, D. (1991). *Simians, cyborgs, and women: The reinvention of nature.* New York: Routledge.

Harris-Perry, M. (2014). How dangerous is harassment in 140 characters? MSNBC. http://www.msnbc.com/melissa-harris-perry/watch/how-dangerous-is-anonymous-online-harassment--347801155546

Harvey, S. (2001). Marching for the vote: Remembering the woman suffrage parade of 1913. In *American women: A Library of Congress guide for the study of woman's history and culture in the United States.* Washington, DC: Library of Congress.

Hillier, L., Mitchell, K. J., & Ybarra, M. L. (2012). The internet as a safety net: Findings from a series of online focus groups with LGB and non-LGB young people in the United States. *Journal of LGBT Youth, 9*(3), 225–246.

Jamieson, K. H., & Cappella, J. N. (2008). *Echo chamber: Rush Limbaugh and the conservative media establishment.* New York: Oxford University Press.

Kimmel, M. (2017). *Angry white men: American masculinity at the end of an era.* New York City: Nation Books.

Lupton, D. (1995). The embodied computer/user. In M. Featherstone & R. Burrows (Eds.), *Cyberspace/cyberbodies/cyberpunk: Cultures of technological embodiment* (pp. 97–112). Thousand Oaks: Sage Publications.

Macintosh, L., & Bryson, M. (2008). Youth, MySpace, and the interstitial spaces of becoming and belonging. *Queer (Re)Presentations, 5*(1), 133–142.

MacKinnon, C. (1979). *Sexual harassment of working women: A case of sex discrimination*. New Haven: Yale.

Mantilla, K. (2013). Gendertrolling: Misogyny adapts to new media. *Feminist Studies, 39*(2), 563–570.

Maxwell, Z. (2012, January 14). Stop telling women how not to get raped. *Ebony*. http://www.ebony.com/news-views/stop-telling-women-how-to-not-get-raped#axzz4ZvRNaDY6/

McPherson, M., Smith-Lovin, L., & Cook, J. M. (2001). Birds of a feather: Homophily in social networks. *Annual Review of Sociology, 27*, 415–444.

Megarry, J. (2014). Online incivility or sexual harassment?: Conceptualising women's experiences in the digital age. *Women's Studies International Forum, 47*, 46–55.

Millar, M. S. (1998). *Cracking the gender code: Who rules the wired world?* Toronto: Second Story Press.

Mirk, S. (2014, June 3). A new report reveals the realities of street harassment. *Bitch Media*. Available: https://bitchmedia.org/post/street-harassment-realities-report-statistics-america

Mustanski, B., Lyons, T., & Garcia, S. C. (2011). Internet use and sexual health of young men who have sex with men: A mixed-methods study. *Archives of Sexual Behaviour, 40*(2), 289–300.

Nakamura, L. (2002). *Cybertypes: Race, ethnicity, and identity on the internet*. New York: Routledge.

Negroponte, N. (1995). *Being digital*. New York: Knopf.

O'Brien, J. (1999). Writing in the body: Gender (re)production in online interaction. In P. Kollock & M. Smith (Eds.), *Communities in cyberspace* (pp. 76–106). New York: Routledge.

Papacharissi, Z. (2002). The virtual sphere: The internet as a public space. *New Media & Society, 4*(1), 9–27.

Perrin, A. (2015). Social media usage: 2005–2015. Pew Research Center. http://www.pewinternet.org/2015/10/08/social-networking-usage-2005-2015/

Sarkeesian, A. (2015, March 21). What I couldn't say panel at all about women. *Feminist Frequency*. Available: https://feministfrequency.com/2015/03/21/what-i-couldnt-say-panel-at-all-about-women/

Sennett, R. (1977). *The fall of public man*. New York: Knopf.

Spender, D. (1995). *Nattering on the net: Women, power, and cyberspace*. North Melbourne: Spinifex Press.

Women Who Tech. (2012). Infographic. http://www.womenwhotech.com/womenintechinfographic

Wylie, M. (1995). No place for a woman. *Digital Media, 4*(8), 3–6.

Zickuhr, K., & Smith, A. (2012). Digital differences. Pew Internet & American Life Project. http://www.pewinternet.org/files/old-media/Files/Reports/2012/PIP_Digital_differences_041312.pdf

Zielinski, A. (2017, February 16). Texas senator shatters table trying to silence woman testifying against anti-abortion bill. *San Antonio Current.* http://www.sacurrent.com/the-daily/archives/2017/02/16/texas-senator-shatters-table-trying-to-silence-woman-testifying-against-anti-abortion-bill

3

Limitations of "Just Gender": The Need for an Intersectional Reframing of Online Harassment Discourse and Research

Lucy Hackworth

When studying online harassment of women, most scholarship focuses on gender-specific elements (such as sexism, misogyny, or gender-specific derogatory language). Research has found significant differences between harassment leveled at men and women,[1] and discussions in the field of online harassment therefore aim to highlight the specific experiences of women. In this chapter, I discuss the framing of this field of scholarship, by exploring common terminology, investigating who is included in research, and focussing on how harassment is discussed. Firstly, I introduce the issues, and provide a broad overview of the current research and existing global trends. I then discuss existing critiques of the whiteness of feminism, explore the concept of intersectionality, and raise current concerns that black feminists have raised about the whiteness of *cyber*feminism.[2] I go on to show how attempts to focus on "just gendered" harassment in scholarship ignore the experiences of women whose harassment falls into other categories, or is multilayered. I illustrate that the dominant discourse about online harassment of women can be both simplifying and silencing, and contributes to the erasure of the experiences of women of

L. Hackworth (✉)
Independent Scholar, Adelaide, SA, Australia

© The Author(s) 2018
J. R. Vickery, T. Everbach (eds.), *Mediating Misogyny*,
https://doi.org/10.1007/978-3-319-72917-6_3

color (and women of other marginalized identities). Moreover, it leaves a gap in analyses that do not allow for adequate exploration of the nuances of online behavior and discrimination.

The Evolution of Online Harassment

After the global expansion of the Internet[3] in the 1990s (Zhao 2006, p. 458), early feminist Internet scholars (e.g., Turkle 1995; Stone 1995 in Chun 2002; Hayles 1999) were optimistic about the potential that online interaction held for users to transcend gender and other categories of disadvantage. Yet it quickly became apparent that the online realm was not immune from discrimination and abuse. In 1999, Susan Herring wrote that "gender-based disparity exist(ed)" online, and at times took "extreme forms… including overt harassment" (1999, p. 151). Leander and McKim argued that, as a "place", the online realm became "just as sexist, classist (and) homophobic" as offline spaces had been (2003, p. 217). Richards later summarized the dilemma that "digital technologies both subvert *and* reinscribe gender, race and other corporeal hierarchies in virtual space" (2011, pp. 6–7—emphasis added). Online harassment has further increased with the emergence of contemporary online spaces that emphasize social interaction, such as Facebook and Twitter.

Statistically, men and women receive similar amounts of harassment online (Duggan 2014), but when it comes to the kinds of harassment, and the severity, gendered trends emerge. Women are generally the subject of more online criticism, especially those with a high public profile, those who raise issues of feminism and sexism, and those who embody additional marginalized identities. Harassment directed at women includes gendered insults, critiques, and objectification of physical bodies, and sexually explicit and sexually violent threats or content. Studies find that women[4] have been receiving increasing amounts of harassment that is misogynist in content, and that often impedes their freedom of expression and movement online, and *offline*. A study conducted by digital platform *Feminism in India* found that 56% of respondents who had experienced online harassment "experienced derogatory comments about their gender or appearance" (Pasricha 2016). A report of online harassment in Germany found that women were "far more strongly exposed" to sexual harassment and cyberstalking online than men (Staude-Müller et al. 2012, p. 267). An inordinately high percentage of *young* women have experienced harassment online, with an Australian study finding that numbers may be as high as 76% of women under 30 (Norton Symantec 2016).

Because of the uniqueness of women's online harassment, scholars, bloggers, online feminists, and online news media have largely focused exclusively on its 'gendered' nature. Over ten years ago, Biber et al. wrote, in their study of the impact of sexual harassment online, that literature and research about online harassment had been primarily focused on gender, despite the presence of harassment based on other discriminations (2002, p. 33). The motivation for focussing on gendered harassment is similar today. As media and communications scholar Emma Jane writes in her book *Misogyny Online: a Short (and Brutish) History*, "focusing primarily on gendered cyberhate involving male attackers and female targets is necessary because of the overwhelming anecdotal and empirical evidence that women are being attacked more often, more severely, and in far more violently sexualized ways than men" (2017, p. 10). Similarly, Social and Political Sciences scholar Jessica Megarry's argument for the study of 'online sexual harassment' (2014, p. 53) is that "women are currently being excluded from online participation based on their sex" (ibid.). The intent of discussing gender is to show that the "new technological frontier" (Braidotti 2003, p. 255) recreates and fosters sexism in similar ways to that of *offline* space. In particular, scholars seek to highlight the misogynist nature of the harassment, and the way that such content impedes women's involvement online. Yet, despite intentions to highlight inequality, current framing of research causes problems related to who is included and how research is undertaken, resulting in a homogeneity of women's experiences. These problems, which I will shortly expand on, directly correlate with existing critiques of past (white) feminist scholarship more broadly.

The Whiteness of (Cyber)Feminism

There has been much criticism of the first and second waves of feminism for being "rooted in whiteness" (Daniels 2016, p. 4), with many including Professor of Philosophy Naomi Zack arguing that "feminism was by, about, and for, white middle-class women" (2007, p. 193). One of the key frameworks 'designed to combat feminist hierarchy, hegemony and exclusivity' (Nash 2008, p. 2) is *intersectionality*. This is a term coined by Kimberlé Crenshaw in 1989 that draws upon, and summarizes, concepts and ideas of many other scholars, activists and groups (see Lutz et al. 2011 for an overview). It refers to the 'multidimensional nature and complexity of (people's) experience' (Lutz et al. 2011, p. 3) and highlights how specific intersections between categories of difference (such as gender, race, and class) shape people's subject positions and experiences in particular ways. Crenshaw shows, for example, that the intersectional experience of black women "is greater than the sum of racism and sexism" (1989, p. 140). By this she means that there is more occurring than just racism, and just sexism, and that the two don't operate in isolation. Instead, the two intersect, making black women's experience unique, and therefore often overlooked due to problems of categorization. This can be summarized in an example referred to as the 'librarians' dilemma', which is used to explain 'historical invisibility' (Purdie-Vaughns and Eibach 2008, p. 383):

> Imagine a librarian who receives a single copy of a book about black women's history. The librarian must decide whether the book should be shelved in the Women's Studies section or the African-American Studies section. If she chooses to shelve the book in the Women's Studies section it is unlikely that casual browsers interested in African-American Studies will come across the book. Alternatively, if she shelves the book in the African-American Studies section the casual browsers of Women's Studies are going to miss the book. Either way, the story of African-American women's experiences will be missed by a whole group of potential readers. (Purdie-Vaughns and Eibach 2008, p. 383)

Intersectionality as an analytic tool is also used to discuss nuances of other intersecting identities of oppression, such as class and sexuality, and the diverse experiences of those who embody such identities. Not only does intersectionality highlight complexity of experience, but it also speaks to a fundamental principle of feminist scholarship: "the acknowledgement of differences *among* women" (Davis 2008, p. 70—emphasis added). After criticisms emerged that feminism claimed to be representative of all women yet actually spoke primarily for the privileged majority, intersectionality as a concept showed why intersectional analyses were vital, and highlighted the "limitations of gender as a single analytic category" (McCall 2005, p. 1771). Many feminist researchers realized that to discuss gender in isolation from other marginalized identities was not by default the study of all kinds of women, but rather the study of those who fit a privileged and vocal subset.

Recently *digital* feminism, also known as cyberfeminism, has also been critiqued for failing to be intersectional in several ways. Cyberfeminism, a term first used by Sadie Plant in 1994 (Consalvo 2012), is described as being the exploration of the way that 'gendered bodies and relations shape technologies and how we interact with them' (Cottom 2016, p. 215), and relates also to the use and appropriation of technologies by feminists (Paasonen 2011, p. 335). White cyberfeminists have been challenged on the ways that the new realm of online feminisms is reproducing the failures of past feminisms, by ignoring the diversity of women's experiences and voices.[5] In addition, as Daniels argues, "there is scant research on whiteness and women online" (Daniels, in Daniels 2016, p. 7), meaning that there is a lack of reflection on the role that white online feminists are playing on keeping other women's identities invisible. Even less included in scholarship are reflections and critique of the oversights themselves. These criticisms are applicable across any form of feminist Internet activity, but the research of online harassment of women is one for which these arguments are particularly relevant. I will now expand on why this is so.

A Focus on "Just Gender"

Online harassment of women occurs based on a multitude of possible discriminations other than simply being a woman. One study found that 51% of African Americans overall experienced harassment online, compared to 34% of white people (Duggan 2014). Gender and sexually-diverse women and people are at higher risk of online harassment (Marwick 2016), and "transgender people (also) face disproportionate levels of harassment online" (Haimson 2016). The content of harassment itself is often based on such identities, but rarely acknowledged in discussion or research. In addition, harassment received by people who embody multiple marginalized identities is likely to be multilayered in nature (Starr 2014), but these complex experiences of harassment are also largely ignored.

Much of the research about harassment of women online is focused on individual categories. Susan Herring, in her 1999 study *The Rhetorical Dynamics of Gender Harassment On-Line*, was one of the first to study harassment of women in the then emerging 'synchronous' (real-time, chat based) forms of online interaction. Although Herring did observe and note some racist comments toward women (1999, p. 159), her study was primarily focused on highlighting the fact that 'gender harassment creates a hostile social environment for some women on-line', and is therefore "a behavior that we cannot afford to tolerate" (1999, p. 164). More recent studies remain largely focused on single-category analysis, such as studies of racist harassment (Hughey and Daniels 2013), gendered harassment (Megarry 2014; Mantilla 2013; Jane 2014; Citron 2009; Filipovic 2007; Biber et al. 2002), and online gender bias (Kasumovic and Kuznekoff 2015; Fox and Tang 2014; Gardiner et al. 2016). The harassment of women of color online *has* been written about, but within studies of online racism. While some scholars mention race within studies of gender and vice versa (e.g. Gardiner et al. 2016; Citron 2014), scant has been written about multilayered harassment itself. Additionally, although studies exist that have included more specific research terms than just 'women' (Pasricha 2016), the field is dominated by those that don't.

Within the field of scholarship relating to the online harassment of women there have been several attempts by scholars to define harassment of women with specific terminologies. Legal and feminist scholar Jill Filipovic refers to harassment of women as *Internet misogyny*, arguing that "online attacks on female bloggers" remind women of their "secondary status through sexualised insults, rape threats and beauty contests"

(2007, p. 303). Legal scholar Danielle Keats Citron writes about online harassment as being *a uniquely gendered phenomenon* (2009, p. 375), while Biber et al. use the term *gender harassment* which they describe as involving "a range of misogynist behaviours directed at women because of their gender" (2002, p. 34). Online harassment scholar Emma Jane has previously referred to the abuse of women online as *e-bile* (Jane 2014) and, more recently, *gendered cyberhate* (Jane 2015). Political science scholar Jessica Megarry refers to the "aggressive harassment of women online" as *online sexual harassment* (2014, p. 47), while Karla Mantilla (2013) refers to specifically misogynistic abuse as *gendertrolling*. These descriptions reflect a conscious decision to *only* focus on the gendered dimension of harassment targeted at women. Terms used imply that gendered harassment can be experienced on its own, and that misogynist or sexist harassment is something that affects any kind of woman the same way, *because* they are women.

Intersectionality Ignored

As yet, intersectional perspectives largely remain missing from dominant harassment discourse, but some scholars have acknowledged they are needed. Fox et al. (2015), in a study of anonymity in sexist content, do not reference the impact or inclusion of racist content within the study, yet note at the end of the report that "future research should probe the intersectionality of sexism and race on SNSs (social networking sites)" (2015, p. 441). Jane addresses that a "limitation of (her) book is that it focuses on the gendered dimensions of cyber-hate as opposed to those aspects of online hate speech which are homophobic, transphobic, racist, culturally intolerant…" (2017, p. 9), but few online harassment scholars have acknowledged the lack of consideration of intersectional harassment. Jane does acknowledge the "political intersectionality of gender with other social identities" but writes that to try and cover all of these would overlook relevant nuances (ibid.).

Yet, as Sociology scholar Katherine Cross emphasizes, separating harassment based on identities is not really possible:

The racism and transphobia of abuse directed at (some) women is not mere flavoring of the abuse, but rather its very content, and that remains thoroughly unanalyzed. It is not so easy, after all, to say where abuse of a Black trans woman becomes specifically "gendertrolling" as opposed to "racetrolling" or "transtrolling." They're inseparable, and that's rather the point, from the perspective of the abuser: Every part of you is available to them for attack. (Cross 2015)

What Cross is articulating is that experiencing gendered harassment in isolation is really only possible for white, middle-class, heterosexual, cisgender, able-bodied women. Anyone else is likely to experience harassment that is more than "just gendered," yet is rarely reported on as such. Women of color online overwhelmingly experience harassment that is sexist *and* racist (Hackworth 2016, p. 59). Women with disabilities experience harassment that is sexist and ableist, and people who identify as queer will experience harassment that is additionally homophobic. Whilst transgender women and trans feminine[6] people experience online harassment that may correlate with many other women's experiences, they can also be targets for specific abuse. As writer Thorne N. Melcher has argued, trans people online seem to experience not only abuse, but also further harassment (such as account suspension) for responding to abuse (Melcher 2017). This has significant implications for wellbeing, but also many transgender people require online spaces for "opportunity and economic mobility" as a result of, or to avoid, discrimination and abuse in traditional workplaces, and so harassment online has further impacts as well (Clark 2015). In addition to these examples, there are of course many more additional types of harassment based on multiple oppressions, and many more multiple oppressions within these scenarios. By separating harassment into singular identity categories, not only are many women's experiences overlooked, and elements of their harassment left out of research and discussion, but the differences in implications also remain unknown.

An example of this is the case of feminist vlogger and game reviewer Anita Sarkeesian, whose harassment online has been widely discussed by online and print media, was repeatedly attacked in "gendered" ways, but whose harassment also included abuse based on her perceived ethnicity. This content, however, is not mentioned by those who discuss her harassment. In another harassment case, a white woman received abuse that was transphobic in content (Filipovic 2007), yet in Filipovic's study (2007) it was included as an example of harassment based on appearance (i.e., classified as gendered, rather than transphobic or transmisogynist, harassment), without mention of the content as being transphobic. Aboriginal Australian former politician and athlete Nova Peris was attacked online in both racist and sexist ways, but almost all online media reported the abuse as being an attack on race (e.g., Hunt 2016; Olding 2016; ABC News 2016). In a similar fashion, actor and singer Zendaya was included in a tweet suggesting the rape of her and three other women of color, yet media reported only on the misogynistic content, and failed to comment on the obvious racialized elements (e.g., Sullivan 2016 [A]; Brucculieri 2016; Cutler 2016).

It is understandable why it is assumed that to study the "gendered" nature of online harassment is to be inclusive of all women. Yet in actuality, what happens in most studies and discussions is that the majority of the women discussed actually reflect a small *minority* of harassment experienced online. Ultimately, a focus on "just gender" means to actively ignore or leave out harassment based on anything else. The harassment removed or ignored to focus on "just gender" would, by design, include that which is racist, homophobic, transphobic or transmisogynist, ableist, or based on religion or beliefs. This occurs because harassment that is based on more than "just gender" complicates research. As Purdie-Vaughns and Eibach (2008, p. 378) argue, research based on androcentric, ethnocentric, or heterocentric[7] principles means that those who experience multiple (or intersecting) identities will be considered as "non-prototypical members of their constituent identity groups." If women happen to also embody multiple identities, this is rarely highlighted in research about online harassment. Even when such cases are about women whose race or ethnicity (for example) *has* been targeted, their cases are referenced to support a broader argument about gendered harassment, and the racialized (or other) components are left out of reporting and analyses.

Let's take a moment to hypothesize. If a transgender woman of color's harassment was to be considered for a study within the current field of gender-specific online harassment scholarship, only the "gendered" harassment they receive would be included in research. Any *other* harassment they receive (for example racist or transphobic) would, based on research terms, be ignored for the sake of analyzing *only* that which is gender-specific. Perhaps this sounds reasonable: filter out the harassment that is gender-specific and leave other harassment for a different study. Yet, aside from elevating gendered harassment as being more impactful than other types, there remains a glaring oversight: the more marginalized identities one woman embodies, the less likely it is that their harassment will ever *only* include gendered elements. If one's harassment is consistently sexist, racist, and transphobic, where is the space for the analysis and recognition of this? In reality, this woman's experience of online harassment would be left out altogether. Because of privilege, referencing "women" in discussions and scholarship without explicitly stating *which* women, really means to reference the (taken for granted as) "standard" group of women in a researcher's personal context. "Women" in the case of online harassment studies are, because of the focus on "just gender", therefore subconsciously prescribed as white, straight and cisgender.

The Need to Reframe Discussion

Kathy Davis writes that intersectionality "touches on the most pressing problem facing contemporary feminism—the long and painful legacy of its exclusions" (2008, p. 70). As discussed, this critique is precisely what is occurring within the discourse of online harassment of women—namely, that certain women are being excluded. Citron writes that "cyber gender harassment damages women as a group and society as a whole by entrenching gender hierarchy in cyberspace" (2009, p. 390). I would argue that the very concept of 'cyber gender harassment' and other categorical terminologies discussed earlier as a framework for discussion contributes to the entrenchment of racial hierarchy in cyberspace *and* in scholarship. It is therefore imperative to reframe the discussions of online harassment and reconsider terminology and research methods to move towards intersectional and inclusive discussions and analyses of Internet activity.

An intersectional reframing of online harassment research will allow for better insight and more rigorous analyses of online behavior and experience. Online gaming scholar Kishonna Gray writes that current "feminist engagements with technology and culture are *limiting* as they fail to capture race and other identifiers" (in Gray 2016, p. 59—emphasis added). In studies that *have* discussed the intersectionality of harassment, a complexity of experience is highlighted that is missing from related studies of "just gender". A study of sexism in online gaming, for example, shows that those who appeared to be female experienced higher rates of abuse (Kasumovic and Kuznekoff 2015). Comparatively, Gray's (intersectional) gaming research highlights the fact that black women gamers are subjected to specific abuse that is racist *and* sexist (Gray 2012), which indicates a layer of analysis missed by the aforementioned study. Gray documented her own experiences as a gamer and a woman of color, showing that when people became aware she was a woman she was abused on gendered grounds, and when they became aware she was a woman of color the abuse became racist as well (ibid.).

Researchers not only limit their studies by sticking to a singular category framework, but also contribute to the already-present issue of women's visibility online. Women, gender and sexuality studies scholar Tanisha C. Ford expands on the problem with this, arguing that black feminists are particularly at risk of harassment when they speak out online, because they are articulating issues that implicate others in systems of power (in Starr 2014). Because of this, white cyberfeminists and scholars have a responsibility to recognize that they are in a position that affords them more space at the expense of others. This not only includes recognizing that some are experiencing unique and extreme harassment based on multiple marginalized identities, but also that those women's experiences are heard less, and they are also having to combat the issue of white feminist dominance in the online realm.

How Can We Rethink This Field?

Artist Faith Wilding wrote that "If cyberfeminists have the desire to research, theorize work practically, and make visible how women (and others) worldwide are affected by new communication technologies... they must begin by clearly formulating cyberfeminisms' political goals" (1998, p. 12). Given broad awareness of the critiques of the whiteness of feminism prior, it can be argued that cyberfeminism, and the research of cyberfeminists, should be fully aware of the politics of visibility, and the hierarchy and complexity of experiences. Unfortunately, as discussed, this is not the case, and reframing online harassment research must therefore reconsider the field from an intersectional perspective. This includes discussing women's experiences using an "anti-categorical" approach (McCall 2005), and examining "process and power relations" (Cottom 2016, p. 216). As summarized by Lutz et al. (2011, pp. 7–8), "intersectionality not only challenges us to integrate marginalised perspectives but also demonstrates the necessity of understanding relations of rule and power differentials as co-constituted and co-constitutive."

So far, there has not been an in-depth analysis of the online harassment experiences of non-white, or lesbian, or trans women, or women with disabilities. In addition to this, the case studies mostly referred to in scholarship are predominantly those of white women (e.g. Mantilla 2013; Citron 2009; Filipovic 2007). As Jesse Daniels summarizes (2016, p. 26), the challenges faced by women of color are that they are not heard and are ignored, are bullied or abused, and are excluded by white women, sometimes as a result of speaking out. For these reasons it is imperative to publish work in this field that broadens the scope of the harassment and the range of experiences included. It is also important to challenge any ideas that uphold certain cyberfeminists as leading the field over others, and to acknowledge structural power imbalances when it comes to whose voices are heard and upheld as important.

Daniels argues that white cyberfeminists are dominantly portrayed as being the "architects and defenders of a framework of feminism in the digital era" (Daniels 2016, p. 4), and white cyberfeminists have actively contributed to the silencing and overlooking of non-white women's work and experiences. The #SolidarityIsForWhiteWomen campaign, for example, was a direct action against the fact that white online feminists had continually contributed to, and been complicit in, the silencing of black women online. The hashtag, created by online black feminist Mikki Kendall, became the topic of a panel discussion, on which Kendall herself was not initially invited to speak (NPR Staff 2013). This hypocrisy, later amended with a panel adjustment, speaks to the prejudice within cyberfeminism to not only support white cyberfeminists more, but also actively provide space for their voice to be heard, at the expense of other women. For these reasons, it is imperative to reflect on the work of black cyberfeminists (see Cottom 2016), and to implement intersectional approaches and analyses.

An intersectional approach to online harassment research would recognize that considering gender as a single analytical category has limitations, a point that feminist researchers have long been aware of (McCall 2005, p. 1771). Doing so should therefore be avoided when discussing online harassment of women. Nakamura (2008, p. 18) writes that this is vital in Internet research, and that "digital visual culture critique needs to read both race and gender as part of mutually constitutive formations." It is simply not possible to claim that we are studying online harassment of women if we don't acknowledge and include harassment based on other parts of women's identity. I do not mean to discredit the important research being conducted on the gendered vitriol and misogynist content directed at women online, and there is no doubt that there are gendered trends that deserve focus. Rather, I wish to suggest that work should only be reduced to being called "gendered harassment" if the researcher can also commit to highlighting women's diverse experiences, and also comment on the intersectional nature of the harassment they receive. If this seems impossible to do, then it should be acknowledged that the "gendered harassment" they study most likely reflects the experience of specific women. To overcome the problems with using gender as an individual analytic tool, I suggest reframing harassment discourse as the study of 'online harassment of women' or similar. This allows us to then research harassment that women experience that may not actually be gendered in content or nature, but is still impactful to *women*. With regard to practical application and research, researchers must reflect on and acknowledge that certain women are in a position where oppressions intersect. Because of this, it is imperative to specify which women we are talking about, and for, in our research of women's harassment online.

Conclusion

As I have discussed previously, within the existing landscape and literature of online feminism and the study of online harassment, there are problems with *simplistic and homogenous terminology*, *lack of intersectional analyses*, and *erasure or ignoring of non-gendered harassment*. These problems leave certain women's experiences out of discussion, do not allow for rich analyses, contribute to an environment that allows certain women more space, and more of a voice, and do not recognize the politics around white feminist scholars staying silent when it comes to racism. All of these are occurring in a new field of feminist research (online/cyber/digital feminism), but none are new criticisms of feminist scholarship.

Currently within the literature around online harassment of women there are attempts to describe harassment with categorizations that do not allow for the inclusion and discussion of women's diverse and multi-layered experiences. Scholars often refer to harassment of women online from an exclusively gendered perspective, and without intersectional analysis. Not only does doing so imply that harassment based on gender is more impactful than, and separate to, harassment on other grounds, but it also actively removes the experiences of those who embody other marginalized identities. It is not enough to acknowledge that there are different forms of harassment—gender-specific, racist, ableist, transphobic—but rather it is imperative to use language that does not elevate gender based harassment above other forms. If we separate harassment into areas—such as gendered or racist—we render invisible the intersectional harassment experienced by many women online.

Those who, like myself, are white cyberfeminists, cannot continue to discuss and research online harassment of women using non-intersectional, or reductive, terminology and analyses. All researchers and commentators must highlight, listen to, collaborate with, and incorporate the research, voices, and experiences of other women, and recognize the power relations that inform our research and biases. Research frameworks and terms must be altered so as not to contribute to a "whitewashing" of cyberfeminism and to the erasure of women's experiences in online harassment discourse. There is an opportunity, in a still emergent field, to reframe discussions about women's harassment online with a commitment to making visible the diversity of women's experiences, and by refraining from using limiting terminology. Doing so will offer opportunities for an increased richness in analyses and understandings of the complexity of online behaviors and user experiences. It is imperative, also, that white cyberfeminist and Internet scholars reflect on past indiscretions of feminist scholarship and heed criticisms by scholars of color and black cyberfeminists. A commitment must be made to widen and reframe discussions of online harassment, and in doing so acknowledge diversity of experience. By this I do not mean to merely *include* diversity of experience within research, but rather that the methodologies, analyses, and research principles should *start* from a place of intersectionality, and in recognition of previous feminist errors of exclusion.

Notes

1. A criticism of this field that I will discuss is the cis-normative framing of men and women. In addition it is important to note that there is a significant lack of research and acknowledgement of non-binary and gender-diverse people's experiences online.
2. I am a white woman and acknowledge that I write this within the structural context of that which I critique, and that this is not free from being problematic. I also acknowledge that I build upon the work of women of color, some of whom I have mentioned, but almost certainly more that I have missed.
3. I refer broadly to the "Internet" as it is currently understood in its contemporary form.
4. As I will begin to expand on later, an oversight in many quantitative studies of harassment of women online is that the category of "women" is used broadly and without clarification as to *which* women are being discussed.
5. For a comprehensive overview of whiteness and online feminism see Daniels (2016).
6. It is also important to note that a focus on gender that simplifies binary categories of men/women therefore overlooks transmasculine and non-binary experiences.
7. Androcentrism defines the "standard" person as being male, ethnocentrism defines the "standard" ethnicity as the dominant ethnicity of the region, heterocentrism defines the "standard" person as heterosexual.

References

ABC News. (2016, July 13). Nova Peris accepts apology from disgraced chiropractor Chris Nelson. Retrieved 14 July 2016, from http://www.abc.net.au/news/2016-07-13/nova-peris-accepts-chiropractor's-apology/7627240

Biber, J. K., Doverspike, D., Baznik, D., Cober, A., & Ritter, B. A. (2002). Sexual harassment in online communications: Effects of gender and discourse medium. *Cyberpsychology & Behavior, 5*(1), 33–42.

Braidotti, R. (2003). Cyberfeminism with a difference. In M. Peters, M. Olssen, & C. Lankshear (Eds.), *Futures of critical theory: Dreams of difference* (pp. 239–260). Oxford: Rowman & Littlefield Publishers.

Brucculieri, J. (2016, April 7). Zendaya masterfully shut down this troll's rape "joke". *The Huffington Post*. Retrieved 7 April 2016, from http://www.huffingtonpost.com/entry/zendaya-twitter-rape_us_577940dde4b0a629c1aa6600

Chun, H. K. (2002). Othering space. In N. Mirzoeff (Ed.), *The visual culture reader* (pp. 243–254). New York: Routledge.

Citron, D. K. (2009). Law's expressive value in combating cyber gender harassment. *Michigan Law Review, 108*, 373–416.

Citron, D. K. (2014). *Hate crimes in cyberspace*. Cambridge, MA: Harvard University Press.

Clark, K. (Rep.). (2015). Online violence against trans women perpetuates dangerous cycle. *The Huffington Post*. Retrieved 16 August 2016, from http://www.huffingtonpost.com/katherine-clark/online-violence-against-trans-women-perpetuates-dangerous-cycle_b_7562108.html

Consalvo, M. (2012). Cyberfeminism. *Encyclopaedia of new media* (online). Thousand Oaks: SAGE, 2002. 109–110. SAGE Reference, 4 Apr. 2012, Retrieved 26 March 2016, from: http://study.sagepub.com/sites/default/files/Ch17_Cyberfeminism.pdf

Cottom, T. (2016). Black cyberfeminsm: Ways forward for intersectionality and digital sociology. In J. Daniels, K. Gregory, & T. M. Cottom (Eds.), *Digital sociologies*. Bristol/Chicago: Policy Press.

Crenshaw, K. (1989). Demarginalizing the intersection of race and sex: A black feminist critique of antidiscrimination doctrine, feminist theory and antiracist politics. *University of Chicago Legal Forum, 1989*(1), 139–167.

Cross, K. (2015, November 27). Online harassment isn't only about misogyny, regardless of what 'Gendertrolling' implies. *Rewire*. Retrieved 1 July 2016, from: https://rewire.news/article/2015/11/27/online-harassment-isnt-misogyny-regardless-gendertrolling-implies/. Accessed 1 July 2016.

Cutler, J. (2016). Zendaya shuts down troll who asked which celebrity they'd rape. *New York Daily News*. Retrieved 4 July 2016, from: http://www.nydailynews.com/entertainment/gossip/zendaya-blasts-twitter-troll-promoted-rape-article-1.2698356

Daniels, J. (2016). The trouble with white feminism: Whiteness, digital feminism and the intersectional internet. In A. Brock, S. Noble, & B. Tynes (Eds.), *Intersectional internet: Race, sex and culture online, Peter Lang digital edition series*. New York: Peter Lang Publishing.

Davis, K. (2008). Intersectionality as a buzzword: A sociology of science perspective on what makes a feminist theory successful. *Feminist Theory, 9*(1), 67–85.

Duggan, M. (2014). Online harassment. *Pew Research Center.* Retrieved 1 January 2016, from http://www.pewinternet.org/2014/10/22/online-harassment/

Filipovic, J. (2007). Blogging while female: How internet misogyny parallels 'real-world' harassment. *Yale Journal of Law & Feminism, 19*(1), 295–303, article 10. Retrieved 29 August 2016, from http://digitalcommons.law.yale.edu/yjlf/vol19/iss1/10

Fox, J., & Tang, W. Y. (2014). Sexism in online video games: The role of conformity to masculine norms and social dominance orientation. *Computers in Human Behaviour, 33,* 314–320.

Fox, J., Cruz, C., & Lee, J. Y. (2015). Perpetuating online sexism offline: Anonymity, interactivity, and the effects of sexist hashtags on social media. *Computers in Human Behaviour, 52,* 436–442.

Gardiner, B., Mansfield, M., Anderson, I., Holder, J., Louter, D. & Ulmanu, M. (2016). The dark side of guardian comments. Retrieved 4 September 2016, from https://www.theguardian.com/technology/2016/apr/12/the-dark-side-of-guardian-comments

Gray, K. L. (2012). Intersecting oppressions and online communities. *Information, Communication & Society, 15*(3), 411–428.

Gray, K. L. (2016). Solidarity is for white women in gaming. In Y. B. Kafai, G. T. Richard, & B. M. Tynes (Eds.), *Diversifying Barbie and Mortal Kombat: Intersectional perspectives and inclusive designs in gaming* (pp. 59–70). Pittsburgh: ETC Press.

Hackworth, L. (2016) *Acting like 13 Year old boys? Exploring the discourse of online harassment and the diversity of harassers.* Erasmus Mundus Masters in Women's and Gender Studies, University of Utrecht. Retrieved 20 June 2017 from: http://studenttheses.library.uu.nl/

Haimson, O. (2016). *Harassment, threats, and trolling online, transgender experiences with online harassment.* Social Computing Symposium 2016, Microsoft Research. Retrieved 10 August 2016, from https://www.microsoft.com/en-us/research/video/social-computing-symposium-2016-harassment-threats-and-trolling-online-transgender-experiences-with-online-harassment/

Hayles, K. (1999). Toward embodied virtuality. In K. Hayles (Ed.), *How we became posthuman: Virtual bodies in cybernetics, literature, and informatics: Chapter 1* (pp. 1–24). Chicago: The University of Chicago.

Herring, S. (1999). The rhetorical dynamics of gender harassment on-line. *The Information Society, 15*, 151–167. Retrieved 8 August 2016, from: http://ella. slis.indiana.edu/~herring/harassment.pdf

hooks, b. (2000). *Feminism is for everybody: Passionate politics.* Cambridge: South End Press.

Hughey, M. W., & Daniels, J. (2013). Racist comments at online news sites: a methodological dilemma for discourse analysis. *Media, Culture & Society, 35*(3), 332–347.

Hunt, E. (2016, June 23). Chiropractor not rebuked by health watchdogs over racist posts about Nova Peris. *The Guardian* online. Retrieved 5 July 2016, from https://www.theguardian.com/australia-news/2016/jun/23/chiropractor-not-rebuked-by-health-watchdogs-over-racist-posts-about-nova-peris

Jane, E. A. (2014). Your a ugly, whorish, slut' understanding e-bile. *Feminist Media Studies, 14*(4), 531–546.

Jane, E. A. (2015). Flaming? What flaming? The pitfalls and potentials of researching online hostility. *Ethics and Information Technology, 17*(1), 65–87.

Jane, E. A. (2017). *Misogyny online: A short (and brutish) history.* London: Sage.

Kasumovic, M. M., & Kuznekoff, J. H. (2015). Insights into sexism: Male status and performance moderates female-directed hostile and amicable behaviour. *PLOS ONE, 10*(7). Retrieved 14 August 2016, from: http://journals.plos.org/plosone/article?id=10.1371/journal.pone.0131613

Leander, K. M., & McKim, K. K. (2003). Tracing the everyday 'sittings' of adolescents on the internet: A strategic adaptation of ethnography across online and offline spaces. *Education, Communication & Information, 3*(2), 211–240.

Lutz, H., Vivar, M. T. H., & Supik, L. (2011). Framing intersectionality: An introduction. In H. Lutz, M. T. H. Vivar, & L. Supik (Eds.), *Framing intersectionality: Debates on a multi-faceted concept in gender studies* (pp. 1–24). Surrey: Ashgate.

Mantilla, K. (2013). Gendertrolling: Misogyny adapts to new media. *Feminist Studies, 39*(2), 563–570, Retrieved 2 February 2015, from: http://www.jstor.org/stable/23719068

Marwick, A. (2016, November 24). A new study suggests online harassment is pressuring women and minorities to self-censor. *Quartz.* Retrieved 24 June 2017, from: https://qz.com/844319/a-new-study-suggests-online-harassment-is-pressuring-women-and-minorities-to-self-censor/

McCall, L. (2005). The complexity of intersectionality. *Signs: Journal of Women in Culture and Society, 30*(3), 1771–1800.

Megarry, J. (2014). Online incivility or sexual harassment? Conceptualising women's experiences in the digital age. *Women's Studies International Forum,* 47(part A), 46–55.

Melcher, T. N. (2017, November 2). Twitter has a transgender problem. *The New York Times.* Retrieved 12 January 2018, from https://www.nytimes.com/2017/11/02/opinion/twitter-transgender-harassment-problem.html

Nakamura, L. (2008). Introduction: Digital racial formations and networked images of the body. In L. Nakamura (Ed.), *Digitizing race: Visual cultures of the internet* (pp. 1–35). Minneapolis: University of Minnesota Press.

Nash, J. C. (2008). Re-thinking intersectionality. *Feminist Review, 89*(1), 1–15.

Norton Symantec. (2016). Norton study shows online harassment nears epidemic proportions for young Australian women. Retrieved 13 January 2017, from https://www.symantec.com/en/au/about/newsroom/press-releases/2016/symantec_0309_01

NPR Staff. (2013, September 5). Twitter, feminism and race: Who gets a seat at the table? *Code Switch: Race & Identity, Remixed.* Retrieved 22 August 2016, from http://www.npr.org/sections/codeswitch/2013/09/05/219278156/twitter-feminism-and-race-who-gets-a-seat-at-the-table

Olding, R. (2016, July 5). Chiropractor Chris Nelson sentenced for racist posts on Nova Peris' Facebook. *Sydney Morning Herald.* Retrieved July 7 2016, from: http://www.smh.com.au/nsw/chiropractor-chris-nelson-sentenced-for-racist-posts-on-nova-peris-facebook-20160705-gpys9d.html

Paasonen, S. (2011). Revisiting cyberfeminism. *Communications, 36*(3), 335–352. Retrieved 7 June 2016, from: http://www.arifyildirim.com/ilt510/susanna.paasonen.pdf

Pasricha, J. (2016). "Violence" online in India: Cybercrimes against women & minorities on social media. Research paper. Retrieved 14 January 2017, from: https://feminisminindia.com/wp-content/uploads/2016/05/FII_cyberbullying_report_website.pdf

Purdie-Vaughns, V., & Eibach, R. P. (2008). Intersectional invisibility: The distinctive advantages and disadvantages of multiple subordinate-group identities. *Sex Roles, 59*(5–6), 377–391.

Richards, R. (2011). "I could have told you that wouldn't work": Cyberfeminist pedagogy in action. *Feminist Teacher, 22*(1), 5–22.

Starr, T. J. (2014). The unbelievable harassment black women face daily on Twitter. *AlterNet.* Retrieved 17 April 2017, from http://www.alternet.org/unbelievable-harassment-black-women-face-daily-twitter

Staude-Müller, F., Hansen, B., & Voss, M. (2012). How stressful is online victimisation? Effects of victim's personality and properties of the incident. *European Journal of Developmental Psychology, 9,* 260–274.

Sullivan, R. (2016, July 4). American actress and singer Zendaya outs Twitter troll over rape comments. *News.Com.Au.* Retrieved 5 July 2016, from http://www.news.com.au/lifestyle/american-actress-and-singer-zendaya-outs-twitter-troll-over-rape-comments/news-story/16e1a38516cd252cb9623f1a27ece966

Turkle, S. (1995). *Life on the screen: Identity in the age of the internet.* New York: Touchstone.

Wilding, F., & Critical Art Ensemble. (1998). Notes on the political condition of cyberfeminism. *Art Journal, 57*(2), 47–60.

Zack, N. (2007). Can third wave feminism be inclusive? Intersectionality, its problems, and new directions. In L. M. Alcoff & E. F. Kittay (Eds.), *Feminist philosophy* (pp. 193–207). Oxford: Blackwell Publishing.

Zhao, S. (2006). The internet and the transformation of the reality of everyday life: Toward a new analytic stance in sociology. *Sociological Inquiry, 76*(4), 458–474.

4

Mediated Misogynoir: Intersecting Race and Gender in Online Harassment

Stephanie Madden, Melissa Janoske,
Rowena Briones Winkler, and Amanda Nell Edgar

Although race and gender have often been treated as separate issues, scholars have increasingly recognized the ways in which these (and other) issues intersect, impact, and construct a person's standing within the social world (e.g., Andersen and Collins 2006; Weber 2004). While we acknowledge a broader range of identities, here we focus specifically on the intersection of race and gender that have led to the social invisibility of Black women, particularly in online spaces (Macías 2015). Because racism is often investigated through the experiences of Black men, and sexism is investigated as a White female problem, Black women's unique experiences at the intersection of these groups is often

S. Madden (✉) • M. Janoske
Department of Journalism and Strategic Media, University of Memphis, Memphis, TN, USA

R. Briones Winkler
Marketing Department, Vectorworks, Inc., Columbia, MD, USA

A. N. Edgar
Department of Communication, University of Memphis, Memphis, TN, USA

© The Author(s) 2018
J. R. Vickery, T. Everbach (eds.), *Mediating Misogyny*,
https://doi.org/10.1007/978-3-319-72917-6_4

ignored (Sesko and Biernat 2009). To account for the experiences of Black women, the term "misogynoir" was coined by Moya Bailey to "give intersectionality a break from doing a lot of the heavy lifting for Black feminist thought" (Bailey 2013, p. 341). Misogynoir is thus defined as anti-Black misogyny.

It is worth noting that the term misogynoir was popularized within the Black feminist blogosphere (Bailey 2013). Especially for marginalized groups, the "sharing of knowledge between multiple individuals across geographical constraints is one of the most valuable qualities of social media" (Thelandersson 2014, p. 529). While the ability to connect with like-minded individuals can help to elevate voices and experiences, the Internet's publicness can also increase the likelihood of online toxicity towards non-dominant groups (Thelandersson 2014).

Case: Leslie Jones and Twitter

To understand mediated misogynoir, we look to the highly-publicized online harassment of Leslie Jones, a Black U.S. comedian and actress who is a cast member on *Saturday Night Live*. In July 2016, she starred as Patty Tolan in the all-female cast reboot of *Ghostbusters*, a release that led to a surge of harsh criticism, including a review published on conservative news website Breitbart by associate editor Milo Yiannopoulos (2016), who claimed the film is "an overpriced self-esteem device for women betrayed by the lies of third-wave feminism" with Jones' character as the "worst of the lot" by her portrayal of a "two dimensional racist stereotype" (p. 1). The July 18 review sparked a barrage of comments by Internet trolls who then harassed Jones on Twitter, sending insults such as photos of apes, racist slurs, and even tweets from a fake Leslie Jones Twitter account (Brown 2016a). Although Jones reported several of the accounts to Twitter, a few days after the attacks began, Jones announced that she was leaving the platform altogether, leading to a conversation with Twitter CEO Jack Dorsey (Altman 2016), as well as the permanent suspension of Yiannopoulos' Twitter account (Roy 2016). This new iteration of cyberbullying led to counter-hashtags from Jones' supporters such as #LoveforLeslieJ and #StandWithLeslie (Brown 2016a).

The Impact of Online Communities

To understand the ways in which online users interpreted Jones' experience and worked through their individual identities and meanings, our study focuses on the online reactions to this case, specifically in blog comment sections. Online communities, like the ones that may emerge in blog comment sections, are often characterized by specialized relationships and weaker ties, or a select few people to whom one is especially close, and a general knowledge of and connection to a much larger section of the greater community (Kobayashi 2010). Social media platforms provide a space for conversations and other forms of group interactivity (Saxton and Waters 2014).

Making these online communities the medium of choice can help fulfill users' social needs through interaction with other people, based on social media's focuses on interactivity, responsiveness, spontaneity, dialogue, and proximity (Kent 2010). These social media sites also allow people to interact with like-minded individuals while seeking information (Ancu and Cozma 2009). The potential for the Internet to improve a person's life through these relationships has also emerged as a large motivating factor in favor of using the medium (LaAmanda and Eastin 2004).

Based on this literature review, we pose the following research question:

How is online harassment faced by Black women recognized and/or processed by online blog-based communities?

Method

We completed a qualitative content analysis of the comment sections on eight different U.S. blogs and media outlets covering Jones, specifically two feminist blogs that do not mention race (*Jezebel* and *Bust*), two blogs that focus on race but not specifically gender (*The Root* and *Bossip*), two blogs that focus on the intersectionality of race and gender (*Clutch* and *For Harriet*), and two outlets that focus on neither race nor gender (*Slate* and *The Huffington Post*). We examined a variety of blogs to better understand where divisions and differences in both reporting and commenting may exist, and the impact of those differences on the community. All blog posts selected met the following criteria: (1) Jones was the article's subject; (2) the post focused on her online abuse; (3) there were at least five comments; and (4) the article was published between July 11 (the week prior to *Ghostbusters'* opening weekend) and August 18, 2016.

Results

Five primary themes emerged from the data: *intersectionality, racism, responding to online attackers, identity of attackers*, and *emotional responses*. We explore each theme, and associated sub-themes, in the sections below.

Intersectionality

The theme of intersectionality represented the way in which misogynoir manifested itself in our research data. The two primary themes that emerged were *managing male expectations* surrounding Black women's beauty and an *awareness of intersections* at play in the harassment.

Managing Male Expectations The ways Jones' harassment was discussed revolved heavily around discussions of whether men find her attractive. One commenter demonstrated how race and gender intersect in explaining "the worst thing Milo said to her after she blocked him, he inferred that she looked like a man by saying 'Rejected by another black dude, typical'" (Moran 2016). Other commenters focused on the prevalence of such abuse toward women online. One commenter wrote this type of harassment "happens to women all the time. See also: Gamergate. There is basically a large semi-organized mob of guys out there at all times looking for targets. If they can combine racism with their misogyny, that's like Christmas for them" (Davies 2016). Importantly, the male expectations being discussed were those of White men. One commenter on *Jezebel* wrote that the issue is "not just that it's a black woman in Ghostbusters, it's that she's a black woman who does not fit the narrow beauty standards we force on black women so that white boys will fap to them" ("People Ain't Isht" 2016).

Awareness of Intersections Although not a primary part of the online discourse surrounding Jones' harassment, there were discussions that indicated an awareness of the intersections at play in this situation. As one *Jezebel* commenter wrote, "there will never be words as powerfully hateful as those created to spew at minorities and women. Yet another example of cis white male privilege" (Davies 2016). Similarly, commenters at *Slate* recognized the need to separate dislike for the movie from "misogynistic and racist smears at one of the actresses who did nothing other than perform in the movie" (Wagner 2016). Both race and gender are highlighted in the online abuse rendered toward Jones.

Commenters also discussed a need for solidarity in marginalized communities. For example, one commenter wrote, "putting down another woman is bad enough, but putting down another woman of color, I'm done" ("People Ain't Isht" 2016). However, others felt that this solidarity was not being demonstrated by Jones' White female co-stars whose "silence is a cosign to the racial abuse as far as I'm concerned. White feminism at its finest" (Lutkin 2016).

Racism

More prominent than the theme of intersectionality was the theme of racism. Issues of racism manifested in responses that indicated being *unsympathetic to abuse*, potential of *internalized racism*, and offering up *points of comparison* to other situations.

Unsympathetic to Abuse Many online commenters were unsympathetic to Jones' online abuse because, as one commenter posted, "any celebrity on twitter is literally asking for it... Why Leslie Jones is a special case is a mystery, but it fits a narrative" (Dessem 2016). This commenter further explained that "she is a mediocre comedian who often plays a walking stereotype. She is getting pushed because she has enough diversity Pokemon points" (Dessem 2016). Another poster wrote that "this cannot be the first time her looks, gender or color has been mocked or [subjected] to hateful comments… It doesn't stop the higher you get in the industry, it only gets worse… so toughen up and stop all that public drying Lesdogg" ("People Ain't Isht" 2016).

Internalized Racism Other commenters discussed the internalized racism they see represented by Jones. For example, one *Huffington Post* user wrote, "I'm very liberal, but her comedy does remind me of the old minstrel shows and that old Amos and Andy with the angry Sapphire. Oversexed angry black woman stereotype" (Moran 2016). Similarly, a *Bossip* commenter wrote that "this woman 'shucks and jives' for whytee on SNL every chance she gets. She's more of a racist to herself than any outsider can be… She's hurt because others are just calling out the self hate she endures every time she looks in the mirror" ("People Ain't Isht" 2016).

Point of Comparison Online commenters tried to make sense of Jones' online harassment by offering points of comparison to other Black celebrities, such as Michelle Obama, Whoopi Goldberg, and the Williams sisters. As one commenter wrote on *Bossip*, "even the FLOTUS has been denigrated and degraded by racial insults. You can be ultra-educated, polished, and carry yourself with the utmost dignity and still be subjected to cruelty" ("People Ain't Isht" 2016). Another commenter on *Bossip* asked why they "have never heard of black people trolling white people and calling them racist names on articles… Do we not care as much or we got better shyt to do?" ("People Ain't Isht" 2016).

Responding to Online Attackers

Whether or not they focused on the racial aspects of the harassment, commenters demonstrated strong feelings about online attacks and hate speech both generally and in Jones' case. These will be discussed through themes including *policing reactions,* a *need for coping strategies,* and a need to discuss *Twitter and reporting harassment.*

Policing Reactions Many commenters offered Jones suggestions on how to better handle the situation. One *Jezebel* commenter saw the bigger picture, writing, "a lot of people are telling her to just ignore it because she's a celebrity. because somehow that makes you not a person who can be hurt anymore I guess" (Brown 2016b). Plenty of individuals thought Jones "shouldve [*sic*] been done with them people 96 tweets ago" ("People Ain't Isht" 2016), or that she "has a choice to keep your account private and block those who harass you" (Moran 2016). Others, however, saw the problem from a financial perspective, wondering whether it was that "social media is a viable outlet for actors to reach their fan base" (Drayton 2016) or that "the best revenge tweet would be her sitting in her nice, big house, crying happy, successful tears into the piles of money she is making while those trolls sit back in their mama's basement with a bowl of ramen" (Brown 2016b). Others felt that "the whole 'she should have thicker skin response' is just bullshit assholes use to justify their bullying… she doesn't need to have thicker skin; people need to stop being racist and/or misogynistic assholes" (Lutkin 2016).

Need for Coping Strategies Once the conversation turned to how to stop the harassment, people started wishing for better strategies and "waiting for the day when we come up with a better response to this kind of behavior than 'don't feed the trolls'" (Lutkin 2016). The concern, ultimately, was for Jones and her emotional state, with people believing that "[Jones] shouldn't have to keep quiet. She has the right to be mad as hell. Unfortunately, that did seem to feed [the trolls'] attacks" (Lutkin 2016).

Eventually, commenters called for people to figure out "a better way, because I'm really freaking sick of biting my tongue" (Lutkin 2016).

Twitter and Reporting Harassment There was real debate in the comments of multiple articles about the responsibility of Twitter to take control and action when hate speech occurred. Some *Jezebel* users believed that Twitter tolerated hate speech due to "user engagement. Racists and the people that fight with them are helping Twitter show that it has users who are having conversations with each other, then it takes that data and shows it to advertisers. Nobody cares if the engagement is people yelling hate speech, just so it gets replies" (Davies 2016).

The discussion continued from there and was ranged from both broad beliefs, such as "[Twitter] should make sure to hold everyone accountable" (Drayton 2016) and "I really don't understand why twitter hasn't received more blow back from the press" (Brown 2016b), to very specific suggestions and ideas, including "every social platform needs to hire moderators. For editorial, discoverability, and just plain blocking reasons. A computer algorithm is not a solution—nut up or shut up. (Especially you, Twitter.)" (Lutkin 2016), and the lament that "reporting tweets does nothing—Twitter does nothing. So go tweet words of encouragement!!!!" (Brown 2016b). Multiple commenters on different sites believed that the way to solve problems of online harassment was for Twitter to "tighten up their 'Terms of Use' and make it clear when a user is signing up that they are agreeing that any racist speech or harassment is not tolerated and will result in a ban" ("Leslie Jones talks" 2016).

Beyond a simple frustration with Twitter was the desire to do something with the individuals spouting hate speech on the platform. Many commenters talked about having "an itchy 'report' finger" (Brown 2016b), or how they "reported a bunch last night, and then did another round… this morning" (Brown 2016b). Commenters also suggested sending "a few encouraging & appreciative tweets of my own" (Brown 2016b) or "wondering what would happen if a large enough group of high profile users did quit/deactiviate, even for a day?" (Visser 2016).

Identity of Attackers

Across the comment sections we analyzed, users discussed the identities of trolls as a way of understanding motivation for the attacks against Jones. Specifically, commenters understood attacker identity through several themes, including *hiding behind anonymity, White supremacist discourse, sad self-loathing people,* and *not just White people.*

Hiding Behind Anonymity Commenters across publishing outlets explained misogynoir comments by noting that the Twitter trolls were hiding behind anonymity. One commenter on *Slate*, for example, suggested that "maybe the Internet should not be so easily anonymous. If people want to attack others like this, they should be willing to do it publicly and deal with any backlash" (Wagner 2016). This commenter and others in our sample suggested that Twitter's available anonymity emboldened "s$%tty people" (Wagner 2016) to bully others.

Some commenters noted, though, that Jones' trolls went beyond "[p]eople at their ugliest" (Lutkin 2016). One *Jezebel* commenter argued that "ALL RACISTS ARE COWARDS… [who] can only express themselves from the anonymity of the Internet" (Lutkin 2016). Either overtly or by implication, commenters also argued that the solution to anonymity's emboldening of racist trolls would be to link online communication with offline identities. As one *Clutch* commenter noted, "if the IP address and image/mugshot of these clowns were exposed across the web, we would see an immediate decline in trolling, particularly in black spaces" ("Leslie Jones fights back" 2016). Though users across articles pointed to anonymity as a major facilitator of Jones' racist trolls, those participating in feminist and Black feminist platforms specifically discussed the relationship of racism to trolling.

White Supremacist Discourse One trend that was particularly prominent on *Jezebel* and *Huffington Post* was discussing Milo Yiannopoulos and Donald Trump's roles in promoting White supremacy to the army of Twitter trolls. *Jezebel* commenters called the former Breitbart writer and initiator of the Jones attacks the "Charles Manson of the alt-right" and a "vile, smug, evil, abhorrent, and imbecilic piece of trash" (Lutkin 2016). These commenters argued that Yiannopoulos waged the attack against Jones for fame and attention, and they pointed out that "he saw his followers react the last time he was suspended. He knew what they would do" (Moran 2016).

These commenters also noted that Yiannopoulos was not the only leader encouraging racialized violence; prominent politicians have also incited this type of aggression. One *Huffington Post* commenter observed, "attacks of all kinds are up since a nominee for president has made it cool to be racist again" (Sieczkowski 2016), and a British commenter connected this behavior to increases in overt racism following the EU referendum known as Brexit (Lutkin 2016). In reporting Jones' trolls to Twitter for abusive behavior, one *Jezebel* commenter noticed that "many of the people I reported last night were Trump Republicans… Trump's name was rarely more than one Tweet down from their attack on Leslie" (Lutkin 2016). As one *Jezebel* commenter remarked, Trump "empowered bigots to come out of the shadows" (Lutkin 2016), encouraging online and offline attacks on people of color.

Sad, Self-Loathing People Contrasting commenters who placed the blame on White supremacist discourse, commenters across all articles identified self-loathing as a key motivator for racist trolls. Agreeing with a previous commenter, one *Huffington Post* user remarked that these trolls "*desperately* want to unload their self loathing" (Moran 2016). Similarly, a *Slate* commenter noted that "the abuse makes the abuser feel superior" (Dessem 2016), and this sentiment was supported by a commenter on *Jezebel* who noted that these trolls "lash out at random strangers… [to make] their self-loathing slightly more tolerable" (Lutkin 2016). In other words, these commenters argue that trolls put others down to feel better about their own "really lame lives" (Lutkin 2016).

Not Just White People On one article, commenters questioned the conventional wisdom that racist trolls were necessarily White. Commenters lamented "the shaming and degradation that comes from black people" and noted that "the even more painful and unexpected degradation may come from those who look like them" ("People Ain't Isht" 2016). This pattern of abuse may not be new for Jones, as one commenter recalls seeing her "back during her up and coming stand-up comic days [and witnessing] a host of black men comics clown her for her looks" ("People Ain't Isht" 2016). As one user remarked, nodding to the intricacies of oppression, "darkskin heavy or heavier girls have it hard" ("People Ain't Isht" 2016).

Emotional Responses

The data analyzed also revealed a series of emotional responses coming from commenters who used the Jones case to process their own thoughts surrounding misogynoir in online spaces. These responses ran across a gamut of different emotions that emerged through themes, including *general lamenting and disgust, personal online abuse experiences,* and *showing empathy and support.*

General Lamenting and Disgust Overall, commenters used the Jones case to lament more broadly about how awful the Internet has become when it comes to misogyny and racism against successful Black women. As one commenter posted, "You should have to have a mental health evaluation before creating a twitter-account" (Davies 2016). A commenter on another *Jezebel* article lamented the seeming futility of trying to resolve this problem, stating, "There's no freaking point to it, and it's sad and depressing and makes me feel really hopeless about humanity. But, complaining only seems to encourage them" (Lutkin 2016).

In a related vein, commenters' lamenting also emerged as general disgust toward Jones' online harassers and the supporters behind it. As one user posted, "The vile stuff that is coming at Leslie deserves its own article, because it is disgusting and wrong, and people saying 'just ignore it' are not helping. No one should have to be subjected to that" (Brown 2016b). Another commenter shared similar sentiments, stating: "These ladies are celebrities but they're still human beings, like you and me. No one should have to tolerate that level of abuse for no discernible reason. It's disgusting" ("People Ain't Isht" 2016).

Personal Online Abuse Experiences In a more individualized level of lamenting, some commenters used these spaces to share their own negative experiences with online abuse as a way of showing solidarity and demonstrating that they can relate to this experience. One commenter recounted their experience from the early age of the Internet: "I had my attacks on the Internet in the '90s. It was life-changing. It is hard to see someone go through what I went through long ago" (Moran 2016). Another commenter described a more recent experience related to the terrorist attacks in Nice, France:

> I understand a tiny bit. I had the nerve to tweet at Scott Baio's wife and tell her she was "Classy" for her reaction to the Nice attacks. (She used laughing emojis to describe it.) I was attacked by Scott and dozens of his followers telling me that I'm ugly, I'm dumb, and a "lib-tard." Twitter can be a scary place. I think the Trump effect makes people feel safe in their ignorance and bigotry. After all, that's what his movement is about, White (male) Fright. (Lutkin 2016)

Showing Empathy and Support Not all emotions were completely negative on the blogs. Commenters shared their messages of empathy and support for Jones, from one person on *Jezebel* posting that "I find her delightful and personally feel pain when people don't get her or worse, attack her" (Brown 2016b) to another commenter stating that, "I like this gal. A Lot! She's refreshing, bold, sometimes brash, good looking, smart AND FUNNY" (Moran 2016).

One commenter added a small call to action for those who are unfamiliar with Jones' work: "Lots of love for Leslie! If ya'll don't know her, take a second and use the interwebs to enlighten yourselves and broaden your tunnel vision. #bethechange" (Visser 2016). Another commenter took action in a different way by not only trying to report the abuse, but also posting this message to empathize and articulate how Jones must feel: "I wrote above that I also tried to do my diligence and report people for her. It was emotionally exhausting seeing the hate, I can't imagine how spent she must be after being on the receiving end of it" (Lutkin 2016).

Finally, several users posted comments as if Jones would read them herself, as outward signs of their support, such as this one from *Bossip*:

> Leslie, give your detractors and naysayers as much attention as they deserve—which is none. I saw Ghostbusters over the weekend and I loved it. There were a number of laugh-out-loud moments and the cameos (I wasn't expecting to see so many) were nostalgic to see. Congratulations, Leslie, and I wish you much future success! Your star is rising. :). ("People Ain't Isht" 2016)

Discussion

Our aim in studying blog comments was to see what needs were being fulfilled through the interaction, and to see how interaction and community building happened when individuals found like-minded others (Ancu and Cozma 2009). Dialogue often served to separate commenters from the individuals crafting the harassing messages. Commenting on the blog posts was a way for people to present themselves as different from, or in clear opposition to, those who would say such hurtful, racist, and/or misogynistic comments. Individuals articulated their difference from the trolls by showcasing their willingness to support Jones, by sending her direct messages of support, blocking and reporting her harassers, or simply praising her movie. Following Goffman's (1959) discussions of performative impression management, Hogan (2010) has argued that such reactions can act as a form of online impression management, which may help commenters validate themselves as someone who is not hurtful, racist, and/or misogynistic. This also serves as an important building block in online identity formation, as many of these commenters had interacted before, and would likely continue to do so in the future. Even if the interaction among people within a community is minimal, commenters know others will read what they think and thus develop opinions about them; therefore, online identity management is likely in play, even beyond the larger goal of supporting Jones and calling out negative behaviors.

There was also discussion in the comments about how the race of commenters or harassers played a role; other commenters sometimes self-identified race to support their argument, and most assumed that the harassers were White or perhaps Black people struggling with self-loathing or internalized racism. This mix of individuals added to the complexity of intersectionality and community building online.

Understanding Intersectionality

Through their discussions, particularly those expressed through a lens of Whiteness, online commenters both challenged and cemented the importance of socially constructed beauty standards. On one hand, commenters noted that not only did traditional definitions of beauty play a role in Jones' abuse, but also that those definitions of beauty took on racialized and gendered values. In discussing the ways identity politics have historically created divisions between feminist and anti-racist politics, Crenshaw (1991) argues that "it is not the existence of the categories, but rather the particular values attached to them and the way those values foster and create social hierarchies" (p. 1297). Comments denouncing the ways Jones' appearance may have made her more vulnerable to online attacks are a recognition of the ways the actor's Afrocentric features worked to marginalize her in a business that privileges Eurocentric beauty standards (Shohat and Stam 2014). At the same time, commenters repeatedly referenced other Black celebrities as counterpoints to the argument, comparing Jones to well-known Black women like Kerry Washington, Oprah Winfrey, and Michelle Obama, and their treatment in public forums. Though their point was likely to highlight inequality in the public eye, the reassertion of figures who uphold traditional beauty standards (and the comparison to those who do not) also functions to reiterate and cement those standards. Though perhaps a small step toward building a safer online environment for all women, we suggest that commenters shift their thinking away from visually based value imposed by categories of beauty and instead focus on the contributions of the whole person. Perhaps it does less to advance the intersectional feminist cause to argue that all women are beautiful than it does to argue that beauty is, or should be, irrelevant to a woman's worth.

The discussion of beauty standards as an impetus for Jones' abuse was, in many ways, an acknowledgement of the intersectional oppressions of race and gender at the heart of misogynoir. While we were heartened by the commenters who recognized Jones' experience as an intersectional phenomenon, the attention paid to the intersection of race and gender highlighted a missing axis in Jones' identity: class. Running alongside comments about Jones' race and gender were those that highlighted her relative wealth and used this identity characteristic to dismiss the pain experienced in this kind of abuse. When commenters discussed Jones as "rich and famous," they underscored wealth's role in defining humanity in our contemporary capitalist environment. Jones may not face the kinds of oppression poor women and men experience, but her relative wealth should not be used to dismiss the psychological impacts of misogynoir abuse in these comment sections.

Lack of Humanization via the Online Space

The negative commentary from users also demonstrated the complexity of the online space in regards to identity formation and an overall lack of humanization. The fact that commenters claimed that Jones should get over this experience (or even deserved this harassment) due to her race, gender, and/or socioeconomic status, depicts the dynamic relationship between intersectionality and misogynoir within an online context (Bailey 2013). The commenters in this case argued that Jones is automatically an outsider due to her celebrity status, which not only emphasizes the primary focus on class at the expense of Jones' other identities (as detailed above), but also shows the users' attempts to impose social affiliations (Carr et al. 2013) to justify the negative comments. Thus, because online audiences tend to interpret texts via their own ideological lenses through citing personal experiences and individual needs (Ancu and

Cozma 2009; Kent 2010), commenters attempted to present evidence that what Jones is experiencing should not be relatable because she is not like them.

Twitter has attempted to improve online communities and increase the availability of safe spaces by allowing users to hide tweets that include user-identified keywords from their feed. Soon after Jones' abuse became a national conversation, Twitter introduced a tool allowing users to mute conversations that they would prefer to not participate in. Jones cannot stop the deluge of misogynoir, but if she faces similar attacks in the future, she can now mute the offenders. This is not a perfect option, but a start, certainly, and one that other social media platforms should consider.

Building Empathy Online

The ability to build empathy online is key to laying the foundations of an intersectional discourse. As the results of this study showed, many people used the online comments section to share their personal experiences with online abuse to highlight the extent of the problem. Sharing stories can help build empathy through identification and emotional expression (Maynard et al. 2011). Such confessional and personal narratives can help to humanize the impacts of online harassment.

More specifically, we need to explore how and why this online harassment occurs toward Black women, since mediated misogynoir implicates systems of power that disadvantage Black women offline as well. Therefore, such behavior is not simply a tweet to block or a discourse to ignore. Rather, actively engaging against this type of online abuse is critical, and this engagement should not just occur from those who are part of marginalized communities. Empathy is built from listening to and sharing the pain of these experiences, even if it has not personally affected you. Responding to online harassment is an opportunity for both calling out and calling in (Ferguson 2015). Calling out lets others know that their behavior is problematic and will not be tolerated (Ferguson 2015), whereas calling in is similar, but focuses more on compassion and patience (Trần 2013). Online communities, such as those developed in blog comment sections, may prove to be more productive venues for calling people into difficult conversations that recognize and check certain privileges. While it is important to call out harassment on platforms like Twitter, the type of empathy building necessary to combat this type of abuse online is more likely to be productive in these online spaces.

Conclusion

By focusing on the case of Leslie Jones, we could better understand how online harassment faced by Black women is recognized and processed by digital communities. We found that social class played a large role in dismissing the online abuse, adding an additional layer to misogynoir that is often forgotten. Digitally focused intersectionality studies in the future, then, must focus on how all these aspects of identity interrelate to create oppressive systems, as well as how online harassment elucidates how these intersections are recognized and processed in order to move forward and improve online communities for everyone.

References

Altman, J. (2016, July 25). *The whole Leslie Jones Twitter feud, explained.* Retrieved from http://college.usatoday.com/2016/07/25/the-whole-leslie-jones-twitter-feud-explained/

Ancu, M., & Cozma, R. (2009). MySpace politics: Uses and gratifications of befriending candidates. *Journal of Broadcasting & Electronic Media, 53*(4), 567–583.

Andersen, M. L., & Collins, P. H. (2006). *Race, class, and gender: An anthology* (6th ed.). Belmont: Wadsworth Publishing.

Bailey, M. (2013). New terms of resistance: A response to Zenzele Isoke. *Souls, 15*(4), 341–343.

Brown, K. V. (2016a, July 19). *How a racist, sexist hate mob forced Leslie Jones off Twitter.* Retrieved from http://fusion.net/story/327103/leslie-jones-twitter-racism/

Brown, K. (2016b, July 18). Leslie Jones attacked by racist Twitter trolls. *Jezebel.* Retrieved from http://jezebel.com/leslie-jones-attacked-by-racist-twitter-trolls-1783876740

Carr, C. T., Vitak, J., & McLaughlin, C. (2013). Strength of social cues in online impression formation expanding SIDE research. *Communication Research, 40*(2), 261–281.

Crenshaw, K. (1991). Mapping the margins: Intersectionality, identity politics, and violence against women of color. *Stanford Law Review, 43*(6), 1241–1299.

Davies, M. (2016, July 22). Leslie Jones talks online abuse: 'Hate speech and freedom of speech are two different things'. *Jezebel*. Retrieved from http://jezebel. com/leslie-jones-talks-online-abuse-hate-speech-and-freedo-1784131629

Dessem, M. (2016, July 19). Leslie Jones' Tweets on Monday night were a powerful response to an insane torrent of hate. *Slate*. Retrieved from http://www. slate.com/blogs/browbeat/2016/07/19/leslie_jones_tweets_were_a_powerful_response_to_an_insane_torrent_of_hate.html

Drayton, T. (2016, July 19). On Leslie Jones & Twitter harassment: Here's why racists shouldn't be banned from Twitter. *Clutch*. Retrieved from http://www. clutchmagonline.com/2016/07/on-leslie-jones-twitter-harassment-hereswhy-racists-shouldnt-be-banned-from-twitter/.

Ferguson, S. (2015, January 17). *Calling in: A quick guide on when and how.* Retrieved from http://everydayfeminism.com/2015/01/guide-to-calling-in/

Goffman, E. (1959). *The presentation of self in everyday life.* New York: Anchor Books.

Hogan, B. (2010). The presentation of self in the age of social media: Distinguishing performances and exhibitions online. *Bulleting of Science, Technology & Society, 30*(6), 377–386.

Kent, M. L. (2010). Directions in social media for professionals and scholars. In R. L. Heath (Ed.), *The Sage handbook of public relations* (pp. 643–656). Thousand Oaks: Sage.

Kobayashi, T. (2010). Bridging social capital in online communities: Heterogeneity and social tolerance of online game players in Japan. *Human Communication Research, 36*, 546–569.

LaAmanda, R., & Eastin, M. S. (2004). A social cognitive theory of internet uses and gratifications: Toward a new model of media attendance. *Journal of Broadcasting & Electronic Media, 48*(3), 358–377.

Leslie Jones fights back against racist Twitter trolls. (2016, July 19). *Clutch*. Retrieved from http://www.clutchmagonline.com/2016/07/leslie-jonesfights-back-against-racist-twitter-trolls/

Leslie Jones talks banning Twitter trolls "Freedom of speech & hate speech are two different things" [Video]. (2016, July 22). *Bossip*. Retrieved from http://bossip.com/1335906/leslie-jones-talks-banning-twitter-trolls-freedom-of-speech-hate-speech-are-two-different-things-video/

Lutkin, A. (2016, July 19). A lot of celebrities came out to support Leslie Jones after she spoke up about abuse on Twitter. *Jezebel.* Retrieved from http://jezebel.com/a-lot-of-celebrities-came-out-to-support-leslie-jones-a-1783925746

Macías, K. (2015). "Sisters in the collective struggle": Sounds of silence and reflections on the unspoken assault on Black females in modern America. *Cultural Studies ↔ Critical Methodologies, 15*(4), 260–264.

Maynard, A. S., Monk, J. D., & Booker, K. W. (2011). Building empathy through identification and expression of emotions: A review of interactive tools for children with social deficits. *Journal of Creativity in Mental Health, 6*(2), 166–175.

Moran, L. (2016, July 22). Leslie Jones has this very important message for her racist Twitter trolls. *Huffington Post.* Retrieved from http://www.huffingtonpost.com/entry/leslie-jones-ghostbusters-twitter-seth-meyers_us_5791e54ae4b0bdddc4d404bf

People ain't isht: Actress Leslie Jones exposes racist Twitter trolls "I've been called apes... you won't believe the evil" (2016, July 19). *Bossip.* Retrieved from http://bossip.com/1334878/people-aint-isht-actress-leslie-jones-exposes-racist-twitter-trolls-ive-been-called-apes-you-wont-believe-the-evil/

Roy, J. (2016, July 19). *Twitter bans Breitbart's Milo Yiannopoulos for harassment.* Retrieved from http://www.latimes.com/entertainment/la-et-mn-twitter-milo-yiannopoulos-20160719-snap-story.html

Saxton, G. D., & Waters, R. D. (2014). What do stakeholders like on Facebook? Examining public reactions to nonprofit organizations' informational, promotional, and community-building messages. *Journal of Public Relations Research, 26*(3), 280–299.

Sesko, A., & Biernat, M. (2009). Prototypes of race and gender: The invisibility of Black women. *Journal of Social Psychology, 46*, 356–360.

Shohat, E., & Stam, R. (2014). *Unthinking eurocentrism: Multiculturalism and the media.* New York: Routledge.

Sieczkowski, C. (2016, July 19). Celebs tweet their love for Leslie Jones after racist trolls try to tear her down. *Huffington Post.* Retrieved from http://www.huffingtonpost.com/entry/leslie-jones-love-racist-twitter_us_578e372be4b0a0ae97c36403

Thelandersson, F. (2014). A less toxic feminism: Can the internet solve the age old question of how to put intersectional theory into practice? *Feminist Media Studies, 14*(3), 527–530.

Trần, N. L. (2013, December 18). *Calling IN: A less disposable way of holding each other accountable.* Retrieved from http://www.blackgirldangerous. org/2013/12/calling-less-disposable-way-holding-accountable/

Visser, N. (2016, July 18). Leslie Jones, superstar, calls out racist Internet trolls: I'm not different than any of you. *Huffington Post.* Retrieved from http://www.huffingtonpost.com/entry/leslie-jones-Internet-trolls_us_578d8494e4 b0fa896c3fc684

Wagner, L. (2016, July 19). Ghostbusters' Leslie Jones has left Twitter after racist abuse made it a "personal hell." *Slate.* Retrieved from http://www.slate.com/ blogs/xx_factor/2016/07/19/ghostbusters_leslie_jones_leaves_twitter_due_ to_racist_abuse.html

Weber, L. (2004). A conceptual framework for understanding race, class, gender, and sexuality. In S. N. Hesse-Biber & M. Yaisier (Eds.), *Feminist perspectives on social research* (pp. 121–139). New York: Oxford University Press.

Yiannopoulos, M. (2016, July 18). *Teenage boys with tits: Here's my problem with Ghostbusters.* Retrieved from http://www.breitbart.com/tech/2016/07/18/ milo-reviews-ghostbusters/

5

bell hooks and Consciousness-Raising: Argument for a Fourth Wave of Feminism

Katie Blevins

In a time of increasing interconnectedness, where discourse is dominated by communication technologies such as social media networks, young people find themselves in a unique position of being available and connected both to friends and strangers twenty-four hours a day. In the midst of sharing information about what they had for breakfast, they are also organically growing consciousness-raising communities, embracing feminist activism, and, perhaps, defining a fourth wave of feminism. This chapter makes a theoretical argument for linking together consciousness-raising groups—as articulated by feminist scholar and activist bell hooks, activism, and fourth-wave feminism.

We live in a post-feminist culture, where many young people of the millennial generation—one of the generations most open to social change and differences—have an "I'm not a feminist but…" attitude. Celebrities dominate the mainstream media coverage with statements such as Evangeline Lily's 2014 *Huffington Post* interview, in which she stated "I'm very proud of being a woman, and as a woman, I don't even like the word feminism because when I hear that word, I associate it with women trying

K. Blevins (✉)
School of Journalism and Mass Media, University of Idaho, Moscow, ID, USA

© The Author(s) 2018
J. R. Vickery, T. Everbach (eds.), *Mediating Misogyny*,
https://doi.org/10.1007/978-3-319-72917-6_5

to pretend to be men and I'm not interested in trying to pretend to be a man […] I don't want to embrace manhood, I want to embrace my womanhood" (Blickley 2014).

Some celebrity women express the view that equality is already achieved, rendering feminist activism unnecessary. Actress Kaley Cuoco drew widespread criticism for a 2014 interview to *Redbook* magazine, in which we stated that feminism isn't "really something I think about. Things are different now, and I know a lot of the work that paved the way for women happened before I was around… I was never that feminist girl demanding equality, but maybe that's because I've never really faced inequality" ("Kaley Cuoco-Sweeting's Law of Happiness" 2014).

Despite this, women's everyday experiences are still defined by daily instances of sexism, both small and large. Young women, in particular, often lack the knowledge to counter and speak to these experiences, having internalized life-long messages that the United States is a post-feminist culture. Feminist scholar Susan Douglas (2010) highlights this disconnect by addressing what she terms "enlightened sexism," or that it is not only okay, it is funny, to bring back sexist stereotypes of men and women. But some millennials are mobilizing online and rejecting post-feminist cultural values (Aune 2013, p. 49). The first key aspect to this emerging nexus of community, activism, and feminism in online spaces is the re-emergence of consciousness-raising groups (see also Chap. 17 by Desborough and Chap. 18 by Regehr and Ringrose.

Consciousness-Raising Groups

Consciousness-raising groups were informal gatherings for women in different communities, places where women could vent about sexism and social inequalities, as well as places where women could heal from daily injustices against them (hooks 2000, p. 7). Although these groups played pivotal roles in earlier iterations of feminism, they fell out of vogue after the second wave of feminism, as feminism became more centrally-organized and then moved into academia.

The shift to more centralized feminism led to widespread gains for the movement in terms of mainstream visibility and policy objectives, but it also led to a loss of visibility for women who *were not* white and upper-middle class. Additionally, the movement itself became less political. According to the prominent feminist scholar bell hooks (2000), the "dismantling of consciousness-raising groups all but erased the notion that one had to learn about feminism and make an informed choice about embracing feminist politics to become a feminist advocate" (p. 7).

In bell hooks' 2000 book, *Feminism is for Everybody*, she laments the loss of consciousness-raising groups. hooks argues that these groups were vital to the early formation of the Women's Rights Movement: "Feminists are made, not born. One does not become an advocate of feminist politics simply by having the privilege of have been born female. Like all political positions, one becomes a believer in feminist politics through choice and action" (p. 7). Consciousness-raising groups also became a "site for conversion," where women were actively brought into feminism through these important communities (hooks 2000, p. 8).

Losing consciousness-raising groups decreased feminist activism, relegating feminism to a nearly apolitical, and often undesirable, label. As scholars Rebecca Munford and Melanie Waters (2014) point out, "while feminism is not dead, it is not nearly as visible as it once was" (p. 18). Many women, even those who openly identify as feminists, do so from the relative comfort of an apolitical stance (hooks 2000, pp. 10–11).

Though hooks was not content to document the fall of consciousness-raising groups. She saw these communities as essential to a progressive movement addressing lingering issues relating to sexism. In *Feminism is for Everybody*, she argues that "when [the] feminist movement renews itself, reinforcing again and again the strategies that will enable a mass movement to end sexism and sexist exploitation and oppression for everyone, consciousness-raising will once again attain its original importance" (hooks 2000, p. 11). Now, young people are using social media as a way to overcome barriers to activism by congregating in new, grassroots consciousness-raising groups.

There are several key features of consciousness-raising groups as outlined by bell hooks. First, they are a place for members to vent about everyday sexist experiences. The organic structure of consciousness-raising groups encourages widespread sharing of incidences that might otherwise be considered minor within the larger feminist movement. Aside from airing grievances, this process also serves as a point of empathy and community building.

The "Everyday Sexism Project," begun by Laura Bates in April 2012, shows the success of using social media to address daily instances of sexist discrimination while building a strong online community. According to the website, "The Everyday Sexism Project exists to catalogue instances of sexism experienced by women on a day to day basis. They might be serious or minor, outrageously offensive or so niggling and normalized that you don't even feel able to protest. [...] By sharing your story you're showing the world that sexism does exist, it is faced by women everyday and it is a valid problem to discuss" ("Everyday Sexism Project"). Within one year, the project was rolled out to 17 different countries and received tens of thousands of submissions (Cochrane 2013). Joining the "Everyday Sexism Project" page on a social media platform allows users to see updates. It also allows users to comment on stories (generating discussion), share the stories on their own social media accounts (bringing the conversation to their personal social circles), and feel more connected to the community.

The second feature of consciousness-raising groups is that argumentative discussions are both a necessary and a productive part of these groups (hooks 2000, p. 8). In an online space, the combination of anonymity and access has resulted in an atmosphere where argumentative discussions are the norm. Most social media interactions allow for heated discussion to take place. The current atmosphere is definitely a more extreme version of the discussions hooks spoke of in the original consciousness-raising groups.

The *benefit* of such extreme discussion could be contested in this new iteration of consciousness-raising. While many people are drawn to and empathize with victim accounts and stories, the inherently open nature of social media platforms leaves them vulnerable to criticisms, threats, and harassment from trolls who are often participating for the sole purpose of antagonizing feminists. Perversely, the experience of being harassed for expressing feminist viewpoints in social media is a unifying and galvanizing experience for participants in these groups.

The *drawback* is that the relative anonymity of social media has also opened participants up to harassment. One example familiar to many in the feminist community is the #Gamergate storm of 2014. Gamergate began when several prominent women who work in the video game industry became the targets of online trolls—individuals who post incendiary rhetoric, often to provoke a response. Although trolling of women in the male-dominated video game profession is hardly unique, the ferocity of the threats—death, rape, hacking, and public posting of personal information—led several women to flee their homes and go into hiding (Rott 2014). Much of the discussion using the #Gamergate hashtag took place on social media, with supporters of the trolls criticizing the women on platforms like Twitter and Reddit, while others used the hashtag to reply to the trolling.

In light of this harassment, the benefits of open argumentative discussion take on a more problematic light. Although many women and men were drawn to the plight of the victims of #Gamergate, online trolling is what allowed the situation to escalate to the point where one commentator from Gawker, Sam Biddle, said if he had experienced such an onslaught that he would be "locked in a closet rocking back and forth" (Wu 2015).

The third feature of consciousness-raising groups is that they have the fundamental objective of converting individuals to feminist politics (hooks 2000, p. 8). Despite criticisms of "slacktivism," the Pew Research Center has established that social media are platforms used for mainstream political activism. In a 2013 study, Pew found that 39% of U.S. adults had participated in some kind of political activity using a social media site in the 12 months prior to the survey (Smith 2013). Of particular note, 21% of civically-engaged social media users reported belonging to an online group "that is involved in political/social issues, or working to advance a cause" (vs. 12% for the general population) (Smith 2013). Within these communities, users are able to discuss and learn about the specific actions that should be taken. This leads to the fourth feature of consciousness-raising groups: that they establish realistic expectations for change (hooks 2000, p. 8).

Although digital activism lacks the broad, organized goals of the feminist campaigns of the 1960s and 70s—the Equal Rights Amendment, reproductive justice, and equal pay—these online groups focus on small, meaningful changes. For example, Twitter has long been criticized for supporting violent and sexist content. Although the company cites freedom of speech and expression as reasons not to censor content, victims of "revenge porn" have been lobbying for Twitter policies to change.

Most of the outcry came from users who banded together to encourage Twitter to respond to revenge porn, "intimate, and possibly explicit, images or video posted publicly without consent" (Tsukayama 2015). In March of 2015, Twitter acknowledged that while the company has been problematic in its treatment of harmful content, they were revamping user guidelines to ban revenge porn on the social media platform. Twitter's policy shift, while limited in nature, is indicative of the meaningful changes digital activism can enact.

Fifth, consciousness-raising groups should be non-hierarchical. There are no set leaders and all voices are heard equally by other members (hooks 2000, p. 8). This is true online to a certain extent. For example, the 243,000 users who currently follow the "Everyday Sexism Project" have equal standing in terms of that community. Comments, retweets, and responses can be seen by all members. Most social media groups operate in a similar fashion, a deconstruction of hierarchy due to technology. While some social media sites like Reddit allow comments to be up/down voted by the community based on popularity, most social media communities have a forced democratization.

One criticism that hooks had for earlier consciousness-raising groups is that they needed to be more inclusive of men (hooks 2000, p. 11). She argues that men must be brought in to the feminist fold as active members of the feminist cause. Social media allows for *everyone* with an Internet connection to participate. While men are welcome in online spaces, anonymity also allows for a decreased emphasis on an individual's gender.

These online consciousness-raising groups have contributed as a new way for young people to participate in feminist activism. Some of these modern consciousness-raising groups are more than social gatherings based around issues of sexism, they are also re-politicizing young people, and bringing them to the feminist cause through social media activism.

Activism and Social Media

In 2008, only 29% of Americans used some form of social media. As of 2013, Pew Research Center reports that number as 72% (Duggan 2013). Women are more likely to be social media users than men—one of the few media forms with consistently higher usage by women. While previous research on feminism and new media focused on long-form modes of communication, mostly blogs and message boards, the overwhelming adoption of social media is even more important.

Social media—platforms that allow individuals to participate in linked social networks—have opened additional opportunities for alternative viewpoints to be widely promoted. Social movement media is vital to countering mainstream media, which can contain narrow and often inaccurate views of race, sex, and gender. Activism in this context is the "engagement in activities designed to foster social change or, alternatively, to resist it" (Tindall and Groenewegen 2014, p. 2). While social movements involve participation of collectives (individuals or organizations), activism refers to individuals or small groups.

Online activism is not always regarded in a positive way. Not everyone sees social media participation as evidence of effective activism. Skeptics point out that social media provides no uniting focus, and is "merely fostering informal sociability with no specific institutional power" (Downing 2011, p. 363). The combination of fragmentation and lack of formal organization leads critics to label digital activism as less viable than traditional activist channels. Derisive terms like "slacktivism" or "arm-chair activism" focus on the perceived limited impact of digital activism in the "real world" (Tindall and Groenewegen 2014, p. 7).

In contrast, here are five characteristics of digital activism that make it worthwhile. First, the "use of digital technologies, such as mobile phones and Internet-enabled devices, in campaigns for social and political change" encourages participation from individuals in activist endeavors (Tindall and Groenewegen 2014, p. 4). Second, the visual nature of digital activism (indeed most online activities) gives prominence to social/political issues in a way that makes them easily seen by individuals. Third, that the ability to customize and direct content is also unprecedented in the online space. Fourth, so-called "user-generated content," which refers to users who generate media that "circumvent[s] the gatekeeping of commercial media and traditional channels of political discourse with self-produced content," signals a readiness to produce and participate on a new level via social media platforms (Downing 2011, p. 363).

Finally, and perhaps most importantly, the shift to digital activism indicates a lessening in reliance on institutional activism as "movement entrepreneurs" act to participate in an "increasingly diverse set of movement activities" (Tindall and Groenewegen 2014, p. 5). Instead of relying on large, centrally organized bodies to guide and produce activism like many previous social movements, digital activism does not rely on this institutional model. Individuals—regardless of their offline affiliations and status—can, and do, engender activist policies using digital media. The result is a shift toward the individual, where the focus is on "direct action politics" (Tindall and Groenewegen 2014, p. 5). This results in increased participation in activism by overcoming the individual's barriers to participation.

One of the most obvious benefits of this approach is the ability for geographically-dispersed individuals belonging to marginalized groups to connect and challenge hegemonic discourses (Kostiuchenjo and Martsenyuk 2014, p. 571). Digital activism via social media provides a place where a collective identity can be built for these otherwise disparate users (Tindall and Groenewegen 2014, p. 4). This allows marginalized groups to participate and form more cohesive communities, regardless of geographic limitations. There are far-reaching implications for the potential of smaller, marginalized groups—such as communities for transgender individuals—to succeed in social media.

As a result, these digital networks can function as "expressions of new collective identities, both resistant and transformative" (Thornham 2007, p. 123). One of the potential benefits of social media is its relative anonymity, or, at the very least, a physical distance between the individual activist and the cause they are supporting (Tindall and Groenewegen 2014, p. 3). Since one barrier to activism is that the individuals are reluctant to publicly support controversial causes, digital activism offers a way for individuals who might otherwise be reluctant to publicly endorse a cause to participate in a less threatening way.

It is important to put consciousness-raising groups and social media activism into context: the young people participating have never lived at a time where feminist activism marched routinely in the streets, at least not in the U.S. In a post-feminist media landscape, they have reconciled the disconnect between their everyday lived experiences with sexism by taking to social media and forming informal communities to express their discontent. This is important because these feminists are changing the landscape *of* feminism, reinvigorating a movement for a new generation and possibly starting a new wave of feminism.

Fourth Wave of Feminism

Feminist scholars have dwelled on the generational rifts between feminists, as well as differences between academic-based feminism and activist-based feminism. In terms of feminist "waves," Western feminists have been identified (and sometimes shoe-horned) into broadly defined generational categories. From the first-wave of U.S. suffragettes of the 1910s and 1920s, to the second wave's focus on broad social issues in the 1960s–80s, and finally the third-wave micropolitics of the 1990s–2000s, feminism has grappled with fragmented interests and objectives. One result is that many feminist scholars are preoccupied with "anxieties about the past, concern for the future and an overarching uncertainty" about the status of feminism and its ability to enact meaningful change (Munford and Waters 2014, p. 20).

The apparent rift between "academic" theorists and "activist" media-makers is in some ways marked by the differences in second- and third-wave feminists (Downing 2011, p. 197). Specifically, that "while older women became feminists as a result of personal experience or social activism, younger women's exposure to feminism came either through the academic, in the form of a university education, or through American popular culture" (Thornham 2013, pp. 32–33). The third wave is often seen as less overarching in its political aims than the second wave, with the focus lying on the individual feminist's needs, or micropolitics.

Scholar Kristin Aune (2013) points to some of the cultural pressures millennials face that inhibit them from pursuing political agendas. These can range from the commodification of women (consumption as a source of power and fulfillment) to changes in gender expectations (no longer mother/daughter/wife, but have-it-all consumer.) She argues that this cultural landscape has resulted in young women's distancing from even the third wave of feminism, which came to the forefront in the 1990s.

One of the unintentional results of these generational rifts is the fragmentation of feminist objectives and a widespread societal acceptance of a post-feminist landscape, where "sexism had been vanquished" and feminism made obsolete (Downing 2011, p. 197). Post-feminism emphasizes the past, or the "dead history" of feminist politics (Munford and Waters 2014, p. 170). Susan Douglas notes this in her 2010 book, *Enlightened Sexism: The Seductive Message that Feminism's Work is Done*, when she derisively questions and answers, "The notion that there might, indeed, still be an urgency to feminist politics? You have totally got to be kidding" (p. 8).

Even within the academic community, widespread incorporation of basic feminist concerns has led to a brief overview of the history of feminism in many humanities courses, but little discussion regarding any present-day relevance (Thornham and Weissmann 2013, p. 2). At the same time funding has been cut for women's studies departments and programs. Many undergraduate students in the U.S. may spend some time learning the history of feminism—but fewer students learn that there is still a need. Specifically, the "incorporation of feminism and gender studies into the metanarrative of media studies has led to what she [the author] calls the 'depoliticization of academic feminism,' as students discover it alongside and embedded in other key movements and issues" (Thornham and Weissmann 2013, p. 3).

So, is there a fourth wave of feminism and how would such a wave be characterized? Thus far, fourth-wave feminism has largely been identified by the young people who affiliate with it online. In discussion boards and via social media, young women and men are distancing themselves from the third wave of feminism and declaring themselves members of the fourth wave. In Jennifer Baumgardner's 2011 book *F 'em! Goo Goo, Gaga, and Some Thoughts on Balls*, she spoke of the transition from third-wave to fourth-wave feminism:

> In place of zines and songs, young feminists created blogs, Twitter campaigns, and online media with names like Racialicious and Feministing, or wrote for Jezebel and Salon's Broadsheet. They commented on the news, posted their most stylish plus-size fashion photos with info about where to shop, and tweeted that they, too, had had an abortion. "Reproductive justice," coined by women of color in the 1990s, became the term of choice for young feminists. Transgenderism, male feminists, sex work, and complex relationships within the media characterized their feminism.

The focus for fourth-wave feminists is on shifting the depoliticizing micropolitics of the third-wave to a "call out" culture online, where individuals challenge sexism and misogyny through a variety of tactics (Muro 2013).

Instead of returning to a centrally-organized social movement, young feminists are forming communities, consciousness-raising groups, and discussing goals that are relevant to their individual, lived experiences. Fourth-wave feminism is not characterized by a changing strategy but by a change in tactics, the "moves one makes while engaged with the opposition" (Garrison 2010, p. 385). Essentially, what distinguishes the fourth wave from the third is the reincorporation of consciousness-raising groups through social media.

Some critics might question basing a new "wave" around a technological advance. In Ealasaid Muro's essay, "Feminism: A Fourth Wave?," she argues that although "the existence of a feminist 'fourth wave' has been challenged by those who maintain that increased usage of the Internet is not enough to delineate a new era [...] it is increasingly clear that the Internet has facilitated the creation of a global community of feminists who use the Internet both for discussion and activism" (Muro 2013). Even as academics challenge the existence of and the need for a demarcation between third- and fourth-wave feminists, young women *and* men are identifying as fourth-wave, and they are engaging with digital activism through social media as a major part of their feminist activities.

The technology, and adoption of technology, is present in high enough numbers to warrant some generalities about millennials' use of social media. Not only are women more likely to use social media in general, adoption rates for teens of platforms like Facebook are 71% in the U.S. (Lenhart 2015). As of 2015, 71% also belong to more than one social network. What is of special interest with regards to issues of intersectionality is that "African-American and Hispanic youth report more frequent Internet use than white teens. Among African-American teens, 34% report going online 'almost constantly' as do 32% of Hispanic teens, while 19% of white teens go online that often." This indicates that digital activism may avoid one of the common pitfalls of feminist activism— over-reliance on the narratives of upper-middle-class white women.

Additional research needs to be done about the new consciousness-raising groups, such as the differences in dialogues between social media platforms. A 2015 study examined the #Ferguson hashtag to see how people were reacting to the police killing of an unarmed black teenager in Ferguson, Missouri. Research showed that on Twitter, the hashtag was primarily used to share news: "86% of the Twitter conversation with that hashtag was directly related to the news in Ferguson, such as the community protests, the U.S. Department of Justice report or the city's police department" (Hitlin and Holcomb 2015). Instagram posts, by comparison, focused "less as a reference to the events in Missouri, and more often as a way for people to discuss or reference issues such as race, police brutality, and politics." Although these platform differences have evolved organically, going forward they are an important component in better understanding where different conversations are taking place and how to better encourage digital activism.

In a time and place where feminism was removed from communities, depoliticized, and generally dismissed in a post-feminist cultural landscape, it is significant that young people are self-identifying as fourth-wave feminists who are active on social media, forming groups and tackling small-scale activism. This indicates a fundamental shift in the approach *to* feminism and must be studied further. That being said, social media as a site of feminist politics is not without its complications.

Limitations

There are clearly some limitations to the argument that social media is integral to the return of consciousness-raising groups and feminist activism that characterizes the fourth wave. The anonymity of social media networks opens users up to continual harassment in the online space. The very values of free speech and an open society also leave many feminist activists vulnerable. Some social media platforms also maintain sexist policies that make feminist activism problematic. Facebook, the largest of the social media platforms, has been criticized for condoning content that explicitly promotes violence against women. Although Facebook routinely removes content that is homophobic or racist, it "continues to deem content encouraging violence against women inoffensive," despite removing many photos of women breastfeeding, stating that the images are pornographic (O'Toole 2010).

A 2013 letter to Facebook, written on behalf of 65 gender equality groups, argued that "Facebook [apparently] considers violence against women to be less offensive than non-violent images of women's bodies, and that the only acceptable representation of women's nudity are those in which women appear as sex objects or the victims of abuse" ("Open Letter," 2013). It is difficult to build a safe space in an online sphere that encourages sexist practices. This dichotomy is one that individuals have attempted to correct, often through additional digital activism. Facebook, for example, responded to the 2013 letter by changing company policy ("Controversial, Harmful, and Hateful" 2013). This shift opens the possibility for safer dialogues to happen in social media spaces, while also demonstrating the power of consciousness-raising groups to enact measurable progress.

Probably the largest limitation to social media providing a true space for consciousness-raising groups is the potential to reiterate patterns of prominence for the dialogues of white, upper-middle-class users. Although this chapter focuses on the application of hooks's characteristics of consciousness-raising groups to social media and political activism, there are many problematic instances of social media being used as a medium for racist discourses. At a fundamental level, even replication of post-racial jokes via meme culture presents worrying problems for creating safe spaces online. For example, Wendy K.Z. Anderson and Kittie E. Grace's (2015) research about consciousness-raising groups on Facebook for working mothers found that patterns of exclusion based on economic and education limited these groups.

Like the previous waves of feminism, fourth-wave feminism cannot answer certain broad criticisms that surround the use of new media for activism. For example, fourth-wave feminism does not solve the issue of fragmented interests. With so many platform options among social media alone, the ability to group into a large social movement remains limited (Zeisler 2013, p. 181). This, combined with the feminist concern about speaking for others and the culture of anonymity online, detracts from the ability of the fourth wave to effect large-scale change.

Possibly the most crucial critique of digital activism is in the lingering of the digital divide (Tindall and Groenewegen 2014, p. 5). Zeisler (2013) cautions against romanticizing new media in the face of a very real lack of access for many in the United States and worldwide. In late 2014, Pew Research Center analyzed the Census Bureau's first estimates of computer use and Internet connections for different geographic areas. The research found that almost 25 million households (21% of all U.S. households) have no regular Internet access at all, either from a home computer/device or elsewhere, such as a library (Rainie and Cohn 2014). Some common reasons for lack of access include: lack of relevance and difficulty of use (reasons often cited by older respondents), expense related to owning a computer or maintaining an Internet connection, and lack of physical access to the Internet (Zickuhr 2013).

Even though 84% of Americans own a computer (defined as desktop, laptop, netbook, or notebook computer) and 73% of Americans have broadband Internet, the numbers suggest stark differences based on geography (Rainie and Cohn 2014). For example, in the ten largest metro areas, the share of broadband adoption (sometimes limited by broadband access) ranges from 73% in Miami to 84% in Washington, D.C. It is worth pointing out that recent 2015 research shows that, especially among young people, there are high adoption rates of smartphone technology. Almost 75% of teens surveyed had access to a smartphone, and

24% regardless of race/gender report that they are online "constantly" (Lenhart 2015). Of this age group, 92% report going online daily, which is far higher than national numbers.

Overall, this research demonstrates that while many individuals could benefit greatly from the potential of digital consciousness-raising groups, there are still some limitations in terms of basic access for over a fifth of all U.S. households. Additionally, almost one-third of all Americans lack access to broadband Internet, diminishing their ability to take part in digital activism. It is encouraging to see recent research indicating that even though civic engagement research shows that those with a higher income and education consistently have higher percentages for political participation, "the gap in political participation between the lowest and highest income groups is generally smaller on social networking sites than it is for other types of political engagement" (Smith 2013). This indicates that basic access to the Internet can bridge some of the gaps between the "haves" and "have-nots" with regard to socioeconomic status. This leads to better opportunities overall for consciousness-raising and activism.

Conclusion

Using bell hooks's descriptions for the characteristics of consciousness-raising groups, this research applied situational examples of digital activism to provide theoretical support for recognizing many digital activists' efforts as consciousness-raising groups. It also situated these groups within a fourth wave of feminism, arguing that consciousness-raising groups should be one of the primary characteristics of millennials' use of technology with regard to feminist activities. By linking digital activism to feminist activism, the ultimate argument is that these new consciousness-raising groups should be integrated as a key tactic of an emerging fourth wave of feminism.

The return of consciousness-raising groups offers exciting possibilities for inclusion in a fourth wave of feminism. In particular, consciousness-raising groups open the door for ground-level activism, where geographically dispersed individuals can group together and enact changes to a variety of community-based policies and approaches to issues important to traditionally disenfranchised communities. The case study of the "Everyday Sexism Project" demonstrates how informing and revolutionizing feminists through social media makes the feminist movement more accessible while fulfilling hooks's hope for a return to consciousness-raising and revolution through activism. Most importantly, perhaps, it validates the contributions of young people who are self-identifying as fourth-wave feminists and attempting to revive activism through digital spaces.

References

Anderson, W. K. Z., & Grace, K. E. (2015). 'Taking mama steps' towards authority, alternatives, advocacy. *Feminist Media Studies, 15*(6), 942–959.

Aune, K. (2013). Third-wave feminism and the university: On pedagogy and feminist resurgence. In H. Thornham & E. Weissmann (Eds.), *Renewing feminisms: Radical narratives, fantasies and futures in media studies* (pp. 47–62). London: I.B. Tauris.

Baumgardner, J. (2011). Is there a fourth wave? Does it matter? *Feminist.com.* Retrieved from http://www.feminist.com/resources/artspeech/genwom/baumgardner2011.html

Blickley, L. (2014, December 9). Evangeline Lilly is 'Not interested in trying to pretend to be a man'. *Huffington Post.* Retrieved from http://www.huffingtonpost.com/2014/12/09/evangeline-lilly-the-hobbit_n_6290220.html

Cochrane, K. (2013, December 10). The fourth wave of feminism: Meet the rebel women. *The Guardian.* Retrieved from http://www.theguardian.com/world/2013/dec/10/fourth-wave-feminism-rebel-women

Controversial, harmful, and hateful speech on Facebook. (2013). *Facebook.* Retrieved from https://www.facebook.com/notes/facebook-safety/controversial-harmful-and-hateful-speech-on-facebook/574430655911054

Douglas, S. (2010). *Enlightened sexism: The seductive message that feminism's work is done.* New York: Times Books.

Downing, J. (2011). *Encyclopedia of social movement media.* Los Angeles: SAGE.

Duggan, M. (2013). It's a woman's (social media) world. Pew Research Center. Retrieved from http://www.pewresearch.org/fact-tank/2013/09/12/its-a-womans-social-media-world/

Garrison, E. K. (2010). U.S. feminism grrrl style! Youth (sub)cultures and the technologies of the third wave. In N. Hewitt (Ed.), *No permanent waves* (pp. 379–402). New Brunswick: Rutgers Press.

Hitlin, P., & Holcomb, J. (2015). From Twitter to Instagram, a different #ferguson Conversation. Pew Research Center. Retrieved from http://www.pewresearch.org/fact-tank/2015/04/06/from-twitter-to-instagram-a-different-ferguson/

hooks, b. (2000). *Feminism is for everybody: Passionate politics*. Cambridge: South End Press.

Kaley Cuoco-Sweeting's law of happiness. (2014, December 30). *Redbook*. Retrieved from http://www.redbookmag.com/life/news/g2507/kaley-cuoco-sweeting-interview/?slide=2

Kostiuchenjo, T., & Martsenyuk, T. (2014). Gender. In K. Harvey (Ed.), *Encyclopedia of social media & politics* (pp. 565–610). Los Angeles: SAGE Publications.

Lenhart, A. (2015). Teens, social media and technology overview 2015. Pew Research Center. Retrieved from http://www.pewinternet.org/2015/04/09/teens-social-media-technology-2015/#fn-13190-1

Munford, R., & Waters, M. (2014). *Feminism & popular culture*. New Brunswick: Rutgers University Press.

Muro, E. (2013). Feminism: A fourth wave? *Political Studies Association*, Retrieved from http://www.psa.ac.uk/insight-plus/feminism-fourth-wave

O'Toole, E. (2010, May 23). Facebook's violently sexist pages are an opportunity for feminists. *The Guardian*. Retrieved from http://www.theguardian.com/commentisfree/2013/may/23/facebook-violently-sexist-pages-twitter-fbrape

Open letter to Facebook. (2013). *Women, action, & the media*. Retrieved from http://www.womenactionmedia.org/facebookaction/open-letter-to-facebook/

Rainie, L., & Cohn, D. (2014). Census: Computer ownership, internet connection varies widely across the U.S. Pew Research Center. Retrieved from http://www.pewresearch.org/fact-tank/2014/09/19/census-computerownership-internet-connection-varies-widely-across-u-s/

Rott, N. (2014, September 24). #Gamergate controversy fuels debate on women and video games. *NPR*. Retrieved from http://www.npr.org/sections/alltechconsidered/2014/09/24/349835297/-gamergate-controversy-fuels-debate-on-women-and-video-games

Smith, A. (2013). *Civic engagement in the digital age*. Pew Research Center. Retrieved from http://www.pewinternet.org/2013/04/25/civic-engagement-in-the-digital-age/

The Everyday Sexism Project. *Everyday Sexism Project*. Retrieved from http://everydaysexism.com/

The Everyday Sexism Project. *Twitter.* Retrieved from https://twitter.com/everydaysexism

Thornham, S. (2007). *Women, feminism & media.* Edinburgh: Edinburgh University Press.

Thornham, S. (2013). Rebranding feminism: Post-feminism, popular culture and the academy. In H. Thornham & E. Weissmann (Eds.), *Renewing feminisms: Radical narratives, fantasies and futures in media studies* (pp. 32–46). London: I.B. Tauris.

Thornham, H., & Weissmann, E. (2013). Introduction: Renewing-retooling feminism. In H. Thornham & E. Weissmann (Eds.), *Renewing feminisms: Radical narratives, fantasies and futures in media studies* (pp. 1–10). London: I.B. Tauris.

Tindall, D. B., & Groenewegen, T. (2014). Activists and activism, digital. In K. Harvey (Ed.), *Encyclopedia of social media & politics* (pp. 1–98). Los Angeles: SAGE Publications.

Tsukayama, H. (2015, March 11). Twitter updates its rules to specifically ban revenge porn. *The Washington Post.* Retrieved from http://www.washingtonpost.com/blogs/the-switch/wp/2015/03/11/twitter-updates-its-rules-to-specifically-ban-revenge-porn/

Wu, B. (2015, February 11). I'm Brianna Wu, and I'm Risking My Life Standing Up to Gamergate. *Bustle.* Retrieved from http://www.bustle.com/articles/63466-im-brianna-wu-and-im-risking-my-life-standing-up-to-gamergate

Zeisler, A. (2013). New media, new feminism: Evolving feminist analysis and activism in print, on the web, and beyond. In H. Thornham & E. Weissmann (Eds.), *Renewing feminisms: Radical narratives, fantasies and futures in media studies* (pp. 178–184). London: I.B. Tauris.

Zickuhr, K. (2013). Who's not online and why. Pew Research Center. Retrieved from http://www.pewinternet.org/2013/09/25/whos-not-online-and-why/

Part II

Research and Case Studies

6

Mainstreaming Misogyny: The Beginning of the End and the End of the Beginning in Gamergate Coverage

David Nieborg and Maxwell Foxman

While reboots are a common phenomenon in Hollywood, the 2016 remake of *Ghostbusters* garnered a remarkable amount of criticism before viewers had even seen the movie. As early as January 2015, Donald Trump, then a reality TV star and real-estate mogul, posed one of his signature rhetorical questions during a "TrumpVlog": "... and now they are remaking Ghostbusters with only women! What is going on?" (Trump 2015). Trump's seemingly off-the-cuff question about the proper role of women in popular culture would be a harbinger of things to come. In the months leading up to the summer release, online commenters started collective campaigns to downvote the *Ghostbusters'* trailer online. Journalists and pundits pointed out that the vile concoction of misogyny and racism, primarily aimed at the all-female leading cast, certainly had not come out of nowhere. This is how *The Atlantic's* culture critic historicized the events:

D. Nieborg (✉)
Department of Arts, Culture and Media, University of Toronto,
Toronto, Canada

M. Foxman
Communications, Columbia University, New York, NY, USA

© The Author(s) 2018   **111**
J. R. Vickery, T. Everbach (eds.), *Mediating Misogyny*,
https://doi.org/10.1007/978-3-319-72917-6_6

"Ghostbusters… has become a rallying cause for a swathe of fans who are beginning to resemble a movement not unlike the Gamergate nightmare that continues to plague the world of video games" (Sims 2016). After *Ghostbusters'* launch, one of the movie's main protagonists, African-American actress and comedian Leslie Jones, was singled out by anonymous trolls in a stream of online harassment and racist attacks culminating in her personal accounts and website being hacked (for an in-depth analysis of Leslie Jones' harassment and misogynoir, see Chap. 4). Again, a critic writing for *Vox* pointed to Gamergate to contextualize the online onslaught befalling Jones, framing it as "the first major battle of the emerging subculture war" (Romano 2016). For mainstream U.S. journalists, Gamergate—a niche misogynistic online movement primarily targeting female game developers and critics—has become synonymous with, if not a benchmark for, mediated misogyny.

As Gamergate is considered paradigmatic of a recent wave of online hate against women and underrepresented groups, this chapter aims to answer two sets of questions. First, how is the Gamergate movement rooted in game culture's history and what do the movement's online origins tell us about mediated misogyny? To answer these questions, our chapter starts by situating Gamergate within the wider ambit of game culture, which has battled gender-based intimidation since industry codification in the 1980s. Gamergate acted as the tinder that inflamed the systemic online harassment of women, a fire that has been smoldering for years. We argue that Gamergate can be seen as "the beginning of the end" of an era in the history of digital games. For decades, the game industry's dominant masculine identity has been influential in shaping game culture, dominant game genres, practices, and discourses (Kirkpatrick 2013). However, audiences, mainstream journalists, critics, and large segments of the industry have recently become more vocal and successful in championing for greater diversity in terms of players, games and developers.

Second, given that mainstream newsmakers invoke Gamergate as a major battleground for a new form of virulent sexism, how are journalists making sense of the movement's emergence and evolution? While Gamergate initially targeted a relatively isolated group of game aficionados (Mortensen 2016), the movement's profile broke into the mainstream, to the surprise of many. Consequently, Gamergate has become a catalyst to discuss a broader set of Internet phenomena that signal "the end of the beginning": a new era in which online misogyny is increasingly recognized, scrutinized, and criticized by leading news organizations. Our chapter addresses this second issue empirically; we compiled, coded, and performed both discourse and content analyses on a corpus of U.S. mainstream media covering Gamergate over the last two years. We included both legacy publications (e.g., *The New York Times* and *Time*) and digital news platforms (e.g., *Vox* and *Slate*). It is this *process of mainstreaming*—the normalization and subsequent citation of Gamergate events and related actors in widely read print and digital outlets—that makes our argument particularly topical.

Not only are Gamergate supporters still active, but its most visible advocates also seem to be thriving in the age of President Trump. While Trump by no means started the harassment surrounding *Ghostbusters* and Gamergate, key people in his orbit were instrumental in both cases. Breitbart News Network and affiliated authors such as Milo Yiannopoulos played an important role in guiding the harassment of Leslie Jones and whipped up support for the Gamergate cause. The appointment as the White House's chief strategist of Steve Bannon, Breitbart's executive chair who had previous business ties to the game industry, even led a few journalists to label Trump as "the Gamergate president." Seen in this light, Trump's election serves to validate and legitimize the institutionalization not only of mediated misogyny, but also anonymous digital harassment as a tool to suppress rational discourse, fact-based journalism, and progressive ideals.

The Beginning of the End

In the slow news month of August 2014, the Gamergate controversy demonstrated what can happen when a male-dominated subculture feels itself under siege. For the uninitiated, Gamergate is best understood as a self-organized, largely anonymous group of "hooligans" engaging in "leisure-centered aggression" against a small group of women and their supporters (Mortensen 2016). The movement's inception was a seemingly quotidian affair: a vengeful boyfriend trying to hurt his former girlfriend by posting hateful diatribes online. The subsequent series of events are "torturously complex" to recount (Burgess and Matamoros-Fernández 2016, p. 79) and Gamergate's agenda is frustratingly incoherent and contradictory. Clearly, gamers felt that their domain was under attack by unruly women and "Social Justice Warriors" who were perceived as trying to take their games away (Braithwaite 2016). The movement was born and raised online, with social media and message boards serving, ironically, as a safe space for male gamers to congregate and share a perplexing sense of victimhood anonymously.

For a short while, Gamergate coverage was relegated to niche game publications whose authors were intimately familiar with the historical trajectory of game culture. In what seemed to gamergaters like a coordinated effort among games critics and journalists, the "beginning of the end" was announced in a string of blog posts and opinion pieces. Collectively, the articles declared "gamers are dead" (Mortensen 2016), thereby questioning the dominance of the hypermasculine nature of the gamer identity. Instead, a more diverse group of players, playing a more diverse set of games on a wider array of platforms would be the new norm. Under the banner of "ethics in games journalism," Gamergate proponents used this series of progressive proclamations as a battle cry to foment support and lash out against a small group of female developers and critics—Brianna Wu, Anita Sarkeesian, and Zoe Quinn—as well as their supporters. What made mainstream journalists pay attention to Gamergate's emergence may have to do with its particularly aggressive and admittedly effective tactics. Ultimately, Gamergate supporters created "a campaign of systematic harassment" (Massanari 2015, p. 2), and, as Burgess and Matamoros-Fernández (2016) found when "issue-mapping" over 230,000 tweets, they were "absolutely not concerned only or even primarily with 'ethics in games journalism'" (p. 92).

In this chapter, our interest lies with how mainstream journalists discursively shaped and framed Gamergate once it reached the homepages of their digital news platforms. As Braithwaite (2016) notes, Gamergate made "this kind of 'ordinary' harassment newsworthy, calling our collective attention to the sustained abuse many people endure in order to participate in online spaces" (p. 7). Studying mainstream coverage is not only instructive because it taps into a number of media frames about geeks, anonymous trolls, and gamers, but also because it offers clues to the larger question of how similar instances of mediated misogyny are, and might be, constructed by mainstream journalists.

Gamergate's tropes and tactics can be seen as the unholy matrimony between two overlapping subcultures, each with its own history and discursive practices. On the one hand, there are those who put the "gamer" in Gamergate; a group for whom the self-identified moniker of being a "real" (i.e., male) "gamer" not only holds great subcultural value, but who use that identity to aggressively police others. Seen in this light, the events of August 2014 were "unsurprising" to those studying the intersection of game culture and gender (Chess and Shaw 2015). Physical and virtual game spaces, from industry gatherings to the online chat rooms on Xbox Live, have been traditionally unwelcoming to women (Consalvo 2012; Taylor 2008). As the ultimate prelude to Gamergate, one of its most high-profile targets, media critic Anita Sarkeesian, faced sustained threats and harassment throughout 2012 when "online gamers (presumably male)" reported her online accounts as terrorism and sent her "pornographic images of her being raped" (Mantilla 2013, p. 567). In Gamergate, many of the aggressors found their scapegoat to direct an existing campaign of hate, with the ultimate goal to silence women for having the gall to profess their opinions on video games.

On the other hand, the *Ghostbusters* controversy demonstrates that the Gamergate movement is far from unique in the context of digital culture. The tactics employed and the anxieties tapped into by gamergaters share a number of affinities with online subcultures that extend beyond the world of games. They include the "toxic technocultures" of message boards (Massanari 2015) and, more recently, the rise of the so-called "alt-right." Disruptive, aggressive, and hurtful online behavior has a long and somewhat complicated history, which often is associated with subcultural movements. For instance, in her in-depth study of online "trolling," understood as intentional disruptive behavior by anonymous antagonists, Phillips (2015) recognizes the prevalence of white males in the development of Internet philosophy (p. 124). She explicitly places maleness at the center of the trolling attitude and rhetoric. The misogynistic point of view is discussed by trolls in competitive terms and signals a desire to "defeat one's opponent" (p. 125)—a perspective that is strikingly similar to discourses surrounding digital play and resonates with Braithwaite's analysis of Gamergate's discursive traits. Phillips also describes online trolling's origins within a hacker and geek culture that revolved around 4chan and similar online message boards (p. 122), whose anonymous members played a vital role in the ascendance of the Gamergate movement and its mythology.

Pointing toward Phillips' earlier work, Mantilla (2013) offers the notion of "gendertrolling" as a specifically misogynistic subset of more generic forms of trolling. Gendertrolling is not only done for "fun," but also comes from a set of "sincere beliefs" held by trolls about the position and place of women within society and (online) subcultures. Exactly because it is so heartfelt, gendertrolling is particularly vicious and destructive. It is one of the reasons why the Gamergate episode made for such an appealing story to cover for many mainstream reporters. As journalists were soon to find out, the Gamergate phenomenon converges eerily with Mantilla's definition of gendertrolling as having an "unusual intensity and scope," uttering "credible threats" and "gender-based insults" toward women speaking out. It was this amalgamation of online hate speech and gaming subcultures that mainstream journalists encountered and conveyed to the larger public.

How to Study (Online) Hate?

In order to analyze the mainstreaming of online misogyny and the evolution of Gamergate coverage, we engaged in a multimodal analysis of mainstream news surrounding Gamergate. First, we conducted a content analysis of a corpus of mainstream U.S. publications. In order to construct this corpus, we selected all articles that explicitly used the term "Gamergate" from September 2014, when significant coverage of the movement began, through early June 2016.[1] Our publications were drawn from Pew Research's top 45 online news entities from 2015 (Pew Research 2015). The list included both legacy publications, which provide digital and non-digital content (such as *The New York Times* and

Boston Globe), and digitally native news outlets, whose work only exists via online and mobile media (such as *BuzzFeed* and *Slate*). Our pool of publications also included magazines and more traditional daily news coverage, both of which are on Pew's list. Given the online roots of the Gamergate movement and its focus on a digital medium—games—we delineated between legacy and digitally native news in order to glean how publications without a digitally exclusive focus might differ in their coverage from their online-only counterparts. We did not study other English-speaking publications because we recognized that there are explicit historical differences between, and values present in, mainstream U.S. publications and news outlets worldwide (Schudson 2008). Along with a few publications that did not write about the events surrounding Gamergate at all, we were left with 1,283 articles from 37 outlets. The focus of our content analysis was to survey the position and timing of Gamergate coverage within a publication. To that end, we investigated the sections in which articles appeared, the dates the term was invoked, and which authors wrote the articles.

Second, a media discourse analysis was performed on six publications—*The Atlantic*, *The New York Times*, *Slate*, *Time*, *USA Today*, and *Vox*—chosen because they represent a variety of legacy and digital native media, magazine and newspaper-style content, and different kinds of readership. A total of 208 articles were coded as part of the qualitative analysis using NVivo software. In the first phase of open coding, both researchers individually analyzed the text for codes that stayed closed to the specific language of the publications. We then compared codes in a second phase to deduce several central themes. Finally, we selected the codes that were most relevant from those themes to formulate answers to our research questions.

Our discourse analysis primarily focused on how mainstream media framed Gamergate, or how journalists and other newsmakers constructed, promoted, and consistently relied upon singular narratives (Entman 2007, p. 164) surrounding the movement. Media frames shape both the actions of those framing and those framed. For instance, in his foundational work, Gitlin (2003) recognizes that the common media frames surrounding the Students for a Democratic Society—a leftist organization advocating for participatory democracy in the 1960s—both characterized the social movement as radical, but ultimately also shaped the direction of SDS; more pacifist and moderate members left the organization, while media coverage attracted more extremist members. Framing may play a similar role in shaping the attitudes of Gamergate activists and activities, particularly as the subject of gaming moved from the purview of the enthusiast press to a wider public. Therefore, within our coding process, we narrowed our focus to examine how the movement and its specific actions were defined, covered, and utilized to describe wider cultural phenomena.

The End of the Beginning

Gamergate brings to the fore a number of important questions concerning journalism, misogyny, and gaming (Braithwaite 2016; Perreault and Vos 2016). Our particular interest surrounds the content of coverage. How did journalists discursively shape and frame the movement? The results of our content analysis reveal that Gamergate became a widely cited event for a diverse group of journalists in mainstream outlets as well as across many different sections of online publications. That being said, the events surrounding Gamergate and their high-profile targets became the beat of only a few journalists. For instance, at the *Los Angeles Times*, 44% of the 39 articles featuring Gamergate were written by a single author, Todd Martens (Fig. 6.1). Similarly, over 43% of coverage at digital native outlet *Vox* was written by two authors and 45% of coverage came from Caitlin Dewey and Alyssa Rosenberg at *The Washington Post* (Fig. 6.2); the publication contributed the third-highest number (along with *The Huffington Post*) of articles about the subject (106 in total) with 8.26% of the articles published overall.[2] This relatively small cadre of authors tended to already cover games and technology as part of their beat. For instance, much of Martens' work appeared on the "Hero Complex" blog, which reports on games, technology, and "geek culture."

Still, Gamergate permeated mainstream coverage, as demonstrated by the quantity of writers who invoked the movement from 2014 through 2016. For instance, while *Washington Post* reporters Dewey and Rosenberg undertook most of Gamergate news, the term was mentioned by 32 of their colleagues. The diversity of authors was even more noticeable at

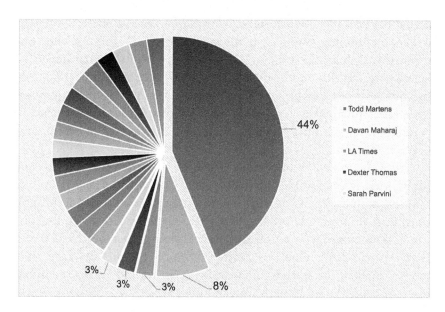

Fig. 6.1 Percentage of individual author contributions at the *Los Angeles Times*

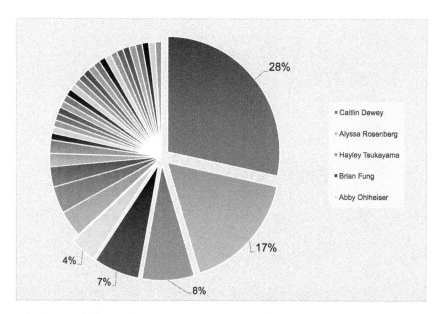

Fig. 6.2 Percentage of individual author contributions at The Washington Post

digital native outlets. For instance, *The Huffington Post* had 69 different writers mentioning Gamergate, whereas *Vice* had 76 authors who contributed to 135 articles (Fig. 6.3). Along with authorship, the subject of Gamergate was not confined to a single news section. While 18.5% of the articles were published in technology sections, similar numbers appeared in other areas of news websites: 8% of articles were published in entertainment sections, just under 7% in news, nation or world, and 4.6% in opinion.

Although evoked by newsmakers consistently over the term of our study, there were specific moments when Gamergate received intense scrutiny from the mainstream press. Two major periods provide a rough timeline to understand how journalists used Gamergate to weave the subject of online misogyny into mainstream coverage. October 15, 2014 to November 7, 2014 witnessed nearly 19.5% of the total coverage. This interval marked the start of mainstream reporting and details the initial threats against the three main women under attack: Wu, Sarkeesian, and Quinn. Digitally native outlets published twice as much as their legacy

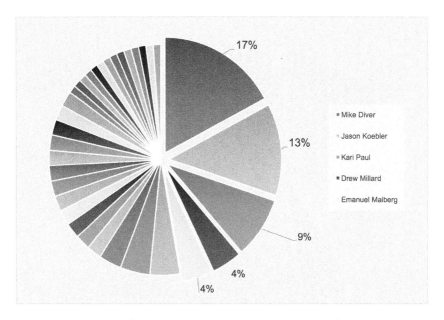

Fig. 6.3 Percentage of individual author contributions at *Vice* (Not all single contribution authors are represented in figure for the sake of ease of viewing.)

counterparts within the first year: 604 articles compared to 312. The early wave of reporting concentrated on explaining both the attacks and the movement itself. For instance, a *Vox* article characterized Gamergate as starting "after indie game developer Zoe Quinn and gaming critic Anita Sarkeesian were both horribly harassed online" and also stated that gamergaters themselves represent "a substantial, vocal movement that believes the generally left-leaning online gaming press focuses too much on feminism and the role of women in the industry, to the detriment of coverage of games" (VanDerWerff 2014).

Such characterization persisted throughout the year and was reiterated when reporting on attacks by gamergaters on celebrities. For instance, in October 2014, when actress Felicia Day was "doxxed"—with personal information, such as her home address, being posted online—by Gamergate trolls, she was quickly aligned with the three figureheads. A *New York Times* opinion article described Day's doxxing (without explicitly using the term) immediately after discussing Sarkeesian's cancellation of a talk at Utah State University due to credible death threats made against her. The article concludes: "Other game designers, journalists and cultural critics have been threatened, or have faced hacking attempts on their online accounts… Video games are unquestionably poorer than they were two months ago when this strange and disheartening series of events began" (Suellentrop 2014).

Another widely reported instance arose when Ellen Pao resigned as CEO of Reddit after the site took down revenge pornography from its forums. A *USA Today* writer used Pao's resignation as an example of the effects of Gamergate attacks: "The issue of online harassment extended beyond gaming, and nearly two years after the peak of #gamergate frenzy, it still continues for some women. Reddit CEO Ellen Pao resigned in July after she said she was harassed online, including death threats" (Snider 2016). Such quotes cemented the connection between Gamergate activities and misogyny online (Fig. 6.4).

A second major spike in coverage came one year later, when 84 articles were published in just over four days. These articles concerned the upcoming 2016 South by Southwest (SXSW) music and technology festival in Austin, Texas, where two panels on misogyny, trolling, and gaming were canceled due to Gamergate-related intimidation. The announcement of

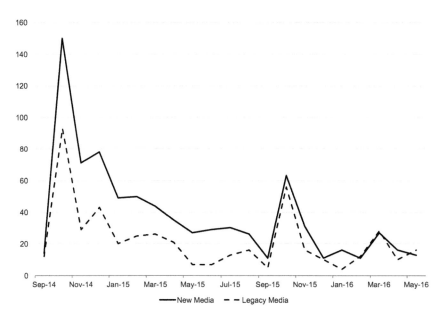

Fig. 6.4 Timeline of mainstream articles featuring Gamergate published from June 2014 to May of 2016

the cancellations saw the most articles published on a single day (34 articles on October 27, 2015). Legacy media slightly outpaced their online counterparts in SXSW coverage, publishing 43 of the 84 articles. The festival provided an opening for wider media analysis. *The New York Times* wrote about the cancellations:

> Other women in the gaming community have faced similar online harassment, which, they say, goes far beyond name calling and has moved into the realm of violent threats and rampant misogyny… Even events attempting to discuss and curtail the harassment of women online and in the gaming community are targets. (Dougherty and Isaac 2016)

This example highlights an elision between "online" and "gaming" activities, as the authors move between the two subjects and also write about the gaming community in the broader context of online misogyny.

Gamergate as Shorthand

What our analysis reveals is how mainstream outlets utilized these two events—the initial attacks on game developers and the cancellation of the SXSW panels—to shed light on Gamergate's evolution. The initial attacks provided a template for characterizing other modes of mainstream gender-based harassment, and the canceled panels tied those modes to the wider phenomenon of online misogyny and trolling as well as for an expansion and reintroduction of Gamergate. Thus, SXSW offered mainstream journalists a wider frame in which to encounter Gamergate, despite the fact that the movement was already a year old and individual stories of its targets had already been explored in depth. Gamergate became shorthand for broader instances of mediated misogyny.

The shift from covering Gamergate's emergence to using Gamergate as shorthand serves a dual role. For reporters, this reframing allowed an assertion of public authority over the movement, which could now be explicitly understood as a mainstream, no longer solely a niche or "gamer," issue. It also gave journalists a lens through which to speak about a wider culture of online misogyny in recognizable terms. Furthermore, for the victims of Gamergate, it situated misogyny as something commonplace—moving it from a singular set of events to the "end of the beginning"—a recognition of a mundane, yet reprehensible aspect of online culture.

Over the duration of our analyzed texts, we found a clear discursive shift in how Gamergate was defined. In the first phase of coverage, journalists were attempting to make sense of the verbal aggression: "[t]he #GamerGate movement... claims that women criticizing misogyny in video games will lead to the death of the gamer and that (largely young, white and male) gamers are under attack" (Dockterman 2014). The language surrounding Gamergate spotlighted what seemed to be a localized phenomenon, and its specific dangers involved issues of gaming. For instance, in an article about women abandoning the "gamer" moniker, a *New York Times* writer stated, "As harassment veered into threats of violence and rape, the controversy drew news media attention, and set off debates over how bad misogyny in gaming had become" (McPhate 2015).

Throughout, the Gamergate attacks were relegated to the subculture of "gaming," which, because of its history of exclusionary practices towards women, was considered to be misogynistic in the first place.

Those who thought Gamergate would be a story of "a summer of hate," or an isolated case of gamers gone rogue, soon found that the story had legs. Over the course of several months, the characterization of Gamergate began to veer from its focus on a localized series of events. Instead, the label was increasingly applied to describe a broad swath of sallies against women. For example, the word "toxic" was invoked in all six publications we discursively analyzed, which is particularly apt considering the ways in which game culture is described as toxic (Consalvo 2012) and online communities as "toxic technocultures" (Massanari 2015). Similarly, a *Time* article recalled the Gamergate attacks and those on Brianna Wu specifically to make a larger claim: "Any woman who is using the Internet for her professional life or for her personal life has come across that moment where there is all of the sudden a hateful or sexist comment coming back at you" (LaFrance 2016). In the end, the term Gamergate itself was redefined. Instead of referencing games journalism, "ethics," and game culture—subjects which gamergaters put at the forefront of their movement—it became a moniker for harassment and online misogyny.

This transformation appears to be necessary for journalists to create both a cohesive and mainstream narrative of the movement. No longer a subcultural phenomenon, Gamergate has come to represent the greater issue of persistent online harassment. Consequently, the story of Gamergate was able to carry more mainstream appeal to readers who were not necessarily interested in games; the subject of online harassment involved a broad range of fields and industries, including business, technology, and culture, as well as the more pervasive issue of shameful treatment of women online (LaFrance 2016).

The discursive shifts in Gamergate coverage undertaken by mainstream journalists not only cemented their authority about the movement, but also established the meaning of the event to a wider public. Such a view is reaffirmed in Perreault and Vos' (2016) study of Gamergate journalists. While their work primarily focused on the intent and reaction of authors from both the mainstream and enthusiast press, the authors provided valuable insights into how journalists approached the subject of games. They described a "paradigm maintenance" and "repair" by games journalists surrounding Gamergate; newsmakers covering the movement saw themselves as mediators, translating the event between enthusiasts and the wider media (ibid.).

What is therefore surprising to those familiar with game culture, and slightly deviates from Perreault & Vos' assertions on paradigm maintenance, is that the tendency to rescript Gamergate events to appeal to a greater audience superseded deeper investigations into gender issues within the subculture. Somewhat unexpectedly, given decades of negative reporting on gaming, journalists eschewed traditional frames surrounding mainstream games coverage. For instance, we found few examples of the traditional utopian (games are educational) or dystopian (games are a health hazard) constructs that tend to surround games according to previous assessments of mainstream game coverage (Williams 2003). While journalists covering the issue could have easily tapped into existing narratives by following the moral panic script that historically marked game-related news, they collectively chose to free themselves from such strictures. Alternatively, Gamergate coverage can be read as a demarcation of the beginning of the end of a decade-long struggle to mainstream game culture.

Mainstreaming Misogyny

A jilted man harassing his ex is a fitting beginning for an incoherent movement that has one undeniable goal: to silence women and deny them their place within digital culture. *Slate* aptly identified the movement as an instance of "Cheeto-breath bigotry" (Waldman and Newell 2014). Yet, for its victims, and there are many, Gamergate was not a passing controversy, but the start of an ongoing culture war that extends far beyond the world of gaming and continues to the present day. For those who think that Gamergate is over, think again. It might not be receiving sustained coverage as it once did, but its infrastructure, ideology, and methods are very much intact; its members are primed to take on the next battle.

Mainstream journalists primarily frame the clash as one between a "movement of dead-enders" versus three outspoken feminists. Recent studies (Burgess and Matamoros-Fernández 2016; Massanari 2015), however, note the involvement of a much wider group of actors, including industry insiders, academics, advertisers, journalists, and platform operators (e.g., Reddit and 4chan). For all these groups, Gamergate should serve as a sobering warning sign. Studying the domain of popular culture comes with a new set of challenges, as entering the sphere of "geek masculinity" (Braithwaite 2016) means a potential engagement with a formidable opponent. We speak from personal experience when we say that the meritocratic ideals of intellectuals are no match for the conspiratorial logic of what Mortensen (2016) calls a "tempocracy": an online subculture "controlled by those who have the most patience and time, strongest dedication to their own opinions, and most ruthless ways to silence their opponents" (p. 9).

Our analysis shows that, unlike countless other instances of mediated misogyny, which are either normalized or ignored in the context of mainstream media coverage, Gamergate not only received significant attention, but also acted as a platform for highlighting similar instances of misogyny online. Amid the initial confusion of what Gamergate stood for, it became immediately apparent to mainstream journalists that this was, to paraphrase Mantilla (2013), a phenomenon to systematically harass and silence women, and deny them access to what until recently was a male-dominated space. Paradoxically, by adopting Gamergate as a stand-in for online harassment, mainstream journalists were allotted a powerful new frame to express their opinions about the toxic quality of social media interactions. Such reframing may seem innocuous or even dilute the subject of Gamergate, but we found the opposite. Journalists were able to use the movement's proponents and their alleged cause of games journalism's ethics to expound on larger issues concerning online misogyny. The mainstreaming of Gamergate coverage exposed many of game culture's underlying tensions for all to see, discuss, and ultimately contest.

The fact that Gamergate essentially became a meme is a double-edged sword. The mainstream coverage of Gamergate serves as an instructive case study for activists and educators to help comprehend how news events evolve, how to contribute to them, and how to position oneself. It highlights the still-vital role of translation and interpolation that the mainstream media provides, and the interplay between new and old media outlets in shaping and reshaping discussions of online misogyny. Ultimately, Gamergate suggests the end of the beginning of a new era of online harassment, which leads us to our final, less encouraging point.

Despite Gamergate bringing to light and characterizing a wide variety of misogynistic activities, the solutions to address such activities go far beyond the tactic of exposure. As Mortensen (2016) notes: "... [Gamergate] taught us how technology designed for increased openness can be utilized to create echo chambers and to silence opposing voices" (p. 13). By invoking the right codes, for example labeling "opponents" as Social Justice Warriors, online hate mobs can be resurrected in a matter of hours. Seen in this light, Mr. Trump could indeed be considered a president befitting the Gamergate era, especially when one considers the way both the Trump campaign and his followers leveraged social media to spread disinformation and to aggressively police "political correctness." Thus, the spirit of the Gamergate agenda may very well thrive during the Trump presidency, whether it be through the online harassment tactics of a subset of his supporters worldwide, the president's own misogynistic remarks, or the strong connections between the movement and high-level White House confidantes such as Steve Bannon. The emergence and mainstreaming of Gamergate coverage, then, serves as a painful yet powerful historical marker in the mainstreaming of misogyny.

Notes

1. To ascertain whether Gamergate was covered by a publication, we used internal search engines on a news outlet's website and searched the domain through Google.com. We then removed any duplicates that were not syndicated across mainstream publications.
2. *Vice* published the most articles utilizing the term, with 10.5% of total coverage.

References

Braithwaite, A. (2016). It's about ethics in games journalism? Gamergaters and Geek masculinity. *Social Media + Society, 2*(4), 1–10.

Burgess, J., & Matamoros-Fernández, A. (2016). Mapping sociocultural controversies across digital media platforms: One week of #gamergate on Twitter, YouTube, and Tumblr. *Communication Research and Practice, 2*(1), 79–96.

Chess, S., & Shaw, A. (2015). A conspiracy of fishes, or, how we learned to stop worrying about #GamerGate and embrace hegemonic masculinity. *Journal of Broadcasting & Electronic Media, 59*(1), 208–220.

Consalvo, M. (2012). Confronting toxic gamer culture: A challenge for feminist game studies scholars. *Ada: A Journal of Gender, New Media, and Technology, 1*(1). http://adanewmedia.org/2012/11/issue1-consalvo/

Digital: Top 50 Online News Entities. (2015, February). Pew Research Center. *Pew Research*. Retrieved from https://web.archive.org/web/20160221050146/http://www.journalism.org/media-indicators/digital-top-50-online-news-entities-2015/

Dockterman, E. (2014, October 15). The comic book world is getting safer for women, but the gaming world isn't. *Time*. Retrieved from http://time.com/3507153/comic-con-women-gaming/

Dougherty, C., & Isaac, M. (2016, March 13). SXSW addresses online harassment of women in gaming. *The New York Times*. Retrieved from http://www.nytimes.com/2016/03/14/technology/sxsw-addresses-online-harassment-of-women-in-gaming.html

Entman, R. M. (2007). Framing bias: Media in the distribution of power. *Journal of Communication, 57*(1), 163–173.

Gieryn, T. F. (1983). Boundarywork and the demarcation of science from nonscience: Strains and interests in professional ideologies of scientists. *American Sociological Review, 48*(6), 781–795.

Gitlin, T. (2003). *The whole world is watching: Mass media in the making and unmaking of the new left, with a new preface* (2nd ed.). Berkeley: University of California Press.

Kirkpatrick, G. (2013). *Computer games and the social imaginary*. Malden: Polity Press.

LaFrance, A. (2016, May 20). When will the internet be safe for women? *The Atlantic*. Retrieved from http://www.theatlantic.com/technology/archive/2016/05/when-will-the-internet-be-safe-for-women/483473/

Mantilla, K. (2013). Gendertrolling: Misogyny adapts to new media. *Feminist Studies, 39*(2), 563–570.

Massanari, A. (2015). #Gamergate and the Fappening: How Reddit's algorithm, governance, and culture support toxic technocultures. *New Media & Society,* 1–18. doi:https://doi.org/10.1177/1461444815608807.

McPhate, M. (2015, December 16). Women who play games Shun "Gamer" label. *The New York Times.* Retrieved from http://www.nytimes.com/2015/12/17/technology/personaltech/women-who-play-games-shun-gamer-label.html

Mortensen, T. E. (2016). Anger, fear, and games: The long event of #GamerGate. *Games and Culture,* 1–20. doi:https://doi.org/10.1177/1555412016640408.

Perreault, G. P., & Vos, T. P. (2016, September). The GamerGate controversy and journalistic paradigm maintenance. *Journalism,* doi:https://doi.org/10.1177/1464884916670932.

Phillips, W. (2015). *This is why we can't have nice things: Mapping the relationship between online trolling and mainstream culture.* Cambridge: MIT Press.

Romano, A. (2016, August 26). The Leslie Jones hack is the flashpoint of the altright's escalating culture war. *Vox.* Retrieved from http://www.vox.com/2016/8/26/12653474/lesliejoneshackaltrightculturewar

Schudson, M. (2008). *Why democracies need an unlovable press.* Cambridge/Malden: Polity.

Sims, D. (2016, May 18). The ongoing outcry against the ghostbusters remake. *The Atlantic.* Retrieved from http://www.theatlantic.com/entertainment/archive/2016/05/the-sexist-outcry-against-the-ghostbusters-remake-gets-louder/483270/

Snider, M. (2016, March 10). After Furor, SXSW prepares to talk online harassment. *USA TODAY.* Retrieved from http://www.usatoday.com/story/tech/news/2016/03/10/after-furor-sxsw-prepares-talk-online-harassment/81417566/

Suellentrop, C. (2014, October 25). The disheartening GamerGate campaign. *The New York Times.* Retrieved from http://www.nytimes.com/2014/10/26/opinion/sunday/the-disheartening-gamergate-campaign.html

Taylor, T. L. (2008). Becoming a player: Networks, structures, and imagined futures. In Y. Kafai, C. Heeter, J. Denner, & J. Sun (Eds.), *Beyond Barbie and Mortal Kombat: New perspectives on gender, games, and computing* (pp. 50–65). Cambridge: MIT Press.

Trump, D. J. (2015, January 28). Indiana Jones and Ghostbusters—what's wrong???#TrumpVlog. [Facebook] Retrieved from https://www.facebook.com/DonaldTrump/videos/10155136336740725/

VanDerWerff, T. (2014, September 6). Why is everybody in the video game world fighting? #Gamergate. *Vox*. Retrieved from http://www.vox.com/2014/9/6/6111065/gamergate-explained-everybody-fighting

Waldman, K, & Newell, J. (2014, October 21). Planet money uncovers one surprising reason the internet is sexist. *Slate*. Retrieved from http://www.slate.com/blogs/future_tense/2014/10/21/planet_money_episode_on_why_female_coders_drop_out_can_help_explain_gamergate.html

Williams, D. (2003). The video game lightning rod. Constructions of a new media technology, 1970–2000. *Information, Communication & Society, 6*(4), 523–550.

7

"I Realized It Was About Them … Not Me": Women Sports Journalists and Harassment

Tracy Everbach

A clearly uncomfortable man stares at a woman sports writer, clears his throat and reads aloud the words from a tweet: "One of the players should beat you to death with a hockey stick like the whore you are." The segment is from a video featuring sports journalists Julie DiCaro and Sarah Spain. Produced in 2016, it depicts a series of unassuming men reading threatening and humiliating tweets the women received simply for doing their jobs (Just Not Sports 2016).

Also in 2016, former Olympic softball gold medalist Jessica Mendoza became the first woman to announce Major League Baseball games regularly on ESPN. Tweets about her first regular broadcast included derogatory comments such as "Jessica Mendoza ruined my opening day experience. Thanks @SportsCenter" (Matthew Moore, @Mooretweets, April 3, 2016), "@_jessicamendoza this seriously is like nails on a chalkboard, please stop talking" (Kyle, @ktrout05, April 3, 2016), and "Shut up Jessica Mendoza. Bitch." (Mike, @PanicCityMike, April 3, 2016).

T. Everbach (✉)
Mayborn School of Journalism, Digital/Print Journalism, University of North Texas, Denton, TX, USA

© The Author(s) 2018
J. R. Vickery, T. Everbach (eds.), *Mediating Misogyny*,
https://doi.org/10.1007/978-3-319-72917-6_7

Resistance to women sports journalists is nothing new. Women have long been minorities in sports media (Hiestand 2008; Lapchick et al. 2015; Lapchick 2016). They make up only about 12% of sports columnists and 8.5% of sports editors in the United States. Women produce only about 10.2% of U.S. sports journalism (Women's Media Center 2017). In addition, female athletes are virtually ignored. Coverage of women's sports makes up a minuscule amount of overall sports media—less than 2% (Cooky et al. 2013). A biannual "report card" evaluating sports journalism gave the industry an F in gender diversity (Lapchick et al. 2015).

Women who work in sports media report on-the-job discrimination and fewer promotions than men (Hardin and Shain 2005, 2006; Miller and Miller 1995; Smucker et al. 2003). Women are often relegated to the sidelines in sports reporting and are judged by their appearance rather than their talent and knowledge—exemplified by *Men's Fitness'* "Hottest 40 Female Sports Reporters" list, which stated, "From former models to just kick-ass chicks, this list cannot be beat" (Haines, n.d.).

The male-dominated environment of the sports world influences women journalists who work within it. Hegemonic masculinity, a concept in which an idealized and often-toxic version of masculinity allows men to maintain hierarchical status over women, continues to rule the sports media industry. Hegemonic masculinity also presumes and prefers heterosexuality as a norm (Connell and Messerschmidt 2005). Online harassment is a common device used to subjugate women sports journalists. This study, featuring 12 in-depth interviews with women who currently work or formerly worked in sports media, examines the effects of social media abuse and outlines strategies they use to cope with it.

Locker Room Breakthrough

Women in the workplace, including women journalists and other media workers, have faced gender-based harassment on the job for decades (Brown and Flatow 1997; Everbach and Matysiak 2010; Flatow 1994; McAdams and Beasley 1994; Miller and Miller 1995). Women sports journalists who broke the locker room barrier in the 1970s and 1980s met resistance and harassment from athletes, team owners, and fans, including physical attacks and verbal threats (Everbach and Matysiak 2010). For example, in 1990, a group of New England Patriots players harassed Lisa Olsen, a sports writer for *The Boston Herald*, in a locker room by taunting her and displaying their genitals. After news media reported on the incident, the team's owner, Victor Kiam, called Olsen a "classic bitch" (and later denied he said so). Fans chanted at Olsen during games and made threatening phone calls to her home (Kane and Disch 1993).

Throughout the 1990s and 2000s, women sports journalists confronted abuse from fans, players, coaches, and other media workers. In a 1996 study, Walsh-Childers, Chance, and Herzog concluded that two-thirds of women sports journalists had experienced gender-based harassment. McAdams and Beasley (1994) surveyed Washington, D.C.-based women journalists and discovered sexual harassment had been a problem for 60% of them. Brown and Flatow (1997) found that co-workers were more likely to harass women than supervisors, and that younger women more often were targets of harassment. Types of harassment Brown and Flatow identified included: physical (e.g., unwanted touching), verbal (e.g., sexual comments), threatening (e.g., soliciting sexual favors in return for job rewards), nonverbal (e.g., making sexual gestures), and environmental (e.g., display of suggestive photos).

Miller and Miller (1995) surveyed members of the Association for Women in Sports Media (AWSM) and discovered that women sports journalists experienced sexual harassment in newsrooms, often in the form of sexist language, received unequal job treatment, and felt "invisible" in their departments. Ten years later, a survey of the same organization's members again discovered a majority had experienced job discrimination and some had faced harassment from peers, athletes, coaches, or sports professionals and administrators (Miloch et al. 2005; Pedersen et al. 2009). Hardin and Shain (2006) found from a survey of focus group interviews that women sports journalists continued to face harassment and discrimination. However, the journalists said those factors would not lead them to leave their jobs. Instead, they were concerned about lack of personal and family time with little payoff, such as promotions, raising questions about retention of women in the industry. The same women reported feeling like "second-class citizens" in newsrooms (p. 329). A 2003 survey of AWSM members cited lack of opportunity for promotion as a reason they would leave sports journalism (Smucker et al. 2003).

Hardin and Shain (2006) concluded that the masculine culture of sports spurs hostility toward women in sports media from both peers and fans. The authors also wrote that women in sports newsrooms face a "double bind": they must meet contradictory cultural expectations, such as empathy and passivity, but also professional standards that emphasize aggressiveness and detachment (p. 324).

Online Harassment on the Job

As news and sports media have moved content online, so have ways to denigrate women journalists. In fact, abuse of women in general is more visible than in the past, with social media and online comment forums allowing harassers to display their aggression publicly. The term "cyber harassment" is defined as online behavior that causes emotional distress to another person. Women are most often the targets (Citron 2009; Van Laer 2014). Online aggression against women includes threats of violence, violent images, the posting of women's addresses to target them, and other forms of abuse. Such harassment often is trivialized and dismissed by society and by law enforcement (Citron 2009) as "locker-room talk" or "pranks," or in counter-arguments that men receive abusive messages as well. The truth is that online harassment of women is a form of sex discrimination that may cause long-term damage to its targets. It is meant to silence and humiliate women who try to enter male-dominated spaces (Barak 2005; Vitis and Gilmour 2016).

Some social media companies have taken small actions. In January 2017, Twitter suspended the account of pharmaceutical company founder Martin Shkreli for harassing Lauren Duca, a *Teen Vogue* writer. Shkreli had superimposed his own face on a photo of Duca's husband, as well as sending other hostile social media messages (Hunt 2017; Vernon 2017). Shkreli was well known because he had drastically raised the prices of his company's drugs; for example, an HIV treatment pill from $13.50 to

$750 each (Walters 2015). Shkreli was not the only person harassing Duca; she had received threats, derogatory comments, and other abuse after writing an opinion piece critical of then-presidential candidate Donald Trump, accusing him of "gaslighting" America.

Such attacks against women are designed to intimidate them and serve to reinforce socially constructed beliefs that women are inferior to men. They undermine women's agency, professional goals, and identities. "Despite the destructive nature of these cyber assaults, the public often refuses to take them seriously" (Citron 2009, p. 391). Citron, a law professor, argues that cyber harassment is a civil rights violation. Some free speech advocates assert that the civil libertarian nature of online communication is a "free-for-all" in which all forms of speech should be tolerated (Mkono 2015). The irony is that while the largely unregulated Internet allows users to harass others, it also opens spaces for disenfranchised voices to be heard. This paradox also exists in sports media.

Hegemonic Masculinity in Sports

White male workers always have dominated sports journalism (Creedon 1994; Lapchick et al. 2015). When women enter this sphere, they challenge men's power and control. Resistance to women's entry into the sports realm serves "to subvert and contain the threat of women's presence in a site so central to male power and privilege" (Kane and Disch 1993, p. 33). Kane and Disch point out that women sports journalists must observe unwritten rules, including not becoming too friendly with athletes, lest they be accused of sexual interest; keeping their head and eyes down in locker rooms; and having male "protectors," who will call out others who harass women. Women's gender difference, including their lack of power, becomes reinforced by these actions, according to Kane and Disch (1993).

Sport is a social sphere in which maleness and masculinity are accepted as superior. As Disch and Kane (1996) point out, "sports that require muscle mass, strength, and speed are more prestigious than those that emphasize beauty and flexibility" (p. 294). This emphasis on male superiority is connected to the exclusion of women journalists, including in the newsroom, locker room, and press box (Miloch et al. 2005). The idealized image of male athletes is an example of the social construction of male power in Western culture (Connell and Messerschmidt 2005; Hardin et al. 2009). So-called "feminine" qualities are denigrated in favor of traits seen as "masculine"—strength, domination, and aggression (Hardin et al. 2009). Under this social construction, heterosexual men are valued, while women and LGBTQ people are seen as outsiders. The fact that men compose an overwhelming majority of sports journalists serves to reinforce this culture of hegemonic masculinity in sports media. Even when women journalists are athletes themselves, hegemonic masculinity persists, as exemplified by the negative social media responses to Jessica Mendoza, the Olympic medalist, when she became an ESPN baseball announcer.

Despite their marginalization in sports journalism, some women find and write compelling stories about topics that their male colleagues tend to ignore. For instance, Karen Crouse, a writer for *The New York Times*, says she focuses on players as humans rather than as statistics, a perspective that helped her write a story about a New York Jets defensive back who was sexually abused as a child (Everbach and Matysiak 2010). Many women journalists say athletes are more comfortable talking to them about their personal lives than they are to male journalists, who tend to be more interested in the intricacies of the game rather than in telling stories (Cramer 1994; van Zoonen 1998).

Method

This study is based upon interviews with 12 women who currently work in, or formerly worked in, sports media. Some of them, including Jemele Hill of ESPN and Christine Brennan of *USA Today*, are high-profile sports journalists with established careers. Others are younger and just at the beginning of their careers. I gathered perspectives from women of different generations and different levels of experience to determine what they had in common. I recruited participants by contacting individual women sports journalists and asking them for interviews, by posting on women journalist listservs, crowdsourcing on social media, and asking journalists for personal referrals. The participants agreed to participate in telephone or Skype interviews. The interviews were conducted between July 2016 and September 2016 and lasted from 30 to 60 minutes. All participants were asked the same series of questions, with follow-up questions varying. The women made the choice whether to be identified by name or anonymously in the study. Four participants, all younger women, chose not to be named, while the other eight agreed to the use of their names. The participants ranged in age from 21 to 65 and included Melissa Ludtke, the subject of the 1978 lawsuit that first allowed women sports journalists access to locker rooms.

After the interviews, I examined transcripts of the conversations and extracted themes from them to determine how comments and social media messages affect women sports journalists in their work and how they cope with harassment. I followed the qualitative coding protocol suggested by Hesse-Biber (2017): first, identifying descriptive codes, or labels or tags, in the interview transcripts. Next I organized the descriptive codes into categories, or categorical codes. On a third reading of the transcripts, I culled the categorical codes into the over-arching analytical codes—the main themes.

Results

The four analytical codes, or main themes, were identified as:

1. Persistent sexism in sports media. Women sports journalists continue to face harassment and demeaning treatment on the job.
2. Social media—blessing or curse? While most women journalists said they received mainly positive social media comments, the harassment causes them distress because of its threatening and abusive nature. In some cases, women said they suffer self-doubt because their qualifications and work product consistently are challenged.
3. Strategic troll management. Women employ various strategies to protect themselves and find support and encouragement amid the abuse.
4. Solutions. The women offered several recommendations to stop the abusive and unequal treatment in sports media.

Persistent Sexism in Sports Media

All 12 participants acknowledged that women are treated as outsiders in the profession, sometimes by fans, sometimes by athletes and coaches, and sometimes by co-workers and employers. The women spoke of unfair and unequal treatment in the profession that is their passion. Disturbingly, some of the younger participants said they had left or were thinking of leaving the industry because of harassment and/or inequity. Several women, from the oldest participant to the youngest, recalled sexual rumors that had been spread about them on the job. Melissa Ludtke, 65, who was the plaintiff in *Ludtke and TIME Inc.* v. *Kuhn*, the 1978 lawsuit that allowed women journalists to access locker rooms, recalled that media coverage about her was cast in "moralistic terms."

> I was either the vixen who was going to come in and tempt these players, or I would be cast as the hardened woman who is going to stop at nothing to barge into places she doesn't belong. I was characterized as this person I didn't see myself as, an obstinate, pushy, dominant person. There I was in my Laura Ashley dress, just trying to fit in. (Personal communication, September 16, 2016)

The youngest participant, Alex Francisco, 21, recalled being propositioned in her first college newspaper interview with an athlete. "He said, we could do lunch, or you could come by my house later tonight at 7:30 or 8. I said that was not appropriate for the project, and he said, 'Why not? You can interview me and we can make out later'" (personal communication, July 28, 2016). Francisco reported that her main concern at the time was that her journalism professor would be angry with her for not getting the story. Tabby Soignier, 31, a former newspaper sports writer, said she often was called a "bitch" by readers in online comments and on social media, and at one point, as a college beat writer, had been accused of having sex with a player (personal communication, July 29, 2016). Rumors of sexual involvement with players or sexual motives for wanting the job troubled several of the women. Jessica Quiroli, who writes about Minor League Baseball, said some players badgered her when she tried to conduct interviews in the locker room and others unfairly accused her of having sex with team members.

> The commentary, the comments, when I have walked into the clubhouse, there have been moments where I felt humiliated or uneasy. There was an incident where I walked out. When I walked in, there was a lot of shouting and I couldn't take it, so I walked out, and a player said, 'Oh, you don't want to see us naked?' And I said no, I don't. (Personal communication, July 19, 2016)

Some of the participants left sports journalism. A 26-year-old photojournalist for a niche sports organization who did not want to be identified by name said a string of on-the-job incidents, including someone who accused her of being sexually involved with a 15-year-old boy, led her to quit. She also said men involved in the sport told her she should have sex with athletes to get information from them. "I was so depressed doing it [her job]. When I was at the track, I would think, what are they saying about me? It affected my self-worth and made me feel bad about my work" (personal communication, August 9, 2016). A 24-year-old who didn't want her name used said her supervisor would tell sexual jokes in the office and other men who outranked her would accuse women employees of flirting with players. "I left early because the mistreatment. I don't think I was taken seriously or recognized for my abilities" (personal communication, July 27, 2016).

Jenni Carlson, 41, a sports columnist, was famously singled out at a news conference and berated publicly in 2007 by Oklahoma State University football coach Mike Gundy, who was unhappy with a column she wrote. She also has received letters, phone calls, comments on stories, and social media messages that criticized her ability to write about sports because she is a woman. "I thought there would come a time when I had worked long enough that people would stop making it about my gender." That time has not come (personal communication, August 10, 2016).

Jemele Hill, 40, co-host of the ESPN2 show *His and Hers*, has faced a double dose of discrimination based on race and gender, including physical threats. "There certainly is an element of racism, sexism and misogyny that I deal with on my job… If you're a woman, you are more worried about your physical safety" (personal communication, August 9, 2016).

Social Media: Blessing or Curse?

Most of the participants reported overwhelmingly positive experiences with social media, except for a small percentage of users who sent them abusive, negative, and harassing comments. Most viewed social media as a way to interact with their audiences and to find sources and information. Much like the women in the "More Than Mean" video described at the beginning of this chapter, their experiences online were interrupted by a handful of abusive men, likely empowered by the anonymous and impersonal nature of social media platforms. Social media, a tool that can be so helpful to journalists' work, has become another way for misogynists to tell women they don't belong in sports.

Almost all the participants said men on social media platforms or in online comments have implied they are unqualified for the job because they are women. Gina Mizell, 28, a college sports reporter, said she feels pressure to never make a mistake in her work because "I am going to be accused of not knowing the sport because I am a woman. Does every person who covers the courts need to be a lawyer? Does everyone who covers education need to be a former teacher? Does everyone who covers the president have to be a former president?" (personal communication, September 15, 2016).

Abusive users feel empowered because they can comment without using their true identity. Even when they use their names, they are separated from their targets. "All those people would never say it to my face," Jemele Hill said. "I realize it is just them being suckered in by the anonymity and lack of accountability that the medium provides." Harassers may be motivated to attack because don't think they will suffer consequences. "People feel like they have that open connection to you, but the anonymity is there and people think they can say whatever they want," Jenni Carlson said. "Just because we have free speech doesn't mean we are free from the repercussions of what we say."

Male journalists also receive harassing messages, but the ones directed at women tend to be more vicious and personal. Jemele Hill said her male co-anchor receives racial comments, as she does, but none about his maleness. "As a woman, you have a target on your back." Noted Gina Mizell: "It seems to get more personal with women. It seems more pointed, more about your gender. The criticism my male colleagues get is, they disagree with their opinion, but not who they are." Christine Brennan, 58, a longtime *USA Today* sports columnist and commentator for CNN, ABC, CBS and NPR, acknowledged similar behavior:

> Sports fans are passionate, and passion is good; otherwise I would not have a job. But a very small minority of them are crazy and lose their minds online. They seem to target women and minorities in an inordinate way ... I think these guys are the last vestiges of male chauvinism from another life. (Personal communication, September 2, 2016)

Strategic Troll Management

The participants described various strategies to deal with harassment and abuse, including not reading online comments, blocking or muting harassers, developing a "thick skin," asking for help from employers, and/ or bonding with other women sports journalists for support.

Jenni Carlson said she doesn't read the comments on stories she writes because "I have seen the most mundane story, mundane topic turn into an off-the-rails conversation." On social media, "If people are not adding to the conversation and are mean, spiteful, or annoying, I can mute people. A lot of stuff is out there I don't even see or read." Jemele Hill said she ignores name-calling messages. However, she has been physically threatened more than once and needed protection from her employer's (ESPN) security force. Security officers have monitored her social media accounts and warned her tormentors to back off. Christine Brennan noted that she never interacts with harassers or abusers online. "My advice to anyone is to never engage with any of these people. They are absolutely meaningless." She said that before social media, she received abusive mail from people who tried to intimidate her when she covered the NFL team from

Washington, D.C. "I saw stuff coming back, hateful, nasty stuff, with the b-word, the c-word." She also doesn't read the comments on her columns. "I quickly realized the cesspool that the Internet is." Brennan tells young women in sports media, "Don't for one minute allow these people to affect your beautiful lives."

Several of the women said they had developed hardened attitudes to deflect the abuse. Jenni Carlson noted, "There are some people who think I shouldn't be telling them anything about sports. I have developed a really thick skin." Jemele Hill said she has become desensitized:

> I guess the sad thing is, I've gotten used to it [harassment]. I say this to younger female journalists, especially those of color. I tell them I have been conditioned to just deal with it. I don't feel comfortable telling them the same thing—they shouldn't have to deal with it, they [abusers] just shouldn't do it in the first place.

The participants seek support from various places, including family, friends, co-workers, and other women journalists. A professional group, Association for Women in Sports Media (AWSM), founded in 1987, supports journalists and journalism students with an annual conference, internships, scholarships and advocacy work (see AWSMonline.org). Some women journalists have formed their own groups online. Jessica Quiroli formed one such collective of women sports journalists on Twitter:

> After I saw the hashtag #allmalepanel, I was thinking about a series of live events where fans ask journalists questions, and there were very few women on those panels. I thought, what if we have a forum with just women? Let's do this on our own and give ourselves a voice. That's the great thing about social media—you can get on a bullhorn without being asked.

A 26-year-old sports writer who didn't want her name used joined Quiroli's Twitter group after she complained about on-the-job harassment to superiors, who ignored her. A groundskeeper called her a "bitch" in front of players and coaches and more than once she heard men say that she attends games to have sex with players. She said the women in the group "give each other advice, we talk to each other. It just helps us to focus on the work. There's not that many of us in the industry and we have to look out for each other" (personal communication, July 16, 2016).

Jenni Carlson said the best way to deal with harassment is to remind herself she isn't the problem, the harassers are. "I realized that was about them—their insecurities, their issues, their upbringing—not me. Let them live in whatever misogynistic world they live in and it's not about me." Gina Mizell said that if comments start to bother her, "I ask, why is this person on the Internet having any bearing over how I feel?" Then she talks to friends about it. Jemele Hill said self-preservation is her strategy: "I try to make sure no one can invade my physical space and I try to block it from my mind; otherwise I won't be able to do the job I love."

Solutions to Halt Abuse

The participants said that social media companies, media employers, and fans all can contribute to solving the harassment and abuse problem. The women expressed frustration that companies haven't enacted simple solutions to protect them and allow them to do their jobs without being hounded online. Jemele Hill said social media corporations such as Facebook and Twitter could and should prevent abuse by more closely monitoring user posts.

> They could be a lot more stringent on what people say. I know they are leaning on users to report it themselves. I think there is a certain part of them [companies] that benefits from that level of comment. If these people feel that sense of freedom of speech they are going to be more likely to comment.

Gina Mizell also noted social media companies could do much more to curb harassment and abuse, especially since current practices put the burden on victims to report it. Christine Brennan said media companies should not have allowed random commenters on their sites in the first place.

It's extraordinary that people write these things on our columns. It's extraordinary that newspapers gave up this real estate. You used to have to put your name and phone number on a letter for it to be published. Then newspapers went the other way in a panic-stricken reaction to get clicks.

Sports fans and other social media users also should take actions against abusers and support women sports journalists, the participants said. People on social media have "too much tolerance for cyber bullying," Jemele Hill said. "I think social media users need to police each other and support others. We all could do a better job and stop giving them the attention they seek." Jessica Quiroli suggested fans participate in halting the abuse.

> The main thing is calling them out, so it's just not us yelling out into the world. We actually need male sports fans to support us—female sports fans, too. Sports fans in Major League Baseball and the NFL are 50% female, so our voices are really important.

Quiroli said media companies should support their women employees. The 26-year-old sports writer who didn't want to be identified advised: "If you see a female sports reporter, give her the benefit of the doubt. Just be nice to each other. It isn't that hard."

While sports have a competitive nature, reactions don't have to be hostile. Fans can channel their excitement in different ways, Jenni Carlson pointed out:

> This is what sports does to people. I wish people were more passionate about education and government than what jersey their favorite player is going to wear next year. It affects people in ways you'd never imagine. But that's how people choose to funnel their passions. Here we are.

Brennan said she focuses on the positive. "We need to look at the big picture. Millions of young women are coming out to do sports and they are going to do sports for the rest of their lives. A lot of them want to be sports media people."

Discussion

These in-depth interviews with women sports journalists confirmed what previous studies found—that women who work in sports media face stereotyping, harassment, and abuse. Adding to previous studies about harassment is the relatively new dimension of social media platforms, which provide more opportunities to subordinate women through criticism, insults, and threats. The anonymity and distance provided by social media has empowered users to hurl whatever abuse they want at women, including obscene names, insults, racial and gendered remarks, and physical threats, including rape and other violence. The constant abuse and discrimination, meant to demean and humiliate women, drives some women away from the profession, particularly younger women. Unfortunately, this suppression of women's voices preserves the industry's male domination, even though women journalists are as qualified and talented as men. Women often write human interest stories that men fail to report. Still, the hegemonic masculinity of the sporting world implies that women don't belong and that males are superior.

This study also examined the mechanisms women use to cope with abuse. The women journalists who stayed in the profession long-term developed strategies and support for dealing with the on-the-job mistreatment, such as bonding with other women and forming organizations, as well as using social media tools to block or ignore harassers. They endured far more hostility than their male colleagues did while doing the same jobs. Hegemonic masculinity maintains that women don't belong in sports journalism, and this research confirmed that barriers continue prevent them from being accepted as equals. As Gina Mizell noted, "That's our society. I feel we have a long way to go in creating equality between women and men... It's not just across sports media."

On a positive note, the women in this study reported many more supportive comments and reactions to their work than negative ones. This implies that a small group of social media users is targeting women with hostility and aggression. While such harassment is sometimes defended under the guise of free speech or free expression, social media companies and media organizations have the right and the capability to regulate comments posted on their platforms. As the women pointed out, social media companies as well as the women's employers could take further actions to crack down on online abuse, threats, and harassment so that they could do their jobs without these distractions. Companies could develop algorithms that identify hateful, threatening, or violent speech and remove abusers from their platforms, as Twitter did with Martin Shkreli in 2017. It should be noted that removing one or two people from a social media platform is not likely to spur significant remedies for victims of online abuse. In addition, media companies could provide more security and support for their employees, as ESPN did when Jemele Hill received physical threats. It is surprising that many companies have not taken these simple steps to protect their employees and those who use their platforms.

Half of the women in the U.S. report being sports fans (Jones 2015), and more than half the nation's population is composed of women. Women's voices add rich perspectives to sports journalism and women are talented interviewers, reporters, analysts, editors, and writers. They should be able to do their work without having to face threats and harassment intended to silence them. As these interviews showed, women in sports media simply want a respected place on the team.

References

Barak, A. (2005). Sexual harassment on the internet. *Social Science Computer Review, 23*(1), 77–92. https://doi.org/10.1177/0894439304271540.

Brown, C. M., & Flatow, G. M. (1997). Targets, effects, and perpetrators of sexual harassment in newsrooms. *Journalism and Mass Communication Quarterly, 74*(1), 160–183.

Citron, D. K. (2009). Law's expressive value in combating cyber gender harassment. *Michigan Law Review, 108*, 373–415.

Connell, R. W., & Messerschmidt, J. W. (2005). Hegemonic masculinity: Rethinking the concept. *Gender and Society, 19*(6), 829–859.

Cooky, C., Messner, M. A., & Hextrum, R. A. (2013). Women play sport, but not on TV. *Communication & Sport, 1*(3), 203–230. https://doi.org/10.1177/2167479513476947.

Cramer, J. A. (1994). Conversations with women sports journalists. In P. Creedon (Ed.), *Women, media and sport: Challenging gender values* (pp. 159–180). Thousand Oaks: Sage.

Creedon, P. J. (1994). Women, media and sport: Creating and reflecting gender values. In P. Creedon (Ed.), *Women, media and sport: Challenging gender values* (pp. 3–27). Thousand Oaks: Sage.

Disch, L., & Kane, M. J. (1996). When a looker really is a bitch: Lisa Olson, sport, and the heterosexual matrix. *Signs: Journal of Women in Culture and Society, 21*(2), 278–308.

Everbach, T., & Matysiak, L. (2010). Sports reporting and gender: Women who broke the locker room barrier. *Journal of Research on Women and Gender, 1.* https://digital.library.txstate.edu/handle/10877/4427.

Flatow, G. M. (1994). Sexual harassment in Indiana daily newspapers. *Newspaper Research Journal, 15,* 32–45. https://doi.org/10.1177/073953299401500304.

Haines, J. (n.d.). Hottest 40 female sports reporters. *Men's Fitness.* http://www.mensfitness.com/women/40-hottest-sports-reporters

Hardin, M., & Shain, S. (2005). Female sports journalists: Are we there yet? "No.". *Newspaper Research Journal, 26*(4), 22–35.

Hardin, M., & Shain, S. (2006). "Feeling much smaller than you know you are": The fragmented professional identity of female sports journalists. *Critical Studies in Media Communication, 23*(4), 322–338.

Hardin, M., Kuehn, M. K., Jones, H., Genovese, J., & Balaji, M. (2009). "Have you got game?" Hegemonic masculinity and neo-homophobia in U.S. newspaper sports columns. *Communication, Culture and Critique, 2,* 182–200. https://doi.org/10.1111/j.1753-9137.2009.01034.x.

Hesse-Biber, S. N. (2017). *The practice of qualitative research* (3rd ed.). Los Angeles: Sage.

Hiestand, M. (2008). In sports announcing, women are left on sidelines. *USA Today.* http://usatoday30.usatoday.com/sports/2008-09-17-women-announcing_N.htm

Hunt, E. (2017, January 8). Martin Shkreli suspended from Twitter for alleged harassment of Lauren Duca. *The Guardian.* https://www.theguardian.com/us-news/2017/jan/09/martin-shkreli-suspended-from-twitter-for-alleged-harrassment-of-lauren-duca

Jones, J. M. (2015, June 17). As industry grows, percentage of U.S. sports fan steady. http://www.gallup.com/poll/183689/industry-grows-percentage-sports-fans-steady.aspx

Just Not Sports. (2016, April). #MoreThanMean – Women in sports face harassment. [Video]. https://www.youtube.com/watch?v=9tU-D-m2JY8

Kane, M. J., & Disch, L. J. (1993). Sexual violence and the reproduction of male power in the locker room: The "Lisa Olson incident". *Sociology of Sport Journal, 10*, 331–352.

Lapchick, R. (2016). *The 2016 race and gender report card for Major League Baseball.* http://nebula.wsimg.com/811d6cc2d0b42f3ff087ac2cb690ebeb?A ccessKeyId=DAC3A56D8FB782449D2A&disposition=0&alloworigin=1

Lapchick, R., Guiao, A., Salas, D., Sanders, D., Howell, E., Robinson, L., Simpson, M., Nelson, N., Cabral, N., Van Berlo, V., Robbins, M., & Moyer, B. (2015). *The 2014 Associated Press sports editors racial and gender report card.* http://nebula.wsimg.com/038bb0ccc9436494ebee1430174c13a0?AccessKe yId=DAC3A56D8FB782449D2A&disposition=0&alloworigin=1

McAdams, K., & Beasley, M. (1994). Sexual harassment of Washington women journalists. *Newspaper Research Journal, 15*, 127–132.

Miller, P., & Miller, R. (1995). The invisible woman: Female sports journalists in the workplace. *Journalism and Mass Communication Quarterly, 72*(4), 883–889.

Miloch, K. S., Pedersen, P. M., Smucker, M. K., & Whisenant, W. A. (2005). The current state of women journalists: An analysis of the status of careers of females in newspapers sports departments. *Public Organization Review: A Global Journal, 5*, 219–232.

Mkono, M. (2015). "Troll alert!": Provocation and harassment in tourism and hospitality social media. *Current Issues in Tourism*, 1–14. https://doi.org/10.10 80/13683500.2015.1106447.

Pedersen, P. M., Lim, C. H., Osborne, B., & Whisenant, W. A. (2009). An examination of the perceptions of sexual harassment by sport print media professionals. *Journal of Sport Management, 23*, 335–360.

Smucker, M. K., Whisenant, W. A., & Pedersen, P. M. (2003). An investigation of job satisfaction and female sports journalists. *Sex Roles, 49*(7/8), 401–407.

Van Laer, T. (2014). The means to justify the end: Combating cyber harassment in social media. *Journal of Business Ethics, 123*(1), 85–98.

Van Zoonen, L. (1998). One of the girls? The changing gender of journalism. In C. Carter, G. Branston, & S. Allen (Eds.), *News, gender and power* (pp. 33–46). London: Routledge.

Vernon, P. (2017, January 9). The Media Today: Twitter's abuse problem isn't going away. *Columbia Journalism Review.*

Vitis, L., & Gilmour, F. (2016). Dick pics on blast: A woman's resistance to online sexual harassment using humour, art and Instagram. *Crime Media Culture*, 1–21. https://doi.org/10.1177/1741659016652445.

Walsh-Childers, K., Chance, S., & Herzog, K. (1996). Sexual harassment of women journalists. *Journalism and Mass Communication Quarterly, 73*(3), 559–581.

Walters, J. (2015, September 22). Martin Shkreli: entrepreneur defends decision to raise price of life-saving drug 50-fold. *The Guardian*. https://www.theguardian. com/business/2015/sep/21/entrepreneur-defends-raise-price-daraprim-drug

Women's Media Center. (2017). *The status of women in the U.S. media 2017.* http://wmc.3cdn.net/10c550d19ef9f3688f_mlbres2jd.pdf

8

Misogyny for Male Solidarity: Online Hate Discourse Against Women in South Korea

Jinsook Kim

The chapter discusses how misogynistic discourses have been constructed and reproduced in a male-dominated online community in South Korea (hereafter, Korea). The conservative community website *Ilbe* (an abbreviation of the phrase *The Daily Best Storage* in Korean; http://www.ilbe.com/) will be analyzed to illustrate the processes whereby hate discourse is devised and distributed. This website, created in 2010, collects the best daily posts from the bulletin board of the popular website *DC Inside*. According to the web-rating site *Rankey* (https://www.rankey.com/), *Ilbe* ranked first among humor sites and was Korea's third-largest online community as of October 2016.

In recent years, concerns about the far-right online community have arisen in Korea. The *Ilbe* community is well known as a "base camp" for conservative and right-wing users, promoting such hate discourses as misogyny, xenophobia, and regionalism (Um 2016; Yun 2013). The mass media have focused on sensational and offensive words and postings on

J. Kim (✉)
Department of Radio-Television-Film, University of Texas at Austin, Austin, TX, USA

© The Author(s) 2018
J. R. Vickery, T. Everbach (eds.), *Mediating Misogyny*,
https://doi.org/10.1007/978-3-319-72917-6_8

Ilbe, including use of the term *samilhan,* Korean for "women must be beaten every three days." As a result, the *Ilbe* community has been regarded as a home for a number of extremists.

Misogynistic discourse is not, however, confined to a few extreme sites, but is prevalent in Korea; in a recent survey by the Korean Women's Development Institute (Sang-su Ahn et al. 2015), 83.7% of respondents reported exposure to misogynistic language and content on the Internet. Moreover, misogynistic terms coined in the *Ilbe* community now circulate widely in Korea: for example, 93.7% of respondents were familiar with the gendered expletive *kimchi-nyeo* (Sang-su Ahn et al. 2015).

I accordingly argue that online misogyny is not limited to the extreme conservative right wing. While the *Ilbe* community deliberately stokes controversy to garner attention, posts and comments on liberal male-dominated online communities, popular news portal sites, and social network sites (SNSs) likewise manifest prejudice toward women. Online misogyny must therefore be viewed not as exceptional extremist speech, but as a socially-constructed collective discourse that resonates with broader contexts in Korea. My main argument in this chapter is that the increase in online misogynistic discourse reflects crises in hegemonic masculinity and anxiety over changing gender relations in Korea and this increase thus serves to reestablish male solidarity through hate discourse against Korean women.

I examine the main board on *Ilbe* using textual and discursive analysis. The *Ilbe* community consists of various boards devoted to politics, celebrities, humor, and so on. Users can recommend a post as the best daily post or choose the downvote button to express disapproval. A post sent to the main *Ilbe* board receives dozens to hundreds of votes, which means that it represents a shared opinion. By using an internal search engine, I collect, translate into English, and analyze posts containing specific keywords related to women and misogyny, including "kimchi girl," "kimchi bitch," and "Korean women" from September 2013 to August 2015.

New Media Technology and Gender

Earlier media scholars expected that anonymity and fluidity of identity online would create an egalitarian space on the Internet: the cyborg would transcend the gender dichotomy of male/female; cyberspace was to be a "genderless utopia" (Orgad 2005). However, critical media scholarship has revealed that online identity is not separate from offline power relations; indeed, cyberspace reinforces and reproduces inequality in terms of gender and race (boyd 2011; Shohat 1999; van Zoonen 2001).

Korean feminist researchers describe cyberspace in similar terms. In the early 1990s, relatively few Korean women participated in online activities; according to a 1998 survey, only 25% of Internet users were female (Kim 2012). This gender digital divide, in terms of sheer numbers, has diminished in the present century, but women still do not feel safe on the Internet because personal attacks, sexist postings, verbal abuse on women's online communities, online sexual violence, and stalking have increased at the same time. As scholars point out, not only physical and structural, but also cultural and physiological factors have influenced women's participation in cyberspace. Thus, Spender (1995) notes there exists a "cultural domination of masculinity in online spaces," especially in terms of linguistic styles and conventions (Wakeford 1997). The male-dominated culture forces female users to the margins of cyberspace in Korea (Kim and Kim 2008), so that online communities have become gendered as either male-dominated or exclusive to women (Kim 2015).

Misogyny, Masculinities, and Male Bonds

This study interprets growing online misogyny in relation to a crisis in hegemonic masculinity and the restoration of male bonds. Connell (2005) rejects essentialist approaches to masculinity in favor of the social construction of a hierarchy of masculinities within a society. Hegemonic masculinity is, among other things, "the configuration of gender practice which embodies the currently accepted answer to the problem of the legitimacy of patriarchy, which guarantees (or is taken to guarantee) the dominant position of men and the subordination of women" (p. 77). Hegemonic masculinity thus often relates to misogyny. According to Sedgwick (1985), male bonding, or "homosociality," is accompanied and heightened by homophobia and misogyny as part of the effort to maintain hierarchy in male domination. Because it is difficult to distinguish homosociality from homosexuality, fear of the latter and the exclusion of femininity reinforce the former. Thus, Kendall (2002) shows how hegemonic masculinity and the objectification of women identify and maintain online communities as male spaces.

Numerous studies make clear that online misogyny patrols and polices gender borders and reinforces the male-dominated online atmosphere by limiting women's presence, silencing women's and feminist voices, and attacking female public figures (Citron 2014; Filipovic 2007; Jane 2014a, b; Mantilla 2013, 2015; Turton-Turner 2013). Moreover, its history shows that online misogyny in Korea not only attacks individual women (Kim 2012; KwonKim 2000) but also develops a social discourse which justifies gender discrimination (Kim 2015; Um 2016; Yun 2013). Kim and Choi (2007) demonstrate that anti-feminist discourse reinforces hegemonic masculinity in Korean online discussion boards. Male users' hostile discourse about feminism, women's organizations, and the Ministry of Gender Equality and Family constructs feminists as an abnormal societal category. E.H. Kim (1998) interprets the misogynistic attitudes of Korean men "as part of the practice of constructing and reiterating a masculinity that needs continuous reinforcement precisely because it is something men could lose. Indeed, the men's sense of the ultimate fragility and instability of patriarchal ideology may be what made them so eager to argue for what are supposed to be universally shared notions of masculinity" (p. 72). These theories about misogyny and masculinity are useful for analyzing the ongoing production and distribution of misogynistic discourse on the Internet in Korea as a strategy to restore the male bond and hegemonic masculinity.

Ban on *"Boming-out"*: The Principle of Exclusion of Female Users

The *Ilbe* community bans users from identifying themselves as women. On the analogy of the expression "coming out" in reference to self-disclosure of sexual orientation or gender identity, *boming-out* is formed from the Korean prefix *bo* (from *boji* "pussy") and English "coming out"; it refers to users expressing female identity. The following quotes show how *Ilbe* users justify this practice as a community rule:

Bomingban [a ban on *boming-out*] is not a measure for the exclusion of women but for gender equality. Because most users are men, applying this principle only to women is a more efficient way to main gender neutrality.

Bomingban does not mean that *Ilbe* bans women. *Ilbe* only bans the self-disclosure of female identity. So, female users may participate unless they reveal themselves as women.

When a user is suspected of being a woman, others expose and share her posting as an example of *boming-out* and attack her with malicious comments. Further, the user may be reported to the manager of the *Ilbe* community for violating community rules. If the user is judged to be in violation, the manager blocks access to *Ilbe* either temporarily or permanently, ostensibly as a measure to prevent indiscriminate *boming-out*. However, because they are unseen and unidentifiable, "online participants can never be sure that others' virtual identities are trustworthy" (Anahita 2006, p. 2). Even in the *Ilbe* community, directly expressing one's identity as a woman is rare; more commonly, users accuse each other of being female. For instance, the following are regarded as examples of *boming-out*: "Don't criticize women's abortions; you guys have also some responsibilities," and "Don't you think you are going too far in disparaging women?" Either raising a women's issue or challenging male-dominated opinions can be read as an expression of female identity. Because of the absence of spatial boundaries, online communities try to establish a fixed identity (Anahita 2006). *Ilbe* users patrol that site's border and control its male-dominated culture and identity through the ban on *boming-out*, which both excludes female users and suppresses attitudes favorable to women.

Ilbe has an explicit *Bomingban* rule, but historically many Korean online communities have also been male-dominated. Female users have been excluded and their voices silenced through online hate speech and sexualized attacks, particularly, and unsurprisingly, in relation to gender issues in such contexts as military service[1] (Kim2012; KwonKim 2000; Yun 2013). According to research on the online community *DC Inside*, the precursor to the *Ilbe* community, online cultures maintained a masculine ethos even before the formation of *Ilbe* (Lee 2012). Thus, for example, a dispute among online communities is termed a "war," an overwhelming victory in the war is called "sightseeing" in accordance with a pun; the hidden meaning is "rape" because the Korean words for sightseeing (*gwangwang*) and rape (*ganggan*) sound similar. The numerous female users on many *DC Inside* boards used to pretend to be men to pass as members of the community. Thus, while the *Ilbe* community was particularly blunt in its exclusion of female users through the ban on *boming-out*, male-dominated online culture is nothing new.

Re/Production of Misogyny Online: Focusing on *"Kimchi-nyeo"* Discourse

Online Misogyny as Social Discourse Within this male-dominated online environment, misogyny in Korea develops into social discourse that stereotypes women and justifies misogynistic hate speech and sexualized attacks. This discourse began with the coining of a series of derogatory terms for women based on the word *-nyeo* (girl/woman). The first of these was *gaeddong-nyeo* (dog poop girl) (Hwang and Kang 2014; Yun 2013). In June 2005, a posting on the online humor site *Uggin-Daehak* (*College Humor*) condemned a young Korean woman who allegedly refused to clean up her dog's excrement on a subway. Photos and an account of the incident spread rapidly in online media, and users accused the woman of irrational and anti-social behavior. Within a few days, her personal identity and private information were revealed as a means of punishment, and she and her family were attacked by other users (Krim 2005).

What is important in terms of my larger argument is that the condemnation expressed in this epithet was not directed simply against a person, but against a woman: the suffix "*-nyeo*" (girl/woman) in "dog poop girl" adds the misogynistic implication that Korean women in general are selfish, irrational, and irresponsible. This impression was reinforced by the subsequent *-nyeo* terms that surfaced online (Hwang and Kang 2014). For example, *loser-nyeo* (loser girl) in 2009 became a type after a woman claimed publicly that "short men are losers; men should at least be 180cm tall" during a television program. What these examples demonstrate is that the consistent use of *-nyeo* in these contexts is part of a process of establishing new targets of misogyny: the figure of the *-nyeo* deserves criticism, for which reason misogynistic hate speech and attacks are justified. Furthermore, these individual attacks began to develop a social discourse in which the targets of blame expanded to include young Korean women as a group. Thus, for example, *doenjang-nyeo* (soybean paste girl) has been widely used since 2005 for the purpose of stigmatizing and condemning certain young women as vain, extravagant, and materialistic (Song 2014); the characteristics of these women are generally understood as follows: they like to drink Starbucks coffee that costs as much as an entire meal; they choose foreign luxury brands regardless of their quality; lacking their own economic means, they are dependent on their male partners. Unsurprisingly, it has also induced self-censorship in women, who naturally wish to avoid being thus stigmatized (Hwang and Kang 2014).

***Kimchi-nyeo* as a "Racial Trait"** The term *kimchi-nyeo/nyeon* (girl, woman/bitch) became a buzzword in the *Ilbe* community. Because kimchi is a traditional Korean food, *kimchi-nyeo* signifies Korean women as a whole. In the precursor online community *DC Inside*, foreign countries and their people are named after their representative food. For instance, Turkey is "kebab country," India is "curry country," and Japan is "sushi country." This online terminology shows how ethnicity, food, and gender are related and mobilized in people's thinking. These representative foods are often gendered, not only because cooking and food have traditionally been regarded as "women's work," but also because women have been symbolized as the "cultural carriers" of ethnic groups and "the transmitters of its cultures" (Yuval-Davis et al. 1989, p. 9). Interestingly, in the process of this stereotyping of foreign countries, Korean users started to call Korea itself "kimchi country."

Building on previous -*nyeo* epithets, *kimchi-nyeo* discourse has expanded the target of blame from some young women to all Korean women, serving as a stereotype for all of the supposed negative aspects of the female image. In *kimchi-nyeo* discourse, Korean women's characteristics are defined as a *jongteuk* (racial trait). This term comes from the online game *World of Warcraft*, which is very popular in Korea. These racial traits of *kimchi-nyeo* are hard to summarize because they cover a wide range of characteristics regarding contemporary women and are constantly increasing in number. *Kimchi-nyeo* proceeds from *doenjang-nyeo* (soybean paste girl), suggesting that Korean women who appeal to men and encroach on men's rights while insisting on gender equality are selfish and conniving: they feel no social responsibility, lack etiquette, are selfish, gold digging, addicted to cosmetic surgery, sexually promiscuous, have no shame with regard to abortion, and so on (Yun 2013).

In the *Ilbe* community, the term *kimchi-nyeo* is, in fact, used as an expletive, and examples of this discourse are uploaded almost every day. Typical postings include: "many Korean women are addicted to cosmetic surgery because they only want to seduce men"; and "Korean women see marriage as a business and judge men based only on their economic status." Through *kimchi-nyeo* discourse, *Ilbe* members justify their hate speech against Korean women. The neologism *samilhan*, "women must be beaten every three days," then appeared as a kind of response.

Moreover, the term *tal-kimchi* (ex-*kimchi*), "sensible woman" was coined in the *Ilbe* community to describe women who no longer display the characteristics of a *kimchi-nyeo*, whose opinions are congruent with those of the *Ilbe* community, and who therefore denounce the selfishness of other women. In this way, *Ilbe* users reinforce the idea that the characteristics of the *kimchi-nyeo* are ones that all reasonable women must either avoid or abandon. However, because the concept of the *kimchi-nyeo* embraces virtually all Korean women and negative conceptions of their femininities, it is impossible to find a Korean girlfriend or wife who does not display at least some *kimchi-nyeo* characteristics. Therefore, many *Ilbe* users turn to foreign women as examples of the sensible ex-*kimchi*.

"Sushi-nyeo" as an Idealized Wife As a form of hate speech, *Ilbe* users frequently contrast the unique *jongteuk* (racial traits) of Korean women with those of foreign women to insist that the former are selfish and lack sense. With regard to military issues, for instance, Korean women are often compared to Israeli women, who serve in the armed forces alongside the men. The abstract term "foreign women" is thus mobilized in an arbitrary manner; in contrast with Korean women, they are sometimes portrayed as independent and rational, and at other times as docile and submissive. Japanese women, referred to by the aforementioned ethnic epithet *sushi-nyeo* (sushi girl), are often mentioned in discussions of the ideal spouse.

In the *Ilbe* community, desire discourse using Japanese women is (re) produced in several ways. First, postings about dating or marital life with Japanese women usually receive envious responses from *Ilbe* users. These postings include both television and newspaper stories about Korean male celebrities who have married Japanese women and also personal stories of ordinary *Ilbe* users. Typical titles of posts written by Korean men married to Japanese women include "A date with a *sushi-nyeo*," and "My married life with a *Sushi-nyeo*." Interestingly, a similar narrative structure recurs in many stories of Japanese brides: (1) the difficulty of finding an unselfish Korean girlfriend (often including stories of betrayal by a Korean woman); (2) dating and falling in love with a Japanese woman; (3) lacking the financial resources for married life; (4) receiving emotional and financial support from the Japanese woman and her parents; and (5) enjoying a happy married life despite economic hardship. The moral of these stories is, of course, that Korean men should seek Japanese wives, or at least that Korean wives are deficient in some way. This narrative structure revives the myth of romantic love and the ideology of traditional gender roles. The desirable wife is often portrayed doing such "women's work" as cooking and supporting her in-laws. At the same time, these stories make love, rather than money, the important consideration in choosing a bride. What is distinctive from traditional gender roles is that, unlike in a traditional middle-class ideology, Japanese women here both earn money and fulfill gendered women's roles, all without complaint.

One poster of marital stories lived with his wife's Japanese family and was unable to earn money because of his poor grasp of the Japanese language. One comment asked sarcastically, "Why do you envy him? Because he is treated well by his wife's parents without having to do any work?" Responses to this comment were as follows:

> Unlike *kimchi-nyeon* [bitch], I envy her [the Japanese wife] in that she made an effort to marry him and earn money for herself although her husband did not have enough money. If she were a *kimchi-nyeon*, she would have decided to break up with her boyfriend. "I've been thinking a lot but it's really hard to marry you. Love you but, blah, blah." This is obviously what a *kimchi-nyeon* would say.
>
> I envy him meeting a woman who does not have a *kimchi-nyeon*'s way of thinking. I think our mothers' generation was like the Japanese woman. If a husband was facing difficulties, the wife also worked hard for the family. How about these days? *Kimchi-nyeon*, the bitch, sees her husband as her father or guardian, treats her husband like an ATM, a simple moneymaking machine. Furthermore, she complains and neglects her duty as a wife regarding sexual intercourse, housework, and cooking. This is how a *kimchi-nyeon* acts. They abandon their duties and only take their own interests into account. No wonder I envy him.

In this way, the characteristics of the *sushi-nyeo* and the *kimchi-nyeo* are continually contrasted. In the *Ilbe* community, postings frequently bear such titles as "Behavior differences between a *kimchi-nyeo* and a *sushi-nyeo*," and can include specific situations such as "discussing the military issue," "giving a gift," and "sex." This comparison also appeared in a cable news story in 2013 on *TV Chosun* titled "Men argue for new gender discrimination." Three categories were used to distinguish the supposed differences between the stereotypes: dating expenses, wedding expenses, and breakfast after marriage. Korean women are described as assuming that men will pay the costs of dating and the wedding and the house in which the couple will live and also as being unreliable in providing their husbands with breakfast. Japanese women, by contrast, are described as sharing all expenses of dating and marriage because of their impatience with empty formalities and vanity and belief that a happy family is more important than material possessions; of course, they also serve breakfast assiduously. In this process, Japanese women are stereotyped as being faithful, subservient, and willing to sacrifice for, but economically independent from, their men, and the stories and data reinforce this fantasy irrespective of actual facts. The preference for Japanese over Korean women can thus be read as an effort to reaffirm traditional notions of femininity and as a reflection of anxiety over the male breadwinner ideology. These stereotypes, of course, essentialize Japanese women culturally, internalizing Orientalism. The manner in which Korean men idealize and romanticize Japanese women thereby demonstrates that hate speech directed against Korean women is related to fantasies and stereotypes of foreign women.

Practicing Online Misogyny

In the *Ilbe* community, *haeng-gay*, a term describing users who "act out," is praised in the context of acting to defend the community's values. In terms of misogyny, *haeng-gay* users promote action in several ways. First, building on the earlier discussion, they create and disseminate neologisms. Women are often called *boji* (pussy) in the *Ilbe* community, and the prefix *bo* is used to coin terms about them. Thus, misogyny is known as *bohyum* (hatred of pussy), and women who think of their gender as a form of power and are said to exploit men are called *boseulachi* (pussy titleholder). Such sensational and provocative expressions create a strong impression and are poised to become popular slang. In Korea, feminists have been labeled with such extreme terms as *ggolfemi* (feminazi) and *femi-nyeon* (feminist bitch), a move that virtually precludes the possibility of airing differing opinions (Kim and Choi 2007). These neologisms only serve to ridicule and deprecate women. Online users become accustomed to misogyny through daily and casual use of these words, which also serves to normalize misogyny. As the terms "sightseeing" and "racial trait" make clear, many newly-coined words originate in gaming (Lee 2012), a fact that helps to account for the rapidity with which they spread among online users already habituated to such language. Similar is the neologism *samilhan*, an acronym of "women must be beaten once every three days" from an old Korean saying that "women and dried fish should be beaten once every three days [to make them amenable]." The neologism revives the older misogynistic narrative. *Ilbe* users usually upload images relevant to their postings, and for *samilhan* stories they often use composite pictures of a programmer who was accused of beating his wife in a stark example of how online hate speech parallels physical violence.

Second, many *Ilbe* users make use of extensive data gathering and dramatic presentations to bolster their claims. Typical postings are uploaded with so-called *injeung shots* as verification. Thus, for instance, the post titled "A breakfast served by my *sushi-nyeo* wife" included images of the dishes in the meal, to which other users responded with envy. Other supporting evidence includes statistics, graphs, and figures and screenshots from offline and online media (television, news articles, and SNSs and other online communities) about Korean women. Despite its doubtful origins, many *Ilbe* users place credence in this evidence. Documentation renders hate speech against Korean women a "fact" rather than mere propaganda. Much of the data, however, is fabricated. In July 2013, for example, a posting was uploaded to an SNS making the false claim that the Ministry of Gender Equality and Family in Korea had announced the introduction of women-only roads: "The ministry is planning a road exclusively for women. The road will have walls to protect women from sexual predators, robbers and perverts. Men who enter such roads will be slapped with a fine of up to 300,000 won ($268)" ("Gender Ministry Says Controversial Kakao Account is Fake" 2013). Such false reports often spread rapidly as justification for and promotion of misogynistic discourse online. The stereotypes and supporting evidence are particularly effective because online communication tends to include provocative content.

Such hate discourse often results in offline action, including threats and retribution against female users. As seen in the *gaeddong-nyeo* incident, female victims of "cyber witch-hunting" can become targets of online attacks (Hwang and Kang 2014). *Ilbe* users often share specific female users' URLs, known as "coordinate points for targeting," with other users to coordinate attacks that can include malicious comments and the disclosure of personal information, including their addresses and phone numbers. One *Ilbe* user also performed a one-man demonstration, carrying a misogynistic picket in front of Korea's largest women's university to chastise young Korean women (Kim 2013).

Crisis of Hegemonic Masculinity and Restoring Male Bonds

The proliferation of online misogyny in Korea can be read in the context of the economic crisis and anxiety about challenges to hegemonic masculinity (Kim 2015). The Korean economy has been in decline since the crisis in the late 1990s, while the global economic downturn and neoliberal policies have increased the wealth gap. Accordingly, perceived threats to the male breadwinner ideology and the crisis of hegemonic masculinity are being exacerbated in Korean society (Kim 2001). Some young men call themselves losers in a self-mocking manner while expressing resentment toward young women. A study of "loser culture" and masculinity in Korea (Sang-uk Ahn 2011) shows that these young men's frustrations focus on young women who refuse to like, date, or marry them. Such a reading relates the phenomena discussed here to class issues regarding men in contemporary Korean society. Middle-class-based hegemonic masculinity becomes an unachievable goal for the coming generation, since, in its terms, "real men" must possess wealth. Many scholars have noted the strong link between class and masculinities (Morgan 2005); "if masculinity in contemporary Korea is measured by earning ability, poor men are by definition not masculine" (Kim 1998, p. 86). In this sense, seeming self-deprecation among young men is an aspect of hate speech toward Korean women. Hatred toward women is not restricted, however, to economically vulnerable classes, but is widespread among Korean men: 54.2% of men and 66.7% of male teenagers reported sympathizing with the views expressed in hostile speech against women

(Sang-su Ahn et al. 2015). As Connell (2005) points out, although only a small number of men can actually meet the standards of hegemonic masculinity, the majority of men "benefit from the patriarchal dividend, the advantage men in general gain from the overall subordination of women" (p. 79). These men are thus complicit in the hegemonic project.

As the economic crisis has fractured the long-held notion of male breadwinners and dependent women, growing discourse of a crisis of masculinity is seen as the rise in women's status as a result of gendered antagonism within Korean society. In this context, Korean women are no longer perceived as weak and in need of the protection by Korean men, but rather as exploiters of them (Kim and Choi 2007). A recent survey shows that Korean men identify women in their twenties and thirties as the group that receives the most benefits, and this response is significantly higher among those who sympathize with online misogynistic posts (Sang-su Ahn et al. 2015). Indeed, it has come to play a powerful role in hate speech against Korean women. Many Korean men try to identify the objects of blame as the people who reap benefits disproportionate to their qualifications and abilities, people who were once regarded as the weak in society, that is, women. Thus, they ascribe their sense of incompetence and victimhood, not to the capitalist system or neoliberal policies, but to women who they see as preventing them from receiving their due. In this context, men's rights organizations, including *Man of Korea*, began to appear in the mid-2000s founded on the notion that support for women in society and from the government leads to reverse discrimination and that men are the real victims. Affirmative action and women-friendly policies such as the gender quota system are cited as examples of the benefits and privileges that Korean women enjoy, irrespective of the persistence of sociostructural gender inequality. Moreover, the growing male crisis discourse often makes women a scapegoat for the crisis while ignoring existing male privilege. During the economic crisis in the late 1990s, for example, male workers were protected so that female workers were the first to be laid off in Korea (Cho Han 2000).

The rise of the rhetoric of reverse discrimination, of privileged women and exploited men, however, needs to be read in terms, not of gender inequality, but of inequality among men (K. Um 2011). The disconnect between material conditions and the hegemonic ideology render the notional brotherhood no longer tenable. Thus, this can explain the drive to restore traditional manhood through hate discourse toward Korean women. *Ilbe* users try to initiate and prolong "wars" against women to reaffirm their masculine identities and boundaries. As Kim (1998) argues, "The same patriarchal attitudes and practices that bound men together in turn set women against one another" (p. 89). Ongoing controversies over such gendered issues as the veterans' advantage system can similarly be read as verification and confirmation of the hegemonic masculinity. In sum, consistent production and distribution of misogynistic discourse serve to restore male bonds and with them hegemonic masculinity.

Conclusion

This chapter has explored how online misogynistic discourse has been constructed and reproduced in a male-dominated online community. As online culture in Korea has been male-dominated, female users have been unable to express and identify themselves as women in the *Ilbe* community. Moreover, through the principle of exclusion, the *Ilbe* community controls the site's border and its male-dominated culture and identity.

Starting with series of -*nyeo* (girl/woman) neologisms, misogynistic discourse has expanded in scope from a few women to all Korean women, whose characteristics have been defined as unique racial traits in *kimchi-nyeo* discourse. Hate speech against Korean women is thus often accomplished through comparisons with foreign, especially Japanese, women. The analysis of the *kimchi-nyeo* and *sushi-nyeo* stereotypes shows that misogynistic discourse reinforces traditional gender roles and femininity while reflecting anxiety over changing gender relations and male roles.

Although this chapter uses the *Ilbe* community as a starting point, contemporary online misogynistic discourse is not limited to one conservative site but belongs to the broader social discourse in Korean society. This chapter has further offered a reading of the production of misogynistic discourse in the context of the ongoing economic crisis and threatened hegemonic masculinity. These changing social environments can explain the drive to maintain hegemonic masculinity and to reestablish male solidarity through hate discourse against Korean women. However, as Connell (2005) argues, hegemonic masculinity is not fixed but rather represents a contestable position in gender power relations. Conversely, the rise of misogynistic hate discourse has catalyzed growth in anti-misogyny and feminist activism both online and offline (Kim 2017). Further research is needed to shed more light on the responses of Korean female users to the prevailing misogynistic discourse and the ways in which they criticize and challenge hegemonic masculinity.

Note

1. Since military service is compulsory for all able-bodied adult men, the issue is often read as gendered in Korea. A telling example is the controversy surrounding the army veterans' advantage system, which privileged veterans in terms of the civil service exam and hiring and was declared unconstitutional, on the grounds that it violated the equal rights of women and the disabled, in 1999, though the topic remains highly controversial online.

References

Ahn, S. (2011). *Emergence of loser culture and reconfiguration of masculinity in Korea*. Seoul: Seoul National University.

Ahn, S., Kim, I., Lee, J., & Yun, B. (2015). *Basic research on Korean Men's life (II): Focus on the conflict in values of young men concerning gender equality* (No. 30). Seoul: Korean Women's Development Institute.

Anahita, S. (2006). Blogging the borders: Virtual skinheads, hypermasculinity, and heteronormativity. *Journal of Political and Military Sociology, 34*(1), 143–164.

boyd, d. (2011). White flight in networked publics? How race and class shaped American teen engagement with Myspace and Facebook. In L. Nakamura & P. Chow-White (Eds.), *Race after the internet* (pp. 203–221). New York: Routledge.

Cho Han, H.-J. (2000). "You are entrapped in an imaginary well": The formation of subjectivity within compressed development – A feminist critique of modernity and Korean culture. *Inter-Asia Cultural Studies, 1*(1), 49–69. https://doi.org/10.1080/146493700360999.

Citron, D. K. (2014). *Hate crimes in cyberspace.* Cambridge/London: Harvard University Press.

Connell, R. W. (2005). *Masculinities* (2nd ed.). Berkeley: University of California Press.

Filipovic, J. (2007). Blogging while female: How internet misogyny parallels real-world harassment. *Yale Journal of Law and Feminism, 19,* 295–303.

Gender Ministry Says Controversial Kakao Account is Fake. (2013, July 31). *The Korea Herald.* Retrieved from http://khnews.kheraldm.com/view.php?ud =20130731000898&md=20130803004155_AT

Hwang, S., & Kang, J. (2014). A qualitative study on the discourse of on-line woman interpellation. *Korean Journal of Broadcasting and Telecommunication Studies, 28*(4), 356–388.

Jane, E. A. (2014a). "Back to the kitchen, cunt": Speaking the unspeakable about online misogyny. *Continuum, 28*(4), 558–570. https://doi.org/10.108 0/10304312.2014.924479.

Jane, E. A. (2014b). Your a ugly, whorish, slut. *Feminist Media Studies, 14*(4), 531–546. https://doi.org/10.1080/14680777.2012.741073.

Kendall, L. (2002). *Hanging out in the virtual pub: Masculinities and relationships online.* Berkeley: University of California Press.

Kim, E. H. (1998). Men's talk: A Korean American view of South Korean constructions of women, gender, and masculinity. In E. H. Kim & C. Choi (Eds.), *Dangerous women: Gender and Korean nationalism* (pp. 67–118). New York: Routledge.

Kim, H. M. (2001). Work, nation and hypermasculinity: The "woman" question in the economic miracle and crisis in South Korea. *Inter-Asia Cultural Studies, 2*(1), 53–68. https://doi.org/10.1080/14649370120039452.

Kim, S.-A. (2012). Digital technology and young women's political participation. *Issues in Feminism, 12*(1), 193–217.

Kim, H.-A. (2013, September 30). Ilbe member picketing in front of Ewha Womans University "You are sluts, betraying comfort women." *Donga Newspaper.* Retrieved from http://news.donga.com/3/all/20130930/579205 10/2?ref=false

Kim, S.-A. (2015). Misogynistic cyber hate speech in Korea. *Issues in Feminism, 15*(2), 279–317.

Kim, J. (2017). #iamafeminist as the "mother tag": Feminist identification and activism against misogyny on Twitter in South Korea. *Feminist Media Studies, 17*(5), 804–820. https://doi.org/10.1080/14680777.2017.1283343

Kim, S.-A., & Choi, S.-Y. (2007). Construction and re-production of masculinities in Korean cyberspace: Comparative study on the difference between community board and discussion board. *Media, Gender & Culture, 10*, 5–41.

Kim, S., & Kim, Y. (2008). A study of gender discourse and gender characteristics in cyber public sphere. *Media, Gender & Culture, 10*(0), 5–36.

Krim, J. (2005, July 7). Subway fracas escalates into test of the Internet's power to shame. *The Washington Post*. Retrieved from http://www.washingtonpost.com/wp-dyn/content/article/2005/07/06/AR2005070601953.html

KwonKim, H. Y. (2000). Veterans' extra point system and cyber terrorism. *Women & Society, 11*(1), 133–145.

Lee, K.-H. (2012). *We are the DC: Gift, war and power in cyberspace*. Seoul: Imagine Publications.

Mantilla, K. (2013). Gendertrolling: Misogyny adapts to new media. *Feminist Studies, 39*(2), 563–570.

Mantilla, K. (2015). *Gendertrolling: How misogyny went viral*. Santa Barbara: Praeger.

Morgan, D. (2005). Class and masculinity. In M. S. Kimmel, J. Hearn, & R. Connell (Eds.), *Handbook of studies on men and masculinities* (pp. 165–177). Thousand Oaks: SAGE.

Orgad, S. (2005). The transformative potential of online communication. *Feminist Media Studies, 5*(2), 141–161. https://doi.org/10.1080/14680770500111980.

Sedgwick, E. K. (1985). *Between men: English literature and male homosocial desire*. New York: Columbia University Press.

Shohat, E. (1999). By the bitstream of Babylon: Cyberfrontiers and diasporic vistas. In H. Naficy (Ed.), *Home, exile, homeland: Film, media, and the politics of place* (pp. 213–232). New York: Routledge.

Song, J. E. R. (2014). The soybean paste girl: The cultural and gender politics of coffee consumption in contemporary South Korea. *Journal of Korean Studies, 19*(2), 429–448. https://doi.org/10.1353/jks.2014.0026.

Spender, D. (1995). *Nattering on the net: Women, power, and cyberspace*. North Melbourne: Spinifex Press.

Turton-Turner, P. (2013). Villainous avatars: The visual semiotics of misogyny and free speech in cyberspace. *Forum on Public Policy: A Journal of the Oxford Round Table, 2013*(1), 1–18.

Um, K. (2011). (Im)possibility of new masculinity after neo-liberalism. In H. Y. KwonKim (Ed.), *Masculinity and gender* (pp. 147–166). Seoul: Jaeum & Moeum Publishing Company.

Um, J. (2016). Strategic misogyny and its contradiction – Focusing on the analysis of the posts on the internet community site Ilgan best Jeojangso (daily best storage). *Media, Gender & Culture, 31*(2), 193–236.

van Zoonen, L. (2001). Feminist internet studies. *Feminist Media Studies, 1*(1), 67–72. https://doi.org/10.1080/14680770120042864.

Wakeford, N. (1997). Networking women and grrrls with information/communication technology: Surfing tales of the world wide web. In J. Terry & M. Calvert (Eds.), *Processed lives: Gender and technology in everyday life* (pp. 51–66). London/New York: Routledge.

Yun, B. (2013). Ilbe and misogyny. *The Radical Review, 57*, 33–56.

Yuval-Davis, N., Anthias, F., & Campling, J. (1989). *Woman, nation, state.* Houndmills: Macmillan.

9

Don't Mess with My Happy Place: Understanding Misogyny in Fandom Communities

Gwendelyn S. Nisbett

In the summer of 2016, during the height of the blockbuster movie season, a social media battle broke out about the new version of *Ghostbusters*. What started as fan grumbling about the all-female cast and staying true to the original film bubbled over into an all-out assault on cast member Leslie Jones. Many male fans of *Ghostbusters* trolled the cast and the movie, but focused much of its attention on creating racist and sexist remarks about Jones.[1] (For an in-depth analysis of Leslie Jones' harassment and misogynoir, see Chap. 4.) It may have come as a bit of a shock that fandoms and fans—the perceived realm of the docile nerds and geeks—could be so territorial and brutal. By fall of 2016, male fan outrage had moved to the increase in female leads in the latest *Star Wars* franchise movies (*Rogue One* and the most recent trilogy).

Though these high-profile examples garnered attention, misogyny in fandoms has been an ongoing problem. Geek culture has traditionally been dominated by one group—young white males—and the recent

G. S. Nisbett (✉)
Mayborn School of Journalism, University of North Texas, Denton, TX, USA

© The Author(s) 2018
J. R. Vickery, T. Everbach (eds.), *Mediating Misogyny*,
https://doi.org/10.1007/978-3-319-72917-6_9

171

influx of an increasingly diverse audience has resulted in a backlash (Massanari 2015; Todd 2015). Massanari (2015) refers to this as geek masculinity whereby white men seek to reify their domination of genres like video games and science fiction and lash out against those they view as intruders, particularly women. Women, as seen in the recent #GamerGate scandal, are vilified, objectified, and violently harassed simply for existing in a space formerly dominated by men (for more on #GamerGate and its consequences, see Chap. 6). And communities and media are perpetuating this culture (Perreault and Vos 2016).

Misogyny is not a new phenomenon in pop culture, but little research has examined sexism from the perspective of the fandom experience. The rise in social media fandoms and convergence culture has inspired recent research on the fandom communities, particularly as gendered and diverse spaces (Condis 2015). The goal of this chapter is to explore misogyny in pop culture fandoms from the fan perspective.

Fandoms are loosely organized communities of people who unite and engage around a pop culture artifact or phenomenon. Example fandoms include communities interested in shows like *Star Trek* (i.e., Trekkies) or pop culture giants *Doctor Who* (i.e., Whovians) and Harry Potter. Fandoms also include video games, comic books, and anime. Many of the biggest fandoms include media across many platforms (e.g., Pokémon).

In recent years, aided by social media, fandoms have increased in popularity (Driscoll and Gregg 2011; Jenkins et al. 2013). More than just comic book nerds and Trekkies, people from around the world can now connect and share in a common pop culture interest. From *Star Wars* to *Game of Thrones* and *Sherlock*, fans are also an increasingly important component in pop culture media production and success (Jenkins et al. 2013). This is due in part to fandoms not being simply a fan base or a targeted consumer audience. Fandoms, as Jenkins et al. (2013) argue, are distinct from mere fans, which they define as "individuals who have a passionate relationship to a particular media franchise": fandoms are made up of "members who consciously identify as part of a larger community to which they feel some degree of commitment and loyalty" (p. 166).

Understanding fandoms is important on multiple levels. On an individual level, fandom is linked with deep psychological attachments (i.e., parasocial relationships) to the pop culture texts we love the most. In a world full of divisiveness and stress, escaping reality—even for a moment—is a wonderful gift. It is not unusual for people to lose themselves in a good book or a favorite video game, binge-watch a television show or count down the days before the release of a favorite film. We all love something in pop culture—that which reflects our hopes and fears, where we can escape to, and where we can find acceptance. Fandoms attract people because they can find a positive and accepting community.

This attachment to the community is what makes misogyny in all its vestiges so destructive. Imagine your favorite pop culture fandom—for instance, you fall in love with a television show. As a hobby or even as a diversionary tactic to avoid the day's stresses, you seek out information on your favorite show. What are the back stories on the characters, who are the actors, what is the latest news, what are the best fan theories? Imagine joining a Facebook fan group and then creating a fan blog on Tumblr or posting a fan theory on Reddit. Now imagine getting shunned or trolled, belittled and harassed because you do not fit the mold of what a fan should be or look like. This project seeks to understand how misogyny manifests in fandoms and how it impacts community members.

On a broader social level, fandoms are an example of convergence culture that can wield power over both fandom communities and the media with which they are associated (Jenkins et al. 2013), and arguably have subsequent influence over social attitudes and debates. Indeed, Kligler-Vilenchik (2015) found that political discussions inspired by the fandom *Harry Potter* inspired further interest and mobilization into actual political engagement. Moreover, Jenkins et al. (2013) argue "[f]andoms are one type of collectivity (in that they are acting as communities rather than as individuals) and connectivity (in that their power is amplified through their access to networked communications) whose presence is being felt in contemporary culture" (p. 166). Fandoms in many ways influence storylines and casting decisions, which in turn can have a broader impact on less engaged consumers. For example, fandoms may desire more diversity in casting decisions; both the *Harry Potter* and *Doctor Who* franchises have cast more women and people of color as the series progressed.

This chapter explores the potential for misogyny and gendered spaces within fandom communities. What should be safe places to interact with fellow fans can become segmented and inaccessible, with some fandoms regarding women as second-rate or objects. This chapter first presents a background on the importance of fandom communities situated in the theoretical framework of parasocial interaction phenomenon (Horton and Wohl 1956; Rubin and Perse 1987) mixed with convergence culture (Jenkins 2006).

Second, a case study of fandom community participants is presented. In order to explore fandom culture among actual participants, data were collected at a large fandom convention (i.e., comic con). Comic cons are a cultural phenomenon increasing in popularity and are an example of fandom convergence culture. Where they once may have been the realm of comic book enthusiasts and super fans, comic cons are massive weekend-long events catering to thousands of fans from surprisingly diverse backgrounds.

Lastly, the normative implications are explored with an emphasis on what community members can do to create a more positive space. Moreover, beyond the realms of the fandom, understanding and promoting equality can seep into other facets of popular culture.

Importance of Fandom Communities

Fandom communities, with social media as a catalyst, have become more popular than ever. Gone are the days of the lonely geek with a comic book; fandom communities are attracting a wide spectrum of people from the newly interested genre consumer to the ultra-enthusiastic cosplayer.

Pop culture scholar Henry Jenkins (2006) argues that fandoms are an example of convergence culture, whereby traditional media (e.g., *Harry Potter* the book collection and film series) collides and collaborates with new media (e.g., social media about *Harry Potter*), thus making consuming pop culture "a collective process" (p. 4). Television shows, films, and books representing traditional media mix with online paratexts and fan-generated content to create examples of convergence culture. As convergence cultures, fandom communities exist in many planes, from traditional media to social media to the material world. This collective nature allows pop culture franchises to continue catering to their fandoms while community members create paratexts that influence media producers. An example of this is the long-running *Doctor Who* franchise, where executive producers were inspired by fan-made art and incorporated it into the opening credits of the show.

But, why are people so attached to their fandoms? In a world that is increasingly mediated and, arguably, increasingly detached from interpersonal relationships, fandom is important. Through pop culture, people are potentially developing meaningful (albeit one-sided) relationships with media figures and characters—a phenomenon known as parasocial interaction (PSI) (Horton and Wohl 1956; Rubin and Perse 1987). Fandom can generate attachments that feel very real—even though the media figure does not respond, people feel as if their favorite celebrity or character is a good personal friend (Cohen 2004, 2009; Grant et al. 1991; Rubin and Perse 1987; Rubin et al. 1985).

PSI pertains to the short-term interactions that people have with media figures in which a person sees and actor or character and feels a connection (Rubin and Perse 1987; Rubin et al. 1985). Parasocial relationships (PSR) are long-term one-sided relationships that a person develops with a media figure (Giles 2002; Schramm and Hartmann 2008). PSR is distinguished from PSI in the size and scope of the relationship (Schramm and Hartmann 2008).

When fans join an online fan community or attend a fan convention to see their favorite actor, they are likely experiencing PSR. Relationships with media figures can mimic those (or even replace) actual interpersonal relationships (Cohen 2003, 2010; Derrick et al. 2009; Giles 2002). Through fandom, people are drawing upon PSR to engage in actual social relationships, both online and in person. Prior to online fan communities, people who had similar interests could consume media about their favorite show, film, celebrity, or book, and perhaps chat with friends about it, but they rarely had contact with fellow super fans. Even large comic con events are a fairly new phenomenon in terms of scope, size, and popularity. Through social media, people from all over the world can connect and interact with fellow fans.

Moreover, in conjunction with parasocial factors, narrative transportation is an important component of fandom. Fandom can function as a way to escape our everyday lives, where people feel free to explore interests and identities (Green et al. 2004). Through transportation, people can escape their mundane lives, get lost in the narrative, and emerge changed and enlightened (Green et al. 2004). Because of transportation, people can learn, grow, and be persuaded to change their viewpoints without resisting (Slater and Rouner 2002). Transport also makes the narrative, and the relationships within the story, seem more real, thereby making the experience feel more genuine (Green and Brock 2000).

Through fandom, people can extend this function of narrative transportation via paratexts about the original text. For instance, community members create new content, artwork, and fan fiction to supplement the original content. Even though original content may be limited, narrative transportation can persist through ongoing productive of paratexts created by and catering to the fandom community. In a sense, you can get lost in your fandom.

Fandom also helps us negotiate our feelings about other people that we do not understand. The Parasocial Contact Hypothesis (PCH) (Schiappa et al. 2005, 2006) suggests that as parasocial contact increases with media figures embodying an out-group attribute, feelings of tolerance increase for that out-group. For example, a character that addresses a stereotype or stigma can help audiences understand those stereotypes and stigmas. Hoffner and Cohen (2014), in a study about the show *Monk*, found higher PSI was linked with a more sympathetic appraisal of people with mental health issues. Fandom can extend the impact of PCH, thus extending the potential benefit of addressing a stereotype or stigma.

Given the potential personal and interpersonal benefits of fandom, understanding misogyny and the impact of misogyny on community members is a worthwhile topic. What may be considered a person's retreat, place for friendship, or place to better understand the world may be marred by the presence of hostile or belittling behavior. Given this, the following research question is asked:

RQ: *How do members of pop culture fandoms negotiate gender and misogyny within fandom communities?*

Misogyny in Fandom Communities: A Case Study

This project seeks to further explore misogyny within pop culture through an examination of fandom communities. As a case study, data were collected at a large internationally well-known fandom convention (Alamo City Comic Con) in October 2016. Respondents were recruited at a comic con for a number of reasons. First, as Jenkins and co-authors (2013) noted, there is a difference between a fan and a member of a fandom. Comic cons cater to fandoms—they bring in famous celebrities, host panels about the minutia of fandom media, and sell pop culture merchandise. For their part, attendees are willing to pay steep admission prices to enter and meet celebrities, wait in long lines for hours to attend panels or meet celebrities, and many dress up as their favorite characters (known as cosplay). These are not people who simply like a show or who have read a book; these are actively engaged members of communities where they are both consumer and creator of pop culture artifacts and texts. Simply recruiting respondents online would not have had the same level of validity because it would be hard to gauge whether a respondent was truly a member of a fandom. Second, conventions draw a diverse crowd of people. Respondents include men and women from a variety of backgrounds and age groups. Third, in-person recruitment allowed for quality control in data collection compared to online data collection.

Procedure and Participants Respondents (n=64) included 60% women and 40% men, ranging in age from 18 to 65. In terms of ethnicity, 65% were white, 5% Black, 2% Native American, 24% Hispanic, and 4% mixed/other. Each participant first read a consent form and agreed to take part in the study. The survey first asked for demographic and fandom participation information. Participants then answered a set of five open-ended questions about fandom motivation, the people in fandoms, interactions with other fandom members, and differences in men and women in fandoms. The project was approved by the university Institutional Review Board and followed all ethical guidelines.

Analysis Strategy Study responses were coded using Braun and Clarke's (2006) thematic analysis strategy. A second coder was recruited for the purposes of analysis validity. Responses were first coded using an open-coding style to derive themes. Subsequent coding rounds analyzed sub-categorization of themes and redundancy of themes. Both coders continuously discussed theme content, theme titles, and differences in theme perceptions. Coding continued in iterative rounds until coders were in agreement and themes became redundant.

Thematic Analysis Findings

The thematic analysis resulted in three main themes emerging: women as second-tier fans; objectification of women fans; and response to misogyny.

Women as Second-Tier Fans A major theme was the notion that women are not fully accepted within what was traditionally a very male-dominated culture. While women enjoy and participate in fandoms, they feel as though they are not perceived to be true fans. This manifested in a number of ways. First, women are perceived as not as dedicated and knowledgeable about fandoms as their male counterparts. As one respondent noted, "most men are surprised to hear a woman know just as much as the males" (Female A).

Second, women were also perceived as not being serious about the fandom and not true fans. One respondent said: "There are women who do enjoy comics/shows, and men sometimes underestimate women and how they are actually interested in these fandoms" (Female D). This was shared among men as well as women, as one respondent commented:

> Men in a way feel that a lot of this stuff is mainly men, but women love it too and make as much of an effort as men do to be in or participate in these fandoms. (Male A)

There was also a perception that women have to prove their fandom, as one respondent noted:

I believe a proper fandom should see everyone as an equal. The point of a fandom is to come together over something we enjoy. I think women are treated differently from men when they have to prove themselves to be a fan of something. (Male F)

Different fandoms have different perceptions of women members. Some fandoms tend to be dominated by men—video game and comic book fandoms were cited as examples of this. One female respondent offered, "Video game [fandoms] do not welcome females" (Female G). Added another respondent, "You see more men because it isn't always 'acceptable' for women to play video games" (Female T). This perception that women do not really belong in a fandom can lead to hostility. One respondent noted, "I feel men can be more aggressive on social media in these fandom communities" (Female H). Another respondent commented:

I like to believe that most people in a fandom are pretty understanding. It is other people who are often the rudest or most sexist. I do also feel that women are always viewed as 'less into it' than their male counterparts. (Female S)

Some fandoms were perceived as more open and friendly to women while others were perceived as more sexist. Some fandoms are obvious about misogyny, in both content and fandom. Anime was cited as an example where women are oversexualized. One respondent remarked:

Misogyny is rampant in some fandoms. I notice it especially in the anime/ Japanese sort of fandoms. And in general, I've experienced quite a bit of misogyny in nerd culture. It tends to be underestimated because men in fandoms tend to be "nice guys" not the stereotypical macho dude. I'd like to see it talked about more. (Female X)

Some fandoms see less overt misogyny, but it seeps through in other ways. One respondent noted, "seems less true for *Doctor Who*—the message of the show and fandom is everyone is important and by extension, deserving of respect" (Female C). However, another *Doctor Who* fan added about misogyny:

I have not encountered this except in some of the Moffat (*Doctor Who* and *Sherlock* producer) forums dealing with his treatment of women. I prefer not to engage in them, since passions run too high. (Male B)

In response, women may augment their behavior, as one respondent noted: "As a woman, I tend to use gender neutral usernames as an avoidance of any negative interactions" (Female B). Women may also be drawn to some fandoms more than others because of the perception they are not allowed nor appreciated. One respondent noted: "It's easier to enjoy a sci-fi fandom as a female versus a comic fandom as a female" (Female Z).

Objectification in Cosplay Objectification of women also emerged as a major theme. This centered primarily around the activity of cosplay and the social media associated with posting photos. Cosplay, the fan act of dressing like beloved characters, was the source of objectification and sexualization for women, but not necessarily men. This was a theme for both social media posts about cosplay and in-person cosplay at fan events. For men, the act of representing a character was accepted and applauded. One participant noted:

Today I saw a man dressed as Eleven [a female character] from *Stranger Things*. I laughed, but then came to the conclusion he was a true fan, and I can respect that. (Male G)

Another male fan noted cosplay was generally a positive activity, saying, "people just rocking whatever they are wearing without shame—it's awesome!" (Male K) Women did not seem to have the same overall positive view of cosplay. Though many enjoy the activity, others had reservations or problems. Female fans recognized the imbalance between female and male cosplayers. One respondent offered this comparison: "Women get more attention on their cosplay because they show breasts and boobs." And then added: "Men on the other hand do go all out on their outfits, they do get attention, but not as much as women" (Female U). This appears to impact how some women participate in cosplay, noting one respondent:

As much as I enjoy dressing up, I make sure to be modest as possible because so many people judge a plus size woman in costume. (Female J)

Cosplay for women appeared to create tension between those women embracing sexualization and women who found it offensive. There was a perception that some women play into the objectification of cosplay to get more attention, as one respondent noted: "I notice the females who are half naked tend to get the most attention" (Female N). This had the chilling effect for women who wish to participate without sexual undertones. One respondent noted:

Most of the comic book characters are portrayed with a more revealing outfit when it comes to girls. Most of the girls out there just cosplay to be famous and show everything. I'm not ok with this, this makes the rest of us girls that work hard on cosplay bad. (Female K)

Apathy Toward Misogyny A persistent theme emerged in regard to people dealing with misogyny in their fandoms—respondents generally did not feel empowered or inspired to deal with the problem. Many found it easier to push it away, avoid problems, and downplay the problem of fandom misogyny.

Many fandom community members were indifferent to the presence of misogyny. One respondent said in reference to misogyny, "[t]here probably is, but I personally have never noticed it, but then I have never looked or worried about it" (Female K). Some even adopted a mindset of resignation that misogyny was just something to cope with. For example, one respondent said, "Makes me mad, but everyone has their own opinion" (Female M). Another respondent remarked on sexism, "I think there is—but it's how you approach it" (Female L).

There was a difference in the way men and women regarded misogyny in fandoms. One male participant remarked: "it does not bother me, we are all equal." He later added, in reference to social media fandom spaces, "some only sexualize the women actresses or impose on others ideas that go against gender equality" (Male E). Remarked another, "Everyone has the right to have different points of view" (Male C).

Another subtheme focused on the desire to avoid confrontation or problems. One respondent remarked: "As long as we talk about the things we are supposed to talk about" (Female P). Another noted, "I tend to avoid that side of things because it is deeply problematic" (Female I). There was a persistent desire for the issue not to impact the fandom. One respondent commented:

> I'm sure there are some, but I don't really care. As long as someone has fun being in a fandom, I don't care how people view it. (Female V)

Discussion

Overall, findings suggest that misogyny and gendered spaces exist within fandom communities. Unsurprisingly, perhaps, the traditionally male-dominated pop culture realms of comic books, science fiction, and video games continue to present barriers to women, even though these genres attract an increasingly diverse audience (Todd 2015). This builds upon previous research finding hegemonic male dominance in geek culture (Massanari 2015). In many of these fandoms, women are regarded as not good enough to be fans. They face judgment and scorn about their level of knowledge and skill. Even if women are super fans, they are treated as though they will never truly understand the intricacies of the fandom. Given this, they often face micro-aggressions suggesting they do not know enough or are not committed enough. Massanari (2015) argues that even though geek men fail to uphold masculine traits of physical and romantic prowess, they embrace hegemonic masculinity in terms of intellect: "geek masculinity often embraces facets of hyper-masculinity by valorizing intellect over social or emotional intelligence" (p. 4). This group of geek men, who are often marginalized themselves, are trying to hold onto and perpetuate their form of hypermasculinity by belittling and marginalizing female fans. While each fandom is different, with some being more offensive, the notion of women not fitting into the fandom because of a lack of fandom knowledge was the strongest and most persistent theme.

Not all fandoms were regarded as equally offensive or gendered, and much of this was attributed to the content of the media consumed. In some genres, misogynistic media was linked with misogynistic attitudes toward women in the fandom. Anime and video game fandoms, which often have violent and sexist content, were cited as being the most misogynistic. A subtheme suggests that women will hide their sex identities in online interactions in order to avoid harassment. Todd (2015) argues that the video game industry is highly misogynistic in both sexist content and within the industry itself. This appears to have spread to the fandom, even though video games are popular among an increasingly diverse audience. Trolling and the type of harassment experienced during #GamerGate appear to be happening on a smaller scale within fandom communities.

Other fandoms were cited as being less gendered and/or less hostile to women. Science fiction fandoms appeared to be more welcoming, and much of this was attributed to the tone of the media that strives to be more inclusive. For instance, *Doctor Who* was referenced as valuing and respecting all cultures. *Star Wars*, a franchise that recently cast both women and people of color in critical lead roles, was also cited as a fairly respectful fandom. It very much appears that attitude within the media shapes attitudes within the fandom, which can have subsequent impact on media production.

Another major theme was objectification of women, specifically in the fan activity of cosplay. Cosplay is often a sign of a fan's commitment and creativity. It is as if women are discouraged from being the nerdy "know-it-all" fan and encouraged to objectify themselves through the practice of cosplay. This is a reflection that male fandom members are perpetuating a corrosive form of hegemonic geek masculinity which prefers women to remain as objects rather than becoming full-fledged members of the community. Findings show that women who know a lot about fandom canon and create intricate costumes are shunned and harassed because male fandom members regard them as second-tier members.

Moreover, cosplay is an interesting intersection between offline spaces and social media. Respondents cited cosplay as a fun part of comic con because many fans are dressed up and it adds to the festive nature. Though some women opted to dress more conservatively for comic con, most cited social media cosplay as the biggest problem. Social media cosplay—creating and posting cosplay images simply for social media circulation—was cited as having problems with trolling and harassment. Woman who are overweight or regarded as less attractive by the geek misogynists are barraged with insults and degrading remarks. Many women cited the harassment as so problematic that they changed the way they cosplay dress and altered their social media use, which subsequently hampered the fun and enjoyment they received from this fandom activity. Social media cosplay was also a place of tension where some women regarded other women as caving to objectification and presenting more risqué versions of costumes. It appears even some women were perpetuating misogynistic cultural norms because objectification is rewarded and feminine individualism is scorned in fandom communities where women are second-class citizens.

Lastly, the third major theme to emerge pertained to how people deal with instances of misogyny within their fandom. Members of various fandoms suspected or recognized that misogyny exists within their ranks, yet they did not want to deal with it. They found it easier to push it away. Very few cited a desire to take an active and vocal role in speaking out against misogyny. Findings suggest many did not want to disrupt the community they generally enjoy—they adopted the attitude of ignoring and coping with instances of misogyny or barriers to female participation.

Implications

While popular culture fandom is not a new phenomenon, social media has facilitated an explosion in fandom communities and fandom activities. Social media is crucial to fandom communities because it enables communication between fans and circulation of paratexts (Geraghty 2015). Furthermore, as an example of convergence culture, social and traditional media are intertwined—constantly interacting and feeding into building the community. Given this, it is important to recognize that misogyny within fandoms can be a destructive presence.

Drawing from the case study results, fandom members should be concerned with cultivating a more tolerant and fair community. The themes suggest that women are still regarded as second-tier community members and are often objectified. Yet the desire to speak out, fight back, and start a dialogue within these communities appears minimal. Many are apathetic or reticent, preferring not to disturb a place of enjoyment and happiness. Yet addressing misogyny within fandoms is important on a both a personal and societal level.

At the personal level, fans can and often do have deep emotional attachments to their favorite media figures (via phenomena like PSI, PSR, and narrative transportation), which is why it can be regarded as a happy place for many people. Sexism, harassment, and objectification invade a person's peace of mind.

On a societal level, fandoms potentially have the power to shape media and change culture. One major critique of convergence culture is that it does not venture into cultural aspects that enact political and social change (Hay and Couldry 2011). Jenkins et al. (2013) argued, in defense of convergence culture, that "[f]andoms seek to direct the attention of the media industries and, in the process, shape their decisions—a goal they pursue with varying degrees of success" (p. 166). Perhaps activism within fandom is a pathway to civic engagement. Recent research found a link between political speech within the *Harry Potter* fandom and increased civic engagement and mobilization (Kligler-Vilenchik 2015).

Fandoms can address the problem in a number of ways. First, women are, and should continue to become, more vocal members within their fandoms. And this should go beyond subcommunities that are female dominated or women-centric. In many ways, fandom activities like fan fiction are gendered spaces (Driscoll and Gregg 2011), but fan fiction and "ships" do not necessarily appeal to all women. By being more visible members of fandoms as a whole, women can better support one another to address trolling and hostile behavior. Moreover, male fandom members should speak up against aggressive and belittling behavior, and support female perspectives in fandom communities.

Second, fandom members should call upon leaders, including the producers, artists, and celebrities associated with their fandom, to start a dialogue about the persistent problems within their communities. Fandoms may not fully understand the power they have over the media and over their communities, yet they have a form of collective power by virtue of their allegiance to the community and connection via social media. Fandom members can not only voice concerns regarding canon and casting; they can also help shape media and communities that address misogyny, thereby influencing media creation and social conversation on a wider scale. As communities change and become more tolerant spaces, perhaps the corrosive and hostile aspects of social media (e.g., trolling) can change as well.

Note

1. This subsequently snowballed into the actor being trolled by people outside and indifferent to the movie and the fandom.

References

Braun, V., & Clarke, V. (2006). Using thematic analysis in psychology. *Qualitative Research in Psychology, 3*, 77–101.

Cohen, J. (2003). Parasocial breakups: Measuring individual differences in responses to the dissolution of parasocial relationships. *Mass Communication & Society, 6*(2), 191–202.

Cohen, J. (2004). Parasocial break-up from favorite television characters: The role of attachment styles and relationship intensity. *Journal of Social and Personal Relationships, 21*(2), 187–202. https://doi.org/10.1177/0265407504041374.

Cohen, J. (2009). Mediated relationships and media effects: Parasocial interaction and identification. In R. L. Nabi & M. B. Oliver (Eds.), *The SAGE handbook of media processes and effects* (pp. 223–236). Thousand Oaks: Sage.

Cohen, E. L. (2010). Expectancy violations in relationships with friends and media figures. *Communication Research Reports, 27*(2), 97–111. https://doi.org/10.1080/08824091003737836.

Condis, M. (2015). No homosexuals in Star Wars? BioWare, 'gamer' identity, and the politics of privilege in a convergence culture. *Convergence: The International Journal of Research into New Media Technologies, 21*, 198–212.

Derrick, J. L., Gabriel, S., & Hugenberg, K. (2009). Social surrogacy: How favored television programs provide the experience of belonging. *Journal of Experimental Social Psychology, 45*(2), 352–362. https://doi.org/10.1016/j.jesp.2008.12.003.

Driscoll, C., & Gregg, M. (2011). Convergence culture and the legacy of feminist cultural studies. *Cultural Studies, 25*, 566–584.

Geraghty, L. (2015). *Popular media cultures: Fans, audiences and paratexts.* Retrieved from http://www.eblib.com

Giles, D. C. (2002). Parasocial interaction: A review of the literature and a model for future research. *Media Psychology, 4*(3), 279–205. https://doi.org/10.1207/S1532785XMEP0403_04.

Grant, A., Guthrie, K., & Ball-Rokeach, S. (1991). Television shopping: A media system dependency perspective. *Communication Research, 18*(6), 773–798. https://doi.org/10.1177/009365091018006000.

Green, M. C., & Brock, T. C. (2000). The role of transportation in the persuasiveness of public narratives. *Journal of Personal and Social Psychology, 79*(5), 701–721.

Green, M. C., Brock, T. C., & Kaufman, G. E. (2004). Understanding media enjoyment: The role of transportation into narrative worlds. *Communication Theory, 14*, 311–327.

Hay, J., & Couldry, N. (2011). Rethinking convergence/culture: An introduction. *Cultural Studies, 25*, 473–486. https://doi.org/10.1080/09502386.2011.600527.

Hoffner, C. A., & Cohen, E. L. (2014). Portrayals of mental illness on the TV series *Monk*: Presumed influence and consequences of exposure. *Health Communication, 30*, 1046–1054.

Horton, D., & Wohl, R. R. (1956). Mass communication and parasocial interaction. *Psychiatry, 19*, 215–229.

Jenkins, H. (2006). *Convergence culture.* New York: New York University Press.

Jenkins, H., Ford, S., & Green, J. (2013). *Spreadable media: Creating value and meaning in a networked culture, Postmillennial Pop.* New York: New York University Press. Retrieved from http://www.ebrary.com.

Kligler-Vilenchik, N. (2015). From wizards and house-elves to real world issues: Political talk in fan spaces. *International Journal of Communication, 9*, 2027–2046.

Massanari, A. (2015, October 1–18). #Gamergate and the fappening: How Reddit's algorithm, governance, and culture support toxic technocultures. *New Media & Society*. Online First. doi:https://doi.org/10.1177/1461444815608807.

Perreault, G. P., & Vos, T. P. (2016, September). The GamerGate controversy and journalistic paradigm maintenance. *Journalism*. doi:https://doi.org/10.1177/1464884916670932.

Rubin, A. M., & Perse, E. M. (1987). Audience activity and soap opera involvement a uses and effects investigation. *Human Communication Research, 14*(2), 246–268. https://doi.org/10.1111/j.1468-2958.1987.tb00129.x.

Rubin, A. M., Perse, E. M., & Powell, R. A. (1985). Loneliness, parasocial interaction, and local television news viewing. *Human Communication Research, 12*(2), 155–180. https://doi.org/10.1111/j.1468-2958.1985.tb00071.x.

Schiappa, E., Gregg, P. B., & Hewes, D. E. (2005). The parasocial contact hypothesis. *Communication Monographs, 72*(1), 92–115. https://doi.org/10.1080/0363775052000342544.

Schiappa, E., Gregg, P. B., & Hewes, D. E. (2006). Can one TV show make a difference? *Will & Grace* and the parasocial contact hypothesis. *Journal of Homosexuality, 51*(4), 15–37. https://doi.org/10.1300/J082v51n04_02.

Schramm, H., & Hartmann, T. (2008). The PSI-process scales. A new measure to assess the intensity and breadth of parasocial processes. *Communications: The European Journal of Communication Research, 33*(4), 385–401. https://doi.org/10.1515/COMM.2008.025.

Slater, M. D., & Rouner, D. (2002). Entertainment-education and elaboration likelihood: Understanding the processing of narrative persuasion. *Communication Theory, 12*(2), 173–191. https://doi.org/10.1111/j.1468-2885.2002.tb00265.x.

Todd, C. (2015). GamerGate and resistance to the diversification of gaming. *Women Studies Journal, 29*, 64–67.

10

Misogyny in the 2016 U.S. Presidential Election

Dustin Harp

Much of United States and the rest of the world closely watched the 2016 presidential election, expecting to witness Democratic nominee Hillary Clinton make history in her bid to be the first woman president. In a turn of events disheartening for many who thought Clinton would win, the election was eventually won by the Republican candidate Donald Trump. While throughout the campaign numerous reasons arose to bolster an anti-Trump faction, this chapter concentrates on one especially troubling aspect of Trump and the campaign: the misogynistic behavior of the candidate and anti-Clinton voters. The attitudes and behavior of Trump and various citizens toward women, along with critics' interpretations and accusations of that behavior as misogynistic, played out in a contemporary environment of mainstream, partisan, and social media discourse alongside alternative voices and satire news programs.

One particular incident involving Trump and recorded vulgar comments about women marks a focus for this chapter, while other examples

D. Harp (✉)
Department of Communication, University of Texas at Arlington, Arlington, TX, USA

© The Author(s) 2018
J. R. Vickery, T. Everbach (eds.), *Mediating Misogyny*,
https://doi.org/10.1007/978-3-319-72917-6_10

serve to illustrate the pervasiveness of this attitude toward women. This moment in history offers a means for examining how misogyny functions in our cultural discourse and also how feminist ideologies counter this contempt for and prejudice toward women. Ideology, as understood and applied in this chapter, means "a set of beliefs and expressions that present, interpret, and evaluate the world in a way designed to organize, mobilize, and justify social and political action" (Fastiggi 2013, p. 328). Further, ideology is "a body of ideas characteristic of a particular social group" (Eagleton 1991, p. 1).

The focus of the chapter is to investigate the ways misogyny, which rests within a patriarchal ideology, emerged in public mediated discourse during the presidential campaign. It also examines how alternative feminist voices countered that conversation to provide a robust discussion about women, gender, power, and equality. Discourse serves as a central concept in the chapter, which in the context of this discussion is understood through cultural theorist Michael Foucault. Discourse at its simplest is written or spoken communication or debate. Foucault, however, offers a more complex understanding of the term, explaining that discourse describes ways of establishing knowledge, ways of thinking, and means for producing power (Foucault 1977). As defined by Foucault, discourse refers to "a form of power that circulates in the social field and can attach to strategies of domination as well as those of resistance" (Diamond and Quinby 1988, p. 185).

There are various examples of misogyny that occurred in discourse related to the presidential election (and that occur every day). This chapter examines several before focusing on one prominent example to illustrate the ways in which misogyny is both still allowed and excused in American culture. The chapter also explores how feminist ideologies counter and critique misogyny. The particular incident under extensive scrutiny in this chapter is the comments President Donald Trump made about women during a 2005 outtake of a television entertainment news program titled *Access Hollywood*. The conversation took place as part of a taping session with one of the show's co-hosts, Billy Bush, and it is presumed that Trump, then a reality television star, was unaware a microphone was recording at the time of his comments. The lewd conversation never aired until weeks before Election Day 2016.

This chapter examines these misogynistic comments made by Trump along with other incidents of misogynistic discourse during the campaign and the various discourses that excused this behavior toward women. However, rather than simply focus on the misogyny present in American culture, this chapter looks at how alternative voices (or ideologies) in the mediated public sphere—from mainstream media to satire and social media—countered this misogyny and prompted a dialogue about important issues related to women, gender, and power. (For an analysis of how women who supported Hillary Clinton in 2016 fought against misogyny on social media, please see Chap. 19.)

Mediated Public Spheres

The public sphere is a concept typically understood within the framework of Jurgen Habermas' writings. The simple idea behind the public sphere is that it is a public space where a "society engages in critical public debate," though Habermas was originally talking about eighteenth-century bourgeois society (Habermas 1989, p. 52). The original conceptualization of Habermas' public sphere has been criticized for the narrow way it understood society, since women and other marginalized groups were excluded from this public debate. Feminist theorist Nancy Fraser is among numerous scholars who have updated and expanded on the original concept. Fraser argued that the bourgeois public sphere idealized through Habermas did not open up the political realm to everyone, and instead insured political power of the few through rule by the majority's ideology. Among Fraser's contribution to the concept is her notion of the existence of multiple public spheres. She termed the concept "subaltern counterpublics" and argued that marginalized groups formed their own public spheres (Fraser 1991). She explained these are "parallel discursive arenas where members of subordinated social groups invent and circulate counterdiscourses to formulate oppositional interpretations of their identities, interests, and needs" (Fraser 1991, p. 123). This concept is important for understanding the analysis within this chapter as it considers the discourse of two competing ideological perspectives—patriarchy and feminism—as they exist in the broader mediated cultural discourse.

Within the context of these theories of the public sphere, patriarchal and feminist discourses are engaged in critical debate, formulating oppositional interpretations in a struggle to define women, position them properly, and establish their role in the world.

When formulating these theoretical perspectives, both Habermas and Fraser conceptualized the public sphere in spatial terms. However, Habermas (1989b) did argue that the public sphere needed "specific means for transmitting information and influencing those who receive it" (p. 136). In this sense, he illustrated how newspapers were of particular importance to the public sphere. More recent theorists of the public sphere have considered mediated or virtual public spheres. John Thompson (1995) is among those theorists to criticize the original notion of the public sphere for its focus on face-to-face interactions. Thompson argued that "mediated publicness" is a characteristic of modern society. The main characteristics of this newly conceptualized public sphere include that it is despatialized (as there is a rupture of time and space), it is nondialogical (or unidirectional), and there is a wider and more diverse audience. "Mediated publicness" offers an important addendum for reconceptualizing the public sphere in a contemporary media environment where along with newspapers and traditional broadcast, social media forms an important part of mediated discourse. The Pew Research Center reported 70% Americans use social media to connect with one another (Pew 2017). As Thompson (1995) explained, "the development of communication media provides a means by which many people can gather information about a few and, at the same time, a few can appear before the many" (p. 134).

With these theoretical perspectives forming a framework, I define the mediated public sphere as one that encompasses the expansive contemporary media environment—from television to print and web-based discourse—as a virtual space for public deliberation. Within this framework, I also understand this mediated public sphere to be made up of various subaltern counterpublics. It is within this broad and ubiquitous mediated sphere that patriarchal and feminist ideologies form a discourse about women, proper gender roles and identities, and power. Through an exploration of incidents of misogynistic discourse during the 2016 presidential election, this analysis investigates how these competing ideologies struggle for meaning in the mediated public sphere. Specifically, the research asks what major themes about gender emerged in the discourse and what do these say about broader gender issues within our culture?

Methodological Approach

The methodological approach for this study is a discourse analysis from a feminist and cultural studies perspective. It allows a researcher to take into account the broad discussion in media, including but not limited to mainstream news, social media, and satire. Discourse analysis is a form of textual analysis "that, beyond the manifest content of media, focuses on the underlying ideological and cultural assumptions of the text" (Fürsich 2009, p. 240). The method involves a deep engagement with texts, starting with what Stuart Hall (1975) called "the long preliminary soak" (p. 15) and uses semiotic, narrative, thematic, or rhetorical approaches to textual analysis. Rather than randomly select texts for analysis (as is common in quantitative content analysis), researchers conducting textual analysis often strategically select and present texts that illustrate the overall argument (Fürsich 2009). As the intention of this research is to first illustrate *how* and not how often or how much misogynistic discourse occurred during the election and second to illustrate how ideological struggles related to gender, power, and proper roles occurred, this method of strategic selection fits the goals of the research well. Throughout the election, I scanned and collected mediated discourse for ways gender emerged in the public conversation. I was methodical in my gathering of this data, which is part of a larger project. Within the context of this data collection, I paid particular attention to moments when misogyny appeared in the discourse. Once I encountered a mediated moment of interest, I would then systematically search for related mediated discourse. For example, when news of the lewd Trump tape first broke, I gathered stories from various news and media outlets, via Google searches and also by following various social media outlets. I combed through social media sites (including searching Twitter hashtags that became popular in the wake of the news), and viewed various satire broadcasts. I purposefully gathered stories from the most popular mainstream news media sites, as well as from known alternative (and partisan) news sites, such as Jezebel and Breitbart. I also conducted Google News Archive searches for the dates October 7–15, 2016 using the search term "Trump Tape" and an additional search of the news archive for the same dates using the search term "Trump Assault," since the word "assault" quickly became tied to the conversation. These various searches rendered thousands of texts for analysis. To illustrate the numbers of results on the topic: Google News Archive searches for just one date and one of these search terms rendered as many as 22,000 results in less than a minute. While it was impossible to read and analyze every text in our mediated world that addressed the Trump tape, I gathered and analyzed texts until my analysis reached a saturation point. Saturation in qualitative research is the point in a researcher's examination of data when more data will not lead to new information related to the research question. In other words, it occurs when a researcher stops discovering new findings (Fusch and Ness 2015).

The texts analyzed were vast and absolutely not exhaustive of the mediated texts that mention, discuss, or debate the issue. The point was to capture and highlight the broad discourses throughout the election related to misogyny and the incident with then presidential candidate Donald Trump and to identify major themes within this discourse. Through this method, the research offers an illustration of the various and most prominent perspectives regarding misogynistic mediated discourse during the election. The chapter illustrates ways in which misogyny persisted, was talked about, debated, and rebuked in mass media and on social media platforms.

T-Shirts, Signs, BernieBros and Ageist Misogyny

Trump supporters throughout the election illustrated their misogyny literally, flaunting T-shirts and signs that clearly spelled out their contempt for Hillary Clinton, and for women in general. On October 12, 2016, an article in The Cut noted some of "the most misogynistic gear spotted at

Trump rallies" (Landsbaum 2016). The article shows two young Florida men holding signs that read, "Don't be a pussy Vote for Trump." In this case, the word pussy stands in as a means to feminize any person who does not vote for Trump. This term is especially used to describe men who are not deemed masculine enough. In this sense to be feminine is negative. Misogyny is also on full display on a political button that read "Life's a Bitch Don't vote for one" and displayed a photo of Hillary Clinton. This slogan naming Clinton a bitch is one of a few to use the term in association with Clinton, including the popular "Trump that Bitch." Text accompanying another image disturbingly noted that the man wearing a T-shirt that read "She's a cunt, vote for Trump" attended the rally with his wife and three children. Another sign displayed outside of a rally in Florida simply stated, "Trump vs Tramp." Each of these slogans used derogatory gender terms—bitch, cunt, and tramp—to refer to Clinton. These gendered words are typically used to describe women who are strong, uncompromising, angry, or uninterested in pleasing men.

Another way in which misogyny appears in talk about Clinton is in relation to Monica Lewinsky (a White House intern who had a sexual relationship with President Bill Clinton). For example, a high school boy wore a T-shirt to a rally that on the front read "Hillary Sucks but not like Monica" (a crude reference to oral sex) and on the back said, "Trump that Bitch" (Landsbaum 2016). A sign outside of a Trump rally in Cincinnati noted "If Hillary won she'd sit at the same desk Monica sat under!" again, yet more subtly, referencing oral sex. While most of these T-shirts seemed to be worn by men, women are also able to display misogyny, as evidenced by the woman at a rally in Green Bay who wore a shirt stating, "Hillary couldn't satisfy her husband can't satisfy us." In each of these slogans Clinton's intimacy with her husband becomes a focus and means for discrediting her ability as a politician. Perhaps displaying the most hate for Clinton was the man standing in an undisclosed location who proudly displayed a T-shirt that read, "I wish Hillary had married OJ"—a reference to the former football star who was acquitted of murdering his ex-wife in 1995. According to the photographer, that man clarified that he wished Clinton was dead (Landsbaum 2016). Together these clear signs of misogyny offer a disturbing tale of hatred toward women in American culture. And while certainly within the public discourse condemnation of these slogans and signs existed, they clearly illustrate that misogyny is alive and well in the United States.

Misogynistic behavior during the election, however, was not confined to Trump supporters. In October 2015, *The Atlantic*'s Robinson Meyer coined the term BernieBro to describe a particular faction of Bernie Sanders supporters—Sanders, a self-proclaimed socialist, fought against Clinton for the Democratic nomination (Meyer 2015). In a snarky column, Meyer described this type of Sanders supporter: white, male, social media and Internet savvy, well educated, and financially secure. As the campaign progressed, another attribute became attached to the BernieBro moniker—sexism and hostility in the form of misogyny—as the BernieBros morphed into a social media mob. Women reporters, campaign workers, and supporters of Clinton, along with Clinton herself, were repeatedly attacked using many of the same vulgar and sexist terms Trump supporters had brandished on their signs and T-shirts. The harassment became so frequent and severe that the Sanders campaign actually asked their supporters to "be respectful when people disagree with you" (Rothkopf 2016). A *Newsweek* journalist described the climate this way: "Violence. Death threats. Vile, misogynistic names screamed at women. Rage. Hatred. Menacing, anonymous phone calls to homes and offices. Public officials whisked offstage by security agents frightened of the growing mob" (Eichenwald 2016).

The focus paid to Clinton's age illustrated another, if more subtle, means in which misogyny surfaced during the elections. As one *The Washington Post* columnist noted, "A woman her age is supposed to be invisible. But Hillary Clinton, who is 68, refuses to disappear—and there is no shortage of people who despise her for it" (Dvorak 2016). Ageist misogyny has a long history in American culture, as youthful women are valued, albeit primarily as objects of masculine desire, and older women are criticized for and devalued because of their age. An illustration of this ageist misogyny is seen in another *The Washington Post* story that quotes a Trump supporter calling Clinton a "crotchety old hag" (Johnson 2016). This criticism is problematic because rather than focus on Clinton's work as a politician, the focus is on her age. Much was made throughout the election of her age and in conjunction her weak constitution—including many conspiracy theories about her precarious health—even though both Trump and Sanders are older than Clinton.

Trump Grabs the Spotlight

While evidence of misogyny crept into our public discourse throughout the presidential campaign, it reached a crescendo on October 7, 2016, just weeks before the election ended, when *The Washington Post* obtained and released an audiotape and video of Trump talking about grabbing women by the "pussy" and trying to "fuck" a married woman. The full transcript includes the following lines from Trump:

> I moved on her like a bitch. But I couldn't get there. And she was married. Then all of a sudden I see her, she's now got the big phony tits and everything. She's totally changed her look.
>
> You know, I'm automatically attracted to beautiful—I just start kissing them. It's like a magnet. Just kiss. I don't even wait. And when you're a star, they let you do it. You can do anything.
>
> Grab 'em by the pussy. You can do anything. ("Transcript: Donald Trump's Taped Comments" 2016)

Mainstream news quickly covered the leaked tape, and before long, the vulgar comments by Trump were a primary part of the public discourse, being addressed not only in various news outlets, but also on late-night talk shows and satire programs, and throughout social media. The tape became public on a Friday and saturated news and social media throughout the weekend and in the weeks following. It was taken up not just by the news, but by various media platforms, including satire and comedy. For example, *Saturday Night Live*, a long-standing late-night live sketch comedy television show that parodies contemporary culture and politics, opened its show by mocking Trump's apology. That Sunday, Trump and Hillary Clinton faced off in their second televised presidential candidate debate, where Trump's comments were addressed as well by both the moderator of the debate and Clinton.

Very quickly, three dominant narratives about Trump's comments on the tape emerged—two of which were intertwined and in opposition to the third. One was structured by Trump's assertion, while expressing remorse, that his words were just "locker room talk." In a released statement on the same day as the story about the leaked tape, as reported in *USA Today*, Trump explained, "'This was locker room banter, a private conversation that took place many years ago,' the GOP presidential nominee says. 'Bill Clinton has said far worse to me on the golf course—not even close. I apologize if anyone was offended'" (Cooper and Schouten 2016). This released statement—and the Trump campaign—created the "locker room talk" framing of the leaked conversation, which then replayed throughout the mediated public sphere. *ABC News* published the story under the headline "Trump brags about groping women in vulgar remarks caught on tape, chalks it up to 'locker room banter'" (Keneally 2016). By Saturday morning, Trump had also released a recorded apology in which he continued to downplay his behavior as normal—saying it was what men do when they are together in spaces free from women's ears. This framing continued from within the campaign and was reported throughout the media. For example, reports surfaced of Trump's son, Eric Trump, on the campaign trail Monday excusing his father's conversation with the "locker room talk" narrative. During a broadcast interview with CNN's Anderson Cooper ten days after the release of the original tape, Melania Trump, Donald Trump's wife, reinforced this narrative. Specifically, she said, her husband was "egged on" by Bush "to say dirty and bad stuff" into "boy talk" (Bradner 2016). Further, she told Cooper, "I heard many different stuff—boys talk. The boys, the way they talk when they grow up and they want to sometimes show each other, 'Oh, this and that' and talking about the girls" ("Melania Trump entire CNN interview" 2016).

While Trump, his family, and people from the campaign told the story of "locker room talk," that justification was not prominent in mainstream news organization's opinion sections. Rather, this explanation was primarily found in news stories attached to quotes from people within or associated with the campaign. In other words, few reporters or media personalities supported this narrative. A few media professionals, however, defended Trump's "locker room talk" explanation. For example, evangelical host Pat Robertson said on the *700 Club* that Trump was "just trying to look macho" (Edwards 2016a). On CNN, Corey Lewandowski (a political commentator for One America News Network and Fox News Channel and former CNN political commentator) told his "co-workers, 'That's what is said in a locker room. Guys, don't kid yourself'" (Edwards 2016b). Senator Jeff Sessions, a Republican from Alabama, also made news and further reinforced Trump's perspective when he circulated this same narrative, explaining that Trump apologized for his "very improper language" but that it was not describing sexual assault (Kirkland 2016).

Throughout social media and at Trump's rallies that received news coverage, this narrative of "locker room talk" and the notion that the actions of assertive or aggressive men can be explained away with the "boys will be boys" narrative persisted. Unsurprising to many, Twitter hashtags related to the Trump tape comments appeared minutes after the news broke. One particularly prominent hashtag, #GrabHerByThePussy, illustrates how social media allows citizens (and not just media professionals) to enter into the conversation. Under the hashtag (and throughout social media outlets more generally) people were offered a means for reinforcing the "locker room talk" trope. For example, GingerSnap @ RedheadAndRight tweeted, "Tonight millions of neutered, beta-males are Googling what is the definition of #grabherbythepussy. #TrumpTape" (GingerSnap 2016). In this tweet the writer refers to a popular culture narrative of de-masculinized men who are "betas" in opposition to "alpha" men—tough and aggressive men. This Tweet reinforces the myth that there is one true form of masculinity, hyper-masculinity where "boys will be boys."

The Daily Show, a late night comedy show, aired a segment just days after the tape was leaked in which Jordan Klepper, playing the part of a news reporter, asked Trump supporters at a Trump rally in Pennsylvania what they thought of his "locker room talk" (*The Daily Show* 2016). Because of the nature of media in contemporary society, particular stories and clips from one media outlet may be covered by various other media outlets, creating a kind of domino effect in terms of the numbers (and types) of audience members who see the original content. This particular segment received wide media coverage and garnered a much larger audience than simply those who watch *The Daily Show*. For example, this clip was shared via social media while also being written about in publications including *The Huffington Post*. In the clip real people offer sincere answers to Klepper's questions. One man says "You know what, so what he wants to grab pussy. I want to grab pussy. I wish I could grab as much pussy as he has" while another man reacts to Trump's vulgar comments by saying "I think it's just locker room talk. Guys in a bar talk that way when they see a pretty girl." A couple of women Klepper talks to also concur that what we hear on the so-called Trump tape is just how men talk, one explaining "that what boys do." Again, these are real people offering sincere answers and not scripted answers for the show. While *The Daily Show* is a comedy and the segment is meant to mock the Trump supporters, the piece also serves to reinforce Trump's original framing of the incident in the mediated public sphere and illustrates that he and members of his campaign staff are not alone in their thinking.

The language and rationalization for Trump's vulgar comments about women relies on a common trope about men that constructs and reinforces gender stereotypes. The phrase "locker room talk" represents an idea that there is a particular and acceptable way that men talk and boast about women when they are together free from women; it is code for "boys will be boys." In this case Trump and his campaign explained the crude talk as a natural and normal way for boys/men to talk about girls/women. The narrative also suggests all men behave this particular way and that it is an accepted and understood marker of masculinity.

As quickly as people consumed the news, two additional prominent narratives surfaced about the leaked Trump tape. One of the alternative discourses framing and explaining Trump's words asserted that his comments described sexual assault. As Vox.com reported just three days after the tape became public: "Let's be clear: 'Sexual assault' is absolutely the right way to describe what Trump says on those tapes. It's possible that Trump was boasting to Billy Bush in 2005 about something that didn't happen, but when Trump claims he 'can do anything' to women because he's a star, including 'grab 'em by the pussy,' he is describing sexual assault. That is what you call it when someone grabs a woman and touches her genitals without her consent" (Crockett 2016). This narrative swiftly took hold in the mediated public sphere, with commentary in mainstream news outlets, feminist publications, and television programs, as well as in satire and comedy. In an article titled "Trump's biggest debate lie was calling sexual assault 'locker room talk,'" in the *Chicago Tribune* after the second debate between the two candidates, one writer said "talking about sexually assaulting women is not locker room talk," (Huppke 2016). This framing of the Trump comments became particularly prominent in the media sphere and could be found in news, opinion, and entertainment mainstream and alternative media as well as social media.

Resistance to Trump's narrative of "locker room talk," which became repeated throughout media, took on another form besides the one likening his comments to sexual assault. The other dominant narrative within this framework, and closely aligned with the sexual assault discussion, critiqued Trump's notion of what men talk about in locker rooms. For example, within only days of the leaked tape, a popular animated television show airing on Sunday nights, *Family Guy*, referenced and mocked Trump's "locker room talk" explanation. In the television show, one of the characters, Peter, is on the now-infamous bus with Trump and Billy Bush. As explained in *The Daily Beast,* "Peter suggests some 'locker room talk,' but when Trump starts talking about 'moving on' women, he responds, 'Whoa, whoa, whoa, that's not 'locker room talk.' I meant like 'good play,' 'good pass,' like that kind of thing" (Wilstein 2016). The author writing about this episode for *The Daily Beast* started his article by explaining, "Even Peter Griffin knows that wasn't 'locker room talk.'" A 1 minute and 32 second CNN story posted on Facebook on October 18 featured six teen boys who had posted a picture of themselves in a locker room wearing "Wild Feminist" T-shirts received more than 3.5 million Facebook likes and nearly 30,000 shares. In the video, one of the teens said that in the aftermath of Trump's comments about locker room talk they posted the picture to bring awareness to the fact that women deserve the same rights as men. Various other athletes, including many professionals, took to social media to obliterate the idea that locker room talk included talking about women in the manner Trump did on the leaked tape. For example, Houston Astros pitcher Collin McHugh posted the following on his Instagram account:

> I feel the need to comment on the language that Donald Trump classified the other day as 'locker room talk,' given my daily exposure to it. Have I

heard comments like Trump's (i.e. sexist, disrespectful, crude, sexually aggressive, egotistical, etc.) in a clubhouse? Yes. But I've also heard some of those same comments other places. Cafes, planes, the subway, walking down the street and even at the dinner table. To generalize his hateful language as 'locker room talk' is incredibly offensive to me and the men I share a locker room with every day for 8 months a year. Men of conscience and integrity, who would never be caught dead talking about women in that way. You want to know what 'locker room talk' sounds like from my first hand perspective? Baseball talk. Swinging, pitching, home runs, double plays, shifts. The rush of victory and the frustration of defeat. Family talk. Nap schedules for our kids. Loneliness of being on the road so much. Off-season family vacations…. (Young 2016)

This discourse explaining how men talk in locker rooms opened up a counternarrative to the traditional (patriarchal) "boys will be boys" culture of masculine aggression and power over women. In doing this, it allowed for another model of masculinity in juxtaposition to the hyper-masculine and aggressive man. Men took up this alternative narrative, as they were able to speak from experiences in locker rooms. More women participated in the discourse that described Trump's comments as a description of sexual assault. This discursive construction of the event illustrated a means by which a feminist perspective countered a traditional patriarchal understanding of gender roles and relations and placed the lewd comments within the context of a culture of rape and violence against women. As Samantha Bee explained on *Full Frontal with Samantha Bee*, which aired on the Monday after the release of the tapes, Trump's comment "wasn't just lewd remarks, Trump was literally explaining a time tested strategy for sexual assault" (Lutkin 2016). Also in the wake of the Trump tape, on October 10, the *Boston Globe* published an opinion piece by Anita Hill titled, "What we can still learn from sexual harassment" in which she writes "… the fact that large swaths of Americans believe this to be even vaguely defensible is no different than what many women recount in their claims of sexual harassment and in some cases worse," (Hill 2016).

Perhaps most powerful in all of the public mediated discourse in response to Trump's excuse of "locker room talk" that renamed it sexual harassment was the #NotOkay Twitter hashtag. This began when Canadian writer Kelly Oxford Tweeted "Women: tweet me your first assaults. they aren't just stats. I'll go first: Old man on city bus grabs my 'pussy' and smiles at me, I'm 12" (Domonoske 2016). Oxford reported, "that over the course of a single evening, a million women had responded to her call-out." The next day, on October 8, she tweeted "women have tweeted me sexual assault stories for 14 hours straight. Minimum 50 per minute. harrowing. do not ignore. #notokay" (Domonoske 2016). Other women then shared their stories of sexual assault with the hashtag #notokay. The stories can be viewed on Oxford's Twitter timeline and include a litany of stories about sexual abuse and rape. Others shared in alternative public spaces. For example, on *Medium*, one woman posted an essay titled "Tales of Rape Culture: My story, 37 and just realized I was raped nearly two decades ago" (Borodin 2016). In the piece, the author writes, "I never grew up thinking I would not be believed... I simply grew up, like the majority of women, in a culture so toxic even smart, educated outspoken women are conditioned to just accept that 'boys will be boys.'" She then goes on to name the many incidents of sexual harassment in her life. This response to the Trump tape is significant for two reasons. First, it illustrates how alternative spaces (subaltern counter publics in the words of Fraser) are built within the broader mediated public sphere (mediated publicness). Second, it offers an illustration of how a competing ideology—in this case a feminist understanding of rape culture in opposition to a "boys will be boys/locker room talk" mentality that sits firmly within patriarchy—takes up space and offers alternative ways to understand the world.

Conclusion and Solution

As the chapter illustrates, there are many examples of misogyny during the 2016 presidential election, offering an argument for how Clinton's gender worked against her. The chapter, however, also offers examples of struggles against misogyny in U.S. culture. The varied mediated discourse in reaction to Trump's vulgar comments in which he alternatively participated in "locker room talk" or offered a strategy for sexual assault, illustrates how a struggle for meaning plays out in a mediated public sphere. Theories of the public sphere offer ways to think about how different groups and ideologies might come together to discuss issues important to the lives of citizens. As mediated publicness explains, with a contemporary media society, the conversations are rarely face-to-face but rather despatialized, meaning they do not occur in one space and at one time. They are also not unidirectional, so that rather than news media delivering news to an audience, citizens join in and affect the conversation, as did Oxford when she asked women to tell her their stories about sexual harassment on Twitter. Finally, there are wider and more diverse audiences in our contemporary mediated society.

Beyond illustrating how public discourse occurs in contemporary mediated spaces, this chapter demonstrates how struggles over our understanding of gender and appropriate roles and behaviors are still playing out in American society. What is evident with the analysis of this misogynistic discourse of Donald Trump is that a struggle between traditional gender norms—patriarchy and men's dominance over women and their bodies—is central to U.S. cultural discussion. While the chapter discusses many ways misogyny surfaced during the elections, it focuses on one incident to illustrate the public discursive struggle against misogyny. In doing so, the example represents a broader story about masculinity and misogyny and its presence in contemporary U.S. culture. What then do I say about misogynistic words and behavior throughout the election, contemporary American culture, gender roles, and media discourse? The unfortunate news is that a man who speaks of women as Trump has (as there are many instances where Trump has been called out for his treatment of women) can still in the year 2016 be elected president. The more encouraging news is that when misogynistic behavior and comments are brought into the mediated public sphere, there are spaces for alternative (feminist) re-articulations of the event. With Trump's comments came a lively and important cultural discussion about sexual assault, misogyny, and men's appropriate ways of being. As this chapter illustrates, in contemporary U.S. society, a broad array of voices is allowed the ability to change how we define and understand the world around us. Within this context it is essential that citizens continue to participate in mediated public discourse in order to end hypermasculinity and misogyny. One last directive: vote.

References

Borodin, T. (2016, October 12). Tales of rape culture: My story, 37 and just realized I was raped nearly two decades ago. *Medium*. Retrieved from https://medium.com/@taliaborodin/tales-of-rape-culture-my-story-37-and-just-realized-i-was-raped-nearly-two-decades-ago-dee582add4bb#.25a80zhur

Bradner, E. (2016, October 18). Melania Trump: Donald Trump was 'egged on' into 'boy talk.' CNN. Retrieved from http://www.cnn.com/2016/10/17/politics/melania-trump-interview/

Cooper, A., & Schouten, F. (2016, October 7). Trump apologizes for video bragging about groping women. *USA Today*. Retrieved from http://www.usatoday.com/story/news/politics/onpolitics/2016/10/07/trump-washington-post-women-billy-bush-video/91743992/

Crockett, E. (2016, October 10). Trump's campaign manager: Please stop calling Trump's 'pussy' comments 'sexual assault.' *Vox*. Retrieved from http://www.vox.com/2016/10/10/13223722/trump-debate-kellyanne-conway-tapes-pussy-sexual-assault

Diamond, I., & Quinby, L. (Eds.). (1988). *Feminism and Foucault: Reflections on resistance*. Boston: Northeastern University Press.

Domonoske, C. (2016, October 11). One tweet unleashes a torrent of stories of sexual assault. National Public Radio. Retrieved from http://www.npr.org/sections/thetwo-way/2016/10/11/497530709/one-tweet-unleashes-a-torrent-of-stories-of-sexual-assault

Dvorak, P. (2016, October 6). Hillary Clinton is a 68-year-old woman. And plenty of people hate her for it. *The Washington Post*. Retrieved from https://www.washingtonpost.com/local/hillary-clinton-is-a-68-year-old-woman-and-plenty-of-people-hate-her-for-it/2016/10/06/fac46ee8-8bd9-11e6-bf8a-3d26847eeed4_story.html?utm_term=.a5dbcff00fa4

Eagleton, T. (1991). *Ideology*. London: Verso.

Edwards, D. (2016a, October 10). Pat Roberston: It's 'macho' for trump to grab women 'by the p*ssy' without permission. *RawStory*. Retrieved from http://www.rawstory.com/2016/10/pat-robertson-its-macho-for-trump-to-grab-women-by-the-pssy-without-permission/

Edwards, S. (2016b, October 12). Men are talking. *Jezebel*. Retrieved from http://jezebel.com/men-are-talking-1787630555

Eichenwald, K. (2016, May 18). Get control, senator Sanders, or get out. *Newsweek*. Retrieved from http://www.newsweek.com/2016/06/03/bernie-sanders-get-control-get-out-race-461195.html

Fastiggi, Robert L. (Ed.). (2013). Ideology. In *New Catholic encyclopedia supplement 2012–2013: Ethics and philosophy* (pp. 328–330). Farmington Hills: Gale.

Foucault, M. (1977). *Discipline and punishment*. New York: Pantheon.

Fraser, N. (1991). Rethinking the public sphere: A contribution to the critique of actually existing democracy. In C. Calhoun (Ed.), *Habermas and the public sphere* (pp. 109–142). Cambridge, MA: MIT Press.

Fürsich, E. (2009). In defense of textual analysis: Restoring a challenged method for journalism and media studies. *Journalism Studies*, 10(2), 238–252.

Fusch, P. I., & Ness, L. R. (2015). Are we there yet? Data saturation in qualitative research. *The Qualitative Report, 20*(9), 1408–1416. Retrieved from http://nsuworks.nova.edu/cgi/viewcontent.cgi?article=2281&context=tqr.

GingerSnap. @RedheadAndRight. (2016, October 7). Tonight millions of neutered, beta-males are Googling what is the definition of #grabherbythepussy. *#TrumpTape*. Retrieved from https://twitter.com/RedheadAndRight

Habermas, J. (1989). *The structural transformation of the public sphere: An inquiry into a category of bourgeois society*. Cambridge, MA: MIT Press.

Habermas, J. (1989b). The public sphere: An encyclopedia article. In S. E. Bronner & D. Kellner (Eds.), *Critical theory and society: A reader* (pp. 136–142). New York: Routledge.

Hill, A. (2016, October 11). What we can still learn from sexual harassment. *Boston Globe*. Retrieved from http://www.bostonglobe.com/opinion/2016/10/10/what-can-still-learn-from-sexual-harassment/jCF5rxYbFMgE3bOKR984pI/story.html

Huppke, R. (2016, October 9). Trump's biggest debate lie was calling sexual assault 'locker room talk.' *Chicago Tribune*. Retrieved from http://www.chicagotribune.com/news/opinion/huppke/ct-debate-trump-clinton-locker-room-huppke-20161009-column.html

Johnson, J. (2016, October 4). As Clinton gains, trump supporters seem to hate her more than ever. *The Washington Times*. Retrieved from https://www.washingtonpost.com/politics/as-clinton-gains-trump-supporters-seem-to-hate-her-more-than-ever/2016/10/04/07470fd6-871b-11e6-92c2-14b64f3d453f_story.html?tid=a_inl&utm_term=.5ebad71b7856

Keneally, M. (2016, October 7). Trump brags about groping women in vulgar remarks caught on tape, chalks it up to 'locker room banter.' ABC News.

Retrieved from http://abcnews.go.com/Politics/trump-caught-tape-vulgar-language-women/story?id=42655874

Kirkland, A. (2016, October 10). GOP senator on trump tape: What he's describing is not sexual assault. *Talking Points Memo*. Retrieved from http://talkingpointsmemo.com/livewire/senator-jeff-sessions-trump-grabbing-women-not-sexual-assault?utm_content=buffer9a2eb&utm_medium=social&utm_source=twitter.com&utm_campaign=buffer

Landsbaum, C. (2016, October 12). The most misogynistic gear spotted at trump rallies. *The Cut*. Retrieved from https://www.thecut.com/2016/10/the-most-misogynistic-things-people-wore-to-trump-rallies.html

Lutkin, A. (2016, October 11). Sam Bee's take on Pussygate was worth the wait. *Jezebel*. Retrieved from http://jezebel.com/sam-bees-take-on-pussygate-was-worth-the-wait-1787660364

Melania Trump entire CNN interview (Part 1). (2016). CNN. Retrieved from http://cnn.com

Meyer, R. (2015, October 17). Here comes the Berniebro. *The Atlantic*. Retrieved from https://www.theatlantic.com/politics/archive/2015/10/here-comes-the-berniebro-bernie-sanders/411070/

Pew Research Center. (2017). Retrieved from http://www.pewinternet.org/fact-sheet/social-media/

Rothkopf, J. (2016, January 29). Bernie Sanders' campaign is concerned about the "BernieBro," as they maybe should be. *The Slot*. Retrieved from http://theslot.jezebel.com/bernie-sanders-campaign-is-concerned-about-the-berniebr-1755911898

The Daily Show. (2016, October 14). Jordan Klepper fingers the pulse – Donald Trump's locker room talk. Retrieved from https://www.youtube.com/watch?v=Ih2Nn9VB2Xk

Thompson, J. B. (1995). *The media and the modernity: A social theory of the media*. Cambridge: Polity Press.

Transcript: Donald Trump's taped comments about women. (2016, October 7). *The New York Times*. Retrieved from http://www.nytimes.com

Wilstein, M. (2016, October 15). 'Family guy' mocks the infamous trump tape: 'That's not locker room talk.' *The Daily Beast*. Retrieved from http://www.thedailybeast.com/articles/2016/10/16/family-guy-mocks-the-infamous-trump-tape-that-s-not-locker-room-talk.html

Young, M. (2016, October 10). Collin McHugh explains what Astros' 'locker room talk' is like. *Houston Chronicle*. Retrieved from http://www.chron.com/sports/astros/article/Collin-McHugh-Astros-locker-room-talk-Donald-Trump-9960977.php?cmpid=twitter-desktop

11

Technology-Based Abuse: Intimate Partner Violence and the Use of Information Communication Technologies

Megan Lindsay Brown, Lauren A. Reed, and Jill Theresa Messing

Over the past 15 years, information communication technologies (ICTs) such as mobile phones, smart phones, laptop computers, and tablets have become commonplace. The majority of US adults utilize ICTs on a daily basis for connecting with others, gathering information, and organizing their daily lives (Fox and Rainie 2014). ICTs can have both positive and negative impacts on social relationships; in the case of intimate partnerships, research has begun to explore how ICTs may act as a context and as tools for abusive relationship behaviors. Intimate partner violence (IPV) is a significant problem for women in the United States, with more than one in three women reporting some form of victimization by a partner and 24.3% reporting experiences of severe physical violence (Black et al. 2011). Women who are severely abused are more likely to experience poor health and mental health outcomes and to be killed by their intimate partner (Campbell et al. 2003). Perpetrators of IPV can use

M. L. Brown (✉) • L. A. Reed • J. T. Messing
School of Social Work, Arizona State University, Phoenix, AZ, USA

© The Author(s) 2018
J. R. Vickery, T. Everbach (eds.), *Mediating Misogyny*,
https://doi.org/10.1007/978-3-319-72917-6_11

209

technology to further terrorize victim-survivors through harassment, stalking, and monitoring (Southworth et al. 2007).

Research on IPV, however, has not kept pace with the rapidly expanding culture of technology. Currently, the research literature has focused on how online and technology-based abuse experiences affect adolescents, young adults, and college students. Thus far, the literature suggests that the ubiquity of ICTs may invite abusive behaviors (such as monitoring, controlling, and stalking) in otherwise healthy relationships (Finn 2004; Reyns et al. 2010; Lindsay et al. 2013; Lyndon et al. 2011). Research specifically examining the impact of technology use among women who have identified as being in an abusive relationship is scant (Belknap et al. 2011; Dimond et al. 2011; Eden et al. 2015; Finn and Atkinson 2009). This chapter will review the limited, but emerging research on technology-based abuse among adults and suggest ways in which ICTs can be used as a tool of abuse or, alternatively, can be accessed as a means of support for those experiencing intimate partner violence.

To better understand the current gap in this literature, the following discussion will explore how research has described technology-based abuse experienced by women who identify as IPV victims or survivors (i.e., *victim-survivors*). We use a feminist approach which provides necessary context about IPV victim-survivors as a unique population and attends to women's' and girls' online victimization as a component of a larger culture of gender-based violence (Campbell and Runyan 1998; Rennison and Welchans 2000; McCue 2008; Reed et al. 2010). Due to the lack of research on adult samples, this discussion will draw on research studies about youth, dating abuse, and technology in order to better understand the parallel negative impacts that may exist for adult IPV victim-survivors experiencing technology-based abuse. Four specific forms of online abuses will be described—monitoring, cyberstalking, harassment, and humiliation. Online abuse may also affect women's experiences of physical violence and homicide risk; however, there is limited research focused on the role of mediated communications in exacerbating or mitigating risk and offline violence in relationships involving IPV.

A Gender-Based Framework for Technology-Based Abuse

Feminist researchers emphasize the power and social status afforded to men that creates an inequitable situation for women; in heterosexual intimate relationships, men exploit this power in order to perpetuate violence toward their female partners (Dobash and Dobash 1979). Contemporary theorists point to the need to create more fluid understandings of gender so as not to exclude violence among couples in the LGBT community, or minimize the perpetration of violence toward males (Hunnicutt 2009). Yet feminist scholars maintain that the social performances socialized around heterosexual relationship scripts and traditional forms of authority underlie the power and control dynamics central to intimate partner violence (Johnson 2008; Hunnicutt 2009).

Although some research describe equal rates of IPV perpetration by women and men, or posit that women more often perpetrate some forms of IPV, feminist scholars emphasize the importance of looking at the context and consequences around IPV before concluding that there is gender symmetry (see Kimmel 2002 for a review). A more recent review concluded that IPV is more often perpetrated by men than women, citing studies of arrest reports, homicide data, self-report from large nationally representative surveys of crime victimization and child maltreatment, and self-report survey data that includes sexual violence (Hamby 2014). Only self-report surveys using "partner-specific behavioral checklists" find equal rates of physical violence perpetration by women and men (Hamby 2014). Additionally, IPV results in more dangerous and severe outcomes for women and girls in comparison to their male counterparts, including homicide and physical injury (Reed et al. 2010). Given the disproportionate effects at the population level, many researchers, practitioners, and advocates continue to emphasize the importance of protecting women and children from this epidemic. Experiences of online abuse, if present, often occur in a constellation of other violent and abusive tactics to exercise excessive power and control in the relationship (Johnson 2008).

Online spaces, while supporting new social opportunities, also mimic the preexisting problems within society such as gender inequality and gender-based violence. General online abuse targets women with whom the harassers do not have a personal relationship and may, indeed, be worsened as attackers feel emboldened by the anonymity afforded by the Internet and few legal or social consequences (Marwick and Miller 2014). Studies of online harassment have demonstrated that perpetrators frequently attack women and other marginalized groups (Marwick and Miller 2014). Research on youth has suggested that digital media are a place in which the norms present in mainstream media are further reinforced and normalized (Manago et al. 2008), including gendered beliefs about dating, sex, and relationships. This implies that Internet culture is a reflection of the patriarchal power structure and that the danger that exists for women offline is amplified and recreated through ICT use. The same gender-based framework used to explain physical, sexual, psychological violence and homicide, therefore, should be used to examine the power and control that is facilitated or enabled by ICT use and online culture. Online abuse may be a universal problem, but it is likely that women bear the disproportionate consequences of that abuse. For example, Reed et al. (2016) found that high school girls who experience online abuse from a dating partner were more likely to be distressed and report negative emotional responses from these incidents than boys experiencing the same behaviors. Further, girls and women who are victimized by an intimate partner offline, particularly those that are at high risk for injury and homicide, are likely to be the most vulnerable online as well (Marganski and Melander 2015; Reed et al. 2016; Zweig et al. 2013).

Information Communication Technologies as a Context and Tools for IPV

During the past decade, the prevalence, frequency, and manner in which people use ICTs have increased rapidly. Cell phone ownership in the U.S. went from less than 30% in 2000 to 85% of adults by 2010 (Duggan and Smith 2013; Smith 2010). Households have been shifting away from the use of landline telephones, especially among young people and people of color: 41% of 18–29 year olds report as cell-phone-only households (Duggan and Smith 2013). In addition to the sharp increase in cell phone owner-ship, more U.S. adults are now online. Between 1995 and 2014, the number of Internet users across the U.S jumped from 14% to 85% (Fox and Rainie 2014). Currently, 71% of Americans go online every day, compared to 29% in 2000 (Fox and Rainie 2014). The number of smart phone users has similarly grown, with smart phone use reported by 68% of Internet users; 34% of U.S. adults who rely primarily on mobile devices to go online (Fox and Rainie 2014; Duggan and Smith 2013). One of the most popular online activities is the use of social media, with 71% of adult Internet users on Facebook and 52% of adults having more than one social media account (Duggan and Smith 2013). Young adult women ages 18–29 are at high risk for IPV and are also the highest users of ICT in the U.S. (Duggan and Smith 2013; Fox and Rainie 2014).

The use of ICTs has become so ubiquitous that the culture of day-to-day life has shifted for nearly all Americans, yet there is a dearth of research on how widespread use of ICTs has impacted the abuse and help-seeking experiences of victim-survivors going through intimate partner violence. Only six studies have focused on technology-based abuse among women with severe IPV histories or those identifying as victims or survivors of intimate partner violence. These exploratory stud-ies, which are summarized in Table 11.1, have documented victim-survivor experiences of technology-based abuse (Belknap et al. 2011; Dimond et al. 2011; Finn and Atkinson 2009; Southworth et al. 2007; Woodlock 2016; Zaidi et al. 2015).

Across these six studies, a notable strength is the authors' abilities to highlight the emotional turmoil, life complications, and helplessness that technology-based abuse creates in the day-to-day lives of women. However, these studies also have limitations that warrant further quanti-tative and qualitative research. Four of these studies were conducted with U.S. women, and each collected data before 2010 (Belknap et al. 2011; Dimond et al. 2011; Finn and Atkinson 2009; Southworth et al. 2007). Due to the rapidly changing nature of technologies, it is difficult for researchers to keep pace. Since 2010, the use of Internet-connected mobile phones and the frequency of social media use have increased

Table 11.1 Summary of studies focusing on technology-based abuse among women with severe IPV histories

Citation	Sample and Site	Key findings
Woodlock (2016)	n=46 victim-survivors, n=152 domestic violence advocate	78% of victim-survivors report harassing texts and phone calls 56% of victim-survivors report having location tracked 84% of women receiving unwanted contact self-reported it negatively impacted their mental health Victim-survivors experiencing technology-based abuse also reported emotional, physical, sexual, and financial abuse
Zaidi et al. (2015)	n=49 immigrant women, community partner centers	Cell phone and tech knowledge assisted in seeking help Expansion or maintenance of social support networks Access to service agencies Tech-savvy abusers Perpetrator policing survivor's ICT use
Belknap et al. (2011)	n=236, court involved (filed a police report)	Abuser controlling phone/breaking phone Monitoring phone calls Threatening messages via phone Economic hardship after broken ICT
Dimond et al. (2011)	n =10 shelter residents	Social media used to monitor post break-up (via mutual contact) Threatening text messages Harassment via social media ICT used for support A variety of perception regarding privacy
Finn and Atkinson (2009)	n=339 shelter residents	Threatening emails sent Abuser pretending to be victim-survivors in a chat room Monitor/access email account Online purchases without victim-survivors' permission
Southworth et al. (2007)	Media anecdotes	ICT used for stalking and terrorizing victim-survivors GPS used during stalking Sending threatening messages

considerably (Fox and Rainie 2014). This shift may change the nature and context of abuse. For example, Woodlock (2016) reported that, among victim-survivors in Australia, a high proportion were victimized by online abuse and ICTs furthered a variety of abuse tactics. Anecdotal information indicates that social media offers new ways to perpetrate abuse—especially as a means for humiliation and manipulation among the victim-survivors' networks of friends and family (Woodlock 2016). Therefore, there is ample space in the literature for more recent research on online abuse among more diverse populations of adult victim-survivors.

Forms of Technology-Based IPV

Previous research has identified common forms of technology-based abuse which can be classified into four types of abusive behavior: monitoring, harassing, stalking, and humiliation. Although there is much competing terminology, the definitions of various forms of technology-based abuse often overlap. As an example, online harassment is defined by Finn (2004) as unwanted messages that threaten, insult, or harass the receiver. This parallels a portion of Reyns et al.'s (2010) definition of cyberstalking—*repeated, unwanted attempts at communications or contact, harassment*; yet these authors also include in their definition of cyberstalking unwanted sexual advances, and threats of violence or physical harm (Finn 2004; Reyns et al. 2010). Below, we attempt to clearly define these four constructs, based both on the ICT literature and research studies focused on issues pertinent to intimate partner violence.

Monitoring Most studies of technology-based abuse include an abuser using ICTs to monitor their partner (Belknap et al. 2011; Dimond et al. 2011; Finn and Atkinson 2009; Southworth et al. 2007; Woodlock 2016; Zaidi et al. 2015). We define monitoring as the use of ICTs to gather information about a romantic partner that creates or enhances a dynamic of control within the relationship.

Monitoring is often reported as the most common form of technology-based IPV and comes in many forms. A survey of women staying in a domestic violence shelter found that 18% of victim-survivors had their email accounts monitored, and 16.9% reported the perpetrator used their password to access an account without the victim-survivor's consent (Finn and Atkinson 2009). Anecdotal evidence discussed monitoring emails directly or by using specific software programs such a "sniffer" in order to gather information about the victim-survivor's communications (Finn and Atkinson 2009). As one victim-survivor describes it: "He would check my phone record… I would be very careful [who I would] talk [to] on [my] cell [phone]…" (Zaidi et al. 2015, p. 95). Victim-survivors surveyed about phone-based abuse also reported perpetrators frequently monitored calls. For example, 57.7% reported their abusers were adamant that they disclose who they were talking to on the phone at least once and 39.5% of the women reported their abusers demanded to know 20 or more times (Belknap et al. 2011). Data on phone-based abuse were collected before 2005. Considering the now readily available information about calling history through cell phone records, these types of behaviors may be more frequent or of a different nature (Belknap et al. 2011). In the most recent study of technology-based abuse and stalking, these types of monitoring activities were described as omnipresence: "perpetrators use mobile technologies to create a sense of being ever-present in the victim's life" (Woodlock 2016, p. 9).

Monitoring activities may also be less direct. Some perpetrators reached out to mutual acquaintances through social network sites to follow up or check on the whereabouts or activities of victim-survivors (Dimond et al. 2011; Woodlock 2016). Victim-survivors in a shelter reported that perpetrators would pretend to be the victim-survivor in a chat room (9.4%) or email conversation (11.5%), vicariously spying by pretending to be the victim-survivor (Finn and Atkinson 2009). Victim-survivors and advocates also report several examples of hacking women's social media accounts, or simply following victims closely on social media (Woodlock 2016). Perpetrators would also check the victim-survivor's browser history (25.1%) (Finn and Atkinson 2009). The most frequently discussed forms of monitoring included monitoring phone calls, email accounts, text messages, and phone records (Belknap et al. 2011; Dimond et al. 2011; Zaidi et al. 2015; Woodlock 2016).

Cyberstalking Following Reyns et al. (2010), we define cyberstalking as the use of ICTs to pursue victim-survivors, and also create a sense of omnipresence (Woodlock 2016). Cyberstalking behaviors go beyond monitoring because they demonstrate an intention to physically follow (or stalk) and terrorize a victim-survivor. Research about cyberstalking outside of the intimate relationship context has implications for research on IPV. In a study using nationally representative data, 19% of those who were stalked offline also reported cyberstalking victimization (Reyns and Englebrecht 2010). Researchers hypothesized that the number of cyberstalking cases would invariably increase over time as ICTs become more widespread. A study of college students found that participants who reported obsessive qualities in their relationship were 6.8 times more likely to use cyber pursuit methods—a measure of unwanted romantic pursuit (Lyndon et al. 2011). Lastly, another study of college students found that women and minority groups were significantly more likely to be victim-survivors of cyberstalking (Reyns et al. 2010).

Studies about cyberstalking victimization among IPV victim-survivors demonstrate that perpetrators may exhibit extreme behavior in order to track their victim-survivors. Notably, many perpetrators are technologically savvy, and some have relied on unexpected methods. Three articles describe perpetrators using GPS to monitor victim-survivors. Both Southworth et al. (2007) and Woodlock (2016) described incidents in which a GPS device was attached to the victim-survivor's car. Dimond et al. (2011) discussed two victim-survivors who were harassed by the use of GPS, and one woman described her perpetrator as so computer savvy she would never be able to escape him (Dimond et al. 2011). Perpetrators can create a sense of fear by continually gathering information and physically showing up, or the abuser may instill fear by persuading the victim-survivor they could show back up at any time (Woodlock 2016). Stalking is a significant risk factor for homicide (Campbell et al. 2007).

Online Harassment Across studies, online harassment was the most common tactic used by a perpetrator. Although harassment is executed in many different ways, the common thread is the intrusion on the victim-survivors' digital space and sense of safety through the use of direct acts of aggression or hostility. These behaviors, unlike monitoring and cyberstalking, are overtly intended to distress and threaten the victim-survivor through a demonstration of power. In one study, Belknap et al. (2011) analyzed police reports for examples of technology-based abuse. The most common harassment tactics were unwanted phone calls and texts or email messages (Belknap et al. 2011; Woodlock 2016). To further illustrate, researchers interviewed a sample of IPV victim-survivors (n = 339) who were accessed by community programs or domestic violence shelters: 23.6% of the sample reported receiving threatening or harassing email messages (Finn and Atkinson 2009). In the most recent study of IPV victim-survivors, 78% reported their abuser used text messages, phone, to harass and belittle them (Woodlock 2016).

In an online harassment study among college students, those reporting harassment also experienced emotional consequences such as depression or anxiety (Lindsay et al. 2015). However, among those who received harassing messages from a significant other, only women experienced an increase in feelings of fear and fear linked to depression (Lindsay et al. 2015). In a study of adolescent digital dating abuse, behaviors that are parallel to harassment (e.g., receiving multiple unwanted messages) caused more emotional distress and negative behavioral impacts among teen girls than boys (Reed et al. 2017). Online harassment studies among youth, using larger samples and more sophisticated statistical models show a distinct pattern—the emotional impact is intensified when the harasser is an intimate partner and gender is an important indicator of that impact (Reed et al. 2017).

One example of technology-based harassment involved a harasser continuously calling his intimate partner from ever-changing, anonymous phone numbers to prevent the victim-survivor from blocking the calls (Southworth et al. 2007). Also, 9.4% of victim-survivors reported instances of identity theft by their harassers (Finn and Atkinson 2009). In a more recent study of victim-survivors in a domestic violence shelter, the researchers hypothesized that part of the reason women reported text messaging as the most common type of abuse was because it is the hardest to prevent (Dimond et al. 2011).

Humiliation Technology allows a partner to employ humiliation as a form of abuse more readily than face-to-face interactions. First, ICTs allow a partner to easily reach a meaningful audience of social ties known to the victim-survivor. Secondly, new technologies make gathering and recording private information relatively easy and inexpensive (Southworth et al. 2007; Woodlock 2016; Zaidi et al. 2015). Of victim-survivors surveyed, 39% reported their partner shared embarrassing and private photos without permission, and 33% had their abuser post negative information about them using social media (Woodlock 2016). Advocates confirmed that these humiliation tactics seemed to becoming more prevalent as they worked with victim-survivors (Woodlock 2016).

Examples of humiliation often overlap with other forms of intimate partner abuse. For instance, one woman reported that her partner hid cameras in the home and then published nude images online (Woodlock 2016). This experience served both to humiliate the victim-survivor and to monitor her. As discussed above, an intimate partner may hack into a victim-survivor's accounts and pretend to be her. This monitoring also includes humiliation, when an abusive partner spreads or shares hurtful information with those in the woman's social circle (Finn and Atkinson 2009; Woodlock 2016). Making private and sensitive information public is not only a breach of trust, but also an attempt to undermine social ties outside the relationship and potentially isolate the woman (Woodlock 2016). Another woman described that the majority of the abuse with her intimate partner was sexual violence; her perpetrator would then further abuse the victim-survivor through sharing videos of the sexual abuse online (Woodlock 2016).

Several studies have provided examples of youth using sext messages or explicit photos and videos to manipulate or shame young girls (Hassinoff 2012; Press 2011). Recently, the discussion of sext exploitation has shifted toward a gendered framework pointing out the context in which "slut shaming" is used as a form of bullying; feminist discussions emphasize greater emphasis on consent rather than categorizing the behavior as deviant (Hassinoff 2012; Henry and Powell 2015; Lippman and Campbell 2014; Press 2011). Research on sexting among youth finds that girls are often caught in a "double bind" in which they receive social pressure to send sext messages, and are often socially judged harshly whether or not they send such messages (Lippman and Campbell 2014). Girls also experience more distress than boys from being pressured to send a sext (Reed et al. 2017). Little attention has been paid to the exploitations of adult women and how these experiences may create negative repercussions for those victimized. Women who identify as victim-survivors are likely to disproportionately represent the worst instances of online sexual exploitation and abuse (Henry and Powell 2015; Woodlock 2016).

Information Communication Technologies and Risk for Homicide

The most serious form of intimate partner violence is femicide (Campbell and Runyan 1998; Radford and Russell 1992; Russell and Harmes 2001). This is one of the leading causes of premature death for women in the United States (Hoyert et al. 1999). Although there was a steady and significant decline in the proportion of male homicide victims killed by an intimate partner (a 53% decrease from 1980–2008), the proportion of female victims killed by an intimate partner began to increase in 1995 and, since 1980, there has been a 5% increase in the proportion of female victims killed by an intimate partner (Cooper and Smith 2011). In 65% of femicide cases, the victim-survivors reported previous IPV, making IPV the single largest risk factor for intimate partner femicide (Campbell et al. 2003; Moracco et al. 1998; Pataki 1997).

ICTs play a role in femicide as a tool for threatening femicide and a means of justifying femicidal responses in abusive partners. Separating from an abuser is one of the most dangerous times for victim-survivors (Campbell et al. 2007). They often experience increased threats from their partners during this time, including threats to kill (Campbell et al.

2007). Threats to kill are one risk factor associated with intimate partner femicide, and abusive partners commonly threaten to kill their partners via telephone and voice messaging services (Southworth et al. 2007; Dimond et al. 2011). ICTs enable abusive partners to terrorize, threaten, stalk, harass, and maintain power over the victim-survivor after the relationship has ended (Dimond et al. 2011; Woodlock 2016). Stalking is also a risk factor for femicide and ICTs are used as a tactic for stalking (Campbell et al. 2007; Southworth et al. 2007; Woodlock 2016). For example, in one incident, a perpetrator read his wife's emails and found out his wife was leaving him and where she planned to go. He used this information to stalk and kill her (Southworth et al. 2007). It is important, therefore, to examine the various forms of technology-based abuse in relation to homicide risk.

Information Communication Technologies as Support for Victim-Survivors

Despite the increased opportunities for abuse that they provide, victim-survivors identified information communication technologies as a lifeline during and after abuse (Southworth et al. 2007; Zaidi et al. 2015). Victim-survivors were able to call for help after abuse or prevent abuse by reminding their abuser that they could contact police (Belknap et al. 2011).

ICTs also allowed victim-survivors to expand and maintain their social support networks (Belknap et al. 2011). For example, when staying in a shelter, one woman accessed her sister's Facebook page in order to feel connected to her family (Dimond et al. 2011). In another study, almost half of the victim-survivors (46%) said that their mobile phone was partly responsible for helping them escape the violence (Zaidi et al. 2015). Similarly, in a sample of women involved in court cases for domestic violence victimization, the vast majority (79.8%) used their cell phones to get information about their case, and half of them used their phone multiple times to gather information (Belknap et al. 2011).

Conversely, some victim-survivors found ICTs to be risky and expensive. In two studies, victim-survivors reported that their abusive partner broke their cell phone or computer and that replacing items caused significant financial hardship (Belknap et al. 2011; Zaidi et al. 2015). Although victim-survivors expressed a desire to stay online, some felt that the risk of using ICTs was too great and opted to remain offline and use pseudonyms when getting new mobile phones (Belknap et al. 2011).

Three studies have examined online resources for victim-survivors, the quality of websites, and potential dangers when seeking help online (Finn and Banach 2000; Westbrook 2007; Sorenson et al. 2014). Additionally, online intervention programs have been introduced that use mobile phone applications and other web-based tools (Eden et al. 2015; Lindsay et al. 2013). Specifically, a safety decision aid, available online only, found that women who used the online tool reported lower decisional conflict and had significant reduction in uncertain feelings about their situations (Eden et al. 2015). Developing the safety decision aid as a smart phone application for college-aged women found similar positive results; repeatedly those testers trying the app agreed it was the best way to reach victim-survivors of this age group (Lindsay et al. 2013; Alhusen et al. 2015). Arguments for using technology-based outreach include the benefits of privacy, anonymity, ability to spread information effectively at a low cost, and the potential for web-based counseling services. Concerns include victim-survivors using misinformation, perpetrators monitoring behaviors, and potential for additional experiences with technology-based abuse, especially harassment (Finn and Banach 2000; Westbrook 2007; Sorenson et al. 2014).

Conclusion

Information communication technologies (ICTs) pose unique risks to IPV victim-survivors and addressing IPV in the digital age will require evolving intervention and assessment practices, further research, and new legislation to face these growing challenges. Technology-based abuse should be conceptualized as a new context for in-person IPV behaviors, as most research indicates that these forms of abuse occur in tandem.

Cyberstalking, online harassment, monitoring, and humiliation tactics can inflict real emotional consequences and may indicate that other forms of abuse are occurring.

Understanding technology-based abuse and support behaviors can have meaningful applications in practice settings as well. Findings have the potential to change intervention design and approaches to prevention. Traditional measures and assessment of IPV do not specify whether victimization occurs in person or online, and this contextual information could be significant for intervention and prevention. Additionally, victim-survivors may not readily recognize online abuse as abuse, as it does not look like typical definitions of intimate partner violence (IPV). Practitioners could be missing some essential pieces of their clients' experiences by neglecting to inquire and address technology-based abuse. Because certain behaviors may be more readily observed online, education about technology-based abuse may also enhance and expand the opportunity for bystander interventions.

Future research should continue to synthesize qualitative information and contribute additional quantitative research to further elucidate the prevalence and related characteristics of this type of abuse among adult IPV victim-survivors. Furthermore, this emerging research should be incorporated into design elements for future ICT devices and platforms. The measurement of technology-based abuse through the development of a validated psychometric scale for adults could help practitioners more accurately assess abuse and protect against mental and physical harm, including femicide. Legislation and policy regarding technology-based abuse remains in the early stage throughout the US, and research is necessary for delineating types of technology-based abuse, the relationship of this abuse to other forms of IPV, and homicide risk. Finally, communication between researchers, advocates, and lawmakers will need to remain strong as technology evolves rapidly. Information communication technologies put intimate partners at risk for further types of abuse, and may also be harnessed as a mode of support and social connection for victim-survivors. Attention and research into technology-based abuse will ensure that research and practice around IPV continues to best serve all those who need support.

References

Alhusen, J., Bloom, T., Clough, A., & Glass, N. (2015). Development of the MyPlan safety decision app with friends of college women in abusive dating relationships. *Journal of Technology in Human Services, 33*(3), 263–282.

Belknap, J., Chu, A. T., & DePrince, A. P. (2011). Roles of phones and computers in threatening and abusing women victims of male intimate partner abuse. *The Duke Journal of Gender Law & Policy, 19*, 373.

Black, M. C., Basile, K., Breiding, M., Smith, S., Walters, M., Merrick, M., & Steven, M. R. (2011). *The National Intimate Partner and Sexual Violence Survey (NISVS): 2010 summary report.* Atlanta: National Center for Injury Prevention and Control, Centers for Disease Control and Prevention.

Campbell, J., & Runyan, C. W. (1998). Femicide: Guest editors' introduction. *Homicide Studies, 2*(4), 347–352.

Campbell, J. C., Webster, D., Koziol-McLain, J., Block, C. R., Campbell, D., Curry, M. A., Gary, F., Sachs, C., Sharps, P. W., Wilt, S., Manganello, J., & Xu, X. (2003). Risk factors for femicide in abusive relationships: Results from a multi-site case control study. *American Journal of Public Health, 9*, 1089–1097.

Campbell, J. C., Glass, N., Sharps, P. W., Laughon, K., & Bloom, T. (2007). Intimate partner homicide review and implications of research and policy. *Trauma, Violence & Abuse, 8*(3), 246–269.

Cooper, A., & Smith, E. L. (2011). *Homicide trends in the United States, 1980–2008. Bureau of Justice Statistics (BJS). Department of Justice. Reports & trends* (p. 36). Washington, DC: BJS.

Dimond, J. P., Fiesler, C., & Bruckman, A. S. (2011). Domestic violence and information communication technologies. *Interacting with Computers, 23*(5), 413–421.

Dobash, R. P., & Dobash, R. E. (1979). *Violence against wives: A case against the patriarchy.* New York: Free Press.

Duggan, M., & Smith, A. (2013). *Social media update 2013. Pew internet and American life project.* Retrieved from http://www.pewinternet. org/2015/01/09/social-media-update-2014/

Eden, K. B., Perrin, N. A., Hanson, G. C., Messing, J. T., Bloom, T. L., Campbell, J. C., et al. (2015). Use of online safety decision aid by abused women: Effect on decisional conflict in a randomized controlled trial. *American Journal of Preventive Medicine, 48*(4), 372–383.

Finn, J. (2004). A survey of online harassment at a university campus. *Journal of Interpersonal Violence, 19*(4), 468–483.

Finn, J., & Atkinson, T. (2009). Promoting the safe and strategic use of technology for victims of intimate partner violence: Evaluation of the technology safety project. *Journal of Family Violence, 24*(1), 53–59.

Finn, J., & Banach, M. (2000). Victimization online: The downside of seeking human services for women on the internet. *Cyberpsychology & Behavior, 3*(5), 785–796.

Fox, S., & Rainie, L. (2014). February 2014, "The Web at 25." Available at http://www.pewinternet.org/2014/02/25/the-web-at-25-in-the-u-s

Hamby, S. (2014). Intimate partner and sexual violence research scientific progress, scientific challenges, and gender. *Trauma, Violence & Abuse, 15*, 149–158.

Hasinoff, A. A. (2012). Sexting as media production: Rethinking social media and sexuality. *New Media & Society, 15*(4), 449–465.

Henry, N., & Powell, A. (2015). Beyond the 'sext': Technology facilitated sexual violence and harassment against adult women. *Journal of Criminology, 48*(1), 104–118.

Hoyert, D. L., Kochanek, K. D., & Murphy, S. L. (1999). *Deaths: Final data for 1997.* Hyattsville/Maryland: US Department of Health and Human Services, CDC, National Center for Health Statistics.

Hunnicutt, G. (2009). Varieties of patriarchy and violence against women: Resurrecting "patriarchy" as a theoretical tool. *Violence Against Women, 15*(5), 553–573.

Johnson, M. (2008). *A typology of domestic violence.* Boston: Northeastern Press.

Kimmel, M. S. (2002). "Gender symmetry" in domestic violence: A substantive and methodological research review. *Violence Against Women, 8*, 1332–1363. https://doi.org/10.1177/107780102762478037.

Lindsay, M., Messing, J. T., Thaller, J., Baldwin, A., Clough, A., Bloom, T., et al. (2013). Survivor feedback on a safety decision aid smartphone application for college-age women in abusive relationships. *Journal of Technology in Human Services, 31*(4), 368–388.

Lindsay, M., Booth, J. M., Messing, J. T., & Thaller, J. (2015). Experiences of online harassment among emerging adults emotional reactions and the mediating role of fear. *Journal of Interpersonal Violence.* 0886260515584344.

Lippman, J. R., & Campbell, S. W. (2014). Damned if you do, damned if you don't…if you're a girl: Relational and normative contexts of adolescent sexting in the United States. *Journal of Children and Media.* https://doi.org/10.1080/17482798.2014.923009.

Lyndon, A., Bonds-Raacke, J., & Cratty, A. D. (2011). College students' Facebook stalking of ex-partners. *Cyberpsychology, Behavior and Social Networking, 14*(12), 711–716.

Manago, A. M., Graham, M. B., Greenfield, P. M., & Salimkhan, G. (2008). Self-presentation and gender on Myspace. *Journal of Applied Developmental Psychology, 29*, 446–458.

Marganski, A., & Melander, L. (2015, November 25). Intimate Partner Violence Victimization in the Cyber and Real World: Examining the Extent of Cyber Aggression Experiences and Its Association With In-Person Dating Violence. *Journal of Interpersonal Violence*. First Published November 25, 2015. https://doi-org.ezproxy1.lib.asu.edu/10.1177/0886260515614283

Marwick, A. E., & Miller, R. W. (2014). Online harassment, defamation, and hateful speech: A primer of the legal landscape. *Fordham Center on Law and Information Policy Report*, (2).

McCue, M. L. (2008). *Domestic violence: A reference handbook*. Santa Barbara: ABC-CLIO.

Moracco, K. E., Runyan, C. W., & Butts, J. D. (1998). Femicide in North Carolina, 1991–1993 a statewide study of patterns and precursors. *Homicide Studies, 2*(4), 422–446.

Pataki, G. (1997). *Intimate partner homicides in New York state*. Albany: State of New York.

Press, A. L. (2011). Feminism and media in the post-feminist era: What to make of the "feminist" in feminist media studies. *Feminist Media Studies, 11*(01), 107–113.

Radford, J., & Russell, D. E. (1992). *Femicide: The politics of woman killing*. New York: Twayne Pub.

Reed, E., Raj, A., Miller, E., & Silverman, J. G. (2010). Losing the "gender" in gender-based violence: The missteps of research on dating and intimate partner violence. *Violence Against Women, 16*(3), 348–354.

Reed, L. A., Tolman, R. M., & Ward, L. M. (2016). Snooping and sexting: Digital media as a context and tool for dating violence among college students. *Violence Against Women, 22*, 1556–1576.

Reed, L. A., Tolman, R. M., & Ward, L. M. (2017). Gender matters: Experiences and consequences of digital dating abuse victimization in adolescent dating relationships. *Journal of Adolescence, 59*, 79–89.

Rennison, C. M., & Welchans, S. (2000). Intimate partner violence. *Violence Against Women, 1993*, 98.

Reyns, B. W., & Englebrecht, C. M. (2010). The stalking victim's decision to contact the police: A test of Gottfredson and Gottfredson's theory of criminal justice decision making. *Journal of Criminal Justice, 38*(5), 998–1005.

Reyns, B. W., Henson, B., & Fisher, S. W. (2010). Stalking in the twilight zone: Extent of cyberstalking victimization and offending among college students. *Deviant Behavior, 33*(1), 1–25.

Russell, D. E., & Harmes, R. A. (2001). *Femicide in global perspective.* New York: Teachers College Press.

Smith, A. (2010). *Americans and their gadgets. Pew internet research.* Retrieved from http://www.pewinternet.org/2010/10/14/americans-and-their-gadgets/

Sorenson, S. B., Shi, R., Zhang, J., & Xue, J. (2014). Self-presentation on the web: Agencies serving abused and assaulted women. *American Journal of Public Health, 104*(4), 702–707.

Southworth, C., Finn, J., Dawson, S., Fraser, C., & Tucker, S. (2007). Intimate partner violence, technology, and stalking. *Violence Against Women, 13*(8), 842–856.

Westbrook, L. (2007). Digital information support for domestic violence victims. *Journal of the American Society for Information Science and Technology, 58*(3), 420–432.

Woodlock, D. (2016). The abuse of technology in domestic violence and stalking. *Violence Against Women,* 1077801216646277.

Zaidi, A. U., Fernando, S., & Ammar, N. (2015). An exploratory study of the impact of information communication technology (ICT) or computer mediated communication (CMC) on the level of violence and access to service among intimate partner violence (IPV) survivors in Canada. *Technology in Society, 41*, 91–97.

Zweig, J. M., Dank, M., Yahner, J., & Lachman, P. (2013). The rate of cyber dating abuse among teens and how it relates to other forms of teen dating violence. *Journal of Youth and Adolescence, 42*, 1063–1077.

12

Leave a Comment: Consumer Responses to Advertising Featuring "Real" Women

Amanda Mabry-Flynn and Sara Champlin

It is well known that the majority of female models featured in advertising are considered "ultra-thin," often weighing 20% less than the average American woman. In recent years, developments in technology and image production have created ways to make models even smaller—by altering images in post-production using computer software such as Photoshop. Images of models become "impossibly gorgeous" by having their faces, waists, hips, and other body parts edited through airbrushing techniques, as well as cropping, manipulating lighting, and other adjustments (Donovan 2012). This is misleading for consumers who use these images to evaluate the credibility or effectiveness of products promoted in advertisements. Brown (2015) argues that specifically using manipulated images of celebrities or models "add[s] a sense of believability to

A. Mabry-Flynn (✉)
Charles H. Sandage Department of Advertising, University of Illinois at Urbana-Champaign, Champaign, IL, USA

S. Champlin
Mayborn School of Journalism, Advertising, University of North Texas, Denton, TX, USA

© The Author(s) 2018
J. R. Vickery, T. Everbach (eds.), *Mediating Misogyny*,
https://doi.org/10.1007/978-3-319-72917-6_12

what is an unattainable beauty" (p. 88). Exposure to ultra-thin models through media is recognized as having a negative impact on women's perceptions of personal body image (Grabe et al. 2008). Over time, body dissatisfaction can lead to numerous negative health outcomes (Grabe et al. 2008), including disordered eating and attitudes toward eating (Johnson and Wardle 2005), mental health concerns, and decreased self-esteem (Johnson and Wardle 2005; Paxton et al. 2006).

In response to this, several brands have stepped forward to create mass-mediated campaigns that promote positive self-esteem and body image among women. Foci of these campaigns featuring "real women" include incorporating female models of all body shapes and sizes, deciding to no longer manipulate images of models, and utilizing taglines or advertising copy that supports these efforts (e.g., "the real you is sexy"). Examples of intentional and long-running efforts in which the brands rally around women celebrating their appearance and self-esteem include Dove's Campaign for Real Beauty and "aerie Real," a campaign for American Eagle's lingerie line, Aerie. Other brands, such as Target, Always, Bongo Jeans, Seventeen Magazine, and ModCloth, have made public agreements or commitments to be inclusive with their model selection or, in some cases, to not alter photos. Additionally, female celebrities such as Kate Winslet, Vanessa Hudgens, and Emma Roberts make public efforts to not work with brands that alter images or include only a limited selection of female models. Though there is clearly an increasing conversation regarding the unrealistic depiction of women in advertising at the industry and policy levels (Waller 2015), such real women campaigns remain the exception rather than the rule. This may be related to an uncertainty brands and advertisers feel about the responses these types of campaigns will garner from consumers.

Appealing to Consumer Aspirations

The goal of advertising is typically to influence potential consumers' attitudes about a brand in order to persuade them to purchase a particular product or service. Advertisers employ various persuasive tactics in order to create a positive impression of a brand. When a tactic successfully influences attitudes, and ultimately, purchase behavior, it is not surprising that it becomes a technique used in many subsequent campaigns.

One way ads can effectively influence attitudes is by appealing to a consumer's aspirations by demonstrating how a product or service can help them reach an important goal. For example, most parents believe it is important to feed their children a healthy meal, but may have difficulty finding time to cook a healthy dinner every night. This consumer insight can help advertisers of brands ranging from family-friendly restaurants to frozen vegetables create campaigns that focus on how their product or service will help parents achieve the goal of providing healthy meals for their family even when short on time. Another common way aspiration is used in advertising is through athlete and other celebrity endorsements. If an amateur swimmer sees an ad for a brand of swimwear featuring Michael Phelps, he may be more inclined to consider purchasing that swimwear because he associates it with the success of a highly-decorated Olympic athlete. Similarly, fashion ads often tap into a woman's desire to appear stylish and well-dressed. By featuring attractive models who appear to be well put together, they are working to persuade consumers that their brand can help make the audience look just as fashionable. Research has shown that when consumers can identify with the persona projected by a brand or product (e.g., a mom who cares for her family, an aspiring athlete, an attractive and well-dressed woman), they are more likely to have a positive opinion of it (Festinger 1954).

However, it has been argued that advertising doesn't simply appeal to innate human desires and aspirations, but rather it plays a key role in *creating* unrealistic expectations that women often feel forced to achieve. Research has consistently found that women are portrayed differently than men in advertising (Browne 1998; Kang 1997; Lafky et al. 1996; Monk-Turner et al. 2008). Women in ads are more likely to be sexualized (e.g., wearing revealing clothing or postured in a manner that suggests sexual readiness) and objectified (e.g., only some parts of the body are shown or the woman is the equivalent of a prop) than men, which reinforces the perception that a woman's value is largely related to her physical appearance and attractiveness to heterosexual men. Taken in isolation, a single ad that sexualizes or objectifies a woman may have little impact, but when the innumerable examples of these types of ads are considered collectively, they have the power to influence the way women are perceived at a societal level (Kilbourne 1999). For example, when women are perceived as less than human—as objects meant for the gratification of men—it may be easier for violence against them to be justified (Kilbourne 1999). Thus, the use of "aspirational" models may be perpetuating misogynistic and damaging attitudes toward women. In addition to depicting unrealistic images of female bodies, advertising has historically depicted and communicated with women through housewife or homemaker stereotypes. Previous research suggests that this practice results in decreased perceptions of women as leaders, analytical, and as people who enjoy complex tasks when compared to advertisements where women were not depicted using stereotypes (Kilbourne 1990). These findings only compound the concerns discussed earlier that exposure to images of ultra-thin and impossibly gorgeous models has been shown to have detrimental effects on girls' and women's mental health.

This type of research on the adverse effects of limited female representation in advertising has raised the consciousness of many consumers—a trend brands have taken notice of in recent years. The emergence of real women campaigns and other brand-based initiatives aimed at helping raise women's self-esteem and stymieing other negative outcomes is undoubtedly driven, at least in part, by the desire for brands to capitalize on these concerns (Banet-Weiser 2012). In her critique and analysis of modern brand cultures, Sarah Banet-Weiser (2012) notes the inherent contradiction between brands like Dove that communicate a brand ethos of helping women feel beautiful no matter their age or appearance, while at the same time encouraging the purchase of products that purport to help women adhere to a prescribed cultural standard of femininity and beauty. Dove is one example of a brand that has worked to commodify feminist ideals by positioning consumers' purchase behaviors as a form of social activism (Banet-Weiser 2012).

Despite the potential contradictions around the corporate motivations behind changing advertising strategy, American consumers' purchase decisions can have a very real impact on how advertisers represent various segments of society, such as "real" women. In light of the concerns around women and girls' well-being, some consumers in the U.S. have actively demanded that advertisements incorporate a broader range of models in terms of size, shape, ability, and race/ethnicity in order to better reflect American women. It is important to explore consumer reaction to brands that have created real women advertising campaigns—for cultural critics and advertisers alike. While real women campaigns are often celebrated for their intentions to depict true images of women, there are also many instances in which the models or brands are attacked for these practices. Most often, negative reactions are communicated in the comments section in response to news articles or on social media platforms promoting the campaign. For example, after a *Huffington Post* article featuring Aerie's agreement to drop photo editing of their models, one male commenter posted, "I don't really give a sh**—I just wish they'd stop blaming this 'media ideal' on straight men. This is all the creation of women and gay fashion designers." To the same article, another male commenter posted, "I like photoshop better, I see the regular/real American form everyday… the escape is nice." These examples depict a highly misogynistic lens applied to content aimed at celebrating women for who they are whereby men are reinforcing the idea that women in ads should be presented in a way that is gratifying to heterosexual men rather than expressing any sort of power or agency of their own. Negative comments in response to real women campaigns are not solely communicated by men. At times, similar comments are made by women, reflecting how misogyny can be internalized and set up women as competitors for men's attention. However, the comments section also provides a space for women and men to push back against this misogynistic rhetoric and engage in dialogue about the motivations behind and effects of real women campaigns.

Case Study Analysis

To further explore how consumers are reacting to real women campaigns, comments from online articles and discussion boards of two real women campaigns were collected: Dove's Campaign for Real Beauty and aerie Real by American Eagle. These campaigns are two of the most prominent examples of efforts made by major brands to shift away from using traditionally ultra-thin models in their advertising. Dove's campaign launched in 2004 as the brand began offering new beauty and skincare products in addition to its well-known bar soaps. The campaign became widely known after a 2006 digital video called "Evolution" was one of the first examples of digital content to go viral. "Evolution" depicts a photo shoot from beginning to end; starting with a bare-faced, "normal"-looking woman and closing on a final image of the same woman who has been made to look like a supermodel after makeup, lighting, and extensive photo editing. The video remains relevant a decade later with over 19 million YouTube views as of January 2018.

Aerie announced the launch of its aerie Real campaign in spring 2014. The campaign features models who have not been altered by Photoshop, which means features like freckles, skin folds, tattoos, etc. are still visible to the viewer. Aerie's chief merchandising officer, Jennifer Foyle, describes "the purpose of 'aerie Real' is to communicate there is no need to retouch beauty, and to give young women of all shapes and sizes the chance to discover amazing styles that work best for them" (Aerie 2014). Although most women in the campaign are professional models, recent examples have also included a number of women that have no professional modeling experience.

In an effort to capture a large span of online user types, comments were collected from a variety of media platforms, including those posted to *Huffington Post* news articles, YouTube videos, and the social media platforms Reddit and Twitter. Comments were evaluated and collected in fall 2016. In order to evaluate the nature of the comments, each author read through all comments collected and independently identified common themes that emerged across all comments made about each campaign. The authors then compared and condensed their notes into four broad themes as they relate to audience reactions to real women campaigns: Positive Progress, The Problem is Only in Your (Female) Mind, It's Not Enough, and It's All About the Bottom Line.

Positive Progress

The general sentiment of the majority of commenters, both male and female, was positive. Many commenters supported the way the ads made them feel or were hopeful about how a shift in advertising practices might impact future generations and body image perceptions as a whole. In response to aerie Real one commenter states:

> Easy to be cynical, but personally I think this is awesome. I remember when I was in high school (like, 6 years ago…) aerie had more 'natural' looking models, which was cool. They were gorgeous, obviously, but they had freckles and they didn't photoshop them to hell and back. I had noticed that recently they'd gone full-throttle on the photoshop and their models were all stick thin and sexy-frowning at the camera. Hopefully this means that trend is reversing!

Some commenters specifically addressed the benefits a real women campaign might have, saying, "But even so, maybe seeing these super skinny underwear clad women will make people more comfortable if they are not retouched. Example: that skinny thing has cellulite??? etc."

Similarly, in a comment related to a digital video called "Choose Beautiful" by Dove's Campaign for Real Beauty, a commenter praised Dove's efforts saying, "Dove is promoting being comfortable in one's own body and not being ashamed of it. There is so much body shaming in the world. At least, some company is doing the opposite of that and promoting self confidence." This video depicts women entering a building that has two doors, one labeled "Beautiful" and the other labeled "Average"; the women then describe why they chose the door they went through and reflect on how that makes them feel and their perceptions of how others view them.

Even though some commenters noted that they would like to see more diverse women in aerie Real ads (see the section "It's Not Enough" below), many remained pleased with the efforts: "They chose some pretty flawless models to go unretouched, but I applaud the effort anyway!" This commenter followed with, "(Maybe flaws are in the eye of the beholder?)" Similar comments were made in response to Dove's "Choose Beautiful" commercial, with one male commenter noting, "Didn't see anyone average. Everyone is beautiful." Others shared similar reactions, indicating that "everyone" deserved to walk through the door labeled "beautiful" rather than the one labeled "average." It is clear that many chose to leave positive comments in response to the efforts put forth by these two brands. The focus on real women in advertising campaigns not only garnered positive feedback regarding the content but also seemed to foster a sense of a supportive online community with commenters rallying together to support these initiatives. Responses were not always positive, however.

The Problem Is Only in Your (Female) Mind

A second notable trend was identified primarily among male commenters. Throughout the comments, at times men suggested or noted that women just need to "get over it" or "get over themselves" when faced with challenges related to body image and gender. Central foci of real women campaigns include showcasing beauty in its many forms and building self-esteem by not re-touching or editing models to unrealistic standards; yet discussions of what others perceived to be "right" and "wrong" when it comes to the depiction of the human body could be found in the comments. One commenter argued that it was not "okay" to be "plus size[d]," and dismissed the concept of "body shaming" altogether, stating, "im positive being overweight is unhealthy it has nothing to do with 'body shaming' so stop saying its okay to be 'plus' size kids are listening."

One of the articles reviewed for this project focused on an Aerie model speaking out about how she feels when men on the street—strangers—tell her to smile. She states,

English men—you know, builders—would sometimes shout, 'cheer up, love' or 'crack a smile,' and I'm like, OK, how dare you try to tell me to smile! Is it for your benefit? I should look smiley and therefore attractive to you? (Hatch 2016)

Her opinions were received with mixed reviews, with many negative responses from men. One male commenter compared a situation in which he was asked to smile to that of the experiences many women have with being asked to smile by men unknown to them. Said the commenter, "As a male, I've had the same thing said to me. I smiled. Problem solved. For some women, it is one of the biggest annoyances in their lives. For me, it was Monday. Get over yourself. I've been called honey, sweetheart, darling, etc. Never bothered me one bit." Another commenter added to this, "1st world problems to the nth degree."

Other male commenters made similar remarks in response to body image campaigns and initiatives, dismissing them as if they do not exist. In one example, a male commenter stated, "kinda getting sick of very attractive people going on about 'body positivity' in an attempt to get a pat on the back." Similarly, another male commenter stated that the Aerie model who did not like when men asked or harassed her about smiling, "should try a different line of work, then, if she wants people to stop telling her what to do with her face and body."

Sometimes men praised campaign efforts but then continued to generalize the problems as stemming from women (in this case, what the commenter described as a subset or type of women),

> As a man yes this is a F******* GREAT step! Im tired of the imphatuation many woman have with plastic lives… The ones who idolize plastic surgery and obscenely expensive clothes and shoes that could literally feed hundreds of starving mouths. Im sick of a culture in women that values such petty and materialistic things and I am so happy to hear of this campaign!

It should be noted that in some examples it was difficult to determine the gender of the commenter because posts were listed under the user's online handle/username. In some cases, it was suggested through the language used; for example, "Soooo women will feel better about themselves if they don't have photoshopped pics? Good grief women, get you shit together." In other instances, commenters were simply confused about the presence of an issue,

What's wrong with portraying your product in a flattering light... obviously the stakes are different, as fashion advertising can actually have the power to define what we see as ideal in people's appearances, and that can have the profound effect of actually dictating people's self-images. But still, we do have a concept of attractiveness in society. It's probably important to make sure that the threshold for what is considered attractive remain realist. But at the same time, to be frank, people like to see attractive people.

In this case, the commenter clearly acknowledges that there is potential for this practice (editing visual images of women to reflect unrealistic body types) to be destructive; yet simultaneously dismisses this as something that is reversible—"people like to see attractive people." Commenters also made sarcastic comments at the efforts of these campaigns, "This 'real women' bullshit." Another commenter similarly disregards the impact of the campaign, "thin and attractive women are women too so I would hope they'd use them...".

Overall, the comments that comprise this theme speak to the idea that some men believe women exaggerate experiences such as street harassment or feelings of pressure to live up to a certain beauty ideal. It may be that since most men do not live through these experiences, it is easier to believe they only exist in the minds of certain women rather than challenge the status quo. However, one male commenter disagreed and tried to empathize with the experiences of women by relating a story:

It is funny. I was recently at a convention where I was sitting at a desk with two men and two women. We were all busy and working when at least 3 different men passed the desk and knocked, only, on the women's desk, and said "smile." Nobody said anything to me or the other guy that was sitting right next to the women. I really got a first hand look at how annoying this must be. The women completely ignored him because I imagine it happens all the time to them but I was irritated.

It's Not Enough

In some cases, commenters found real women campaigns to simply not do "enough" when it came to truly representing real women. Many commenters pointed out that the women included in the aerie REAL campaigns did not truly reflect all types of women; rather, the women featured in the campaign were simply un-retouched models. Commenters voiced a call for the inclusion of a greater variety of women and were often specific about what they wanted to see. For example,

> I'm sorry, but where are the plus size models exactly? Put me in a bikini after gaining 70 pounds during pregnancy and 3 kids later, then dropping the weight, so sagging skin and lots of stretch marks, and I guarantee that Aerie will photoshop me. It's fine for the girls who aren't even a little overweight, but think they're heavy, but for disabled, chunky, or scarred people, not so much. Why do we applaud this stuff anyway?

This commenter suggests that there is perhaps a delineation between the types of bodies advertisers will include in real women campaigns and those that they will not (i.e., featuring "disabled, chunky, or scarred people.") However, several commenters replied to this post and pointed out that other brands have taken steps to include models of a diverse set of backgrounds, including children and adults with disabilities. Said one commenter, "At least they are taking steps to include more diverse body types. There will always be the person that says they can do more. There are other companies that have included disabled and your definition of 'chunky' in their ads—ModCloth, Target, as examples." Interestingly, it is these more diverse initiatives from other brands that may contribute to the expectations consumers develop over time about the types of people that should be depicted in "diverse" advertising. The original commenter follows with, "Companies should always make strides to be more inclusive and body positive, but saying that the girls shown in these images are plus size, or even large, is false. I will applaud them when I can actually see a difference."

Similar skeptical reactions were found in response to Dove's "Choose Beautiful" video, with one post stating, "Thing is nowadays thinking your 'beautiful' is considered being vein. This really doesn't help with anyone's confidence because it makes you think you can never be beautiful and your always 'average.' It's sad to be honest."

In this vein, it may be that brands are viewed as "taking credit" for combating an issue with only a small commitment or acknowledgement. On one hand, Aerie has made an agreement to no longer edit its models, but it seems that many audience members expect that the models selected would not require much editing in the first place. Said one commenter,

> I have to admit, I was looking at these girls and thinking, "What man wouldn't find her attractive?" Because all of them are obviously very good-looking and have great figures (not to mention pretty faces and good skin.). The one girl with the hour-glass shape? Doubt many men would be criticizing her for not being a size 2.

The Dove campaigns received some comparable comments, where commenters questioned the need for a brand to align itself with a specific cause. One commenter stated, "Am I the only one who thinks this is obviously fake?" Others simply felt that what the brands were doing through the advertisements actually exacerbated the issue.

> Disappointed in media influencing superficiality. What about strength and intelligence. Why isn't average just as good as beautiful? Why can't they be the same? People are average and beautiful at the same time and there's nothing wrong with either one of those things. Why not think about something important?

These comments demonstrate that efforts specifically designed to promote self-esteem among women and shift advertising industry practices are still met with hesitation from many audiences. It may be that what viewers perceive as small efforts or hints at impending change can lead some to become skeptical of the underlying intentions of the brand. Perhaps these steps can open too many doors for others to become critical or work to dismiss the issue. It seems that people want to see the brands commit, be "all in," and truly fight to be inclusive of all women.

It's All About the Bottom Line

Though large, well-known brands are perhaps some of the greatest mouthpieces to communicate important messages about causes and pro-social initiatives, because of their ties to product sales and marketing (perhaps seen as an ulterior motive), skeptics of the work may point to the brand's need to meet sales goals. Some commenters found it unfortunate that a brand would want to monetize or capitalize on something that should be standard practice. In these cases, commenters pointed out that it seemed inappropriate that products and companies should make money while tying themselves to an initiative such as body positivity or inclusive representation. One commenter lamented, "And of course, the whole point of the body acceptance movement was that someone would find a way to make money off it, not that women would finally be able to quit compulsively shopping for clothes to feel better about how they look." Other commenters argued, "But I do have a problem with the idea that ads should show the average woman in the lingerie. Marketing works by associating extraordinary ideas with the product, not the ordinary."

Still others point out the mismatch between the purported purpose of aerie Real, to show that women are beautiful as they are, and the products the brand actually offers its customers, "Umm the biggest size they have in that store is a 12." Another commenter indicates that she appreciates the campaign, but is frustrated by the relatively limited size offerings, "I think it is awesome but going into the store I could not find anything in my size. I am a size 12. How about actually catering to people who are not skinny?"

Similarly, other commenters were turned off by the branding initiatives attached to otherwise sentimental or moving advertisements, "This was heart warming a flawless until the ad dove came up cuz tht just ruined the moment." Several commenters also pointed out the inconsistent principles of Dove's parent company, Unilever, because it owns the brand Axe as well, which is known for highly sexist advertising,

> Dove is owned by the same people that own Axe. There might be some great ads by Dove about women empowerment—but it is all just a

marketing scheme. The company doesn't give two shits, as long as you buy their product.

Overall, this theme tapped into a skepticism that brands were genuine in their efforts to actually "help" women feel better about their bodies:

This is called pandering. Aerie is a sub brand of American Outfitters which is just another corporation exploiting cheap labor selling overpriced clothes for suckers. The only reason they aren't using models is because of the "backlash trend" where woman are sick of the photoshopped, retouched images, so in the name of empowerment, companies like this or Dove market their product as being "pure". It's manipulative at best.

Conclusion

Advertising is pervasive in women's lives. Depictions of women in advertising have the power both to fuel ongoing societal misogyny *and* to help move beauty norms toward inclusivity. The use of ultra-thin and impossibly gorgeous models is pervasive in advertising aimed and men, women, and even children. Media scholar and critic Jean Kilbourne has spent decades collecting examples of ads that portray women in this way and suggests "the obsession with thinness is most deeply about cutting girls and women down to size. It is only a symbol, albeit a very powerful and destructive one, of tremendous fear of female power" (Kilbourne 1999, p. 137). She argues that as women have achieved greater equality throughout history, there has been a concurrent emphasis on valuing their thinness. This focus on diminishing women's physical presence reflects a patriarchal society's attempt to diminish women's social power and maintain the status quo in which men remain firmly in control of the marketplace, politics, and public spaces in general (Kilbourne 1999).

Although the movement of some brands toward using more "real" women in their campaign efforts is a step toward inclusivity and can encourage women to take up space rather than diminish themselves, change does not come without at least some resistance. The findings from this study help provide insight into how real women campaigns are received by people of all genders and how people use these online spaces to engage in dialogue about the positive and negative outcomes associated with this type of advertising. More specifically, the comments explored for this chapter demonstrate the complexity of consumer responses to real women campaigns. While for some consumers these efforts represent a positive and encouraging step toward inclusivity and realism, for others they are disingenuous at best and, at worst, manipulative attempts to profit on women's continued concerns about their physical appearance.

Online spaces such as discussion boards and comments sections allow for open and often anonymous reactions to real women campaigns; thus, they may provide a more accurate depiction of consumers' responses. It was not surprising to find many commenters who presented as male lamenting that there is no "need" for real women campaigns and suggesting the problem is largely in the minds of unattractive women. For some commenters, this discourse only seems to emphasize the importance of real women campaigns to shifting societal norms of beauty away from an unrealistic ideal and toward inclusivity. On the other hand, an argument that appeared throughout the comments was that these campaigns still place focus on a woman's physical appearance, which only reinforces the idea that a woman's primary value is based on her looks.

While there have been some regulations placed on the use of "excessively skinny" models in countries such as France, Israel, Spain, and Italy (Stampler 2015), such policies have yet to be implemented in the U.S. This means that advertising is a self-regulated industry that is largely driven by consumers' demands. If real women advertising campaigns are both well received by consumers and lead to increasing sales, it is more likely we will see these efforts increase in the future. When women who are the target audience for these campaigns speak up about both the positive and negative aspects of these efforts through social media, comments sections, and their spending and other consumer behaviors, they can play a meaningful role in shaping real women campaigns that will shift societal norms.

Acknowledgement The authors would like to thank graduate students Xiaohan Hu and Hailey Sutton as well as undergraduate student Amanda Woodard

(University of North Texas) for their help finding media posts and content for this chapter. The authors would also like to thank a team of University of North Texas undergraduate research methods students for sparking this idea based on their class project on consumer perceptions of the Victoria's Secret brand.

References

Aerie. (2014). Intimates line aerie gets real, unveils "aerie Real" spring 2014 campaign featuring unretouched models, challenging supermodel standards. PR Newswire. Retrieved from http://www.prnewswire.com/news-releases/intimates-line-aerie-gets-real-unveils-aerie-real-spring-2014-campaign-featuring-unretouched-models-challenging-supermodel-standards-240777281.html

Banet-Weiser, S. (2012). *AuthenticTM: The politics of ambivalence in a brand culture*. New York: NYU Press.

Brown, A. (2015). Picture [im]perfect: Photoshop redefining beauty in cosmetic advertisements, giving false advertising a run for the money. *Texas Review of Entertainment and Sports Law, 16*(2), 87–105.

Browne, B. A. (1998). Gender stereotypes in advertising on children's television in the 1990s: A cross-national analysis. *Journal of Advertising, 27*, 83–96.

Donovan, K. C. (2012). Vanity fare: The cost, controversy, and art of fashion advertisement retouching. *Notre Dame Journal of Law, Ethics & Public Policy, 26*(2), 581–620.

Festinger, L. (1954). A theory of social comparison processes. *Human Relations, 7*(2), 117–140.

Grabe, S., Ward, L. M., & Shibley Hyde, J. (2008). The role of the media in body image concerns among women: A meta-analysis of experimental and correlational studies. *Psychological Bulletin, 134*(3), 460–476.

Hatch, J. (2016). Aerie model says she'll smile when she feels like it, thank you very much. *Huffington Post*. Retrieved October 3, 2016, from http://www.huffingtonpost.com/entry/aerie-model-iskra-lawrence-says-shell-smile-when-she-feels-like-it-thank-you-very-much_us_57f26557e4b0c2407cdeae8e

Johnson, F., & Wardle, J. (2005). Dietary restraint, body dissatisfaction, and psychological distress: A prospective analysis. *Journal of Abnormal Psychology, 114*(1), 119–125.

Kang, M.-E. (1997). The portrayal of women's images in magazine advertisements: Goffman's gender analysis revisited. *Sex Roles, 37*(11–12), 979–996.

Kilbourne, W. E. (1990). Female stereotyping in advertising: An experiment on male-female perceptions of leadership. *Journalism Quarterly, 67*(1), 25–31.

Kilbourne, J. (1999). *Can't buy my love: How advertising changes the way we think and feel.* New York: Simon and Schuster.

Lafky, S., Duffy, M., Steinmaus, M., & Berkowitz, D. (1996). Looking through gendered lenses: Female stereotyping in advertisements and gender role expectations. *Journalism & Mass Communication Quarterly, 73*(2), 379–388.

Monk-Turner, E., Wren, K., McGill, L., Matthiae, C., Brown, S., & Brooks, D. (2008). Who is gazing at whom? A look at how sex is used in magazine advertisements. *Journal of Gender Studies, 17*(3), 201–209.

Paxton, S. J., Neumark-Sztainer, D., Hannan, P. J., & Eisenberg, M. E. (2006). Body dissatisfaction prospectively predicts depressive mood and low self-esteem in adolescent girls and boys. *Journal of Clinical Child and Adolescent Psychology, 35*(4), 539–549.

Stampler, L. (2015). France just banned ultra-thin models. *Time.* Retrieved December 14, 2016, from http://time.com/3770696/france-banned-ultra-thin-models

Waller, D. S. (2015). Photoshop and deceptive advertising: An analysis of blog comments. *Studies in Media and Communication, 3*(1), 109–116.

13

A Space for Women: Online Commenting Forums as Indicators of Civility and Feminist Community-Building

Joy Jenkins and J. David Wolfgang

For centuries, women's concerns – the home, family, personal relations – were relegated to the private sphere, while men's topics – the workplace, politics, economics – occupied the public realm. When women cross this divide with their views, they have encountered contestation and even condemnation. The rise of online media has presented opportunities and barriers for women sharing their perspectives. The Internet allows diverse individuals to engage with news content on political, social, and cultural topics (Dahlgren 2005) while also providing platforms for journalists to interact with their audiences (Edwards 2002).

Women, however, may perceive online environments as hostile to their participation (Herring 1996; Jane 2016; Penny 2011). In August 2014,

J. Jenkins (✉)
Reuters Institute for the Study of Journalism, University of Oxford, Oxford, UK

J. D. Wolfgang
Journalism & Media Communication, Colorado State University, Fort Collins, CO, USA

© The Author(s) 2018
J. R. Vickery, T. Everbach (eds.), *Mediating Misogyny*,
https://doi.org/10.1007/978-3-319-72917-6_13

the website *Jezebel* issued a public statement to its publisher, Gawker Media, addressing the distress commenters and staff members experienced as a result of viewing and removing misogynist images posted by online commenters (Jezebel Staff 2014). The previous week, *Guardian* columnist Jessica Valenti received threats, name-calling, lewd comments, and harassment in response to a tweet she wrote asking whether any countries subsidize menstruation products (Aran 2014).

These examples and more prompted *Slate* writer Amanda Hess (2014) to declare that women are not welcome online. However, news organizations can create online mediated spaces where women can freely address issues affecting their lives. Using a feminist lens, this chapter addresses the potential for news organizations to facilitate online publics that are not only inclusive of women's concerns but also resist incivility, challenge gender stereotypes, and offer opportunities for empowerment. As a case study, we examined online comments regarding the topic of domestic violence, specifically the 2014 suspension of NFL player Ray Rice after a video was released showing him punching his then fiancée in a hotel elevator.

First, we discuss how online forums associated with news organizations can foster civility, feminist discourse, and online publics. We then describe the Ray Rice case, followed by an analysis of how the online publics emerging in response to news coverage of the incident both reflected and contested expectations for online civility, feminist community-building, and networked publics.

Online Spaces

Although the Internet might provide a safer space for women to engage in group communication because of reduced social cues, women are more likely to perceive online communication as being more hostile and less hospitable (Herring 1996; Jane 2016; Penny 2011). This response may stem from the fact that men dominate online forums (Baek et al. 2011). Women prefer to mask their identity online more than men and feel that anonymity contributes to their ideas being accepted (Flanagin et al. 2002).

Online gender harassment may also discourage women from participating in online discourse (Citron 2009). "Gendertrolling" occurs when a woman speaks out against sexism and may involve coordinated participation of numerous people, gender-based insults, vicious language, credible threats, and intense attacks that are broad and long-lasting (Mantilla 2013). "E-bile" involves sexualized threats, typically including profanity, violent imagery, and gender stereotypes (Jane 2012). The defining and overarching characteristic of online gender harassment is the attempt to exclude women from public discourse (Megarry 2014).

In online spaces, women can behave as active audiences emphasizing plurality and difference (Fenton 2000). They can also share their experiences and address topics of interest while engaging in community-building, or encouraging "individuals with mutual concerns to build alliances" (Antunovic and Hardin 2013, p. 1376). However, women participants have been cast in limited ways, such as consumers, community creators, and collaborators, rather than citizens, activists, intellectuals, and employees (Van Zoonen 2001). Studies should address how women engage with the Internet to reconstruct the gendered distinction between consumption/production and entertainment/information (Van Zoonen 2001), as well as how they use digital media to participate in everyday acts of resistance (Van Zoonen 1991).

Civility in Online Discourse

Civility represents the idea that individuals should be able to engage in discourse despite differences in opinion (Evers 2009). Civility in discourse demonstrates empathy and an obligation toward others while showing respect through curtailing self-interests (Wright and Gehring 2008). Civility involves genuine interactions and sincerely seeking common ground (Wright and Gehring 2008). Three requirements stand out: egalitarian treatment (Baumgarten et al. 2011; Darr 2005); interpersonal respect (boyd 2004; Orwin 1991; Wright and Gehring 2008); and tolerance (McGregor 2004; Rucht 2011; Sinopoli 1995). Online comment moderators help set boundaries (Edwards 2002), bring other voices into the conversation (Parkinson 2004), and encourage mutual respect, but only if the moderator accepts the role of promoting respect (Smith and Wales 2000).

Some feminists, however, critique civility for valuing certain voices over others: "Throughout American history, disenfranchised minorities such as women and African Americans have been regularly accused of incivility just by virtue of daring to show up in public and press their rights claims" (Zerilli 2014, p. 108). That is, as a social norm, civility was developed, and is maintained, by those with power in society. As such, "Those who hold power can express their views within the framework of existing institutions, but those who do not may lack the recognized channels for registering their claims" (Zerilli 2014, p. 108). Furthermore, civil behavior is defined in a way that often prevents those with less power from acting in anti-social ways to overcome inequality (Zerilli 2014).

In contemporary politics, we should be less concerned about the lack of civility in discourse and more concerned about the lack of adequate spaces "in which grievances can legitimately be raised and meaningfully addressed by fellow citizens and their elected representatives" (Zerilli 2014, p. 112). This is an issue not just of physical space but also the strategies, practices, and tone of those who speak up against those in power. Based on previous research, we define civility based on inclusiveness, interpersonal respect, and tolerance for ideas. This definition promotes the need for an egalitarian space where individuals are also allowed to criticize ideas. The distinction between criticizing individuals and ideas is critical in order to allow underrepresented participants to fully express themselves while protecting individuals' dignity.

Online Publics

Online forums develop based on who is present and how participants choose to structure and engage in the conversation. Participants can be considered members of publics, or independent groups of strangers who use discussion to make cultural and social meaning and create new forms of association (Warner 2002). Specifically, networked publics consist of digital spaces unique from traditional publics because the conversations are more public, the texts are more permanent, the content can be easily shared, and more people can participate (boyd 2011). Participants can come and go as they wish, and the context of the conversation can change quickly, resulting in fluid spaces (boyd 2011). Participants in a networked public rely on imagined understandings of their audience, which can lead to misconceptions about the topic and audience, and whether other participants share the same goals (boyd 2011).

This lack of control over context and audience diminishes the boundary between public and private in that participants do not have private conversations, although they may share private thoughts (boyd 2011). Comment forums represent spaces where strangers come together around a shared topic, but the outcome of that conversation is dependent upon who participates, how the context shifts, and whether individuals are willing to participate.

To study civility along with feminist community-building in online publics, we addressed the following research questions: How do online public forums represent the ideals of feminist community-building? How is civility evident in online public discourse related to domestic violence in female-authored news articles? How do online conversations associated with news articles about domestic violence represent the characteristics of networked publics?

Study Design

Feminist critics assess how texts present certain behaviors for women and men as standard, normal, desirable, and appropriate (Foss 1996). Some texts may also describe women's oppression, address the consequences of patriarchy, and consider the commonality of individuals' experiences (Foss 1996). Online forums may represent these qualities, but they may also include constraints, such as sexual harassment, cyberbullying, "gendertrolling," and suppression of women's perspectives. A feminist analysis of online forums addresses the presence of these and other limitations.

We assessed the level of civility with which online commenters addressed a topic of interest to women. In 2014, Baltimore Ravens running back Ray Rice punched his then fiancée Janay Palmer in an Atlantic City, New Jersey, hotel elevator and dragged out her unconscious body

(Sobleski 2014; TMZ staff 2014). After a gruesome video of the incident was published in September 2014, Rice was cut from the Ravens and banned indefinitely by the NFL (Wilson 2014). After the punishment, which Rice appealed, many U.S. news stories addressed domestic violence and why some women choose to stay in abusive relationships (Benbow 2014; Carpenter 2014; Grinberg 2014; Jarrett 2014). Many of these news stories included online forums in which commenters addressed the incident; the responses of Rice, Palmer, and the NFL; and domestic violence. This incident allowed us to study how news organizations bring a private issue affecting women into public view and then invite readers to share their perspectives. Because the issue involved a professional football player – a sphere often reserved for men – it also allowed us to consider statements reinforcing how to be "man" or "woman" (Lazar 2007, p. 150).

We selected stories published between September 8 and September 29, 2014, representing the three-week period after TMZ released the second video. We used the Factiva database to access news and opinion articles published in major U.S. news publications mentioning "woman," "women," "wife," "Ray Rice," and "domestic violence." The search was limited to articles attracting at least ten comments. Additionally, because academic literature and recent press coverage emphasize the negative responses women face when engaging online, we included only articles written by female journalists. These search criteria yielded 21 articles, with the final sample including 1,750 total comments. Publications represented in the sample included *USA Today*, *The Washington Post*, *The Wall Street Journal*, *Time*, *Politico*, and others.

We used a feminist-interpretive lens to consider how the ideals of feminist community-building might be represented through news-mediated public discourse, or "how women may rally together in solidarity to oppose some form of discrimination" (Lazar 2007, p. 150) and potentially form ongoing coalitions. We also studied instances of sexual harassment – including threats, the objectification of women, and making humiliating comments targeting women – toward article authors and commenters and civility – including statements of inclusiveness, interpersonal respect, and tolerance for other perspectives and ideas. This approach allows for an exploration of how the social norms of interpersonal communication are evident in conversations about domestic violence. Lastly, we considered how participants used the unique features of networked publics to build new communities for discussions of domestic violence to understand how open and participatory discourse spaces might advance or inhibit the interests of women who participate.

Analysis

Several components of feminist community-building were evident in the online forums. First, commenters shared personal stories related to domestic abuse. Second, evidence of alliance-building emerged through commenters responding to these stories with advice, encouragement, and empathy. Women also raised awareness about and suggested solutions for addressing domestic abuse. Lastly, commenters invoked particular conceptions of gender, with some reinforcing stereotypes and others questioning them.

Sharing Personal Stories Some commenters discussed experiencing abuse, while others referenced the experiences of a parent or friend, and still others shared insights from working professionally with abuse victims. In many cases, sharing these stories allowed commenters to address misconceptions about domestic violence, such as why victims choose to stay or leave abusive relationships, how the cycle of violence unfolds, and the challenges of navigating life post-abuse. In response to a September 18, 2014, *USA Today* article in which TV personality Meredith Vieira described an abusive relationship, a commenter asked where Vieira's family was when the abuse occurred. Commenter Stephanie F. replied, "But many times you don't know it's happening. I had bruises, black eyes, broken and jammed fingers, broken ribs. You get creative in your explanations as to why your [*sic*] injured." William L. responded, "Thank you for sharing your story! There lis [*sic*] NO EXCUSE for a man laying his hands on a woman unless he is defending himself." Although some commenters responded to abuse stories with mocking or criticism, this response and other supportive messages suggested that the forum could offer a welcoming space for survivors of abuse and their friends and families.

Similarly, a September 19, 2014, CNN article invited "iReporters" to share their stories of being abused or address the abuse of a loved one. GD wrote:

> I will never forget walking out of the bathroom after drying my eyes from crying over a fight, the second I walked out he punched me in the face. Knocking me down, his mother was standing right beside him telling me to run. I ran, he chased me, dragged me down the stairs, she held him back and I finally got away. I didn't leave him.

This commenter followed this with, "I am now married and very happy with my family. Abuse free." This commenter described how abuse can escalate and the victim's thought processes. Other commenters shared similar stories, such as thinknonit: "But I agree with you that the abuse changes a person. I can not bring myself to allow a woman back into my life for fear that she may end up as abusive as my Ex had been." GD responded, "First take time to give yourself a chance to heal. I was single for three years before I even attempted to be with someone again… but please, don't shut out love." The journalist frequently entered the conversation to thank commenters for participating. "Reading your story reminded me a lot of the person I interviewed for the first video. She too found love after abuse" (czdanowicz 2014). In one case, the journalist connected two commenters with similar experiences. "That's an interesting observation, SwankDaddy. One of the other stories from a man, I think it was @Glenn S.'s comment, received a more supportive response. I appreciate you bringing this up, as it's worth discussing!" (czdanowicz 2014).

In this forum, commenters continually engaged and shared their stories and perspectives to enhance understandings of the prevalence of domestic abuse and the ways victims respond to it. This forum also demonstrated that when a news organization invites commenters to address a particular topic and the journalist engages in that discussion, the resulting conversations may be more welcoming and feature less mocking or critical comments than other forums.

Raising Awareness Commenters also used the online forums to raise awareness about domestic violence, such as by offering additional insight and context. In response to a September 12, 2014, *Denver Post* article, Chiefpr said: "Being taught to be completely self sufficient and supporting means never having to stay in a bad relationship. Families, including relatives need to stop brow-beating kids into a relationship or demeaning singles." This commenter addressed the need for children to develop self-esteem and recognize that leaving an unhealthy relationship is acceptable. In a forum associated with a September 11, 2014, *Washington Post* article, commenters addressed assumptions about why victims do or do not leave their abusers. CalypsoSummer said, "It's a pathological situation that can be as hard to stop as anorexia or cutting. It's also extremely dangerous both to be in, and to leave – 75% of women killed by their partners are murdered when they're leaving an abusive situation." The commenter provided a link to additional information about the challenges victims face. Betsey A. said, "If a woman is financially dependent on the man (and often he makes sure she is), then she may feel she can't leave, especially if there are children involved."

Additionally, commenters identified societal reforms that would address causes and consequences of abuse. On September 15, 2014, NBC commenter Kim-2982716 wrote, "Conflict resolution, communication skills and problem-solving with respect for the opposite party should be taught in school along with many other life skills that children are not receiving anymore." Other commenters addressed problems associated with how domestic violence is prosecuted. For example, *USA Today* commenter Ron W. (2014) said, "It should be the law of the land that counseling be mandatory and if physical abuse is evident to Police, charges must be brought against the perpetrator. This should have nothing to do [with] whether the injured party wants to press charges or not." Commenters not only shared their views about domestic violence but also pressed for responses and ideas that would help address the problem. These conversations, however, did not necessarily lead to immediate actions or the formation of ongoing alliances, as conversations continually shifted and were associated with only one article.

Lastly, commenters mentioned inequality more broadly – often invoking and clarifying the tenets of feminism – when addressing domestic violence. These discussions emerged in a forum associated with a September 27, 2014, *Time* magazine article critiquing actress Emma Watson's speech to the United Nations about HeForShe, an initiative calling upon men to support feminism. In response to a commenter who said feminism is not about equality but emphasizes women's needs, onthevraydar15 said, "The fact that you're hung up on 'fem' is exactly why we need feminism." JimmyRhapsody responded, "Exactly. What better indicator that we still live in a patriarchal society than fear of the word feminism? Feminism is about moving in a direction as a society where women and men both have the same opportunities, and expectations, which are currently horribly lopsided." These comments addressed the value of feminism for addressing issues important to both genders. Some commenters self-identified as feminists when making arguments. For example, on September 13, 2014, NPR commenter PA Quinn said, "I'm a feminist. I'm proud to be a feminist – and by the way, you don't have to be a woman to be a feminist." Although discussing feminism and identifying as a feminist might still be stigmatized in some public spaces, the participants often used them to express their perspectives and discuss issues important to them. In some cases, they were met with criticism, but in others, support emerged. Although commenters discursively united under the broad umbrella of feminism, and supported one another's comments in several cases, their conversations did not necessarily suggest the creation of continuing associations through which they could engage in feminist resistance.

Gender Norms We considered how gender norms were expressed or challenged in the forums. One theme addressed the narrative that men, especially those who suffer domestic abuse, cannot be honest about their victimization. On September 19, 2014, CNN commenter whatnext?? said, "As a man it must have been so hard because you are supposed to be strong and manly and to say anything about it may have made you feel inadequate." Commenters also suggested that the view that men cannot be vulnerable contributed to the problem of male victims not getting help. On September 26, 2014, *Time* commenter SashaShepherd said, "It reinforces notions that men are less deserving of help and sympathy. It causes us to not listen when men report very real issues." Despite the focus on male gender norms, few commenters challenged female gender expectations to promote a more egalitarian understanding of gender. As one September 19, 2014, CNN commenter (SwankDaddy) wrote: "Now in the case of men explaining there [*sic*] experiences with violent females or bouts with domestic violence. There are no like or replies. I wonder why. Could it be no woman has empathy or sympathy for a man who has been a victim of domestic violence." The continued emphasis on reminding commenters in the forum that men can also become victims of domestic violence was used more often to dismiss the concerns of women in the articles and forums, stymying potential community-building.

Commenters consistently suggested that the law treats women more leniently in cases of domestic violence, either because a judge assumes that the male is the aggressor or that women can more easily portray themselves as victims. On September 15, 2014, NBC commenter Baddog40 said, "Women can steal a mans money, lie, cheat, steal, antagonize, but they are ALWAYS the victim." This comment represented the idea that a woman's status as a victim is often strategic. Comments focused on female abusers also tended to reinforce stereotypes of women as manipulative, overly emotional, and greedy.

Civility in Discourse

We evaluated civility through the presence of respect, inclusiveness, and tolerance for ideas. We also considered how commenters responded to the female authors of the articles we analyzed, particularly whether they criticized or harassed the authors.

Elevated levels of respect were evident in most forums, showing that participants can be respectful while disagreeing, even if they are not productive at solving problems. A number of commenters tempered their disagreement by using respectful introductory phrases. In response to a

September 26, 2014, *Time* article, for example, casesera said, "From some of your other posts, you seem to have thought a lot about this issue, and I found this response interesting. However, a couple counter-points came to mind in reading it." Rather than dismissing the individual, this commenter legitimized the other commenter, encouraging his or her participation.

However, some expressed disrespectful statements to delegitimize others' perspectives, including other commenters and, in some cases, the authors of the articles. Some commenters believed that allowing individuals to share their experiences with domestic violence gave a voice to people looking for attention. On September 17, 2014, *USA Today* commenter Don H. said, "Here it comes. Every liberal loser coming out with their sob story." In a forum on September 18, 2014, *USA Today* commenter Greg G. said this openness would lead to statements from "every dame with a horror story." Disrespectful commenters attacked with veiled threats rather than rationality. In response to a September 11, 2014, *Washington Post* article, Zyx321 said, "So now this 'gender reporter' decides that once she saw the video it was all totally different, you see. Really? Or was it another excuse to beat some more on the latest favorite target of the man haters, the NFL." Although we did not observe overt threats toward female journalists, some commenters attempted to delegitimize their articles through mocking their perspectives, pointing out where their reporting was lacking, or tying them to the feminist cause. These commenters distracted from the conversation but were greatly outnumbered by respectful participants.

Including a Diversity of Voices Commenters expressed inclusiveness through statements attempting to broaden others' understanding about domestic violence or showing a willingness to accept others. On September 12, 2014, *Denver Post* commenter Dick L. wrote, "There is no excuse for any male ever hitting a woman. Ever. That said, there needs to be more media attention to the fact that men can be, and are victims of DV as well." Statements like this framed violence against men as a topic that should be discussed alongside violence against women. This opened the door for those with minority views to express them. Certain articles showed more inclusivity, raising the possibility that statements welcoming new perspectives encouraged more individuals to engage. Some commenters' openness to including outside voices reinforced the lack of a dominant perspective as the foundation for the discussion and that the context of the conversation depended upon who participated.

Tolerance for Ideas Beyond welcoming new individuals into the conversation, civility also requires tolerance for new perspectives. This was evidenced through statements of support and reflexive remarks that showed an individual had considered another's viewpoint. In a September 17, 2014, NBC discussion of men as domestic violence victims, one commenter attempted to parse out the nuances of the problem. "Lucy, agree with you, and it's not the same percentage of women hitting men, but it's still wrong, and I sort of doubt these writers will give equal mention to men being abused by women" (Steve-1167608 2014). This comment showed the reflexive interest of the commenter in both recognizing the problem and assessing others sharing that perspective.

Tolerant expressions followed the pattern of individuals calling out other commenters for falling short of the ideal. An NPR commenter (T B 2014) said, "It's comments like yours that make men ashamed to report domestic abuse when it does occur. Given your obvious concern about the topic, I thought you would be concerned about abuse in whatever form it takes." Although the commenter acknowledged the individual's concern about the topic, he or she suggested that the original commenter presented a limited argument.

Networked Publics

Two consistent outcomes emerged from the converations about Ray Rice's acts of domestic violence: discussions of the relationship of the NFL to domestic violence; and discussions of domestic violence. These themes raised questions regarding participants' ability to control the audience and whether the context of the conversation could influence how the discussion developed.

The potential audience for the news stories could include both those interested in discussing football and those wishing to discuss domestic violence. Participants' uncertainty regarding who was potentially listening or participating could influence whether individuals participated and certain perspectives emerged. In one case, a commenter argued that the NFL did not have an obligation to protect women. "The NFL Commissioner is hired by the owners, not left wing liberal women's organizations that neither watch, engage, are fans of, or have a stake in the NFL. Go bother someone else. Leave our Sundays alone" (DJC56 2014). When individuals like this participate, and when women are uncertain whether these individuals will become involved, women may struggle to share feminist perspectives. Forums connected to stories about domestic violence and football automatically began with a broad topic that limited commenters' ability to redirect the conversation toward a feminist viewpoint.

In some cases, however, the reporter specifically structured the story around women and domestic violence and referenced the Ray Rice incident as a current event, rather than the focus of the article. These discussions featured a greater prevalence of female participants and feminist perspectives. This approach reduced discussions of football but also gave those who might feel restricted by audience and context opportunities to tell their stories.

Conclusion

These findings addressed not only how commenters with various viewpoints responded to a particular issue but also how they used online forums as sites of feminist resistance (Van Zoonen 1991), raising opportunities to educate people about victims' experiences, illuminating misunderstood aspects of domestic violence, and calling for reforms to aid victims. When some commenters suggested that feminist activism neglects male needs, other commenters reinforced feminist ideologies. In particular, in response to an article critiquing actor Emma Watson's United Nations speech about HeForShe, many commenters criticized feminism for prioritizing women and ignoring inequalities men face. In response, self-identified feminists clarified the tenets of feminism, including its emphasis on supporting people of various genders. Although women's voices have been marginalized in online venues (Megarry 2014), these forums featured active audiences who challenged unequal power relationships (Fenton 2000). It was less clear, however, whether these short-lived conversations resulted in long-term community-building or change.

The forums also spurred discussions that both reinforced and subverted gender stereotypes. Commenters questioned expectations about the roles women play as both victims and perpetrators of domestic violence and the ways they should address domestic violence as a gendered issue. However, online forums also show promise as avenues for unique voices and perspectives. This potential was particularly evident in commenters' continual use of the forums to share personal stories of domestic violence and support one another. These responses reflected female participants as community creators and collaborators as well as citizens and activists (Van Zoonen 2001), but the ambiguity of the online space suggests that commenters of various genders could fulfill these roles.

Women in the forums were also marginalized and told they did not belong or that their perspectives were unwelcome. However, the conversation was drastically different on a CNN article that talked frankly about domestic violence. The journalist specifically asked women to share their experiences, and the conversation was inclusive, diverse, and congenial. The journalist entered the discussion three times and legitimized the women's experiences. Other commenters showed empathy, legitimized the women's stories, and used their personal experiences to demonstrate the effects of domestic violence. This forum appeared to show how a journalist can serve a positive role as a moderator by both setting the boundaries of discourse and encouraging mutual respect (Edwards 2002; Smith and Wales 2000). Further, the journalist specifically drew in people with personal experiences with the issue, reflecting Parkinson's (2004) description of moderators adding other voices to discourse. The consistent presence of supportive individuals seemed to help prevent the silencing effect that Megarry (2014) argues often occurs in male-dominated online discourse. Criticism of the author was also limited.

Although the conversations showed relatively strong levels of inter-personal respect, civility also requires inclusivity and tolerance of new perspectives. The commenters generally showed respect while challenging others' perspectives. This form of adversarial discourse embedded in interpersonal respect prevented inclusiveness and tolerance from becoming normative features of conversations, except in a few cases. However, those engaging in less civil forms of discourse could see the space as a place for expressing minority opinions. This finding aligns with Zerilli's (2014) argument that socially constructed norms of civil behavior might not represent the interests of underrepresented groups. Those quality cases of civility involved situations in which individuals shared personal experiences with domestic violence and encouraged one another.

In many of the discussions, conversations were less personal and more apt to challenge the legitimacy of advocating against violence against women. Additionally, in some cases, commenters aimed to delegitimize the views or reporting of female journalists. The drastic difference in the level of civility between some conversations raises concerns that some factors could influence the civility of the conversation. Whether these challenges involved online gender harassment on the part of male participants cannot be determined, however, because participants' gender is frequently unknown. The fact that only personal testimonial discussions of domestic violence met the idealistic expectations of civil discourse raises questions as to whether civility norms are adequate tools for studying discussions of women's issues from a feminist perspective.

The online forums and their structures could also affect how discussions developed. Networked publics and their success rely upon conversations in which participants are more aware of the potential audience and more able to control the context of the conversation. Conversations in which participants constricted the topic to the narrow context of domestic violence against women included more female participants, allowed for more feminist community-building, and were more civil. This finding suggests that using news stories to drive discourse about important news topics should be handled with more caution – specifically to ensure that participants receive a narrow context for discussion. This approach appears to provide minority participants with more confidence to participate and less fear that others might hijack the conversation.

Although the Internet has been derided as a threatening space for women to share their stories and perspectives, this study offered evidence that news organizations can provide safe and accessible public venues for women and other marginalized individuals to discuss broad topics with personal implications. Within online forums, commenters can share personal experiences, critiques, and suggestions for collective response. In doing so, individuals may create vibrant, diverse, and engaged online communities.

References

Antunovic, D., & Hardin, M. (2013). Women bloggers: Identity and the conceptualization of sports. *New Media & Society, 15*(8), 1374–1392.

Aran, I. (2014, August 9). Female writer faces Twitter backlash after asking about tampons. *Jezebel*. Retrieved from http://jezebel.com/female-writer-faces-twitter-backlash-after-asking-about-1618802000

Baddog40. (2014, September 15). Ray Rice isn't alone: 1 in 5 men admits hitting wives, girlfriends. *NBC*. [Online forum comment]. Retrieved from http://www.nbcnews.com/storyline/nfl-controversy/ray-rice-isnt-alone-1-5-men-admits-hittingwives-n203841

Baek, Y. M., Wojcieszak, M., & Delli Carpini, M. X. (2011). Online versus face-to-face deliberation: Who? Why? What? With what effects? *New Media & Society, 14*(3), 363–383.

Baumgarten, B., Gosewinkel, D., & Rucht, D. (2011). Civility: Introductory notes on the history and systematic analysis of a concept. *European Review of History: Revue europeene d'histoire, 18*(3), 289–312.

Benbow, D. H. (2014, September 10). Like all abused women, Ray Rice's wife had reasons to stay. *Indystar.com*. Retrieved from http://www.indystar.com/story/life/2014/09/10/opinion-ray-rices-wife-had-millions-of-reasons-to-stay/15335631/

Betsey, A. (2014, September 15). Domestic abusers can reform, studies show. *Wall Street Journal*. [Online forum comment]. Retrieved from http://online.wsj.com/articles/domestic-abusers-can-reform-studies-show-1410822557

Boyd, R. (2004). Michael Oakeshott on civility, civil society, and civil association. *Political Studies, 52*(3), 603–622.

boyd, d. (2011). Social network sites as networked publics: Affordances, dynamics, and implications. In Z. Papacharissi (Ed.), *A networked self: Identity, community, and culture on social network sites* (pp. 39–58). New York: Routledge.

CalypsoSummer. (2014, September 11). Janay Rice's pain may help other women escape domestic violence. *Washington Post*. [Online forum comment]. Retrieved from http://www.washingtonpost.com/local/janay-rices-pain-may-help-other-womenescape-domestic-violence/2014/09/11/dc666e10-39d3-11e4-8601-97ba88884ffd_story.html

Carpenter, M. (2014, September 11). Ray Rice case draws national attention to domestic violence, why some victims stay. *Pittsburgh Post-Gazette* online. Retrieved from http://www.post-gazette.com/news/nation/2014/09/11/Rice-case-hashtag-WhyIStayed-draw-national-attention-to-domestic-violence/stories/201409110155

casesera. (2014, September 27). Sorry, Emma Watson, but HeForShe is rotten for men. *Time*. [Online forum comment]. Retrieved from http://time.com/3432838/emma-watson-feminism-men-women/

Chiefpr. (2014, September 12). Victims of domestic abuse live in fear and often blame themselves. *Denver Post*. [Online forum comment]. Retrieved from http://www.denverpost.com/news/ci_26517562/victims-domestic-abuse-live-fear-and-often-blame

Citron, D. K. (2009). Law's expressive value in combating cyber gender harassment. *Michigan Law Review, 108*, 373–415.

czdanowicz. (2014, September 19). Victims of domestic abuse speak out. *CNN*. [Online forum comment]. Retrieved from http://www.cnn.com/2014/09/11/living/domestic-violence-irpt/

Dahlgren, P. (2005). The internet, public spheres, and political communication: Dispersion and deliberation. *Political Communication, 22*(2), 147–162.

Darr, C. R. (2005). Civility as rhetorical enactment: The John Ashcroft 'debates' and Burke's theory of form. *Southern Communication Journal, 70*(4), 316–328.

Dick, L. (2014, September 12). Victims of domestic abuse live in fear and often blame themselves. *Denver Post*. [Online forum comment]. Retrieved from http://www.denverpost.com/news/ci_26517562/victims-domestic-abuse-live-fear-and-often-blame

DJC56. (2014, September 15). UltraViolet group says NFL plan doesn't get Goodell off hot seat. *NBC*. [Online forum comment]. Retrieved from http://www.nbcnews.com/storyline/nfl-controversy/ultraviolet-group-says-nfl-plan-doesnt-getgoodell-hot-seat-n203701

Don, H. (2014, September 17). Meredith Vieira reveals history of domestic violence. *USA Today*. [Online forum comment]. Retrieved from http://www. usatoday.com/story/life/people/2014/09/17/meredith-vieira-reveals-history-of-domestic-violenceexplains-why-she-stayed/15762049/

Edwards, A. (2002). The moderator as an emerging democratic intermediary: The role of the moderator in internet discussions about public issues. *Information Policy, 7*, 3–20.

Evers, A. (2009). Civicness and civility: Their meanings for social services. *VOLUNTAS: International Journal of Voluntary and Nonprofit Organizations, 20*(3), 239–259.

Fenton, N. (2000). The problematics of postmodernism for feminist media studies. *Media, Culture & Society, 22*(6), 723–741.

Flanagin, A. J., Tiyaamornwong, V., O'Connor, J., & Seibold, D. R. (2002). Computer-mediated group work: The interaction of sex and anonymity. *Communication Research, 29*(1), 66–93.

Foss, S. K. (1996). Feminist criticism. In S. K. Foss (Ed.), *Rhetorical criticism: Exploration and practice* (pp. 165–224). Prospect Heights: Waveland Press.

Greg, G. (2014, September 17). Meredith Vieira reveals history of domestic violence. *USA Today*. [Online forum comment]. Retrieved from http://www. usatoday.com/story/life/people/2014/09/17/meredith-vieira-reveals-history-of-domestic-violenceexplains-why-she-stayed/15762049/

Grinberg, E. (2014, September 17). Meredith Vieira explains #WhyIStayed. *CNN*. Retrieved from http://www.cnn.com/2014/09/09/living/rice-video-why-i-stayed/

Herring, S. (1996). Posting in a different voice: Gender and ethics in CMC. In C. Ess (Ed.), *Philosophical perspectives on computer-mediated communication* (pp. 115–145). Albany: State University of New York Press.

Hess, A. (2014, January 6). Why women aren't welcome on the Internet. *Pacific Standard*. Retrieved from https://psmag.com/why-women-aren-t-welcome-on-the-internet-aa21fdbc8d6#.84bjou4a4

Jane, E. (2012). Your a ugly, whorish, slut. *Feminist Media Studies, 14*(4), 531–546. https://doi.org/10.1080/14680777.2012.741073.

Jane, E. (2016). Online misogyny and feminist digilantism. *Journal of Media & Cultural Studies, 30*(3), 284–297.

Jarrett, T. (2014, September 10). Why she stayed: Ray Rice video sheds light on domestic violence. *NBC News*. Retrieved from http://www.nbcnews.com/storyline/nfl-controversy/why-she-stayed-ray-rice-video-sheds-light-domestic-violence-n200266

Jezebel Staff. (2014, August 11). We have a rape gif problem and Gawker media won't do anything about it. *Jezebel*. Retrieved from http://jezebel.com/we-have-a-rape-gif-problem-and-gawker-media-wont-do-any-1619384265

JimmyRhapsody. (2014, September 27). Sorry, Emma Watson, but HeForShe is rotten for men. *Time*. [Online forum comment]. Retrieved from http://time.com/3432838/emma-watson-feminism-men-women/

kim-2982716. (2014, September 15). Ray Rice isn't alone: 1 in 5 men admits hitting wives, girlfriends. *NBC*. [Online forum comment]. Retrieved from http://www.nbcnews.com/storyline/nfl-controversy/ray-rice-isnt-alone-1-5-men-admits-hittingwives-n203841

Lazar, M. (2007). Feminist critical discourse analysis: Articulating a feminist discourse praxis. *Critical Discourse Studies, 4*(2), 141–164. https://doi.org/10.1080/17405900701464816.

Mantilla, K. (2013). Gendertrolling: Misogyny adapts to new media. *Feminist Studies, 39*(2), 563–570.

McGregor, J. (2004). Civility, civic virtue, and citizenship. In C. T. Sistare (Ed.), *Civility and its discontents: Essays on civic virtue, toleration, and cultural fragmentation* (pp. 25–42). Lawrence: University Press of Kansas.

Megarry, J. (2014). Online incivility or sexual harassment? Conceptualizing women's experiences in the digital age. *Women's Studies International Forum, 47*, 46–55.

onthevraydar15. (2014, September 27). Sorry, Emma Watson, but HeForShe is rotten for men. *Time*. [Online forum comment]. Retrieved from http://time.com/3432838/emma-watson-feminism-men-women/

Orwin, C. (1991). Civility. *American Scholar, 60*(4), 553–564.

PA Quinn. (2014, September 13). Domestic violence protections still resonate 20 years after crime bill. *NPR*. [Online forum comment]. Retrieved from http://www.npr.org/2014/09/13/348016597/domestic-violence-protections-still-resonate-20-yearsafter-crime-bill

Parkinson, J. (2004). Hearing voices: Negotiating representation claims in public deliberation. *British Journal of Politics & International Relations, 6*, 370–388.

Penny, L. (2011, November 11). A woman's opinion is the mini-skirt of the Internet. *The Independent*. Retrieved from http://www.independent.co.uk/voices/commentators/laurie-penny-a-womans-opinion-is-the-mini-skirt-of-the-internet-6256946.html

Ron, W. (2014, September 13). Voices: Domestic violence - From the boy next door. *USA Today*. [Online forum comment]. Retrieved from http://www.usatoday.com/story/news/2014/09/12/voices-ray-rice-domestic-violence/15397021/

Rucht, D. (2011). Civil society and civility in twentieth-century theorizing. *European Review of History: Revue européenne d'histoire, 18*(3), 387–407.

SashaShepherd. (2014, September 27). Sorry, Emma Watson, but HeForShe is rotten for men. *Time.* [Online forum comment]. Retrieved from http://time.com/3432838/emma-watson-feminism-men-women/

Sinopoli, R. C. (1995). Thick-skinned liberalism: Redefining civility. *The American Political Science Review, 89*(3), 612–620.

Smith, G., & Wales, C. (2000). Citizens' juries and deliberative democracy. *Political Studies, 48*(1), 51–65.

Sobleski, B. (2014, February 19). Ravens' Ray Rice allegedly knocked out fiancee at hotel. *USA Today.* Retrieved from http://www.usatoday.com/story/sports/nfl/ravens/2014/02/19/ray-rice-girlfriend-unconscious-atlantic-city/5621415/

Steve-1167608. (2014, September 15). Ray Rice isn't alone: 1 in 5 men admits hitting wives, girlfriends. *NBC.* [Online forum comment]. Retrieved from http://www.nbcnews.com/storyline/nfl-controversy/ray-rice-isnt-alone-1-5-men-admits-hittingwives-n203841

SwankDaddy. (2014, September 19). Victims of domestic abuse speak out. *CNN.* [Online forum comment]. Retrieved from https://www.cnn.com/2014/09/11/living/domestic-violence-irpt/index.html

T B. (2014, September 13). Domestic violence protections still resonate 20 years after crime bill. *NPR.* [Online forum comment]. Retrieved from http://www.npr.org/2014/09/13/348016597/domestic-violence-protections-still-resonate-20-yearsafter-crime-bill

TMZ staff. (2014, February 19). Ray Rice dragging unconscious fiancee after alleged mutual attack [Video]. *TMZ.* Retrieved from http://www.tmz.com/videos/0_c5nk3w3n/

Van Zoonen, L. (1991). Feminist perspectives on the media. In J. Curran & M. Gurevitch (Eds.), *Mass media and society* (2nd ed., pp. 33–54). London: Arnold.

Van Zoonen, L. (2001). Feminist internet studies. *Feminist Media Studies, 1*(1), 67–72.

Warner, M. (2002). *Publics and counterpublics.* Brooklyn: Zone Books.

whatnext??. (2014, September 19). Victims of domestic abuse speak out. *CNN.* [Online forum comment]. Retrieved from http://www.cnn.com/2014/09/11/living/domestic-violence-irpt/

Wilson, R. (2014, September 8). Ray Rice cut by Ravens, indefinitely banned by NFL amid video fallout. *CBS Sports.* Retrieved from http://www.cbssports.com/nfl/news/ray-rice-cut-by-ravens-indefinitely-banned-by-nfl-amid-video-fallout/

Wright, R., & Gehring, T. (2008). From spheres of civility to critical public spheres: Democracy and citizenship in the big house (Part I). *The Journal of Correctional Education, 59*(3), 244–260.

Zerilli, L. M. G. (2014). Against civility: A feminist perspective. In A. Sarat (Ed.), *Civility, legality, and justice in America* (pp. 107–131). New York: Cambridge University Press.

Zyx321. (2014, September 11). I criticized the media for showing Rihanna's battered face. But the Ray Rice video changed my feminist views. *The Washington Post.* [Online forum comment]. Retrieved from https://www.washingtonpost.com/posteverything/wp/2014/09/11/how-the-ray-rice-video-changed-my-feminist-views/?utm_term=.43f9f4fca3b3

Part III

Feminist Resistance

14

Combating the Digital Spiral of Silence: Academic Activists Versus Social Media Trolls

Candi Carter Olson and Victoria Lapoe

A few days after the 2016 presidential election, a Google doc of "False, Misleading, Clickbait-y, and Satirical 'News' Sources" went viral. It was created by Dr. Melissa Zimdars, an assistant professor of communication and media at Merrimack College in Massachusetts, for her mass communication students. Within days of the Google Doc's spread across the Internet, Zimdars had received so many threats and so much harassment that she removed the document and took measures to protect herself on her campus. She told Internet news source *The Daily Dot:*

> Firstly, I am currently being doxed/harassed (and indirectly threatened) by readers of some of the websites on the list (as are my colleagues and even one of my students). This kind of activity is *exactly* why those websites

C. Carter Olson (✉)
Journalism & Communication, Utah State University, Logan, UT, USA

V. LaPoe
E.W. Scripps School of Journalism, Ohio University, Athens, OH, USA

© The Author(s) 2018
J. R. Vickery, T. Everbach (eds.), *Mediating Misogyny*,
https://doi.org/10.1007/978-3-319-72917-6_14

271

were included on my list in the first place, and this kind of activity, largely by the alt-right, will likely be a major roadblock to anyone who is critical of them in the future. (Cameron 2016)

Like Zimdars, many academic women increasingly worry that if they engage in certain kinds of conversations, especially about feminist issues, they will face harassment or threats at some point. Zimdars' experience, though, shows that it isn't only activist conversations that draw out the trolls. The horror that Zimdars faced for her list—a teaching tool and not an activist publication—caused her to withdraw her class material for safety reasons.

Research upholds U.S. women's perceptions that they are targets online. A 2014 Pew Research Center study of online harassment found that 26% of women 18–24 had experienced online stalking, and 25% of them had been targets of online sexual harassment (Duggan 2014). While women were significantly more likely to experience online stalking and sexual harassment, men were slightly more likely to receive physical threats and sustained harassment, although women certainly weren't exempt from these forms of digital intimidation. Thirty-seven percent of women, as compared to 44% of men, were embarrassed, called names, or physically threatened online (Duggan 2014). As author Amanda Hess (2014) reported for *Pacific Standard* magazine:

> Just appearing as a woman online, it seems, can be enough to inspire abuse. In 2006, researchers from the University of Maryland set up a bunch of fake online accounts and then dispatched them into chat rooms. Accounts with feminine usernames incurred an average of 100 sexually explicit or threatening messages a day. Masculine names received 3.7.

Women also are minorities in academic teaching and research positions. In fall 2013, women comprised 35% of the 1.5 million faculty members in degree-granting post-secondary institutions, with only 51% of those professors being full-time employees. Of the full-time faculty, in terms of race, 6% of those professors were Black, 5% Hispanic, 10% Asian/Pacific Islander and less than 1% were American Indian/Alaska Native. Mentorship and collaboration are particularly important within academia, especially for underrepresented groups who can use supportive relationships to navigate the academic promotion system (National Center for Education Statistics 2013).

With women and people of color making up a fraction of academia, it is not surprising that some may feel a double bind. Jamieson (1995) defines the double bind as women not being able to be competent in their work and also a mother. This double bind can lead to silencing, a concept that is particularly important to consider in academic contexts, notes Carmen Luke (1994, p. 212). Luke writes, "Women's historical location in the private sphere of muted domesticity and servitude has excluded them from education, from reading, writing and speaking the public tongue of politics" (p. 213). Therefore, women's gendered roles have placed a constant wrap of silence around their speech that has kept them from participating fully in academic discourse. Those limitations include the framing of canonical texts as masculine, thereby leaving women as "'outsider' readers and reproducers"; the framing of men as "more articulate, more able to sustain rationalist argumentation, and more able to provide the 'life experiences' that professors value and respond to," thereby leaving women "feeling inadequate in a competitive academic environment"; and the framing of women's role as primary caregivers of the home and children, thereby leaving them with additional gendered burdens as they attempt to fulfill those roles and their roles as academics. In sum, "The wall of obstacles that many women students face at university is incomparable to men's experiences at university" (p. 213). As this chapter will show, the obstacles facing women are not limited to students. Women scholars at all levels also find themselves negotiating masculine spaces to assert their own voices.

For women academics, who may find professional support and connections on social media, digital silencing can be problematic for their own career advancement. Social media may provide them alternative support and networking opportunities by connecting with others who can give them advice and support. In addition, academics often share teaching and research tools online that can be used to enhance student education, as in the case of Zimdars' list of fake and misleading news websites. Originally theorized by Elisabeth Noelle-Neumann (1974), the Spiral of Silence theory says simply that the more people perceive their own opinion to be in the minority, the more they will tailor their outward behavior and statements to fit with the majority, in turn silencing their own voices.

The question, then, is: How can female academics feel comfortable to speak out within their careers and the digital sphere?

Social Media Perils

This chapter examines women academics' experiences of online harassment and their reactions to threatening behavior in digital spaces. Through this discussion, the authors explore the opportunities and perils social media present for women seeking to advance their careers. Results from interviews and an online follow-up questionnaire complete a discussion about ideas and solutions for aiding women academics' interactions with digital environments. Through this chapter, the authors will show that the simple act of engaging on social media advances women's voices in online spaces and combats gendered digital silences. The deliberate choice to not engage online removes voices from the digital public sphere, in effect reinforcing the prevailing opinion in online communities and silencing debate. Combating the digital Spiral of Silence creates the possibility of safe spaces for advancing the voices of women and minorities and proliferating professional support networks for academics.

Before we discuss the full results of the interview and survey, it should be noted that this topic is one that aroused extreme emotions in our respondents. One survey respondent said, "This is too sensitive to discuss right now." This same respondent began an answer to the question, "What recommendations would you have to keep academics safe online?" with, "I'm not sure that there is a way to keep anyone safe online." The types of threats received by anyone who distributes material online may be explicit and violent, as Zimdars' story illustrates, and they can escalate quickly as people publicly pile onto the rage machine.

Women, in particular, have historically been silenced in many ways, which is why this chapter particularly focuses on women's experiences with a digital Spiral of Silence. Adam Knowles (2015) notes that the

Greeks saw women's silence as both part of their proper deportment and a good indication of their secretive, duplicitous nature that was prone to tricking men. While Greek men's silences showed their self-mastery and "harmony with one's place," women's silence "disturbs any possible harmony, serves forgetting (*lethe*), and denies women the capacity for straightforward truth-saying" (p. 305). In this system, women's voices were ascribed silence because it marked them as a divisive, sneaky "other" and evicted them from Greek citizenship. Women's silences meant they could not belong. "In this polis, the feminine is thus not simply forgotten, as if through a simple lapse of mind, but is structurally marked as the forgotten" (p. 309). Interestingly, this sense of alienation runs through women's voices as they speak about being trolled in online environments today. The level of harassment faced by women like Zimdars causes them to drop out of online conversations, thus removing themselves from the digital society, just as Greek women were removed from their society by the framing of their silences.

Luke (1994) notes that, in opposition to silences, the revived feminist movement of the 1960s was interested in promoting and advancing women's voices. However, just as there are many kinds of voices, there are also many kinds of silences. Discerning the purpose of a silence can be empowering for women. She argues that "In our classrooms, silence as a politics of resistance must be discussed alongside silence as a possible consequence of guilt and/or threat which must be confronted if it is to become silence as a way of listening" (p. 225). Particularly identifying fear as an impetus for silence, though, can reveal women battling harassment and sexual injustice. Andrea Dworkin highlighted this in her ground-breaking 1979 work *Pornography: Men Possessing Women*. She likened the women and girls who escaped from the pornography industry to escaped slaves or fugitives. "They live in jeopardy, always more or less hiding," she wrote. "They write—in blood, their own. They publish sometimes, including their own newsletters. They demonstrate; they resist; they disappear when danger gets too close. The Constitution has nothing for them… The law has nothing for them—no recognition of the injuries done them by pornography, no reparations for what was taken from them" (pp. xvii–xviii.). In the same way, there are few to no protections from gendered digital harassment and trolling. The Internet exists in a nebulous space where individual social media sites make their own rules about harassment and enforce those rules—or do not enforce those rules—as they see fit.

While feminists are frequent targets, no one seems to be protected from trolls. David French, a male author for the conservative magazine *National Review*, wrote a group blog for the *Review* criticizing Ann Coulter, a vocal conservative media personality whose far-right views during the 2016 election cycle frequently parroted the white nationalist movement. French's blog called Coulter's rhetoric "inexcusable" and said "it has no place in the conservative movement" (*Fresh Air* 2016). Soon after, his "Twitter feed basically exploded" (*Fresh Air* 2016):

> I began to see images, for example, of my youngest daughter, who we adopted from Ethiopia many years ago, who at the time was 7 years old— images of her in a gas chamber with a—Donald Trump in an S.S. uniform about to push the button to kill her. I saw images of her Photoshopped or, you know, artist's rendering of her face in slave fields. (*Fresh Air* Oct. 26, 2016)

Other posts called French names and talked about his wife having sex with Black men while he was deployed in Iraq in 2007 and 2008. "It just descended from there," he said (*Fresh Air* 2016). Even though French was ostensibly the target here, both his wife and daughter were the specific targets of the trolls. Note that French himself was not the focus of the troll's pictures, nor was he being framed as having illicit sexual relationships. He was called names but not visually depicted in degrading ways. The trolling flames focused on the bodies and behaviors of the women associated with French.

In a separate incident, well-known feminist author and activist Jessica Valenti announced on July 27, 2016 that she was taking a break from social media after anonymous trolls threatened to rape and kill her five-year-old daughter. She tweeted, "I am sick of this shit. Sick of saying over and over how scary this is, sick of being told to suck it up." She added in another tweet, "I should not have to wade through horror to get through the day. None of [us] should have to" (Piner 2016, paras. 3–5).

As the rape threat against Valenti's child and the images of French's seven-year-old daughter and discussion of his wife's fidelity show, many trolls target the people and things dearest to a victim. These threats are not only computerized rhetoric. They also are designed to tear at a person's semblance of safety and leave her feeling exposed and vulnerable. A person's conscious decision to retreat from digital spaces and silence her voice is not surprising in the face of these kinds of threats.

Spiraling into Silence

The Spiral of Silence theory and Noelle-Neumann have been heavily criticized, particularly because Noelle-Neumann worked for the Nazi paper *Das Reich* and was a "cell leader" of a Nazi student group, although she denied ever being a member of the Nazi party and repudiated Nazi beliefs later in her life (Honan 1997). Noelle-Neumann claimed that her experiences in the Third Reich and the growth of anti-Jewish sentiment prompted her thoughts about the Spiral of Silence. She said, "My scholarly work was indeed influenced by the trauma of my youth… It was precisely the experience of living without freedom that made the field of public-opinion research so fascinating to me" (Honan 1997).

The Spiral of Silence explains how a vocal minority can push its agenda into the mainstream and overpower other viewpoints. Noelle-Neumann (1974) wrote, "Thus the tendency of the one to speak up and the other to be silent starts off a spiraling process which increasingly establishes one opinion as the prevailing one" (p. 44). The extent to which this silencing actually happens in an in-person environment is a point of debate, particularly when researchers factor in cross-cultural modes of communication and the degree to which people are certain of their own opinion (Matthes et al. 2010; Scheufele and Moy 2000). However, more recent conversation has hypothesized that news media's propensity to present a narrow group of opinions leaves media consumers "misled about the real state of public opinion and, prompted by a 'fear of isolation,'" those same consumers "are less likely to express their own viewpoint when they believe their opinions and are ideas are in the minority" (Neuwirth et al. 2007, p. 450). Noelle-Neumann (1979) writes that this silencing, prompted by mediated framing, influences both publicly expressed ideas and behavior, which is pertinent in the case of academic women choosing to not engage with social media for fear of their own safety or the stability of their careers.

Noelle-Neumann (1993) draws on social psychologist's Paul Lazarsfeld's Bandwagon Effect theory, which says that people will join the majority opinion to avoid social isolation. The Bandwagon Effect is an individual response to fear that culminates in social change (Noelle-Neumann 1993). Those with weaker self-confidence and less interest often are more likely to make the last-minute switches. A main component within the Spiral of Silence is the "fear of isolation"; when there is a chance for separation from the majority, a person becomes vulnerable and a social group can punish them for not being with the majority (Noelle-Neumann 1993). This typically occurs when there is a conflict or a chance of change in an event. Fear of isolation includes fear of someone exposing herself/himself and this person must live not only with his/her feelings, but also with the judgment of the masses.

A criticism of the Spiral of Silence by Scheufele and Moy (2000) is that there needs to be more cross-cultural research, and this chapter, in particular, argues for more gender-based research. For example, how one may speak out in Croatia may be different from the United States or Japan. In subsequent research, Spencer and Croucher (2008) found when surveying respondents in France and Spain that people who believed they were in the *minority*, not the majority opinion, were less likely to speak out against a separatist group. In a more recent study published in *China Media Research*, Xiaodong and Li (2016) conducted an experiment testing climate, fear of isolation, and outspokenness, and noted that those in non-dominant opinion climates had greater outspokenness than those in more dominant climates.

Highlighting the limitations of Spiral of Silence research shows the importance of finding voices that are being delimited from discourse, including women's voices. Even before engaging with media, women academics face a system that prioritizes male voices over their own. The portrayal of educational pursuits as a masculinist endeavor has historically been silencing for women in academia, although much of the writing about academia's inequalities has been about students. Elaine Fredericksen

(2000) argues that "girls of any background can and do feel unacceptable in a culture which seems to have been created for boys. School experiences often appear to reinforce rather than weaken these perceptions. As a result, schoolgirls may become increasingly more timid as speakers and writers. In a very real sense, language fails them" (p. 301). In examining women's proscribed spaces in the university environment, Bano et al. (2011) found that both students and instructors were restricted and excluded from full participation in societies. "Women teachers are subjected to innumerable extralegal rules through an insistence on subordination to authority. They are treated to a range of humiliations if they put for their demands. Prevailing codes of language in university circles invisibilise (sic) and undermine women and mainly define them as objects of voyeuristic pleasure and as 'cultured', 'sweet', 'civilized', and 'decent'" (p. 27). Even the work that women are most often assigned within academic environments—teaching and service—is undervalued. Linda Leigh McDowell argues that "an hierarchical ordering of the different tasks that constitute academic work is used to maintain women's subordinate position" (p. 328). In addition, academic women are subordinated through sexual harassment in the workplace and the "social construction of knowledge," that prioritizes historically masculine traits over historically feminine traits.

Therefore, when considering digital Spirals of Silence and academics, it is important to consider that women academics are already working from a position of historical silencing within their institutions. Reaching out to other women across social media platforms provides the opportunity to strengthen and promote women's intellectual work. It also helps women combat imposter syndrome, the feeling that no matter how much a high-achieving woman knows or has accomplished, she somehow still cannot measure up and one day will be discovered as an "imposter." Kate Bahn (2014) argues that female-oriented support groups, including those that are found online in social media sites and elsewhere, "can bolster women's self-esteem by providing safe spaces for discussion and affirmation that yes, they do belong in academia" (para. 13–14). The dual silencing from both institutions and Internet trolls reinforces the ideology that educational pursuits are masculine in nature, and that women's voices should be circumscribed from both realms of discourse. Connections with other women, including connections purely across digital spaces, reinforce women's self-worth and give them a sense of belonging that can lead to increased retention and promotion of women academics.

Digital Spirals of Silence

Online posts and pages are shared, interactive, voluntary, and deliberate communications. These items create a shared online culture, where a person is participating and providing views that may serve within or outside of majority opinion. Carey (1992) discusses a ritualistic view of communication that one shares, participates, and maintains fellowship. With this in mind, online communication may serve as maintenance to majority opinion; communication that is not focused on the sharing of information, but instead on forming a community with agreed-upon beliefs. However, the questions then raised include: how does one account for the silence? If digital spaces reinforce majority opinions, are there spaces where silenced opinions can challenge that opinion's dominance?

In one of the first articles researching relationships between digital media and the Spiral of Silence, Liu and Fahmy (2011) studied the impact of new media on virtual behavior motivation and found that when the likelihood of speaking out online increases, so does the likelihood of speaking out in a physical setting. If a climate is consistent with one's own opinions, participants also appeared more willingly to speak offline. Askay (2015) discovered similar results in terms of an online participatory community. Members of a hospitality travel website suppressed non-positive reviews because of fear of isolation from this community.

When examining work relationships and the Spiral of Silence, a study found that employees felt uncomfortable speaking out about *any* issues (Milliken et al. 2003). The reason for remaining silent included being viewed negatively, facing consequences in the workplace, and damaging relationships. In South Korea, journalists who believed there was a discrepancy between their opinions and Twitter users' opinions were also less willing to voice opinions (Lee and Kim 2014). This study found that journalists' ideologies impacted their perceptions. Journalists who were politically conservative felt they were in the minority and were not as likely as politically liberal journalists to discuss opinions on Twitter.

Interviews with Academics

To examine the pressures and potential pitfalls of social media for academics and who feels safe speaking out and who does not, the authors interviewed 45 scholars, women and men, about their social media use. The interview subjects gathered were a purposive sample based on the characteristics the authors were investigating: specifically academics, gender and digital media use. The authors sent solicitations for participants to the Association for Education in Journalism and Mass Communication (AEJMC)'s Commission on the Status of Women, Minorities and Communication Division, and LGBTQ Interest Group. The authors were particularly interested in feedback from groups whose voices have been marginalized in the academy. Because there were no consistent responses to a query about whether the interview subjects had been harassed online in the first round of interviews, the authors circulated a four-question follow-up Qualtrics questionnaire to all interview participants to receive the broadest response possible. Twenty-seven people responded to the follow-up survey. Of those, 22 were women, three were men, and two did not indicate a gender. This is consistent with the gender breakdown of the original interviews, which consisted of 36 women and nine men. Interviews were conducted between May and August 2015, and the survey was circulated in September and October 2016. Among the survey respondents, seven indicated that they had definitely been harassed, three said maybe, and 15 said they had not been harassed. Both the interview and survey were anonymized. Both men and women academics were sought for this study to compare experiences; as noted, however, our sample was primarily female. The survey asked questions regarding experiences posting on digital media platforms, how academics engaged the public, and peer communication. Specifically, we were interested in what academics shared, what they did not share, where they shared it and why.

The people who were interviewed and responded to the survey reported a wide variety of experiences with digital harassment. One survey respondent reported being attacked both on Facebook and Twitter: "The Facebook harassments were more sexual, comments from strangers. The one time on Twitter I got trolled for my views on Indian politics." One survey respondent reported being stalked online when working as a professional journalist, and another had a social media account hacked by an ex-husband. Another scholar reported being harassed by students online. When other people who were not students had addressed the academic in a "disrespectful way," this person chose to engage to a point, and then blocked the person if the conversation continued to be confrontational. In the original interviews, an assistant professor who frequently posts on progressive issues ranging from LGBTQ rights to racial equity reported getting into confrontational online conversations with people.

> My wife was encouraging me to just unfriend them rather than argue every time because they want to argue race issues or they want to argue about political issues and then I waste time doing that… This is the part of the new living room so if you want to post your own stuff, that's fine post it. It's not an invitation for you to come tell me how horrible of a person I am.

An associate professor and university administrator said her first experience with a troll was someone who reacted with racist epithets to one of her posts inviting people into conversation on a seemingly innocuous topic:

> I had one person call me a "nigger" on Twitter. It was one of these trolls. See this is the thing, I'm not Twitter famous. I'm not like a [recording interference] on their radar, but I said something about like, "what books were you going to read for the summer?" And this guy responded like, "You nigger bitch," or something like that. And I was like… I wasn't astonished. I was like, wow, I have a troll, this is a first.

Based on these conversations, the experience of digital harassment is as diverse for academics as it is for other professions, and many of our respondents have experienced some level of hostility. Some of those attacks were in response to political ideology; others were harassment based on a person's identification with a specific racial or ethnic minority or sexual or gender identity.

Even if it wasn't perceived as outright harassment, many interview and survey respondents reported negative interactions online. One American academic at an international university said, "I don't think I have [been harassed]." However, she then followed up by recounting two recent experiences with online hostility "I tweeted something recently and a guy replied with really something negative and I just ignored it. I was just saying to myself like what are you talking about, but I was like don't even say that to him just move on." One survey respondent called this kind of behavior "usual," noting, "[I've experienced] The usual trolling by friends of FB friends on political posts and even, rarely, a FB friend. Recently, I had to tell a high-school friend that his behavior on the thread was insulting and inflammatory."

The implication here is that trolling is normative and unavoidable, and perhaps that people who are being targeted should respond with the digital equivalent of a shrug. Fighting back seems difficult, as well, since trolls are behind a wall of anonymity and many social media sites' rules do not provide adequate protection. A survey respondent reported digital attacks to Twitter, but the company dismissed it:

> I wrote a column about racism and sexism in the 2016 Olympics and some trolls started tweeting at me and posting messages on Facebook calling me an "idiot" and a "moron." When I got a comment on Twitter that said "I hope you don't procreate," I reported it to Twitter. I got an answer from Twitter a few days later that there had been no violation of their policies.

Digital spaces seem to lack protection, causing people to self-censor or retreat fully from online conversations.

Interestingly, even though 15 survey respondents said they had never been harassed online, among the women interviewed, there was a sentiment that even if they hadn't been harassed online yet, the experience was an inevitable part of participating in social networks. That fatalistic feeling was predominant in survey responses as well. An instructor who identifies as part of the LGBTQ community has been attacked multiple times online. The interviewee noted that she expects negative feedback when online:

> I think it's just part of the territory. I don't know how to explain it other than that of course when you're doing anything online you have to expect you're seeing the best and the worst of everyone, so of course we act differently in online communities than we do in real life. There are people who would argue against that, but I think that you do see the wicked because you're behind this wall of anonymity or pseudo-anonymity.

One academic noted that the worst online encounter she's had so far was confrontational remarks about her work.

> The comment I got, I wouldn't consider it harassment. It was just simply a comment about my work. But that's [harassment] something I fully anticipate eventually will happen. Considering [I am] somebody who studies issues of gender, I anticipate that will unfortunately happen.

Self-Censoring into Silence

Because of this sense of the inevitable nature of online attacks and a lack of protection from social media sites, many of our interviewees and survey respondents take steps to try to avoid trolls by censoring their online comments and participation. A dominant theme from our interviewees was that academics should be careful of what they put online for professional reasons, with a subset of those respondents noting that the self-censorship will protect them from harassment. An administrator and professor at a multi-campus university considers self-censorship a form of defense.

> I try to stay away from things that could get me in trouble, quite frankly. Well, I identify that my views are my own on my blog. I don't identify my university at all. But I really want to be careful about the things that I say. So usually I stick to safe "topics" like parenting and customer service or crisis communication or something like that.

The academic who was called a "nigger" noted that she sees self-censorship as a necessary part of an online engagement strategy:

It's like when one of my graduate student friends, when we were in grad school together, wanted to study the Ku Klux Klan and white supremacy groups. And she was warned, "They will hunt you down, and they will make your life miserable." And I said, "…That's a note for future self: don't do things that are super controversial." Not because I'm not interested in them, but because there's a certain element of my safety. I like my life. I like living. I don't like being harassed. So is it very feminist of me to not engage with those things? Probably not, but also for my personal safety—I have to have some joy and a bit of comfort of anonymity in my own life.

In a climate where trolling is seen as a weapon that can ruin lives, this concern is particularly salient. In the wake of the 2016 elections, it was reported that the Neo-Nazi website "The Daily Stormer" distributed a list of more than 50 Twitter users "who had expressed fear about the outcome of the 2016 election" and told followers to "punish" those users by trolling them until they committed suicide (Chmielewski 2016). A woman associate professor we interviewed said:

One of the problems I think is because of the degree of harassment women often encounter that women are retreating. We know that the research tells us that, and I think that's very unfortunate because it's an important way to be in the world and to communicate with a very, very wide range of people. And I mean it's good for personal development and professional development as well. So it's not just getting your message out, but learning a lot more about a lot of new subjects taking in new ideas. And if women are not a part of that conversation, then their views, their voices are lost or continue to be separated over here.

In addition to women's voices being suppressed in the digital sphere, our participants remarked that women lose opportunities to network and promote their work if they're censoring their online engagements. This is particularly problematic for scholars who are minorities or academics who may be working in isolation. However, those opportunities aren't necessarily available on a person's campus because of the small numbers of people of color, in particular, in the professoriate. An administrator said digital spaces are particularly important for women of color, who use networking strategies to survive and advance in the academy,

> I think we've lost a little bit of that in the sense that people feel "free" to talk about whatever they want to on their wall until they talk about something that offends someone else and then everybody wants to shut everybody down. This is not the place to do this… well if it's not the place then where are we supposed to do it? It's my wall. So if I'm struggling as an academic as a woman of color in academia I should be able to talk about that on my Facebook wall and seek counsel without being made to feel like I'm less than a human being because I'm struggling. And I've seen some young academics try to do it and I've seen the responses and it's really terrible because people are not kind, saying this is not the place for that and I can't believe you want to engage in this conversation… well it needs to happen.

Combating the Spiral of Silence

Many of the academics who participated in this study expressed fear of judgment that would lead to them losing their jobs, so they deliberately choose not to share certain information or engage in online conversations as a form of protection. This self-censorship creates a Spiral of Silence. As noted, most of the people who participated in our research groups identify as women. This means the digital Spiral of Silence identified here is primarily composed of women. Our interviewees and survey respondents universally identified this spiral as a problem. Combating the digital Spiral of Silence allows diverse people to find mentors and support systems, which, in turn, could lead to those people successfully advancing through their academic careers. This would demonstrate to students and faculty that the academy actually does value diverse perspectives.

What does it take to combat the digital of Spiral of Silence reported by our interview and survey respondents? Our survey respondents mentioned a variety of potential solutions, ranging from steps that individuals can take to protect themselves to institutional changes that need to be made at universities. Many of the individual changes, although not all, reinforced the Spiral of Silence identified throughout this chapter, with people recommending that academics simply censor what they post and avoid engaging in controversial conversations. Others encouraged scholars to educate themselves about the various issues. As one respondent wrote, "Read a lot, stay up to date to issues around social media. Don't just be a user." Others advocated that scholars proactively block and filter people and report inappropriate behavior to sites in the hopes that this type of active protection will create a safe space for non-hegemonic voices. Some of these recommendations include:

1. "Post rules of behavior, moderate threads/forums, and block people who violate the rules."
2. "Delete a lot, filter a lot, check all settings often since companies change their rules without notice."
3. "Ignoring when the posts escalate and lodge a formal complaint to Twitter or Facebook requesting to block the person."

Social media sites are constantly updating their policies and interventions when it comes to online harassment, so users need to stay abreast of changes. In 2016, Twitter, notorious for its trolls, instated new user controls over who can see and interact with individuals (Leong 2016), put in place a way for users to report up to five tweets at a time (Olivarez-Giles 2016), and announced a new Twitter Trust & Safety Council in February (Cartes 2016). The more people raise their voices, the more the social media sites seem to be listening and trying to control trolls.

In terms of institutional changes, participants indicated that both universities and social media sites have culpability for the harassment leading to the Spiral of Silence. One survey respondent said, "I think the biggest issue is making sure professors are backed and supported by their institutions and their security systems. Often the cyber-end of things is ignored." Another respondent said, "Universities need to do the best job possible to screen the students they admit and make sure that there are appropriate prerequisites in place for course [sic] covering sensitive and mature material." While some universities provide advice for professors to help students with online harassment, many universities have not publicly endorsed policies for faculty and staff who are being harassed.

The Spiral of Silence is not universal across academics. As some of our interviewees and survey respondents said, they see opportunities for educating people by engaging in controversial topics online. Participating in digital communities creates a space for voices to be heard, and some participants said they have felt empowered by being able to post their views online. One assistant professor said that political posts often bring positive reactions and help to create community. "If anything, I have students and colleagues that are like jazzed up about it. Like one of my students, I posted this rant I got, and she was like, 'look at my badass professor!' So it's been mostly positive." Another associate professor explained that even though she's had negative feedback and had people dismiss her thoughts, she primarily sees the Internet as an important and empowering places for activist academic voices. She summed up what many of our respondents expressed:

> I would just say some other people are just dismissive… "oh well you're just some feminist who doesn't know what's she's talking about." But I would say a majority of people are interested in listening, interested in considering, interested in debating. And you know, to me, if they want to offer an alternative viewpoint and make a strong argument for it, that's great. I'm willing to listen, and I've changed my mind on some issues because of arguments like that. But just defensive statements of, "you don't know what you're talking about?" I do great work, shut up. That's just not helpful at all.

References

Askay, D. A. (2015). Silence in the crowd: The spiral of silence contributing to the positive bias of opinions in an online review system. *New Media & Society, 17*(11), 1811–1829.

Bahn, K. (2014). Faking it: Women, academia, and imposter syndrome. *Chronicle Vitae.* Retrieved from https://chroniclevitae.com/news/412-faking-it-women-academia-and-impostor-syndrome

Bano, S., Nanda, B., Bandyopadhyay, M., & Datta, N. (2011). Women on campus: Negotiating spaces and silences. *Economic and Political Weekly, 46*(53), 27–29.

Cameron, D. (2016, November 17). Viral 'fake news' list deleted after author and students get harassed, doxed. *The Daily Dot.* Retrieved from http://www.dailydot.com/layer8/fake-news-facebook-deleted-alt-right/

Carey, J. (1992). *Communication as culture: Essays on media and society.* New York: Routledge.

Cartes, P. (2016, February 9). Announcing the Twitter trust & safety council. Twitter, Inc. Retrieved from https://blog.twitter.com/2016/announcing-the-twitter-trust-safety-council.

Chmielewski, D. (2016, November 12). White supremacists urge trolling Clinton supporters to suicide. *USA Today.* http://www.usatoday.com/story/tech/news/2016/11/10/white-supremacists-urge-trolling-clinton-supporters-suicide/93617792/.

Duggan, M. (2014, October 22). *Online harassment.* Pew Research Center. Retrieved from http://www.pewinternet.org/2014/10/22/online-harassment/

Dworkin, A. (1979). *Pornography: Men possessing women.* New York: Plume.

Fredericksen, E. (2000). Muted colors: Gender and classroom silence. *Language Arts, 77*(4), 301–308.

Fresh Air. (2016, October 26). Harassed on Twitter: "People need to know the reality of what it's like out there." *NPR.* Retrieved from http://www.npr.org/2016/10/26/499440089/harassed-on-twitter-people-need-to-know-the-reality-of-what-its-like-out-there?utm_source=facebook.com&utm_medium=social&utm_campaign=npr&utm_term=nprnews&utm_content=2052.

Hess, A. (2014, January 6). Why women aren't welcome on the internet. *Pacific Standard.* Retrieved from https://psmag.com/why-women-aren-t-welcome-on-the-internet-aa21fdbc8d6#.tx3wh14xg

Honan, W. H. (1997, August 27). U.S. Professor's criticism of German Scholar's work stirs controversy. *The New York Times* [online edition]. Retrieved from http://www.nytimes.com/1997/08/27/us/us-professor-s-criticism-of-german-scholar-s-work-stirs-controversy.html

Jamieson, K. H. (1995). *Beyond the double bind: Women and leadership.* New York: Oxford University Press.

Knowles, A. (2015). The gender of silence: Irigaray on the measureless silence. *The Journal of Speculative Philosophy, 29*(3), 302–313.

Lee, N. Y., & Kim, Y. (2014). The spiral of silence and journalists' outspokenness on Twitter. *Asian Journal of Communication, 24*(3), 262–278.

Leong, E. (2016, August 18). New ways to control your experience on Twitter. Twitter, Inc. Retrieved from https://blog.twitter.com/2016/new-ways-to-control-your-experience-on-twitter.

Liu, X., & Fahmy, S. (2011). Exploring the spiral of silence in the virtual world: Individuals' willingness to express personal opinions in online versus offline settings. *Journal of Media and Communication Studies, 3*(2), 45.

Luke, C. (1994). Women in the academy: The politics of speech and silence. *British Journal of Sociology and Education, 15*(2), 211–230.

Matthes, J., Morrison, K. R., & Schemer, C. (2010). A spiral of silence for some: Attitude certainty and the expression of political minority opinions. *Communication Research, 37*(6), 774–800.

McDowell, L. L. (1990). *Sex and power in academia.* The Royal Geographical Society (with the Institute of British Geographers), *22*(4), 323–332.

Milliken, F. J., Morrison, E. W., & Hewlin, P. F. (2003). An exploratory study of employee silence: Issues that employees don't communicate upward and why. *Journal of Management Studies, 40*(6), 1453–1476.

National Center for Education Statistics. (2013). Race/ethnicity of college faculty. [Electronic version]. Retrieved November 17, 2016 from https://nces.ed.gov/fastfacts/display.asp?id=61

Neuwirth, K., Fredrick, E., & Mayo, C. (2007). The spiral of silence and fear of isolation. *Journal of Communication, 57,* 450–468.

Noelle-Neumann, E. (1974). The spiral of silence: A theory of public opinion. *Journal of Communication, 24*(4), 43–51.

Noelle-Neumann, E. (1979). Public opinion and the classical tradition: A re-evaluation. *Public Opinion Quarterly, 41*(2), 143–156.

Noelle-Neumann, E. (1993). *The spiral of silence: Public opinion, our social skin* (2nd ed., pp. 11–15). Chicago: University of Chicago Press.

Olivarez-Giles, N. (2016, April 26). Harassed on Twitter? Now you can report up to five tweets at once. *The Wall Street Journal.* Retrieved from http://www.wsj.com/articles/harassed-on-twitter-you-can-now-report-up-to-five-tweets-at-once-1461706377

Piner, C. (2016, July 28). Feminist Writer Jessica Valenti takes a break from social media after threat against her daughter. *Slate.* Retrieved from http://www.slate.com/blogs/xx_factor/2016/07/28/feminist_writer_jessica_valenti_takes_a_break_from_social_media_after_threat.html

Scheufele, D., & Moy, P. (2000). Twenty-five years of the spiral of silence: A conceptual review and empirical outlook. *International Journal of Public Opinion Research, 12*(1), 3–28.

Spencer, A. T., & Croucher, S. M. (2008). Basque nationalism and the spiral of silence: An analysis of public perceptions of ETA in Spain and France. *International Communication Gazette, 70*, 137–154.

Xiaodong, Y., & Li, L. (2016). Will the spiral of silence spin on social networking sites? An experiment on opinion climate, fear of isolation and outspokenness. *China Media Research, 12*(1), 79–88.

15

The Varieties of Feminist Counterspeech in the Misogynistic Online World

Scott R. Stroud and William Cox

Online harassment takes many forms, but at its core is a new media version of the harassment women are routinely exposed to in offline settings. In 2014, the Pew Research Center conducted a study of online harassment in the U.S. that showed one-third of women had personally experienced some type of harassment, and 72.5% of women reported witnessing someone being harassed online (Citron 2014). Most of the harassment towards men occurred in the form of name calling and attempts to embarrass; however, for women, the most common forms of harassment were threats of sexual violence and stalking. Alarmingly, only 40% of the women surveyed by Pew claimed to have addressed their most recent incident of harassment (Duggan 2014). Harassment of any kind is abhorrent, but the harms of online harassment presents women with a double bind: be catcalled outside on the street, or demeaned in the comfort of your living room. On an individual level, harassment can have negative effects on self-esteem and interfere with a person's quality of life. From a group

S. R. Stroud (✉) • W. Cox
Department of Communication Studies, University of Texas at Austin, Austin, TX, USA

© The Author(s) 2018
J. R. Vickery, T. Everbach (eds.), *Mediating Misogyny*,
https://doi.org/10.1007/978-3-319-72917-6_15

293

perspective, harassment creates unsafe spaces and undermines community building.

Women and their allies have not remained complacent in reaction to such harassment online. As the cases of online misogyny multiply beyond comprehension, women have turned to the use of *counterspeech* as a way to undo the harms of other's misogynistic speech. Counterspeech is "the idea that 'bad speech' can be effectively countered or cured with more speech," rather than legal prohibition or government coercion (Richards and Calvert 2000, p. 554). In this chapter, we will say something about the general types of counterspeech being developed as responses to online harassment by examining two recent cases: 1) Anna Gensler's artistic attempt to draw attention and shame to misogynistic men she encountered on apps such as Tinder, and 2) TrollBusters' coordinated attempt to create a visible support network for the female victims of Internet harassment. After examining the general scope of online misogyny as well as these two uses of counterspeech, we will discuss the ethical intuitions— and conflicts—underlying these different uses of force as responses to online misogyny. Counterspeech will be shown to be a rich, albeit normatively complex, path of resistance to harassment online.

The Scope of Online Misogyny

An overwhelming amount of harassment takes place on social media, partially because of its ubiquity, partially because opinion and belief are front-loaded in social media, and partially because social media also allows for the quick distribution of abusive messages to individuals or to groups of targets. We categorize such abuse in two ways: inflammatory and malicious. *Inflammatory harassment* attempts to derail conversations in progress by presenting nonsensical or deliberately provocative arguments and comments. The objective focus of such attacks is to remove the agency of the target, forcing them to either deal with the interruptions or stop their conversation. *Malicious harassment* takes the form of gender-based insults and threats of sexual and physical violence. Where inflammatory harassment seeks to disrupt a public conversation, malicious harassment is targeted at the source and aims to scare the target into silence.

The Internet provides a platform for trolls to recreate the harassment of the offline world. What prompts a user to become an abuser? Initially, online harassment can be explained by the "online disinhibition effect." Suler (2004) argues that "when people have the opportunity to separate their actions online from their in-person lifestyle and identity... they don't have to own their behavior" (p. 322). This enables harassment grounded in a patriarchal mindset that views women as objects. Far from being a simple act, "objectification should be viewed as a cluster concept, involving seven distinct ideas: instrumentality, denial of autonomy, inertness, fungibility, violability, ownership, and denial of subjectivity" (Nussbaum 2010, pp. 69–70). Objectification works as a systematic process for a harasser to take power from their target. In online cases, the harassment is not targeted at content, but at the person producing the content. Even when gender plays no role in the nature of the attacks, men are often the prime agents of online harassment. Hinging on Suler's assertions, it appears "the weak need to affirm themselves, relieving the psychic distress that comes with subordination, by creating a virtual world, an expressive world, in which they hold sway" (Kindlon and Thompson 2009). Objectification serves as a way to seek power over and through other human beings.

The final factor contributing to the harassment of women online comes from the inherent anonymity that the Internet provides. Even without using measures to hide all traces of your identity (such as your IP address), one can still easily create a new name, gender identity, and even choose an unrealistic photo avatar to shape their online self. This is not all for the worse, of course. Many have written on the ethical challenges—and virtues—created by malleable online identity (Baym 2010; Donath 1999; Stroud and Pye 2013; Turkle 1995). It is clearly an important aspect to consider in talking of misogyny online, since such malleable identities allow trolls and other harassers the chance to hide their identity from offline consequences as they create harms for their targets.

Beyond such factors lies significant systemic factors: offline incompetence fostered by a lack of conversation among victims and non-victims, deep tensions with established doctrines of free speech, and a lack of law enforcement training. Authorities do not often recognize the toll that being female takes on online targets (Citron 2014). This leads to a practical challenge: the absence of effective and informed police policy concerning online abuse and harassment enables such abuse to continue to occur. In surveying the range of hate-motivated acts on the Internet, Citron notes, "the majority of law enforcement agencies do not investigate cyber stalking complaints because they lack training to understand the seriousness of the attacks, the technologies used to perpetuate them, and the usefulness of existing laws… Police officers in local and rural communities rarely have any training about the problem of cyber stalking" (Citron 2014, p. 84). Many online activities could be pursued under existing harassment and stalking laws (as addressed in the Conclusion of this book), but this requires a motivated and knowledgeable policy presence. Authorities are also concerned about the uncertain lines between harsh speech and bullying or stalking. Some putative crimes involving speech and expression, such as the posting of revenge porn escape the grasp of many existing laws and may require new legislation (Stroud 2014). The laws that do concern cybercrime focus on fraud, identity theft, and intellectual property rights, not how people interact in heated communicative interactions. All of this adds up to a psychological and legislative free-for-all that enables harassment and exclusion of girls and women in the online world. Operating with such a fostered feeling of impunity not only exacerbates harassment, but also tends to normalize the biases that motivate it. When victims have no recourse, and abusers have no reason to stop, the cycle continues.

The Spectrum of Feminist Counterspeech

Short of possessing a superhuman capacity for ignoring such vitriol online, women must create strategies for responding to digital misogyny. The common question of "how can women respond to online misogyny" must be replaced with a query that marks the sophistication, range, and nuance of such responses. This section will illustrate two ways that women have reacted or acted against online harassment using *counterspeech*, or speech designed to remedy the harms of others' use of speech. The idea of counterspeech has its roots in the liberal philosophy of John Stuart Mill (1859/2002), who famously decried efforts to use government force to coercively silence unpopular opinions. Yet the question of how strategies of counterspeech are enacted and differ from each other is still left unanswered. Additionally, such an investigation will assist us in the final section in the project of analyzing the *types of decisions* evident in using counterspeech as a response to online harassment. This will be important since there is a notable difference in the types of counterspeech available. For instance, does one's counterspeech target the harasser or those who would think highly of the harasser? Or does one's counterspeech build up those who have been harassed? The two cases we will analyze represent recent uses of technological means to respond to hateful online discourse directed primarily at women. Some research has looked at efforts to combat racism and bullying online (e.g., Stroud 2016, in press), but most of these strategies are characterized by the *anonymous* agency of those pursuing a path of speech or action. What is unique about the cases we examine is that their originators or enactors are non-anonymous in their use of speech to counter or remedy misogynistic speech. As we will demonstrate, this brings both benefits and drawbacks to these methods of counterspeech.

One of the more sustained and unusual uses of feminist counterspeech as a remedy to online misogyny occurs in the efforts of the artist Anna Gensler. Gensler was interested in the increasing amount of misogynistic discourse that women were subjected to on dating apps such as Tinder. As Amanda Hess (2014) notes, Gensler met the reality that most women on such dating apps fall into during her six months on Tinder: their mere presence as women on an app that many take as representative of "hookup culture" served as the stimuli for an immediate barrage of pick-up lines. For the most part, these lines were extremely crude, and almost always referenced sexual acts or the female body. For instance, Gensler received texts from "matches" in her city that opened up conversation with her with lines such as "Bet your tight" or "If I was a watermelon, would you spit or swallow my seeds" (Hess 2014). As conversational starting points, these statements are extremely crude and presuppose the only value to the person on the other end of the Internet connection was as a sexual object for the sender. Gensler was shocked at the misogyny she witnessed from simply just being on this app, and searched for a way to respond. She asked, "What is something I can do to make me feel the way that they're making me feel" (Hess 2014)?

The strategy of counterspeech that she created was unique. In order to teach the men bombarding her with unwanted objectifying message the lesson that "objectification is a two-way street," she began to objectify them as sexualized objects. She used their profile picture, drew them naked, and then referred them to the portrait in a following message (Stampler 2014). This was not a private revelation. As Gensler discussed in an interview about her activities, she posted the drawing—coupled with choice pick-up lines and dialogue from the offender—on her publically viewable Instagram account. Thus, when the men saw their image, they were seeing what others are seeing if they followed Gensler's Instagram account. While most did not send her nude pictures, she "just started doodling how I would imagine them naked… except sad-naked. It was the most immature thing I could think of, because their pickup lines are the most juvenile, basic things, but also still oddly offensive" (Hess 2014). These unflattering nude portraits featured recognizable images of the offender's face, as well as his first name and age. Thus, she would pair an objectifying line such as "You are ANNA-tomically what I'm looking for" or "You tryna get the pipe?" with an unflattering nude image of the utterer in an attempt to demonstrate that these "guys are immature and their lines are incredibly juvenile, yet they are still offensive to the women they are aimed toward" (Zarrell and Carrissimo 2014).

When she tried this exercise in counter-objectification on OKCupid (another dating site), Gensler's profile included the disclaimer that "'I'm going to draw you naked if you send me rude messages,' and linked back to her Instagram" (Zarrell and Carrissimo 2014). Strangely enough, such a warning was either unnoticed or disregarded, as men continued to send her objectifying utterances. Some even requested that she draw them nude, which Gensler noted "defeats the purpose" (Buesman 2014). Thus, Gensler continued to draw, name, and shame the men that sent her unsolicited harassing lines. As Callie Buesman (2014) argues, such lines are not simple extensions of what one should expect if one's on such apps; instead, they are "just an extension of the unwanted harassment they face on a daily basis. Simply put, women shouldn't have to constantly field aggressive sexual advances—and, online, it is both constant and aggressive." Most men portrayed in her artistic counterspeech did not appreciate this lesson. Indeed, as Gensler (2014) revealed on her blog, she has been subjected to sustained campaigns of stalking and death threats from certain portrayed individuals, courses of action that authorities have been unable to address effectively.

By objectifying men in a public fashion (through her Instagram account followed by thousands), Gensler was striking a blow against two parties: the men using the objectifying utterances and those third parties observing. These parties, of course, could be skeptical parties concerning the putative abuse that women face; Gensler's artistic renditions of these men would highlight through a range of examples the sort of harassment of women that does exist online. These parties could be sympathetic individuals, who could be rallied to the reality of Gensler's cause through her public shaming of these individuals. In the "act of turning the male gaze back on its perpetrators" (Brooks 2014), men targeted as harassers experience the displeasure of being represented as sexual objects. More than this, they seem disturbed by an *inaccurate* representation of their sexual organs and overall weight; some seem fine with being objectified, as long as it is on their self-interested terms. Thus, Gensler's artistic mode of counterspeech aimed at shaming misogynistic men reveals an interesting underpinning—objectification is integrally related to agency. Some agents see their interest and agential powers as tied to *not* being cast as a sexualized person or object in a public setting, whereas others seem to want to exert their agency through *how* they are rendered as a sexual object. Either way, Gensler's approach works by *publicly* targeting the *harassing individual* in a way that they do *not approve of* or that brings them some sort of *harm*. Her strategy of counterspeech thus relies on shame and publicity to harm those who she judges as morally deserving of such harm, a common operation for courses of online shaming (Ronson 2015).

Another strategy of counterspeech calculated to combat online misogyny came from the actions of Michelle Ferrier. As an African-American journalist in a largely white area of Florida, Ferrier reported on important issues that involved race. This spawned admirers in her online audience, but it also spurred hatred from some readers. One in particular began sending her threatening letters, and Ferrier would later speculate that this person was part of an organized hate group (Kabas 2016b). Her experience was not unique, as the International Women's Media Foundation and the International News Safety Institute reports: almost two-thirds of women journalists that were polled had experienced online "intimidation, threats or abuse in relation to their work" ("Magnitude of the problem" 2016; see Chap. 7 for Everbach's chapter on women journalists). During the "Gamergate" incident, a loosely coordinated backlash of mostly male gamers against female gamers, game reviewers, and journalists, Ferrier saw the way that misogynistic bullying can accumulate in overwhelming amounts on a person's Twitter feed, driving them offline (Kabas 2016b, March 18). She then hatched the plan for a concerted counter to this deluge of Twitter and online negativity: an organization she would dub "TrollBusters" (see Chap. 16 for Ferrier and Garud-Patkar's chapter on TrollBusters).

As Ferrier describes it, "TrollBusters is a just-in-time rescue service for women writers and journalists." It uses "positive messaging and education to create a hedge of protection around targets in online spaces like Twitter," all with the goal of keeping female Internet users online by providing "emotional, technological and other supports to help targets rebuild their digital identity and reputation" (Hare 2016). The way TrollBusters uses speech to counter hateful speech is multifaceted. Its primary method is through flooding an individual being targeted by trolls with positive messages. These "positive, supportive messages" function as a visible "counter narrative to drown out hateful trolling" (Sillesen 2015). Trolls work by degrading and harassing their victims, so the strategy of TrollBusters is to undo this harm, even if they cannot fully remove the troll's or harasser's motive for their caustic speech acts. The TrollBusters "never respond to the harassers' comments, no matter how vitriolic, and instead focus on providing support for the target of abuse." Instead, TrollBusters posts "inspirational quotes, safety tips for dealing with harassment, and general words of encouragement to remind women in the public eye who speaks their minds that they shouldn't be ashamed and they're not alone" (Kabas 2016b, March 18). All of this is done publicly to show the target of abuse and others watching this individual—now or in in the future—that they were supported in this time of unreasonable attack. Will the trolls or harassers be changed or altered due to this use of counterspeech? This is unclear, but it is the effect of silencing women that TrollBusters attempts to meliorate.

TrollBusters also serves as an information source for women online concerning social and legal recourse to dealing with trolls or harassers. They are even branching into locating and "outing" trolls and "troll nests," or sites and groups that organize hateful discourse campaigns online. All of this, however, is secondary to the social support function that TrollBusters aims to provide to targets of online misogynistic abuse. The TrollBusters team responds to a submitted complaint, but their long-term goal is "that women will eventually be able to set up personal S.O.S. teams of friends and family, who can send personal messages" (Sillesen 2015). This social-support approach to keeping women online in the face of online misogyny is growing in popularity, and includes other groups and organizations in addition to TrollBusters. One of these allied organizations is "HeartMob," an operation organized by the anti-harassment group "Hollaback!" to pair supportive women with targeted women (see Chap. 17 for Desborough's work on Hollaback!). Volunteers for HeartMob receive reports of harassment from women online, and then "craft custom messages to users who have posted their harassment stories with encouraging words about appearance, self-esteem, and ignoring the haters" (Kabas 2016a, January 27). Like TrollBusters, the supportive messages come from a community that a targeted individual does not know offline. This is part of the power of the online world—individuals can take up causes, good or bad, easily and at a distance against those they judge worthy of such condemnation or praise. This drives organized campaigns of self-righteous harassers as much as it does the feminist groups organizing counterspeech to support the targets of such campaigns.

What we see emerging from these two strategies of counterspeech is a *spectrum of force* that can be utilized against online misogyny. Gensler's approach operates on the principle that those that hate and harass women should themselves be made to feel a similar harm. Her drawings target specific individuals, the ones judged as transgressing norms of respect due to any human online, and attempt to marshal the opinions of observing others to shame them. Perhaps the public can identify the perpetrator's identity, or perhaps they will simply remain unknown beyond that crude drawing, first name, and age. The former potential brings

Gensler's efforts close to the machinations of those who post nonconsensual porn as a punishment for some relational transgression: both involve revealing private sexual features in public as a way to harm an individual, and both involve a similar logic of addressing harmful actions through another harmful action. Of course, she does not reveal all of the individual's identifying information, but neither do many revenge porn posters (Stroud 2014). A little information may be enough to find this specific person in the age of image search or online mobs acting as sleuths. Gensler's activities use art to bring a sort of hurtful force to bear on the harassing individual. We can call such a use an instance of *targeted negative counterspeech*. It takes aim at a specific individual, and it attempts to negatively—albeit justifiably to many observers—affect their psychological or physical well-being.

The second sort of counterspeech—exemplified by TrollBusters and similar operations—can be contrasted to the pervious type of counterspeech in its target orientation as well as the sort of force employed. TrollBusters also subscribed to a general feminist agenda, and harassment of female journalists undoes much of the progress toward its goals, as it sets back both the target of the harassment and others who may be demoralized in such a quest through observing such online hatred. TrollBusters epitomizes what we can call the *directed positive counterspeech*. It is *directed* insofar as it is adapted to one specific person—the victim of this harassment, and her emotional support needs. It differs from the previous form of counterspeech since those target specific harassers. This strategy is also *positive* in that it seeks to rebuild or increase the self-esteem and emotional valuing of the victim, thereby keeping her online. It ignores anonymous and potentially unreachable trolls and harassers, and instead works to assist the target of the harassment through creating an immediately available support network. The force employed here is not a harm-inducing negative type of force; instead, TrollBusters and other similar entities are using speech to build up specific agents online, just as Internet trolls and mobs use speech to help each other hurt specific targets.

Ethical Conundrums to Online Feminist Counterspeech

Let us explore the normative value of the two approaches detailed. If we have the chance to use our speech to counter online misogyny, which approach ought we to follow? If we are to encourage others to use their expressive powers to combat online hate, what should we advise—and for what reasons? These questions highlight the practical, normative side to online counterspeech, a first-person aspect that implicates agents as speakers beyond the abstract ruminations of theory and general critique. In this concluding section, we will discuss the challenges created or represented by the Gensler and TrollBusters cases, thus expanding what we know about the complex normativity of the *targeted negative counterspeech* and *directed positive counterspeech* types.

The notion of counterspeech occupies complex ethical terrain. In U.S. jurisprudence, it has been clearly linked to the free speech value of the First Amendment and to the solution of the harms of negative speech. For instance, Justice Louis Brandeis concurred in *Whitney* v. *California* that "If there be time to expose through discussion the falsehood and fallacies, to avert the evil by the processes of education, the remedy to be applied is more speech, not enforced silence" (Richards and Calvert 2000, p. 553). But this is too simple for some critics. As Richards and Calvert (2000, p. 554) note, opposition to any normative reliance on counterspeech comes from a variety of quarters, some alleging that there is a lack of time to address the putatively bad speech, there is no guarantee that the recipients of the harmful speech will be reached by counterspeech, there is no equal access to the means of counterspeech for all groups, and that hate speech silences its victims, thereby preventing the workings of counterspeech. What is distinctive about the cases covered in this chapter is the fact that counterspeech did occur, and its targets maintained some sort of agency and efficacy in the face of online harassment. Thus, the normative challenges to counterspeech occur here *inside* of the domain of counterspeech, and sidestep the larger question over counterspeech's usefulness per se.

What are the ethical challenges to the *types* of counterspeech covered in the present analysis? One immediately sees that there are issues that can be raised about the type of force employed and its relevant target. In Gensler's case, one could worry about the meliorative value of the harm caused to these specific misogynistic speakers. Is such harm warranted? Is such harm useful for creating a non-patriarchal society and its related forms of interaction, both online and offline? For the TrollBusters case, the questions are similar: bolstering the victims is fine, but does not the guilty deserve some equitable treatment? Is it useful to allow these specific harassers to go on with their activities without any consequence? If we can conceive of emotional harm and reputational harms as true *harms*, and we can conceive of activities that intentionally cause harm to others as *violence*, we are approaching a fundamental decision point in interpersonal and group ethics. How are we to respond to violent activities, either as a society with its institutions (such as the legal system) or as individuals (with our limited means of physical force or expressive force)? *Normatively speaking about actions within our control, should we do violence to those who do violence to others*? This seems to be the fundamental point of conflict that lies behind our support of or resistance to these types of counterspeech. Even though they stop short of physical violence (e.g., coordinating death threats and sustained paths of physical harm), they do involve or elide the creation of harm. For instance, Gensler's artistic techniques are calculated to embarrass and shame those drawn and named, and there is some chance of this online shame from others being connected to offline identities. Given the latter possibility, it is interesting how close Gensler's technique comes to some practices of revenge porn posting: they both use private issues of sexuality to shame and thereby harm those judged to be worthy of such harm. One of the most important differences, however, comes in the judgment of each offending party. Many people would think those Tinder users who used such crude lines deserved *some* response, whereas few probably have the epistemic grasp on relational facts to say that this ex-partner deserved this type of sexual shaming. But this difference in judgment does not satisfy the inherent question of whether those employing harmful speech deserve harm in return, or what type or level of harm they deserve.

Some observers will perceive Gensler's approach to be the right one— harm those who dare to harm others who do not deserve such treatment. Others will hesitate, recognizing the supposed wrong in both the harasser's treatment and the artist's shaming. The latter sort of observer might be drawn more to the supportive, non-harming form of counterspeech represented by TrollBusters and its message of victim support. Some might even think that the best approach is using *both* negative and positive counterspeech, helping victims and hurting perpetrators. Yet this middle path will not work, at least insofar as we need to resolve the fundamental issue of when violence or harm can be done to others. What we can discern under this divergence in pathways of counterspeech is a struggle at the heart of important approaches to normative ethics. One such approach focuses on the creation of ideal communities or states of affairs. This is the endpoint that activities as means must strive for, and thus provides a consequentialist measure of acceptability for all actions. In our cases, this would be a standard that tells us the unacceptability of online misogynistic harassment as well as the acceptability of an artist's counterspeech designed to shame and harm those individuals. One of the leading exemplars of this sort of intuition is utilitarianism, championed in the western world by individuals such as Jeremy Bentham (1781/2007) and John Stuart Mill (1861/2001). Central to this ethical system is the commitment that the base motivators of human activity are pleasure and pain, and that ideally we ought to strive to minimize the latter and maximize the former. Since all humans are equal in feeling these qualities of experience, utilitarianism trends toward an egalitarian philosophy, aiming for the creation of systems or communities that maximize pleasure and minimize pain. Means are only important, according to this basic reading of utilitarianism, insofar as they create pleasure or alleviate pain. We can see this *intuition* as underlying efforts such as Gensler's drawings—we can create a better state of affairs or community of agents if we create harm for these problematic individuals.

Mill is also noteworthy as one of the first male philosophers to overtly argue for a conception of equality among men and women. He can thus be taken as an early feminist figure, given such imperfect texts as *The Subjection of Women* (1869/1870) that used utilitarianism to argue that it was to society's moral and prudential advantage to enact measures to treat women as equal to men in all regards. This text was developed in collaboration with his wife, Harriet Taylor Mill, although her efforts sadly were not acknowledged in the work published after her death in 1858. The utilitarian view espoused in this book was very progressive for its time, and portrays the "legal subordination of one sex to the other" as "wrong in itself," and argues for the utilitarian advantage of replacing such sexism with "a principle of perfect equality, admitting no power or privilege on the one side, nor disability on the other" (1). Of course, the cases of counterspeech dealt with here push the consequentialist critique of online misogyny beyond legal measures; it deals with opinions and communication, or the use of social approbation or support to create effects. Mill's notion of free speech fits into this reading of effect creation. In *On Liberty* (1859/2002), Mill takes a strong stance prohibiting coercive restraining of unpopular opinions. He is one of the most important advocates of the "marketplace of ideas" idea, arguing that the best (most useful, on utilitarian grounds) response to "clearly" wrong or evil speech is countering speech. By engaging such speech simply as speech to be evaluated, we can show how firm our hold on the good and the true is, and how incorrect the bigots or unpopular others are. Occasionally, they are right, of course, so Mill maintains that it is best for society to allow such unpopular speech, since censoring it out of existence would remove from us the opportunity to gain its truths should we see their light. One could see the utilitarian argument for shaming through speech, though: a viable and justified consequence of vigorous counterspeech is to show the absurdity or evil of some opposed view, and the publicity of such an effort ensures that others would learn from this interaction. Thus, shame being brought about on a shameful opinion exposed through the operations of counterspeech is a fair cost to a system of speech that leads equal speaking agents closer to better opinions and beliefs. On such an account, both directed positive *and* targeted negative counterspeech is normatively justified, as they both play a role as speech-based means in creating a system free of absurd—and potentially harmful—opinions and beliefs.

For those that would support only positive counterspeech, where might their normative intuition lie? We believe that they may find a source of justification in the deontological system of Immanuel Kant. Kant famously grounded his system of ethics not on pleasure or pain, but on the inherent value of humanity as an end in itself (1785/1996). Lest we think that this ethical system is too far removed from human social life, scholars such as Marcia Baron (1995) have given us lengthy explanations about how Kant's arguments for respecting humanity impacts vital issues in feminist philosophy, such as underwriting social claims of care, love, or fellow feeling with other agents. The most important part of Kant's ethics, though, is that some duties of love or respect must be recognized as transcending momentary consequences, putting him at odds with consequentialist views. In emphasizing absolute respect for human agency, his philosophy can be appropriated and extended to feminist approaches to critique of dehumanizing and objectifying activities (e.g., see Hay 2013; Schott 1997). The intuition underlying much of Kant's ethics parallels the thinking of those who may oppose Gensler's efforts, but support positive efforts such as TrollBusters: no matter how awful an agent is, some amount of respect is due to him or her since they are a human agent. This intuition would tell us, no matter how awful you think a trolling attempt is, or how much good can come from shutting this person up through evoking online mobs or shaming attempts, one should not do this to them since they are an intrinsically valuable human. The same sort of reasoning underlies our judgments about how a harasser is so wrong in treating their victim in a certain way; the standard does not change since one's status as a moral agent does not change through previous action. No matter how pure or vile one is, one still deserves respect. Such an intuition would hesitate about shaming perverted, rude, or chauvinistic agents on Tinder, even if we firmly believe the world would be better if those agents were beaten or shamed into silence or rectitude. On such an account, the respect due to all human agents acts as a limiting factor on our use of violence through counterspeech. Just as their harmful speech is wrong, so is our purposefully harmful counterspeech. We must find better ways, such a critic exclaims, such as TrollBusters or non-directed courses of fighting misogynistic views.

This inquiry ends, in one sense, no further than it began. There are still deep issues yet to be decided about the use of counterspeech in the fight against online misogyny. Yet the debate has been clarified, and this is a gain. We can now see that all counterspeech is not the same, even in the domain of feminist responses to online harassment. The cases analyzed in this study—Anna Gensler's use of nude drawings in fighting patriarchy on Tinder and TrollBusters' supportive measures for female journalists and writers—have revealed a structure of possible types of counterspeech. More than this, the general distinction of *targeted negative counterspeech* and *directed positive counterspeech* highlight the different types of force employed on differing agents. More must be said on this, since online modalities of speech and malleable identity will only continue to inspire new and creative ways to harass and harm women on the Internet. Counterspeech will also take advantage of these online powers, but the normative questions will be there for us as well as for those we dub as harassers: how ought we to use the powers of expression and occluded identity online? Thus, we view our efforts here as a starting attempt to follow out the charge of Richards and Calvert, who concluded more than a decade ago that "New media provide new opportunities for counterspeech, and new chances to explore its potential" (2000, p. 586).

References

Baron, M. W. 1995. *Kantian ethics almost without apology*. Ithaca: Cornell University Press.

Baym, N. K. (2010). *Personal connections in the digital age*. Malden: Polity.

Bentham, J. (1781/2007). *Introduction to the principles of morals and legislation*. New York: Dover Publications.

Brooks, K. (2014, April 23). Artist turns creepy online dating exchanges into nude Instagram artworks. *Huffington Post*. Retrieved from: http://www.huffingtonpost.com/2014/04/23/anna-gensler_n_5192977.html

Buesman, C. (2014, April 22). Genius woman responds to OKCupid creeps by drawing them naked. *Jezebel*. Retrieved from http://jezebel.com/genius-woman-responds-to-okcupid-creeps-by-drawing-them-1566157819

Citron, D. K. (2014). *Hate crimes in cyberspace*. Cambridge, MA: Harvard University Press.

Donath, J. S. (1999). Identity and deception in the virtual community. In M. Smith & P. Kollock (Eds.), *Communities in cyberspace* (pp. 27–56). New York: Routledge.

Duggan, M. (2014). *Online harassment*. Retrieved from http://www.pewinternet.org/2014/10/22/online-harassment/

Gensler, A. (2014, June 10). *The truth of the matter*. Retrieved from http://www. annagensler.com/blog/the-truth-of-the-matter

Hare, K. (2016, March 28). Meet the woman drowning out trolls that harass female writers. *Poynter*. Retrieved from: http://www.poynter.org/2016/ meet-the-woman-drowning-out-trolls-that-harass-female-writers/

Hay, C. (2013). *Kantianism, liberalism, and feminism: Resisting oppression*. New York: Palgrave Macmillan.

Hess, A. (2014, April 22). How to get revenge on online dating creeps: Draw them naked. *Slate.com*. Retrieved from http://www.slate.com/blogs/xx_factor/2014/04/22/anna_gensler_gets_back_at_tinder_and_okcupid_creeps_by_drawing_them_naked.html

Kabas, M. (2016a, January 27). Harassment-fighting HeartMob aims to drown out the trolls. *Daily Dot*. Retrieved from: http://www.dailydot.com/irl/ hollaback-online-harassment-heartmob/

Kabas, M. (2016b, March 18). TrollBusters helps protect women writers from online bullies. *Daily Dot*. Retrieved from http://www.dailydot.com/irl/ troll-busters-online-harassment/

Kant, I. (1785/1996). Groundwork for the metaphysics of morals. *Practical philosophy* (trans: Gregor, M. J.). New York: Cambridge University Press.

Kindlon, D., & Thompson, M. (2009). *Raising Cain: Protecting the emotional life of boys*. New York: Ballantine Books.

"Magnitude of the problem". (2016). *Trollbusters*. Retrieved from http://www. troll-busters.com/

Mill, J. S. (1859/2002). *On liberty*. New York: Dover Publications.

Mill, J. S. (1861/2001). *Utilitarianism*. Indianapolis: Hackett Publishing Company.

Mill, J. S. (1869/1870). *The subjection of women*. London: Longmans, Green, Reader, and Dyer.

Nussbaum, M. C. (2010). Objectification and internet Misogny. In S. Levmore & M. C. Nussbaum (Eds.), *The offensive internet, Cambridge* (pp. 68–90). Harvard University Press.

Richards, R. D., & Calvert, C. (2000). Counterspeech 2000: A new look at the old remedy for 'bad' speech. *BYU Law Review, 2*, 553–586.

Ronson, J. (2015). *So you've been publicly shamed*. New York: Riverhead Books.

Schott, R. M. (1997). *Feminist interpretations of Immanuel Kant*. University Park: Pennsylvania State Press.

Sillesen, L. B. (2015, July/August). *Columbia Journalism Review*. Retrieved from http://www.cjr.org/analysis/the_invaluable_service_of_trollbuster.php

Stampler, L. (2014, April 23). This is the most glorious way to respond to creepy Tinder advances. *Time*. Retrieved from http://time.com/73777/ anna-gensler-tinder-response-draw-naked/

Stroud, S. R. (2014). The dark side of the online self: A pragmatist critique of the growing plague of revenge porn. *Journal of Mass Media Ethics, 29*(3), 168–183.

Stroud, S. R. (2016). 'Be a bully to beat a bully': Twitter ethics, online identity, and the culture of quick revenge. In A. Davisson & P. Booth (Eds.), *Controversies in digital ethics* (pp. 264–278). New York: Bloomsbury Press.

Stroud, S. R. (in press). The Jaina rhetoric of nonviolence and the culture of online shaming. In M. Kennerly, & D. Pfister (Eds.), *Ancient rhetorics and digital networks*. Tuscaloosa, AL: University of Alabama Press.

Stroud, S. R., & Pye, D. (2013). Kant on unsocial sociability and the ethics of social blogging. In M. E. Drumwright (Ed.), *New agendas in communication: Ethics in communication professions* (pp. 41–64). New York: Routledge.

Suler, J. (2004). The online disinhibition effect. *Cyberpsychology & Behavior, 7*(3), 321–326.

Turkle, S. (1995). *Life on the screen: Identity in the age of the internet*. New York: Simon & Schuster.

Zarrell, R., & Carissimo, J. (2014, April 22). This artist found an amazing way to get back at men who objectify her on Tinder. *Buzzfeed*. Retrieved from: https://www.buzzfeed.com/rachelzarrell/an-artist-found-an-amazing-way-to-get-back-at-creepy-men-on

16

Trollbusters: Fighting Online Harassment of Women Journalists

Michelle Ferrier and Nisha Garud-Patkar

Michelle Ferrier, a journalism professor at a U.S. university and former newspaper columnist, had been looking at her Facebook feed in the summer of 2014. It contained stories of the women media workers who had spoken out about misogyny in the video game industry and had been subject to rape and death threats online. The backlash by trolls, organized under the hashtag #Gamergate, used Twitter, Reddit, and Internet Relay Channels 4chan and 8chan to fight against these "social justice warriors." The goal of the trolls: to bombard targets online with misogynistic, sexist, and violent threats. Brianna Wu, a video game developer and a writer, who often talked about misogyny in the gaming industry, was one of the women under attack during Gamergate. She was forced to leave her home after harassers sent her threats and packages via mail. The fear of being attacked left a psychological impact on Wu. Even an unexpected knock on the door would send her into a panic. Wu kept a baseball bat

M. Ferrier (✉)
E.W. Scripps School of Journalism, Ohio University, Athens, OH, USA

N. Garud-Patkar
Department of Journalism and Mass Communication,
San Jose State University, San Jose, CA, USA

© The Author(s) 2018
J. R. Vickery, T. Everbach (eds.), *Mediating Misogyny*,
https://doi.org/10.1007/978-3-319-72917-6_16

311

near her door and employed staff to work full-time to handle her tweets and emails (Hedayat 2015). (For an analysis of Gamergate and misogyny, please see Chap. 6.)

Ferrier knew all too well what it felt like to be targeted by threats: she had left her job as a newspaper columnist many years ago because of hate mail and the online harassment she received. What if she could do something to help women journalists feel supported in a way she had not? How could she keep them online and writing even while they were under attack? Ferrier decided to take an experience that had cost her job, her home, and her peace of mind and turn it into good.

Ferrier had been an award-winning columnist for a Florida daily newspaper when she began to receive hate mail. She was the first African-American columnist for the newspaper in 2003 and her picture appeared alongside her weekly column called "Chasing Rainbows." Ferrier's slice-of-life stories of raising her children as an African-American woman in central Florida garnered a diligent following of local fans, but also attracted an undercurrent of society that didn't want to see an African-American woman in the newspaper pages. Arriving both electronically and via the postal service, the hate mail Ferrier began to receive focused on her gender and her race. One letter writer wrote long, racist screeds, manifestos that went beyond critiques of the columns and threatened her and all n****s with an upcoming race war.

"HOW DO YOU GET A NIGGER OUT OF A TREE? CUT THE ROPE!!"
"BEFORE THIS WORLD ENDS, THERE WILL BE A RACE WAR…"
"ALL YOU PEOPLE DO IS CRY BITCH WINE [*sic*], BITCH."
"HAVE YOU PLAYED THE RACE CARD MICHELLE THIS WEEK?"

Ferrier received many letters from the harasser, who for several years continued to send her mail that escalated in violence and hate. Ferrier believed the letters were the work of a hate group that used this vile mail to threaten and intimidate women and people of color. She went to the local police, and the Federal Bureau of Investigation and the Central

Intelligence Agency to get someone to investigate the threats. No one could help her. The hateful letters, though frightening, skirted the letter of the law. Local police were unable to investigate unless there was an actual crime, they said. Ferrier went to professional organizations like the Society of Professional Journalists and the National Association of Black Journalists. These organizations had never before addressed the issue of online harassment of journalists and couldn't offer Ferrier any guidance. Ferrier finally sought out the Committee to Protect Journalists, which championed Ferrier's case to the U.S. Department of Justice. However, with the inauguration of the nation's first African American president, the nation's investigative agencies were tracking a rise in hate speech online and the rise of hate groups around the nation. Organized hate was on the rise, according to the Southern Poverty Law Center. Ferrier finally left her job and her home and moved to another state to become a journalism professor.

However, Ferrier soon realized that racism has no borders. An African-American female student at Ferrier's North Carolina college was walking along the roadside and was threatened by an oncoming car that tried to run the student off the sidewalk. The white male students in the car shouted the N-word at the student as it sped off. The student went to the campus police to report the crime. Ferrier thought about her own experience at the newspaper and how emotionally damaging the experience had been for her. She wanted to explain to her communication students how words could hurt, so she decided to reveal her past to her students, show them the letters she had received, and share the impact on her work and her life.

During the emotionally charged class, Ferrier explained how she began choosing the topics of her column carefully to avoid drawing the hate of this letter writer. She described how her life and the lives of her children and husband changed because of the letters, culminating in her move to North Carolina. Then she asked the students to brainstorm ways that social media and communication tools could be used to bring awareness to campus harassment. They created a hashtag—#NotonMyCampus—and began to tweet supportive messages to the African-American student population. The next class period, students brought cards and letters of support and love to Ferrier.

One anonymous student wrote:

> Not a drop of vengeful talk slipped from your tongue the other day. That is not only more than any other human being can say for themselves, but it is also the very embodiment of courage. You are very brave, madam. And we, as students, would be wise to learn from your character as we are under your teaching this semester.

And another student: "I hope you know that through your story, you serve as a beacon of hope and it is my hope that all of us take that and use it to become lanterns of our own by standing up against intolerance everywhere."

The positive love letters helped Ferrier heal and she wondered if the same strategy could be used to help women journalists facing online harassment.

Challenging Hate with Love: The Birth of TrollBusters

A hackathon for women media entrepreneurs provided the venue for Ferrier to develop an "anti-Gamergate" tool to help women journalists combat online harassment. A hackathon is a short design sprint, usually lasting a couple of days. In January 2015, the International Women's Media Foundation (IWMF) hosted a summit and a hackathon in New York to bring together media professionals, technologists, and female news entrepreneurs to help address barriers and challenges to female-led ventures, including funding ("Why VCs aren't funding" 2016). The IWMF is a Washington, D.C.-based organization that is dedicated to strengthening the role of women journalists worldwide. The organization's website professes that the news media worldwide are not truly free and representative without the equal voices of women. The IWMF summit brought together women publishers, content creators, technology developers, journalists and others to brainstorm solutions. Ferrier attended the summit as a panel moderator for a session on financing startups. She stayed that evening for the hackathon.

Women journalists, front-end developers, designers and educators gravitated toward the ideas they wanted to implement, then worked into the evening developing ideas to pitch before judges the next day. The judges were scrutinizing each pitch on four criteria: usefulness, creativity, technical difficulty and user-friendliness.

Ferrier wanted her team to develop an anti-Gamergate solution. Recent media coverage of Gamergate and attacks on celebrities and women scholars online resonated with the audience of women journalists. Some of them had experienced online harassment themselves. The anti-Gamergate project pitch garnered the interest of three other team members at the hackathon—female journalists from around the globe. The team included Debbie Galant, formerly of Montclair State University's NJ News Commons; Louisa Reynolds, a former IWMF Fellow and a U.K. freelance journalist; Berta Valle, general manager of Vos TV from Nicaragua and our hacker Sneha Inguva, co-founder of Perooz, a browser service to refute false claims in news reports.

Ferrier's idea would combine natural language processing and machine learning to provide just-in-time support to targets of online harassment. Ferrier's solution would use keywords to monitor the feeds of journalists, then used the language to help refine search and rescue on Twitter. Machine learning would build on that knowledge base to teach web crawlers to identify threatening tweets.

The TrollBusters solution would then drown out the nastiness of the trolls with positive messages and legal, technological, or emotional support. In June 2014, a *New York Times* article had revealed that Facebook had been experimenting with users' feeds (Goel 2014). Facebook engineers had tweaked the algorithms to adjust the number and tone of users' feeds, either feeding users more "positive" or more "negative" content. Facebook found that people who were exposed to more negative content posted more negative content. Users who were exposed to more positive content in turn posted more positive content. Mood, they found, was contagious. Ferrier had been following the Facebook research closely and felt that if she could moderate the tone of a users' feed with positive content, TrollBusters posts could make the feed a less inviting environment for trolls.

Ferrier's team worked for 12 hours to define the problem, find statistics, determine what services and supports they could offer technologically and emotionally to women under attack and they hacked and created wireframes to visualize potential solutions. The international team helped put in perspective that trolling was one part of a problem that sometimes included lost jobs and lost lives. And that online harassment is not just an American problem. Within 24 hours, her team developed the prototype with key features and pitched their idea—Troll-Busters.com—as an "online pest control" service that would provide support to women journalists, bloggers and news publishers on Twitter.

Other ideas pitched to the judges included LaunchMeet, a matchmaking site for founders and coders; The Gender Report, a tool to analyze the ratio of female and male sources in news stories; and PitchCoach, a mobile app to help founders perfect the all-important pitch, among others. Team TrollBusters was one of the last to present.

The idea received one of the top cash prizes from Google, a sponsor of the IWMF hackathon. Ferrier then went on to pitch the idea to the Knight Prototype Fund competition and, in May 2015, she received an additional $35,000 grant from the Knight Foundation. Ferrier launched the beta version of Troll-Busters.com in September 2015. Her premise: Counter hate with love. Her tag line: Online Pest Control for Women Writers.

With Troll-Busters.com, Ferrier sought to create a hedge of protection around women journalists at the site of attack. By entering a URL where online harassment is occurring, the target signals the S.O.S. team at Troll-Busters.com that floods the target's Twitter stream with positive messaging and endorsements—fighting hate with love. TrollBusters use memes that provide online protection tips to alert the target and other followers that TrollBusters is monitoring and capturing interactions on the Twitter feed. When Troll-Busters.com is alerted to online harassment through its website or on Twitter, the service sends positive messages and just-in-time education to help the target protect her location and help her document, deflect, and respond to online harassment. Ferrier believed that positive, funny, encouraging, and inspirational messages could help bolster the emotional state of women journalists—diluting the disturbing and violent text and images sent by the harassers.

Using Pinterest and a series of memes providing quotes and tips on online protection, Troll-Busters.com distributes tweets into the tainted Twitter stream, letting the target—and the trolls—know that someone is watching. Using quotes from famous people like scientist Jane Goodall or civil rights leader Martin Luther King, Jr., or instructional memes like "Use an anonymous 'cloak' or browser to wipe your digital footprint." Troll-Busters.com helps equalize the balance of power online by providing just-in-time emotional, technical, and legal supports to women journalists. The service provides referrals to lawyers, psychologists, and technical supports and helps coach targets about next steps. While trolls have anonymity on their side, women journalists have a network of colleagues who have their backs.

The Impact of Online Harassment on Journalism

Digital media have become integral to the workflow of the media industry and journalists. Journalists are virtual newsgatherers, who use social media tools to find new sources, distribute content, and engage with audiences (Ahmad 2010; Bor 2014; Cozma and Chen 2013).

On social networking sites such as Twitter and Facebook, journalists find themselves under attack by online actors commonly called trolls. Digital platforms such as Twitter and Facebook Live have become a haven for perpetrators to remain anonymous and generate online "smart mobs" to attack women, people of color, and traditionally marginalized groups through criticism, taunts, and provocative messages. The messages often move beyond critique—as protected speech—into the realm of online harassment (Clifford 2015; Ferrier 2016; Filipovic 2007; Munoz 2014).

Online harassment is defined as an intentional and overt act of aggression toward another person online, which involves making rude or nasty comments toward someone, or intentionally embarrassing another user in retaliation for a perceived wrong (Ybarra and Mitchell 2004). Tweets, online comments, and Facebook status updates contain threats of violence against journalists, the release of a journalist's personal information (known as doxxing), or expose them to violent content. They may also contain hate speech with sexist, racist, homophobic, anti-Semitic comments. For example, the Anti-Defamation League (ADL) Task Force on Harassment and Journalism conducted a study in October 2016 to capture anti-Semitic language on social media. Using a broad set of keywords, the team found that a total of 2.6 million tweets contained language frequently found in the anti-Semitic speech posted across Twitter between August 2015 and July 2016. Moreover, about 19,253 overtly anti-Semitic tweets were sent to about 800 journalists in the United States during the same period (ADL 2016). In the online gaming community, this activity is called "griefing," where players use varied tactics to intentionally inflict grief on other players by slowing or stopping their gameplay (Hunter et al. 2015). The online harassment of journalists, like "griefing" in virtual environments, can create a chilling effect—journalists may avoid online contact, reduce the media content they create and share, and withdraw from reporting, social media, and other job-related activities.

The term *chilling effect* was first used in the context of the *Wieman* v. *Updegraff* case in 1950 when the state of Oklahoma enacted legislation that all public employees were required to take a loyalty oath swearing they were not directly or indirectly associated with any communist organization (Penney 2016). The legislation deterred citizens' rights to privacy and led to a chilling effect on their rights to free speech. Penney (2016) states that similar cases that dealt with anti-communist state measures during the 1950s and 1960s led to the establishment of a doctrine in First Amendment jurisprudence termed the "chilling effects doctrine."

In a legal context, the term "chilling effect" is an objection evoked against government laws that unintentionally deter the rights of citizens to express their opinions freely. These rights refer to the freedom of speech and freedom of expression as granted to citizens in the First Amendment of the U.S. Constitution. Schauer (1978) said that if a common law sanction aimed at punishing the publication of defamatory factual falsehood has an effect of suppressing the truth or an opinion, then a chilling effect is registered.

Chilling effects are also seen in situations where people or groups have sufficient power to make it difficult for others to express their opinions, such as trolls deterring speech on social media. Schauer (1978) states that when individuals do not exercise their fundamental rights, the whole society is at a loss because the constitutional rights that the First Amendment guarantees are not exercised. Scholars in the field of mass communication have used the chilling effects as a theoretical perspective to examine conflict in intimate relationships (Solomon et al. 2004), online surveillance and Wikipedia use (Penney 2016), and the impact of peer-to-peer scrutiny on social media (Marder et al. 2016). A few scholars have used this perspective to examine Internet trolling and online hostility (Jane 2015). Terms such as "cyber-bullying," "cyber-stalking," "cyber-violence," "trolling," and "flaming" are all subsets or variations of each other and, to a large extent, contribute to the explication of hostility in the digital environment and the silencing of users' self-expression (Jane 2015). When applied to journalists, these activities hinder the operation of a free press.

Online Harassment and the Safety of Journalists

When journalists are targets, the online harassment takes a toll on the news enterprise. The chilling effect on individual journalists and journalistic lines of inquiry can lead to the silencing of diverse voices in the media, the technological takedown of an ethnic media site, or the abandonment of a line of investigative inquiry.

A report on journalists' safety conducted in 2015 by the International News Safety Institute found that all news organizations have become larger targets of violence over the past ten years as their content is routinely retweeted or shared on social media. The institute surveyed 170 international journalists and found that 88% agreed that the safety of journalists and media workers is more of an issue than it was ten years ago, whereas 86% stated that journalists are more likely to be targets of violence, and that social media was a key driver for this violence (Clifford

2015). The National Union of Journalists in Scotland and the University of Strathclyde surveyed 35 broadcast, freelance, and print journalists in May 2015 and found that online abuse increased more than 50 times over the previous year and had extended beyond working hours (Holleran et al. 2015). The Representative on Freedom of the Media, a structure within the Organization for Security and Co-operation in Europe that monitors freedom of expression and free media worldwide, provided recommendations in September 2015 to counter challenges to freedom of expression. Antonijevic (2016), the national program officer at the Organization for Security and Cooperation in Europe, lays out the importance of this issue to journalistic freedoms worldwide:

> As building blocks of democracy, the media are not just information providers—they are the creators of public opinion as well. They are the gatekeepers of fundamental freedoms and also the agenda-setters. Therefore, how they present themselves and what they communicate is of crucial importance, especially if these images and representations not only perpetuate inequalities between women and men in society but also encourage violence against women. (p. 9)

The Dart Center for Journalism and Trauma outlines the serious threat to press freedoms worldwide because of online violence:

> Threats to all forms of violence suppress free speech or create environments in which journalists self-censor thus reducing freedom of the press. Given this clear evidence, we are concerned that adverse reactions to trauma can all lead to the abandonment of important lines of journalistic inquiry and impair journalists' ability to report effectively on such critical issues as human rights abuses, crime, and the public response to natural and man-made disasters. (Dart Center 2014)

According to the same report, the effects on individual journalists and their future are equally damaging:

> We also need to understand that the many of these actions, regardless of the actual physical danger, operate by creating a stressful, disruptive, and at times invalidating environment in which journalists must be vigilant about

self-presentation, privacy, danger, and security of self and loved ones. This psychological pressure, which at its most severe may challenge a journalist's capacity to work effectively and safely, undermines human rights of autonomy, free expression, dignity and justice. (Dart Center 2014)

Hate speech and humiliation are used as weapons to silence journalists and shame them for voicing their opinions (Hagen 2016). Many journalists are not prepared to handle online harassment and many experience fear, discomfort, anger and loneliness. A UNESCO report, *Building Digital Safety for Journalism* (Henrichsen et al. 2015), states that journalists have to bear psychological, convenience, and financial costs due to harassment. Journalists are made to feel unworthy and unfit for their roles as watchdogs of democracy. In spite of the growing incidence of such abuse, many journalists do not report the abuse (Henrichsen et al. 2015). Loke (2011) states that the emerging information and communication technologies challenge journalists to search for tools to combat harassment with, sometimes, little or no help from their organizations. At times, journalists are not aware of the support they can get from their employer or do not think that it is necessary to report the issue. Holleran et al. (2015) found that 40% of the journalists they interviewed did not report the abuse to the company/organization they were working for at the time and that 74% were unaware of the support available from their employer. The respondents stated that they were either unsure who to raise the issue with, thought there was no point because the abuse was very mild, or they weren't intimidated, or thought they (the employer) wouldn't care (Holleran et al. 2015).

The UNESCO report on digital safety for journalists also found that as a result of harassment and intimidation, journalists may be increasingly concerned about their personal security and start using pseudonyms when they publish or stop writing about a story or topic. Some give up journalism or leave their jobs entirely; others may either stop reporting from specific localities, or be forced to relocate (Henrichsen et al. 2015).

Harassment of Women Journalists in the Digital Milieu

Online harassment is a phenomenon that manifests from traditional power structures of oppression in society, including gender, religious, and race-based biases. In 2016, *The Guardian* conducted an analysis of readers' comments posted on its own website and found that articles written by women journalists attracted more abuse and dismissive trolling than those written by men, regardless of the subject of the article. Moreover, the journalists who received the highest abuse were non-white, Muslim, and/or gay (Gardiner et al. 2016). Historically, women journalists have used pseudonyms instead of their given names in order to protect their identity (Desta 2015; MacLean 2016; National Women's History Museum 2007). However, with social media and digital technologies, journalists typically bring their authentic identities to their digital work, blending personal and professional lines and making female journalists vulnerable to abuse and cyberstalking (Holton and Molyneux 2015).

According to the Pew Research Center (2014), women are targets of online harassment more often than their male counterparts and often experience more severe forms of harassment, including bodily threats, reputation damage, and even death threats. In the case of women journalists, bloggers, and publishers, TrollBusters has found that these online attacks can shut down their sites and silence women's voices online. For women journalists, online harassment may also result in emotional stress and may require legal and technological remedies to mitigate the damage to identity and reputation. The activity of these harassers has significant psychological and economic effects on the individual journalists who seek out Troll-Busters.com and for them the online activity creates an ongoing tension. They have told us the rituals and changes to routine and writing assignments they will make to avoid another attack. These women question how they can continue to work in an environment where they are always under attack.

Increasingly, women journalists and women journalists of color worldwide find themselves on the receiving end of misogynistic attacks because of their professional role. Anja Kovacs of the Internet Democracy Project states that women who write about politics, religion, feminism, or sexuality, experience more online abuse than those who write about less controversial topics (Henrichsen et al. 2015, p. 44). Women involved in constructive debates on national issues portray themselves as more intelligent, headstrong, and knowledgeable than their male counterparts. This image often disrupts perpetrators, who believe that women should be submissive and obey men. Often these "feminists" and "SJWs" (social justice warriors) are disciplined through coercive measures such as misogyny online (p. 44).

Women journalists often are the targets of some of the most severe forms of online harassment, such as rape threats, death threats, and hate speech. In 2013, an International Women's Media Foundation online survey of female journalists worldwide found that almost two-thirds of the 149 women journalists polled experienced intimidation, threats, or abuse in relation to their work. More than 25% of these threats took place online and included threats that were "verbal, written, and/or physical intimidation including threats to family or friends." Nearly half (45%) of the journalists who experienced tapping, hacking, and digital security threats said they "don't know" who the perpetrator was, while more than a quarter (27%) said it was a government official, 15% named police as the perpetrator, and 12% selected "other" (Munoz 2014). In "Violence, threats and pressures against journalists and other media actors in the EU" (November 2016), the European Union Agency for Fundamental Rights says that women journalists and bloggers are often targeted specifically because of their gender and/or their ethnicity, and face threats of rape and violence. They call on member states to strengthen their focus on gender in the protection of journalists and on the unique challenges women face in the course of their work (p. 17).

British journalist Mary Hamilton, who experienced sexist and misogynistic conversation on the Internet for the first time as a 12-year-old learned that if she wanted to be taken seriously or avoid threatening sexual advances she had to chose a male name or take up a gender-neutral identity (BBC.com, "Twitter Abuse", 2013). In the Norwegian press, Hagen (2016) found that one in four journalists had received threats in the past five years, with men receiving more threats. However, approximately one in four women and one in 20 men received sexualized comments or threats. Almost twice as many young female journalists (age 26–35) report that they have experienced harassment compared to their male colleagues of the same age. And one-fifth of Norwegian journalists and editors say they feel silenced because of harassments or threats (Hagen 2016).

Similarly, Hagen (2016) concluded that male journalists are more likely to experience physical confrontation than women, while women receive more comments on their appearance and more obscene phone calls. Henrichsen et al. (2015) state that women journalists often receive comments that focus on physical appearance rather than professional accomplishment.

Impact of Online Harassment on Journalists

At the 2015 Online News Association keynote panel on online harassment, writer Laurie Penny stated, "A woman's opinion is the short skirt of the Internet." Just as in physical space, women are under attack online for being female or females of color. Jill Filipovic, who has experienced years of name-calling and harassment for her feminist writing, states, "men are generally attacked for their ideas or their behavior," but with women, harassers "go straight between the legs" (Filipovic 2007, p. 303). As a first-year law student at New York University, Filipovic (2007) found herself targeted on an online message board by people who knew where she had spent her vacations, the ethnicity of her boyfriend, and details about her appearance. Along with regular slurs of "bitch," "whore," and "cunt," Filipovic found her photograph in a bathing suit during a vacation in Greece taken from her personal photo account and posted under "The Most Appealing Women @Top Law Schools." At first, she ignored the comments and stopped visiting the forum; as the slurs and jokes continued, however, Filipovic began to feel withdrawn from her virtual and embodied identity. Along with the natural inclination of taking a break from her writing for six months, she feared the consequences of going to school with her online harassers. She stopped making friends with her new classmates and also skipped a few classes.

Online harassment has both short- and long-term effects. Online harassment damages the confidence and self-esteem of journalists and causes anger, stress and anxiety. Online harassment can also cause significant emotional distress, leading to psychological ailments such as depression (Ford 2013; Henry and Powell 2015). In a study conducted in May 2015 by the National Union of Journalists in Scotland and the University of Strathclyde, 35 broadcast, freelance, and print journalists reported that online harassment damaged their confidence and self-esteem and they experienced feelings of anger, stress, and anxiety. Journalists who had just started their career were contemplating changing their profession. Holleran et al. (2015) state that the consequences on freedom of speech were evident as a few journalists stopped using social media. Additionally, a few reported that the fear of retaliation from covering controversial topics changed their perspectives on whether to pursue the issues and in what manner. Filipovic (2007) states threats also lead to fears about loss of employment and progression in careers among women. The belief is that future employers may come across hate comments, personal photos, or illustrations posted about them on online forums, which reduce their chances of being hired by large firms.

In a report to the Media Leaders Conference of the United Nations Educational, Scientific and Cultural Organization in February 2016, the International Women's Media Foundation reported that violence, both on- and offline, has significant effects on journalists. "Emotional distress is a common side effect of prolonged exposure to violence and living under threat," the report states. "Continued emotional distress can lead to decreased performance at work, bad decision making in volatile situations, risk taking that endangers others and interpersonal tensions" (Brayne 2007; IWMF 2016).

And as freelancers, women journalists face the additional long-term effects of damage to their digital identity, which may prevent potential clients from wanting to work with them (IWMF, Overview, 2016).

Although many journalists take online harassment seriously, there are a few who believe that these threats are never serious and the best way to deal with them to ignore them (Hess 2014). Hanna Rosin, an editor at *Slate*, argues that online harassment is evidence of women's empowerment. She states, "It shows just how far we've come. Many women on the

Internet are in positions of influence, widely published and widely read; if they sniff out misogyny, I have no doubt they will gleefully skewer the responsible sexist in one of many available online outlets, and get results" (Rosin 2012).

Fighting Online Harassment: What Can You Do?

Many of the solutions currently addressing online harassment allow users to block online comments from view or limit access to content on social media platforms. Twitter offers blocking technology that allows you to remove posts from selected users from your feed. In spring 2017, Twitter suspended accounts with anonymous "egg" profile images. These accounts were oftentimes bots that are being deployed by online harassers to find targets and proliferate canned messages. The platform also allows you to report objectionable content. However, journalists do their work in a digital environment and should be employing security measures throughout their workflow to ensure their safety online and off.

1. **Your Name.** Determine if you are going to use your given name or a pseudonym in your professional writings. Or whether you will alternatively use a pseudonym for your online personalities. Your name is a key to your identity and can be used to track you to your physical address and link you to friends and family. Create separate professional and personal accounts for social media.
2. **Your location.** Lock down your physical location by erasing your address and other identifying information on third-party aggregators like Spokeo.com. These sites collect data from voting records and property records like land and home ownership. They also include known relatives along with ages.
3. **Use secure communication with sources and in workflow.** Emails are hackable. Use encrypted channels like Signal for phone and messaging to protect yourself and your sources. Use a Tor browser to erase your digital footprint and workflow.

4. **Learn and practice physical defensive measures** regardless of your assignment or role.
5. **Communicate with management, trusted friends and colleagues** about your attacks and how they can support you. Report direct threats to the police.

About TrollBusters

Since its start in 2015, TrollBusters continues to protect and serve women journalists. After launching her beta version in September 2015 at Troll-Busters.com and yoursoteam.wordpress.com, Ferrier shared her experiences at the Online News Association in 2015, the United Nations World Press Freedom Day in 2015, and the inaugural South by Southwest Online Harassment Summit in 2016. Ferrier launched a pilot monitoring program for women journalists in September 2016 and in November 2016, Ferrier was invited to the European Commission to discuss Troll-Busters.com and protections for women journalists in the European Union. She detailed her story in a chapter called "The Progression of Hate" that she wrote for the 2016 volume of *Attacks on the Press* published by the Committee to Protect Journalists (Ferrier 2016). Ferrier was awarded one of ten community service awards from South by Southwest in Spring 2017 for "using technology for good" and her work on TrollBusters has been featured in major news outlets around the world.

Operating on the web at Troll-Busters.com (www.troll-busters.com/) and YourSOSteam.Wordpress.com or on Twitter @yoursosteam, Ferrier and TrollBusters have provided monitoring, education and training to hundreds of journalists and women writers. Ferrier recently created an infographic "What to Do? Where to Go?" to address the chief concern of targets she worked with at TrollBusters. "These journalists were silenced by their own professional culture that suggested they should be stronger and ignore the attacks," Ferrier said in a radio interview on National Public Radio (2017). "The infographic breaks down the types of threats journalists might face in the online environment and then the next steps they should do to stay safe." Ferrier also created a series of digital hygiene courses to educate journalists about online protection, which are available free at yoursosteam.wordpress.com. As an educator, Ferrier often speaks to students in journalism programs and professionals around the globe, preparing them for the digital culture they operate within as journalists and media workers.

The attention on the issue of online harassment has grown recently with the rise of white supremacist rhetoric in the United States and inflamed political rancor. In particular, the use of Twitter by President Donald Trump and his specific attacks against the media, have created an increasingly unsafe environment for journalists, both on- and offline. In July 2017, President Trump took on CNN on social media, tweeting a meme of himself in a pro wrestling slap-down match against an opponent sporting a CNN-logo head. As reported in *Newsweek* by Zach Schonfeld, the resulting online firestorm resulted in death threats against the journalist who uncovered the identity of the originator of the meme used in the president's tweet (2017).

Ferrier believes that online harassment requires a more nuanced approach to combating different types of hate speech and different types of online actors. She has also advocated for a much more coordinated approach using technological, human, legal and policy changes to provide redress to targets.

Legislators are taking notice as frequent targets of online harassment themselves. Rep. Katherine Clark of Massachusetts has introduced several pieces of legislation to update federal and state cyberstalking laws after her constituent Brianna Wu contacted her during Gamergate in 2014. The new law would target doxxing, the act of publishing a person's personal information on the Internet; sextortion, where users threaten to post sexual images online; and swatting, where law enforcement are prank-called on an unsuspecting target. The legislation also allocates funding for the training of law enforcement officers to identify and investigate online harassment (Mallon 2017).

Ultimately, it will take a coordinated strategy by legislators, online platforms, media management, and journalists themselves to minimize online harassment and its effects. And we each bear our own personal responsibility for creating civil spaces online with every online post.

References

Ahmad, A. N. (2010). Is Twitter a useful tool for journalists? *Journal of Media Practice, 11*(2), 145–155.

Anti-Defamation League. (2016, October 19). Anti-Semitic targeting of women journalists during the 2016 presidential campaign: A report from ADL's task force on harassment and journalism. Retrieved from http://www.adl.org/assets/pdf/press-center/CR_4862_Journalism-Task-Force_v2.pdf

Antonijevic, Z. (2016). The media cannot be truly free if women's voices are silenced. In D. Mijatović (Ed.), *New challenges to freedom of expression: Countering online abuse of female journalists* (pp. 8–12). Vienna: Office of the Representative on Freedom of the Media Organization for Security and Co-operation in Europe.

BBC.com. (2013, July 29). Twitter abuse: Why cyberbullies are targeting women. *BBC.com*. Retrieved from http://www.bbc.com/news/technology-23488550

Bor, S. E. (2014). Teaching social media journalism: Challenges and opportunities for future curriculum design. *Journalism and Mass Communication Educator, 69*(3), 243–255.

Brayne, M. (2007). *Trauma and journalism: A guide for journalists, editors & managers*. London: Dart Center for Journalism and Trauma. Retrieved from http://dartcenter.org/sites/default/files/DCE_JournoTraumaHandbook.pdf

Clifford, L. (2015). Under threat. The changing state of media safety. International News Safety Institute. Retrieved from http://newssafety.org/underthreat/under-threat-the-findings.html#

Cozma, R., & Chen, K. J. (2013). What's in a tweet? Foreign correspondents' use of social media. *Journalism Practice, 7*(1), 33–46.

Dart Center For Journalism & Trauma. (2014). *Trauma & Journalism: A Practical Guide*. Retrieved from https://dartcenter.org/sites/default/files/DCE_JournoTraumaHandbook.pdf

Desta, Y. (2015). A brief history of female authors with male pen names. Mashable. Retrieved from http://mashable.com/2015/03/01/female-authors-pen-names/#nCwK.WBoPPqA

Ferrier, M. (2016). The progression of hate. In Committee to Protect Journalists (Ed.). *Attacks on the press 2016*. Retrieved from https://cpj.org/2016/04/attacks-on-the-press-progression-of-hate.php

Filipovic, J. (2007). Blogging while female: How internet misogyny parallels real-world harassment. *Yale Journal of Law and Feminism, 19*(1), 295–304.

Ford, D. P. (2013). Virtual harassment: Media characteristics' role in psychological health. *Journal of Managerial Psychology, 28*, 408–428.

Gardiner, B., Mansfield, M., Anderson, I., Holder, J., Louter, D., & Ulmanu, M. (2016). The dark side of guardian comments. *The Guardian.* Retrieved from https://www.theguardian.com/technology/2016/apr/12/the-dark-side-of-guardian-comments

Goel, V. (2014, June 29). Facebook tinkers with users' emotions in news feed experiment, stirring outcry. Retrieved from https://www.nytimes.com/2014/06/30/technology/facebook-tinkers-with-users-emotions-in-news-feed-experiment-stirring-outcry.html

Hagen, A. L. (2016). Shame, shock and speech injuries: Online harassment against journalists in Norway. In D. Mijatović (Ed.), *New challenges to freedom of expression: Countering online abuse of female journalists* (pp. 17–21). Vienna: Office of the Representative on Freedom of the Media Organization for Security and Co-operation in Europe.

Hedayat, N. (2015, August 19). Cyberbullying is not a women's issue. It's a human issue. *Glammonitor.* Retrieved from http://www.glammonitor.com/2015/cyberbullying-is-a-human-issue-weve-turned-into-a-womens-issue-3937/

Henrichsen, J. R., Betz, M., & Lisosky, J. M. (2015). *Building digital safety for journalism: A survey of selected issues.* Paris: UNESCO. Retrieved from: http://unesdoc.unesco.org/images/0023/002323/232358e.pdf.

Henry, N., & Powell, A. (2015). Embodied harms gender, shame, and technology-facilitated sexual violence. *Violence Against Women, 21*(6), 758–779. https://doi.org/10.1177/1077801215576581.

Hess, A. (2014). Why women aren't welcome on the Internet. *Pacific Standard.* Retrieved from https://psmag.com/why-women-aren-t-welcome-on-the-internet-aa21fdbc8d6#.hvsqqopi1

Holleran, P., Duncan, S., Davidson, F., & Doherty, J. (2015). Cyberbullying: The media survey. *National Union of Journalists.* Retrieved from https://www.nuj.org.uk/news/cyberbullying-the-media-survey/

Holton, A., & Molyneux, L. (2015). Identity lost? The personal impact of brand journalism. *Journalism, 18*(2), 195–210. (First published November 3, 2015).

Hunter, P., Bowman, N. D., & Banks, J. (2015, September). The enjoyment of griefing in online games. *Journal of Gaming & Virtual Worlds, 7*(3), 243–258.

International Women's Media Foundation. (2016, February). *An overview of the current challenges to the safety and protection of journalists.* Report prepared on the occasion of the UNESCO Media Leaders Conference on the Safety of Journalists, 13–14. Retrieved from https://www.iwmf.org/wp-content/uploads/2016/02/IWMFUNESCO-Paper.pdf

Jane, E. A. (2015). Flaming? What flaming? The pitfalls and potentials of researching online hostility. *Ethics and Information Technology, 17*(1), 65–87.

Loke, J. (2011). Amplifying a public's voice: Online news readers' comments impact on journalism and its role as the new public space (Doctoral dissertation). Retrieved from https://repositories.lib.utexas.edu/bitstream/handle/2152/28469/Loke_dissertation_20112.pdf?sequence=1

MacLean, M. (2016, July 7) History of American women. (Web log post). Retrieved from http://www.womenhistoryblog.com/search/label/Journalists

Mallon, M. (2017, June 30). How Congresswoman Katherine Clark is fighting back against online harassment toward women. *Glamour.* Retrieved from http://www.glamour.com/story/congresswoman-katherine-clark-fighting-back-online-harassment

Marder, B., Joinson, A., Shankar, A., & Houghton, D. (2016). The extended 'chilling' effect of Facebook: The cold reality of ubiquitous social networking. *Computers in Human Behavior,* 60582–60592. https://doi.org/10.1016/j.chb.2016.02.097.

Munoz, E. L. (2014). Violence and harassment against women in the news media: The global picture. The International Women's Media Foundation & International News Safety Institute. Retrieved from http://www.iwmf.org/wp-content/uploads/2014/03/Violence-and-Harassment-against-Women-in-the-News-Media.pdf

National Women's History Museum. (2007). Women with a deadline: Female printers, publishers, and journalists from the Colonial Period to World War I. Retrieved from https://www.nwhm.org/online-exhibits/womenwithdeadlines/wwd5.htm

Penney, J. W. (2016). Chilling effects: Online surveillance and Wikipedia use. *Berkeley Technology Law Journal, 31*(1), 117–182.

Pew Research Center. (2014). Online Harassment (Report). Retrieved from http://www.pewinternet.org/files/2014/10/PI_OnlineHarassment_102214_pdf1.pdf

Rosin, H. (2012). *The end of men: And the rise of women.* New York: Penguin.

Schauer, F. (1978). Fear, risk and the first amendment: Unraveling the chilling effect. *Boston University Law Review, 58,* 685–732.

Schonfeld, Z. (2017, July 7). Donald Trump vs. CNN: How the president is trolling the media into oblivion. *Newsweek*. Retrieved from http://www.newsweek.com/donald-trump-cnn-hanassholesolo-how-president-trolling-media-oblivion-633662

Solomon, D. H., Knobloch, L. K., & Fitzpatrick, M. A. (2004). Relational power, marital schema, and decisions to withhold complaints: An investigation of the chilling effect on confrontation in marriage. *Communication Studies, 55*(1), 146–167.

Why VCs aren't funding women-led startups. (2016, May 24). Knowledge @ Wharton. Retrieved from http://knowledge.wharton.upenn.edu/article/vcs-arent-funding-women-led-startups/

Ybarra, M. L., & Mitchell, K. J. (2004). Youth engaging in online harassment: Associations with caregiver–child relationships, internet use, and personal characteristics. *Journal of Adolescence, 27*(3), 319–336.

17

The Global Anti-Street Harassment Movement: Digitally-Enabled Feminist Activism

Karen Desborough

Across the world feminist activists have been developing an anti-street harassment social movement to resist and end sexual and gender-based harassment in public spaces. While numerous anti-harassment initiatives have mobilized in the last 10–15 years, deploying a diverse and creative range of online and offline resistance strategies, to date there is no academic research on the movement's emergence. This is a surprising omission given the movement's global reach, and the growing recognition of street harassment as a pervasive and harmful social problem (Fileborn 2014, p. 38). This chapter examines the role of digital technologies – the Internet, social media platforms, and mobile phone technologies – in enabling the formation and global expansion of the movement. Recent years have witnessed much debate concerning the influence of digital

I would like to thank Elizabeth Evans, Eric Herring, and Jutta Weldes for providing helpful comments on earlier drafts of this chapter.

K. Desborough (✉)
School of Sociology, Politics and International Studies, University of Bristol, Bristol, U.K.

J. R. Vickery, T. Everbach (eds.), *Mediating Misogyny*,
https://doi.org/10.1007/978-3-319-72917-6_17

technologies on the emergence and outcomes of social movements (Shirky 2009; Gladwell 2010; Morozov 2011). Nevertheless, it is evident that such technologies do not determine social movements (Castells 2012, p. 103). Rather, digital technologies *afford opportunities* for activists organizing and participating in collective action. When technological affordances are leveraged effectively, social movements may emerge (Earl and Kimport 2011, p. 10). "Technological affordance" describes the "special technological capacities of Internet-enabled technologies' and refers to the 'actions or uses that a technology makes easier (and therefore facilitates)" (Earl and Kimport 2011, p. 32). Based on interviews with 32 anti-harassment activists, operative in ten countries,[1] this chapter argues that activists have leveraged the affordances of digital technologies to organize and participate in anti-street harassment activism, thus accelerating the movement's formation and development. The chapter refers specifically to 14 anti-street harassment initiatives (see Table 17.1).

To structure my analysis, I draw on R. Kelly Garrett's (2006) work on the mobilizing potential of digital technologies for collective action. Following a review of the social movement literature, Garrett identified three technology-related mechanisms that can facilitate political

Table 17.1 Anti-street harassment initiatives

Group/individual/campaign	Country	Year emerged/initial anti-street harassment campaign
Blank Noise	India	2003
Hollaback!	Global	2005 (in New York)
Girls for Gender Equity	U.S.	2007 (Street Harassment Summit)
Stop Street Harassment	U.S.	2008
Collective Action for Safe Spaces	U.S.	2009
HarassMap	Egypt	2010
Hollaback! London	U.K.	2010
Hollaback! Berlin	Germany	2011
Bassma (Imprint Movement)	Egypt	2012
I Saw Harassment	Egypt	2012
Chega de Fiu Fiu (Enough with the Catcalls)	Brazil	2013
Feminista Jones	U.S.	2014 (#YouOKSis campaign)
Girls Against	U.K.	2015
HarassTracker	Lebanon	2016

participation. Digital technologies help to first, reduce the costs of organizing and participating in collection action; second, promote collective identity, which helps to foster and maintain participation; and third, and relatedly, enable community formation (2006, p. 204). Garrett's framework largely applies to this study; however, to more adequately explain digitally-enabled participation in anti-harassment activism, I also draw on feminist scholarship in this area.

Reduction of Participation Costs

The first mechanism or affordance involves digital technologies' potential to lower the participation or 'transaction costs' for activists organizing, mobilizing and engaging in collective action (Van Laer and Van Aelst 2009, p. 236). According to Shirky (2009), the reduction of transaction costs – time, money, effort or attention – removes the obstacles to group action, thereby enabling the creation of new and efficient forms of collective action (pp. 18, 22, 48). As he puts it, "the collapse of transaction costs makes it easier for people to get together – so much easier, in fact, that it is changing the world" (p. 48). Now that people are less constrained by participation costs, "group-forming has gone from hard to ridiculously easy, [and] we are seeing an explosion of experiments with new groups and new kinds of groups" (p. 54). Similarly, in a study of seven social movement cases, Bonchek (1995) found that the speed and inexpensiveness of the Internet, and its capacity for many-to-many communication, reduced communication, coordination, and information costs, and therefore facilitated group formation, recruitment and retention (pp. 2–4). In a similar vein, I find that anti-harassment activists have benefited from the "cost-reducing affordance" of digital technologies (Earl and Kimport 2011, p. 15), which, in part, explains the formation and development of many and varying types of anti-harassment groups worldwide.

Hollaback! provides an excellent example of the movement's use of digital technologies to resist street harassment, and to organize efficiently and mobilize people rapidly. Hollaback! began operating in 2005 as a blog where people could share their experiences of street harassment.

Emily May, Hollaback!'s co-founder and executive director, described the creation of the blog as a "breakthrough" and an opportunity to create a "bigger, more global conversation" around street harassment (as cited in Keller et al. 2016, p. 5). Hollaback! has since expanded into a global network operating in 84 cities across 31 countries (Vera-Gray 2017, p. 1), deploying a range of online and offline tactics. Potential participants can easily join the network via the organization's website (which I discuss later) and site leaders receive all their training online. During a three-month period, new site leaders participate in a series of webinars, covering topics that include leveraging social media, dealing with the press and organizing on the ground. In addition, each site is provided with a customized website, which they build and populate with local content. To encourage communication, collective identification, and participation, Hollaback! operates a Listserv and a private Facebook group, as well as a shared Google Drive, through which activists can access informational resources and materials for campaigning purposes (D. Roy, personal communication, April 13, 2014). Debjani Roy, deputy director of Hollaback!, sums up the importance of digital technologies for the development of the global network:

> In my opinion, technology is everything… without it we wouldn't be able to organize in this decentralized way; we wouldn't be able to have regular contact with site leaders; we wouldn't be able to work towards understanding what this looks like on a global scale. The speed of information flow is absolutely necessary to building the movement at the pace that it's been growing. It is impossible without it. (personal communication, April 13, 2014)

Hence, it is clear from this testimony that digital technologies have lowered the coordination, communication, and information costs for Hollaback!, enabling the formation and growth of the global network. Throughout the interviews there were many other examples of activists benefiting from the affordances of digital technologies. Above all, new technologies make communication easier, enabling information to be shared rapidly to large numbers of people across time and space. For instance, according to Holly Kearl, founder and executive director of

Stop Street Harassment, "technology is the core because we started as a website and we do most of our work online… So, without the technology it would be kind of impossible to reach each other at this level and this speed" (personal communication, April 24, 2014). This point is echoed by Julia Brilling, director of Hollaback! Berlin, "it wouldn't be possible without technology. That's the thing, it's all Internet-based. All you need is [a] computer and the Internet… it allows you to connect to so many people instantly, so we reach a lot of people just by posting something" (personal communication, January 12, 2016). Digital technologies have similarly played a critical role in Girls Against's communication and outreach efforts to combat sexual harassment and assault in the live music industry:

> We would be nothing without the Internet. We do everything on there, our campaign is primarily on Twitter. We have a Facebook [page] and do most of our communicating via emails… and messages. That's the only way we've been able to get into contact with important people in the music industry who are going to be the huge catalyst for change. (H. Camilleri, personal communication, February 1, 2016)

Thus, many anti-harassment activists value and effectively utilize the connectivity afforded by the Internet as it enables the transmission of a thought, idea, or information to fellow activists and followers "at a moment's inspiration" (Wellman et al. 2003). Moreover, several groups – among them Bassma, HarassMap and I Saw Harassment in Egypt, and Blank Noise in India – use digital technologies to recruit volunteers and coordinate their volunteer activities. For instance, in Egypt mobile phone messaging services are crucial for the coordination of Bassma volunteers, who form security patrols to prevent attacks on women during protests and religious holidays when mass sexual harassment is common. Co-founder Nihal Saad Zaghloul explains: "mobile phones are very important because this is how we communicate and send each other text messages… We work all day and many of us might not have access to email all day but we have access to SMS [and] WhatsApp" (personal communication, April 4, 2016).

As the quotations above indicate, without digital technologies many anti-harassment initiatives would not have formed and would not be as effective in reaching audiences or in achieving their objectives. This is not to infer that all anti-harassment activists worldwide enjoy equal access to digital technologies, or notice and effectively leverage technological affordances (Earl and Kimport 2011, p. 33). Much has been written about the "digital divide", which shows that Internet access is not equally distributed among groups, but disproportionately benefits the young, affluent, and more highly skilled (Schuster 2013, p. 11; Elliott 2016). According to Joanne Smith, chief executive of Girls for Gender Equity, young people in marginalized communities typically do not have "that kind of a phone to have that kind of an app and in the neighbourhoods that they go home to, they're not going to take a picture of somebody who's harassing them.[2] They're going to find a safe space" (personal communication, April 10, 2014). Hence, digital inequalities exist between movement participants, with privileged actors better able to take advantage of the opportunities afforded by such technologies. Notwithstanding these exclusions, digital technologies have lowered the participation costs for many anti-harassment activists worldwide.

In addition to lowering the financial, temporal, and spatial costs associated with participation, feminist scholars point out that digital platforms, such as blogs and social media applications, afford new opportunities for women and girls to share their experiences in ways that were not previously possible (Keller et al. 2016, p. 6). For young women, especially – a demographic highly affected by street harassment[3] (Fairchild and Rudman 2008, p. 338) – online platforms may provide less intimidating avenues for political engagement than more traditional forms of participation (Harris 2008, p. 492). Further, in the context of street harassment and sexual assault, the Internet can be a "safe space" for women to resist gender oppressions (Fileborn 2014, pp. 33–34). For example, through an analysis of posts to the Hollaback! website, Keller et al. (2016) showed that, protected by the anonymity of the Internet, women were empowered to speak about, and thus make visible, often silenced experiences of street harassment. Moreover, digital technologies allow feminist activists to circumvent traditional media platforms and to counter mainstream narratives that silence women's experiences of street harassment, and enable and normalize sexual violence (Fileborn 2014, p. 33; Clark 2016, p. 789). For instance, Juliana de Faria, journalist and founder of Chega de Fiu Fiu (in English: Enough with the Catcalls), Brazil, submitted an article on street harassment for publication in a women's magazine but was told that the topic was "too politically correct." She explains:

> Thank God for the Internet era: I decided to do it on my own. I decided to go with an online campaign, because I had no money... and I thought it would be an easier and cheaper way to engage people... [The campaign] went viral and several women started writing [to] me. They were sharing their fears and traumas with street harassment, and many of them were sharing their stories for the very first time. (J. de Faria, personal communication, December 4, 2015)

While digital technologies enable activists to bypass mainstream media, at the same time actors and their efforts to resist street harassment may gain positive media coverage from initially unreceptive and even hostile media, helping to promote their cause to a wider audience. For instance, as also discussed in Chap. 1, Chega de Fiu Fiu's 2015 Twitter campaign, #primeiroassedio (in English: #firstharassment), generated more than 82,000 tweets and retweets in five days, attracting significant media attention. The project has since been featured in more than 200 Brazilian and international media outlets, and de Faria has received much international recognition from, for example, the Clinton Foundation and *Cosmopolitan* Magazine who nominated her "one of the most inspiring women in the world" (Chega de Fiu Fiu 2015).

In sum, digital technologies have reduced many of the costs associated with participation, enabling the proliferation and maintenance of new and varying anti-harassment groups worldwide, and affording women new opportunities to speak about and resist street harassment. This is not to infer that there are no longer any costs or barriers to anti-street harassment activism. Many of the interviewees identified a lack of time and money as perennial constraints to participation. Moreover, anti-harassment activists, like most women speaking out about sexism, are at risk of misogynistic online harassment or 'gendertrolling' (Mantilla 2013, p. 565), which can curtail or alter women's political participation. For example, following multiple death threats online, Feminista Jones, who devised the viral hashtag campaign #YouOKSis, decided to redirect her campaigning efforts into offline spaces, such as schools and youth groups (personal communication, February 12, 2016). Hollaback! has taken a different approach; in response to years of gendertrolling, initially in the form of abusive emails, which then escalated into rape and death threats, the leadership team launched HeartMob in 2016 – a platform where users can provide support and show solidarity to victims of online harassment (HeartMob 2017). Finally, it is worth reiterating that while digital technologies have reduced participation costs significantly for many activists, not all actors resisting street harassment have equal access to these technologies.

Promotion of Collective Identity

In this section, I argue that the global anti-street harassment movement has developed a collective identity among movement adherents through digital technologies, which has fostered and sustained political participation. Collective identity refers to "the sense of shared experiences and values that connects individuals to movements and gives participants a sense of 'collective agency' or feeling that they can effect change through collective action" (Staggenborg 2011, p. 22). This is particularly important for anti-harassment activists, who may experience feelings of isolation in a context where street harassment is normalized and trivialized. Digital technologies assist in the development of collective identities by making concerned individuals aware of similar struggles (Garrett 2006, p. 205) through, for example, shared "frames of reference" promulgated on organizations' websites (Van Aelst and Walgrave 2004, p. 95). Holly Kearl, for instance, explains how she came to identify with the experiences, values, and goals of anti-harassment groups through researching the rise of websites resisting street harassment: "I had felt unsafe and annoyed by harassers in public spaces for years before I found out there were groups taking action. So, knowing others were trying to make public spaces safer, a goal I wanted for myself, helped draw me to [the movement]" (personal communication, December 2, 2015).

Consequently, the Internet promotes collective identification as activists observe, learn from each another, and validate each other's actions, which can occur rapidly, and concurrently in numerous places and in numerous ways (Van Laer 2007, p. 8). For example, Julia Brilling was inspired to launch a Hollaback! chapter in Berlin after identifying with content posted on Hollaback! London's website. She explains, "This [was] so good to read. It was so healing, it was so inspiring. It was like 'oh my God, this happened to me as well' and I never knew I could talk about it… This empowerment, this feminist space, this safe space, the community, it's just so helpful" (personal communication, July 26, 2014). Thus, for this activist, the shared sense of "we-ness" or solidarity in having recognized certain shared attributes as salient and important (Nip 2004, p. 206) prompted her to take action against street harassment.

Many of the interviewees commented on the fact that prior to the Internet, women in different sites had little or no awareness of similar struggles against street harassment elsewhere. Emily May, for instance, observes that before the advent of social media only disparate, localised initiatives emerged around street harassment. Yet, "now you're really seeing globally folks having these similar shared experiences and addressing them all around the world in approximately the same timeframes, which is to say within the past ten years or so"[4] (personal communication, May 11, 2016). This explosion in anti-street harassment activism coincides with a renewed interest in feminism in the U.K., the U.S., and other countries, and in response to persistent sexual objectification of and violence against women (Evans 2015, p. 1). Within this context, several interviewees attributed the growth in anti-harassment activism to women's recognition of shared experiences, and the inspiration they have drawn from the actions of others resisting street harassment. As May explains: "it's kind of like success begets success and somebody will say 'oh, it's happened to me' and they'll look around and see other initiatives and they're like 'well, I can do something about this. Maybe I can try this, nobody's doing this thing'" (personal communication, May 11, 2016).

While some scholars doubt the capacity of technology to build identities analogous to those of face-to-face interactions (Pickerill 2003, p. 25), my research indicates that the Internet has promoted collective identification among geographically dispersed women resisting street harassment.

Nay El Rahi of HarassTracker, Lebanon, confirms this view: "[the Internet] makes us feel part of a bigger effort to counter this… very global issue… Knowing that other people are… trying to basically limit its effects, makes us feel that we're on a… continuum of struggle" (personal communication, May 2, 2016). Similarly, Juliana de Faria writes "the Internet… holds the movement together. Because thanks to this incredible tool, we women from all around can share very similar experiences and look, together, for a solution to the problem" (personal communication, December 4, 2015). Hence, for these activists the Internet is a space for sharing experiences, values, and knowledge, enabling women in disparate sites to connect to the movement. This is further evidenced by Feminista Jones' hashtag campaign, #YouOKSis, which provides a space for dialogue and support for black women around their experiences of street harassment. As others have argued elsewhere (Nip 2004, p. 206), #YouOKSis enables direct interactions between women with shared grievances to interpret their experiences and debate possible solutions. Analyzing a sample of tweets from a #YouOKSis Twitter discussion (thetrudz 2014), shows the forging of a sense of common identity and shared meanings around black women's encounters with street harassment. For example, in interpreting understandings of street harassment, several tweeters suggested that the practice entails male entitlement and domination of women's bodies, space, and time. In discussing the prevalence of street harassment, participants typically associated it with pervasive patriarchy and misogyny in society, and discussions on vulnerable targets of harassment prompted several people to reflect that black girls and young black women are most susceptible. The Twitter discussion also generated an exchange of ideas concerning strategies for affecting change.

Community Creation

In this section, I argue that digital technologies have facilitated the formation of various anti-harassment communities, which, in turn, have enhanced political participation. Online communities play an important role in the emergence and development of social movements because of their ability to swiftly connect and organize a member base without regard to geographical location, as well as enabling efficient recruitment of new members (Caren et al. 2012, pp. 170, 187–188). The growth of the Hollaback! network illustrates this point well. While Hollaback! does not actively recruit participants, potential new members can easily sign up by clicking on a "Join the Movement" button on the organization's website (Hollaback! 2016b). Users are directed to a page with suggestions on ways to participate, for example, being an effective bystander, sharing a story of harassment, volunteering at a local Hollaback! site, or starting a new site (Hollaback! 2016c). Those interested in launching their own sites are encouraged to familiarize themselves with Hollaback!'s community values, which espouse a commitment to collective agency, mutual respect, tolerance and trust, solidarity, diversity, intersectionality and participatory, non-hierarchical structures (Hollaback! 2016d). The global expansion of Hollaback! since its inception in 2005 demonstrates how the Internet makes it easy for people to join a community, and to rapidly comprehend and assume the community ethos, and how this "instant ethos" enables many likeminded individuals to quickly connect (Gurak and Logie 2003, p. 31). The Hollaback! site leaders that I interviewed explicitly commented on the sense of community, support, and solidarity they experienced, and how this promotes knowledge exchange and sharing of best practices. For instance, according to Julia Brilling:

> That's the strength of Hollaback! because we are this community… it's so important, we have great conversations, we have our online groups, the way we communicate… is so good, and what's also really, really good, and that's what I love about Hollaback! is that it manages to be… transnational and local at the same time. And it's not only a great resource of knowledge and inspiration, it's a great network. (Personal communication, July 26, 2014)

Julia Gray, co-founder of Hollaback! London, makes a similar point:

> Social media's created a network and the way that the Hollaback online network works means that it's so much easier to spread the word… People are really using it and it's brilliant. It means that people feel like they're not alone because they just go onto the Internet and see that there's this whole

network there… [This] online community has been incredibly important in spreading the message and providing people with that sort of solidarity and that support. (Personal communication, March 28, 2014)

Whilst some contend that online interactions lack the level of trust necessary for establishing strong community ties that are fundamental for collective action (Diani 2000, pp. 391, 397), it is clear from the quotations above that community creation is possible in an online environment, and that community membership has positive impacts on activism. In addition to the existence of a Hollaback! community, I found that a sense of community exists among members of the wider movement, which is based on recognition of and solidarity with others resisting street harassment. As Jasmeen Patheja, founder of Blank Noise, puts it: "because of our shared vision in some spaces or because we know we exist, there is a sense of a global community… and that has only happened through the presence of web. It's more than knowing that X exists, it's sharing and standing there in solidarity with X" (personal communication, December 21, 2015). This reveals an important function of online communities – their ability to foster a sense of belonging among people who do not (or hardly) know each other offline (Wellman and Gulia 1999, p. 341). This sense of collective belonging and identification can help to reduce feelings of isolation experienced by movement participants (Schuster 2013, p. 17), and help to bolster their motivation. This view was articulated by Holly Kearl: "it can feel so isolating and lonely because most people don't get the issue, they don't understand… So, knowing there are other people out there who are fighting the same battles and maybe making progress as well, just knowing that's happening can be very helpful" (personal communication, December 21, 2014). A point echoed by Nihal Saad Zaghloul: "I think that really helps me to continue because it gets really hard sometimes and you feel like you're really alone… and you see the successes of others and then you learn and try to re-strategize" (personal communication, April 4, 2016). Thus, for these interviewees, digital technologies have enabled the creation of a global community of anti-harassment activists. This sense of collective belonging has helped to sustain their morale and participation in the movement.

Additionally, as feminist scholars suggest, digital story-sharing platforms are building communities among women who share their personal experiences of street harassment and sexual assault (Keller et al. 2016, pp. 7, 12; Rentschler 2014, pp. 71, 76, 78; Schuster 2013, pp. 16–18). In the case of Hollaback! (and Stop Street Harassment), for instance, street harassment victims can go online, tell their story and get support from readers who may have faced similar experiences (Wånggren 2016, p. 407). Moreover, interview research with people who had submitted a story to the Hollaback! website found that when participants read other people's accounts of harassment, they "felt that their own experience was validated." Further, reading others' stories helped the participants to realize that it was not their fault, allowing them to shift the blame and burden of the experience, and to feel part of a community (Dimond et al. 2013, p. 483).

In addition to serving a validation function, Carrie Rentschler (2014) argues that these cultures of support may augment site visitors' own capacities for reporting and responding to street harassment and assault, suggesting that the online testimonial culture around sexual violence encourages others to disclose their experiences (p. 76). Juliana de Faria confirms this view:

> A friend of mine complained over Facebook about being harassed on the streets of São Paulo. I was blown away!!! It was the very first time IN MY LIFE that [I'd] seen someone speaking out about it publicly. And in a matter of five minutes, her Facebook post had more than 100 comments of other women. They were sharing similar stories and I felt empowered to share mine too. (Personal communication, December 4, 2015, original emphasis)

Indeed, the growth in anti-harassment activism worldwide can, in part, be attributed to women sharing their stories through online communities, which has made the problem more visible and promoted collective identity among street harassment victims and survivors. As Jasmeen Patheja explains:

I think that a lot of it has happened online and one thing influencing another in terms of one testimony… there's a sense of somebody sitting somewhere else connects with the fact that this has been their experience too, so I guess that if you were to look at the past decade, there's been an overall consciousness raising in understanding and sharing and building dialogue on street harassment because people have also come forward and shared their experiences… one story's affecting the other and it spreads. (Personal communication, December 21, 2015)

While some might view online disclosures of street harassment experiences as little more than 'slacktivism' (i.e., "feel-good online activism that has zero political or social impact") (Morozov 2009), the importance of community validation and support in a context in which victims of street harassment generally lack recognition is important (Rentschler 2014, p. 78). Moreover, accusations of slacktivism assume that actors lack the appetite to commit themselves more fully to a cause (Christensen 2011). However, such assertions rest on traditional (i.e., gendered) definitions of what counts as political participation and where it should be located (Harris 2008, p. 483). Besides, once an individual has participated in a movement, regardless of the size of the contribution, their sense of commitment and obligation to the cause is likely to increase, as well as their sense of community belonging, thus potentially inducing more sustained political action on the issue (Garrett 2006, pp. 206–207; Harlow and Harp 2012, p. 200). Indeed, several of the interviewees explained that their activism was born out of sharing their experiences of harassment online. For instance, Jessica Raven, executive director of Collective Action for Safe Spaces, became politically active through sharing her harassment stories on Twitter and, consequently, developing a feminist consciousness of sexual violence and misogyny. She explains, learning about "the ways that toxic masculinity make women, in particular, and LGBTQ and gender non-conforming people feel unsafe and feel controlled, especially in public spaces… motivated me to want to do more" (J. Raven, personal communication, January 5, 2016).

Conclusion

This chapter examined the ways in which activists' usage of digital technologies has facilitated participation in anti-street harassment activism and, thus, influenced the movement's emergence and global development. I argued that anti-harassment activists have leveraged the cost-reducing affordance of digital technologies, resulting in easier, faster and more widespread activism. This, in part, explains the proliferation of new anti-harassment groups and innovative forms of activism. Additionally, digital technologies have afforded new opportunities for women to participate in anti-harassment activism, and to circumvent mainstream media narratives that minimize street harassment. Digital technologies have also enabled the creation of a collective identity among women over a large, disparate geographical area. Through learning about similar struggles elsewhere and a perception of belonging to a broader group of people with shared grievances, women have been inspired to mobilize against street harassment across the globe. However, future research could test this proposition more directly by examining the extent to which anti-harassment activists exhibit the three elements of collective identities in social movements identified by Taylor and Whittier (1992): a sense of 'we' based on shared characteristics, an oppositional culture to the dominant order, and a collective consciousness around the movement's goals and actions (Nip 2004, p. 206). With regards to the latter element of collective identities, future research should pay particular attention to the ways in which the movement's commitment to intersectionality – the recognition of multiple and overlapping, or intersecting, forms of oppression (Crenshaw 1989) – might impede or interfere with the forging of a common political agenda among different groups of women (Laperrière and Lépinard 2016, p. 375). Finally, I have argued that digital technologies have enabled the formation of communities of (primarily) women resisting street harassment. Online communities have encouraged and helped sustain anti-harassment activism through their ability to quickly connect a member base and to foster community identification and solidarity.

Notes

1. Brazil, Chile, Egypt, Germany, India, Lebanon, Mexico, Peru, the U.K., and the U.S.
2. One of the ways to respond to street harassment advocated by Hollaback! (2016a).
3. Lesbian, gay, bisexual, transgender, queer and intersex (LGBTQI) and gender non-conforming people, are also particularly susceptible to street harassment.
4. Although there is a long history of sporadic feminist resistance against street harassment, especially coinciding with the Suffrage movement in the early 1900s and with second wave feminism between the 1960s and 1980s, it was not until the 2000s that numerous grassroots efforts emerged focused on street harassment specifically (Kearl 2015, pp. xii–xvi).

References

Bonchek, M. S. (1995, April). *Grassroots in cyberspace: Using computer networks to facilitate political participation.* In 53rd Annual meeting of the Midwest Political Science Association, Vol. 6, Chicago.

Caren, N., Jowers, K., & Gaby, S. (2012). A social movement online community: Stormfront and the white nationalist movement. *Research in Social Movements, Conflicts and Change, 33,* 163–193.

Castells, M. (2012). *Networks of outrage and hope: Social movements in the internet age.* Cambridge/Malden: Polity.

Chega de Fiu Fiu. (2015). *Credentials for the Chega de Fiu Fiu Campaign.*

Christensen, H. S. (2011). Political activities on the internet: Slacktivism or political participation by other means? *First Monday, 16*(2). Retrieved from http://firstmonday.org/article/view/3336/2767

Clark, R. (2016). "Hope in a hashtag": The discursive activism of #WhyIStayed. *Feminist Media Studies, 16*(5), 788–804.

Crenshaw, K. (1989). Demarginalizing the intersection of race and sex: A black feminist critique of antidiscrimination doctrine, feminist theory and antiracist politics. *University of Chicago Legal Forum, 1989*(1), Article 8, 139–167.

Diani, M. (2000). Social movement networks virtual and real. *Information, Communication & Society, 3*(3), 386–401.

Dimond, J. P., Dye, M., LaRose, D., & Bruckman, A. S. (2013, February). *Hollaback!: The role of storytelling online in a social movement organization*. In Proceedings of the 2013 conference on Computer supported cooperative work (pp. 477–490). New York: ACM.

Earl, J., & Kimport, K. (2011). *Digitally enabled social change: Activism in the internet age*. Cambridge, MA/London: MIT Press.

Elliott, L. (2016, January 13). Spread of internet has not conquered 'digital divide' between rich and poor – Report. *The Guardian*. Retrieved from https://www.theguardian.com/technology/2016/jan/13/internet-not-conquered-digital-divide-rich-poor-world-bank-report

Evans, E. (2015). *The politics of third wave feminism*. Houndmills: Palgrave Macmillan.

Fairchild, K., & Rudman, L. A. (2008). Everyday stranger harassment and women's objectification. *Social Justice Research, 21*(3), 338–357.

Fileborn, B. (2014). Online activism and street harassment: Digital justice or shouting into the ether? *Griffith Journal of Law & Human Dignity, 2*(1), 32–51.

Garrett, R. K. (2006). Protest in an information society: A review of literature on social movements and new ICTs. *Information, Communication & Society, 9*(2), 202–224.

Gladwell, M. (2010). Small change. *The New Yorker, 4*(2010), 42–49.

Gurak, L. J., & Logie, J. (2003). Internet protests, from text to web. In M. McCaughey & M. D. Ayres (Eds.), *Cyberactivism: Online activism in theory and practice*. New York/London: Routledge.

Harlow, S., & Harp, D. (2012). Collective action on the web: A cross-cultural study of social networking sites and online and offline activism in the United States and Latin America. *Information, Communication & Society, 15*(2), 196–216.

Harris, A. (2008). Young women, late modern politics, and the participatory possibilities of online cultures. *Journal of Youth Studies, 11*(5), 481–495.

HeartMob. (2017). About HeartMob. Retrieved from https://iheartmob.org/about

Hollaback!. (2016a). What to do if you experience/witness harassment. Retrieved from http://www.ihollaback.org/resources/responding-to-harassers/

Hollaback!. (2016b). Home. Retrieved from http://www.ihollaback.org/#

Hollaback!. (2016c). Take action. Retrieved from http://www.ihollaback.org/take-action/

Hollaback!. (2016d). History and values. Retrieved from https://www.ihollaback.org/about/history-and-values/#values

Kearl, H. (2015). *Stop global street harassment: Growing activism around the world.* Santa Barbara/Denver: Praeger.

Keller, J. M., Mendes, K. D., & Ringrose, J. (2016). Speaking 'unspeakable things': Documenting digital feminist responses to rape culture. *Journal of Gender Studies,* 1–15.

Laperrière, M., & Lépinard, E. (2016). Intersectionality as a tool for social movements: Strategies of inclusion and representation in the Québécois women's movement. *Politics, 36*(4), 374–382.

Mantilla, K. (2013). Gendertrolling: Misogyny adapts to new media. *Feminist Studies, 39*(2), 563–570.

Morozov, E. (2009, May 19). Foreign policy: Brave new world of slacktivism. *NPR.* Retrieved from http://www.npr.org/templates/story/story.php?storyId=104302141

Morozov, E. (2011). *The net delusion: How not to liberate the world.* London: Penguin.

Nip, J. Y. M. (2004). The queer sisters and its electronic bulletin board: A study of the internet for social movement mobilization. In W. Van De Donk, B. D. Loader, P. G. Nixon, & D. Rucht (Eds.), *Cyberprotest: New media, citizens and social movements.* London/New York: Routledge.

Pickerill, J. (2003). *Cyberprotest: Environmental activism online.* Manchester/New York: Manchester University Press.

Rentschler, C. A. (2014). Rape culture and the feminist politics of social media. *Girlhood Studies, 7*(1), 65–82.

Schuster, J. (2013). Invisible feminists? Social media and young women's political participation. *Political Science, 65*(1), 8–24.

Shirky, C. (2009). *Here comes everybody: How change happens when people come together.* London: Penguin Books.

Staggenborg, S. (2011). *Social movements.* Oxford/New York: Oxford University Press.

Taylor, V., & Whittier, N. E. (1992). Collective identity in social movement communities: Lesbian feminist mobilization. In A. Morris & C. McClurg Mueller (Eds.), *Frontiers in social movement theory.* New Haven: Yale University Press.

thetrudz. (2014). #YouOkSis: Black women speak up about the violence of street harassment and solutions. *Storify.* Retrieved from https://storify.com/thetrudz/youoksis-black-women-speak-truth-about-street-har

Van Aelst, P., & Walgrave, S. (2004). New media, new movements? The role of the internet in shaping the 'anti-globalization' movement. In W. Van De Donk, B. D. Loader, P. G. Nixon, & D. Rucht (Eds.), *Cyberprotest: New media, citizens and social movements*. London/New York: Routledge.

Van Laer, J. (2007). *Internet use and protest participation: How do ICTs affect mobilization?* Antwerpen: Universiteit Antwerpen.

Van Laer, J., & Van Aelst, P. (2009). Cyber-protest and civil society: The internet and action repertoires in social movements. In Y. Jewkes & M. Yar (Eds.), *Handbook on Internet Crime* (pp. 230–254). London/New York: Routledge.

Vera-Gray, F. (2017). *Men's intrusion, women's embodiment: A critical analysis of street harassment: A critical analysis of street harassment*. London/New York: Routledge.

Wånggren, L. (2016). Our stories matter: Storytelling and social justice in the Hollaback! movement. *Gender and Education, 28*(3), 401–415.

Wellman, B., & Gulia, M. (1999). Net surfers don't ride alone: Virtual communities as communities. In B. Wellman (Ed.), *Networks in the global village: Life in contemporary communities*. Boulder: Westview Press.

Wellman, B., Quan-Haase, A., Boase, J., Chen, W., Hampton, K., Díaz, I., & Miyata, K. (2003). The social affordances of the internet for networked individualism. *Journal of Computer-Mediated Communication, 8*(3). Retrieved from http://onlinelibrary.wiley.com/doi/10.1111/j.1083-6101.2003.tb00216.x/full

18

Celebrity Victims and Wimpy Snowflakes: Using Personal Narratives to Challenge Digitally Mediated Rape Culture

Kaitlyn Regehr and Jessica Ringrose

In October 2015, after reporting a sexual assault in a Facebook post – a post that subsequently went viral across social and news media platforms – Kaitlyn Regehr was labeled a "celebrity victim" by a mainstream media outlet, *Spiked*. Just more than one year later, in November of 2016, Jessica Ringrose took to Twitter to call out sexism and rape culture that she saw populating the digital spaces following the U.S. election, and was aggressively trolled as a result. In this chapter, we take a personal, narrative approach to argue that although the derogatory implication that women lie about sexual assault or, further, try to capitalize on victimhood is not new, abusive attempts to silence women's experiences of sexual violence and their critiques of rape culture have intensified in the digital domain. We unpack both the technological affordances that make feminist critiques of gender and sexual violence possible and explore

K. Regehr (✉)
University of Kent, Canterbury, UK

J. Ringrose
University College London Institute of Education, London, UK

© The Author(s) 2018
J. R. Vickery, T. Everbach (eds.), *Mediating Misogyny*,
https://doi.org/10.1007/978-3-319-72917-6_18

353

increasingly evident postfeminist media discourses that legitimize attacks upon feminist digital consciousness-raising.

The digital sphere has given voice and meeting spaces to communities and activist groups, which have enabled positive social action and social change – take, for instance, the Arab Spring movements and demonstrations in the Middle East and Africa (Gerbaudo 2012). However, while the Internet presents a concentrated space where women's empowered presence is more visible, the subsequent retaliation is often anonymous (Jane 2017). This makes the digital sphere a unique environment that perpetuates – and potentially exacerbates – abuse experienced offline (Mishna 2013), as so-called Internet trolls promote and encourage threats of rape, sexual assault, and physical violence against women online who challenge the status quo.

Narrative research has a history of recording the lived experiences of those involved in social movements (Perks and Thomson 1998; Raleigh Yow 2005). Narrative research is a qualitative method that places emphasis on stories or descriptions of a series of events, which are viewed as essential elements for accounting for an individual's experience (Pinnegar and Daynes 2007). Honing in on the process of voicing sexual violence and rape culture in the digital sphere, our aim is to employ narrative methodological practices in order to contribute to scholarship that illustrates the vitality of the digital sphere for purposes of feminist activism (Harris 2008; Herring et al. 2002; Keller et al. 2016; Phipps et al. 2017; Thrift 2014).

In the first section, we examine research on the Manosphere (Ging 2016) and Internet abuse of women. We acknowledge the Internet as a platform for individuals to voice their experiences with sexual violence or to "come out" as survivors and consider the momentum of these movements. In the second section, through sharing our own personal stories, we trace the demonization of the survivors of sexual abuse and harassment. We further suggest that trolling is not limited to those who report sexual violence, but extends to supporters of survivors and those who speak out against rape culture more generally. Here we explore the denial of rape culture in the digital sphere and the intensification and normalization of these issues following the election of Donald Trump. In the third section of this chapter, we examine one example of this feminist resistance through a discussion of the Facebook group Pantsuit Nation, a community that has mobilized online as a vital answer to this issue.

Pantsuit Nation employs personal narrative approaches and the tradition of storytelling as a means of politicizing, sharing, supporting, and voicing sexual violence and rape culture – themes that are pertinent within the context of the current Trump era.

Speaking Out Against Sexual Violence and the Normalization of Rape Culture in the Digital Manosphere

In 1975, forty years before *Spiked* proposed the phrase "celebrity victim", Susan Brownmiller observed that rape and other forms of sexual violence have traditionally been articulated by men rather than women. Indeed, when compared to other crimes, the numbers of women voicing or reporting sexual violence remains very low (Tjaden and Thoennes 2000; Rennison 2002; Bachman 2000; Fisher et al. 2003; Sinha 2013). These low numbers are often attributed to the traditional mode of reporting – through the criminal justice system, which continuously undermines the severity of rape and sexual assault and affords unequal protection under the law (Renner and Park 2002). To this end, survivors often come to a realization that, despite sharing their experiences, their voices and intentions are not guaranteed to be heard in the justice system (Regehr and Alaggia 2006).

As a result of these factors that problematize the reporting of sexual violence through the criminal justice system, the Internet has emerged as a platform to voice experiences of sexual violence or to "come out" as a survivor. For example, in the article "Speaking 'unspeakable things': documenting digital feminist responses to rape culture," Keller, Mendes and Ringrose examined the hashtag #BeenRapedNeverReported through which women, girls, and a few men, were taking to Twitter to articulate their reasons for not reporting their experiences of sexual violence to authorities (Keller et al. 2016). Over the course of one week, the hashtag #BeenRapedNeverReported had been used over 40,000 times by Twitter users citing the emotional, professional, and, at times, the physical cost of reporting sexual violence. Keller, Mendes, and Ringrose found that participants interviewed in their study gained a sense of solidarity, community, and support through using the hashtag. At the time of writing, the hashtag #BeenRapedNeverReported has been tweeted eight million times. Through these means, survivors have greater control over the messaging and narrative surrounding their experiences. In this way, the concern raised by Brownmiller in 1975, that sexual violence has always been defined by men, is being redressed online though this digital discourse of survivorship. Narratives surrounding sexual violence are being defined and shared by survivors and their supporters rather than by the perpetrators, the legal system, or mainstream media.

However, though survivors have used the Internet as a platform for voicing and fighting back against sexual violence, the reaction or retaliation toward such posts is often anonymous (Jane 2017), making the digital sphere a distinctive space that perpetuates abuse experienced offline (Mishna 2013). Jane suggests that social media has spawned new forms of digital misogyny or "trolling" and that this digital misogyny is not random. Debbie Ging has mapped the presence of what she terms the Manosphere (Ging 2016), a connected online subculture of blogs, forums, and alternative media publications "centred around hatred, anger and resentment of feminism specifically, and women more broadly" (Wilkinson 2016). These commenters commonly associated with Men's Rights Activism (MRA) groups, often throw around terms such as "corrective rape" as a cure for "FemiNazis." Ging suggest that the loose networks of the Manosphere mobilize and reify "narratives of personal suffering (sexual rejection, legal entitlement, humiliation through divorce, suicide/self-immolation)" (Ging 2016, P. 31), which build affective consensus to disregard claims about sexual violence and gender inequality and promote the idea that what is the real issue is "men's plight under feminism" (Ging 2016, p. 31).

Ging has suggested that we have entered a critical moment in gender politics, where the rhetoric of masculinity-in-crisis bumps up against girl power, sex positivity, and biological essentialism (Ging 2009). Jane argues similarly that this backlash is in direct reaction to feminist mobilization online, which interrogates and outs rape culture, domestic abuse, rape, date rape, and sexual harassment. As a result, she positions gendered cyberhate as a derivative of a combination of new technologies, mob dynamics, and systemic misogyny, wherein: "Misogynists have never had so many opportunities to collectivize and abuse women with so few consequences" and "female targets have never been so visible and instantly accessible in such large numbers" (Jane 2017, p. 51).

In the weeks following the US presidential election the Manosphere seems to have been further legitimized and accepted into mainstream culture by way of repetition and affective modulation, as Massumi (2015) argues through repetition of mass media news loops (see Chap. 10 for Harp's research on misogyny in the news during the election). What we might call "Trump Pedagogy" (Ringrose and Showunmi 2016) has served to further normalize some of the most abusive rhetoric in political debate, the digital Manosphere, and the embodied practices of toxic masculinities. For instance, immediate behavioral contagion was evident during the heightened media attention to Trump during his election win. Echoing Trump's by- now infamous slogan, young men at the University of Sydney chanted "grab them by the pussy" on campus to celebrate Trump's presidency (Ringrose and Showunmi 2016). From this perspective, there is a valid concern that rape culture could be sustained and circulate more aggressively in a world where misogyny and performances of aggressive masculinity are acceptable, or in fact rewarded, when the man who publicly stated he would "grab them [women] by the pussy[s]" is now the leader of the free world (Ringrose and Showunmi 2016).

Celebrity Victim and Wimpy Snowflake: The Personal Cost of Speaking Out Against Rape Culture

"To the man on the 207 bus towards Acton" is how Kaitlyn Regehr began what would become a viral Facebook post in search of a Good Samaritan. On Tuesday October 6, 2015, while riding a West London bus, Regehr was groped by a man standing beside her. Having seen the incident, another passenger called out the harasser. He asked if the harasser had any women in his life, and pointed at Regehr, stating, "She could be your mother. She could be your sister." As the 207 arrived at her stop, Regehr mouthed "thank you," but the exchange between the men had become quite aggressive, and she didn't believe the Good Samaritan saw her. As a result, she posted on Facebook stating that she was seeking the Good Samaritan to see if he was OK (the exchange could have become violent) and that she wished to thank and buy him a pint.

On Wednesday, as Regehr held her smart phone in her hand and watched as the post's Facebook shares escalated hundreds by the minute, BBC News, ITV, and the *Daily Mail* began a forceful stream of interview requests. The next day, Regehr's parents in Canada called to express concern when they read about her (the harassment victim) in their morning paper – a story, which ran in newspapers across the world in countries such as Australia, Russia, and Indonesia. However, it was not until actor Ashton Kutcher, with his more than 17 million Twitter followers, shared the story on his Twitter account that Regehr became concerned that the intentions behind her social media post had been misinterpreted. Subsequently, people on message boards theorized that she had invented the event; misogynistic tweets flooded her smartphone, and an article appeared on *Spiked* entitled "Kaitlyn Regehr and the Rise of the Celebrity Victim" (Gill 2015).

The author of the article, Charlotte Gill, mused that Regehr's "post wasn't so much about finding her hero, or gaining an emotional conclusion, but about vanity" (Gill 2015). Gill's underlying claim then is that Regehr was using what is positioned as a supposed act of sexual harassment, to showcase her own desirability "in an age when victimhood has become a fast-pass to fame" (Gill 2015). Indeed, in a familiar postfeminist trope of reviling and attempting to undermine feminist truth claims, Gill goes so far as to suggest: "Contemporary feminism is partly to blame for this development; women are rewarded for spilling their souls and recounting tales of hardship, and gain mass followings from those who relate to their experiences" (Gill 2015).

Tensions around femininity, appearance, and celebrity are used here to question the legitimacy of Regehr's feminism. It is suggested that Regehr's intentions could be compromised by a desire for social media fame and to benefit from her alignment with postfeminist ideals of femininity. Gill positions Regehr as a typical example of a "celebrity victim", a term she employs to define Regehr and "similar" individuals who "have milked their own negative experiences to forge new careers for themselves." Gill cites as a comparable example to Regehr, Charlotte Proudman (a barrister whose work has focused on female genital mutilation, forced marriage, and honor-based violence) and who is "now the *Guardian's* resident moper on a range of issues" (Gill 2015). In this, Gill implies that particular women who speak out about sexual harassment or violence are using it as an attention-seeking device, in which they actively aim to capitalize on 'alleged' claims of sexual violence. The implication here is the same logic that is typically used to undermine rape victims in legal debates – that those who wear a short skirt and sexualize themselves are "asking for it." The undertone of Gill's argument is that Regehr is a narcissist who wants to spread the message that some bloke on the public transit fancied her. Gill seeks to undermine Regehr, and reduce her subjectivity to one of craving heterosexualized attention. The comments under Gill's article concur with this sentiment, employing the term "celebrity victim" to refer to Regehr and her "blatant self-promotion" (Boing, *Spiked* Online Responder, 2016), or referring to her account as typical "old-as-hills 'damsel in distress' storytelling" (Steve Moxon, *Spiked* Online Responder, 2016). Echoing dominant rape culture, the implication made by Gill and her supporters is that Regehr should just shut up and accept the sexual aggression of predatory men as part of the natural order of things.

The theme of discrediting members of the digital feminist community – particularly those who speak out against sexual violence and rape culture – was likewise apparent in an episode of violent trolling directed at Ringrose on November 9 2016, when she took to Twitter to denounce the misogyny and rape culture that she saw populating the Twittersphere as a result of Trump's victory in the U.S. presidential election. Ringrose tweeted and retweeted the hashtag #RacismWon and #sexism, and, further, circulated a blog exploring her concept of "Trump pedagogy" – in which she argues legitimized hate speech is made normal through the mass media affective modulation of Trump rhetoric (Massumi 2015). As a result, Ringrose was intensely trolled for several consecutive days after the election, receiving a stream of violent, demeaning, and sexually abusive tweets. One user, @Warpath, whose profile reads "NEVER Politically Correct, FOREVER Ethically Correct", suggested, "better chop off my testicles, obviously not getting much out of them anyhow." Another

Twitter user suggested that Ringrose should be cleansed from the academic system and another, @YoungGun, dubbed Ringrose a "self-loathing wimpy snowflake" due to her feminist beliefs.

Further, in response to claims that Trump was a rapist @YoungGun states, "just because a woman says it doesn't mean it's true" and a Twitter user by the name of A Man Without Wings suggests, "just because you say something so often you believe it yourself, doesn't make it true to anyone else." Additionally, threats, including those of rape and sexual assault, were directed at Ringrose, finally prompting her to remove the word "feminism" from her Twitter handle. What Ringrose's experience demonstrates is again the misogynistic practice of claiming untruths in order to discredit, undermine, and silence women who openly condemn sexual violence.

Angela McRobbie stated in a recent article that "Anti-feminism has now taken on a much more aggressive edge" (McRobbie 2016), a hostility which "has found a home on the Internet" can also, worryingly, move "from there onto the streets…" (McRobbie 2016). Indeed, when Ringrose's research on feminism in schools appeared in national newspapers, she received hostile comments and abuse from readers, many of whom then took to Twitter in order to troll her account and intensify the criticism. Further, one commenter went so far as to send a hate postcard (which showcased an image of a woman with an arrow through her heart) to her office at University College London. Where news media comment sections are supposedly checked for threats of sexual violence, Twitter is a relatively unregulated space where networked users can create torrents of abuse that increase intimidation; at times, this online harassment can escalate into offline – and potentially physical – consequences.

We are interested in the ways we were (and continue to be) targeted in the virtual sphere, and the ways these digital identities such as the "celebrity victim" and the "self-loathing wimpy snowflake" were thrust upon us as women speaking about, or out against, sexual violence and rape culture. The term "snowflake" is notable here, as it has recently emerged as an insult, often shot from the right to the left, to describe thin-skinned, whining liberals. Further, as *Guardian* writer Rebecca Nicholson has stated, it is a particularly effective insult as you are not just shutting down one's "opinion, but telling them off for being offended that you are doing so" (Nicholson 2016). The feminized nature of the term is also significant in that it positions "snowflake" as weak, frail, and easily offended. Thus, the "celebrity victim" and "snowflake" are both relevant terms within this discussion, as they reflect the archetypal roles often thrust upon women who report sexual assault: The celebrity victim, who attempts to capitalize on the experience and thus can be dismissed; and the snowflake, who is simply overly sensitive and prone to taking offense and, thus, can be dismissed. What both these terms and forms of silencing share are a similarity to offline experiences of sexual assault survivors (Yeager 2012; Ullman and Filipias 2001).

From this perspective, the act of reporting or sharing experiences of sexual violence on social media and speaking out against rape culture is, arguably now more than ever, a brave and defiant act that can be seen as political. Of course, these acts are not limited to the digital sphere but also spill out into everyday acts of political resistance. To demonstrate this, we turn to the next section to the Facebook group Pantsuit Nation, a vital space for sharing and storytelling surrounding issues of sexual violence and rape culture that emerged spontaneously in the days preceding the U.S. election.

Mass Feminist Resistance in Action

In October of 2016, during the lead-up to the U.S. election and in the wake of sexual assault allegations surrounding the then Republican candidate Donald Trump, survivors took to social media to share their stories of sexual violence in a plea to stop the normalization of rape culture. Heartfelt and personal outings as survivors congregated under Twitter hashtags such as #EndRapeCultureNow, and the now out-dated #NeverTrump, and also across other social media platforms.

For example, one woman in Regehr's personal Facebook feed responded to Trump's "grab 'em by the pussy" comments by writing a public post recounting a harrowing experience of being attacked in an empty subway station. She described a man lifting her woolen skirt and attempting to forcefully penetrate her from behind. She articulated the lasting trauma of the event, as she struggled to be alone or ever feel safe and, further, implored readers share her post in order to encourage others not to vote Donald Trump into office. She then went on to outline the normalizing effect of electing a known misogynist and sexually violent individual into the highest office in the country.

The post above offers insight into social media practices as a form of feminist pedagogy that link Trump's behavior to personal experiences of sexual violence. The storytelling posts operate largely for a *personal* social media audience even though the post is "public," showing the public/private boundaries of social media are porous (boyd 2014; Papacharissi 2015). But connectivity was realized in a much wider way when enormous *public* groups quickly formed to enable responses to Trump's sexism and racism during the presidential campaign, most notably the by now unitalicize Pantsuit Nation *Pantsuit Nation*. This closed invite-only Facebook group amassed an incredible following of 3,865,933 members in the few weeks after the election, and has also diverged into smaller regional groups to address more local concerns. Although Pantsuit Nation was initiated with the intention of supporting Hillary Clinton's presidential campaign, it grew to meet the needs of individuals, as the U.S. and the world deals with the aftermath of the presidential campaign. The Pantsuit Nation Facebook page encourages narratives of not only sexual abuse, but also racial and religious bigotry and all manners of sexual violence, including homophobic violence, facing Americans in the aftermath of the election. Its mandate is as follows:

> Pantsuit Nation exists to harness the power of collective storytelling. Millions of voices telling millions of stories. We amplify the voices of those who have historically been underrepresented or excluded. We listen. We empower our members to speak with honesty and without fear of attack. We are strong in our diversity. We invite conversation – true conversation – about the issues that are most fundamental to us and our identities… Taken collectively, stories open us up to the vast and complex realities of what it means to live, work, love, struggle, and celebrate in our country. (Pantsuit Nation 2016)

Here, similar to the Facebook post outlined above and Regehr's post recounted in the previous section, Pantsuit Nation uses emotive – and an arguably very female – age-old tradition of storytelling and oral history, which has been adapted for the digital age. In this way, Pantsuit Nation, as a closed invite-only Facebook group, has created a relatively safe space, and increased options for survivors' articulation, framing, and chosen intention of reporting sexual violence.

Shortly after the election, a 22-year-old Ph.D. student took to Pantsuit Nation to describe an incident from earlier that day. She explained that while riding a public bus, two men grabbed at her arm and began to taunt her. They suggested that she like being grabbed and that she would, therefore, like "it rough." In her post, the student then questioned why she could stand up for others, but was unable to do the same for herself. She concluded by stating that as soon as she arrived home, she opened up the Pantsuit Nation Facebook group in order to find solace. She describes scrolling through the supportive and inspiring stories of others in the group, hoping that this would get her one step closer to being the "nastier woman" she seeks to be.

Like many who take to Pantsuit Nation to share personal narratives of sexual assault, these posters are not reporting to track down or to bring legal implications against sexual abusers, harassers, or predators. They are reporting to be heard. They are reporting to support others. They are reporting in order to situate the harmful nature of normalizing sexual assault and, further, to outline and stress the implications of electing someone accused of sexual assault into a place of great – arguably the greatest – political power. As danah boyd et al. (2010, p. 6) have argued regarding Twitter, users post on a topic or repost others in order "To make one's presence as a listener visible; to publicly agree with someone; to validate others' thoughts; As an act of friendship, loyalty, or homage by drawing attention, sometimes via a retweet request."

The Facebook Pantsuit nation group works in a similar way to Twitter given the high volume of users. The only condition is that one is accepted into the group. The mass liking is part of the Facebook "like economy" (Gerlitz and Helmond 2013), which alerts users of posts that their friends in the group have liked. Likes (and now other hot button responses such as love heart or angry face) generate 100,000s of likes for some of the posts. This massification of likes functions in a similar way to Twitter since "In the Facebook context, liking someone's post – along with other means such as commenting – can be interpreted as a form of support for the user's face-work" (Eranti and Lonkila 2015). We can extrapolate that Pantsuit Nation demonstrates the constantly evolving Facebook platform and capacities of Facebook groups to cultivate activist communities. Indeed, particularly important is how Facebook does not allow for repeated anonymous trolling like Twitter, given that negative commentators can be readily blocked from groups.

Now, however, because of its massive uptake and its value as a social media commodity due to enormous rates of participation in the group, Pantsuit Nation has come under heavy criticism. When its founder, Libby Chamberlain, filed to trademark the name Pantsuit Nation, and subsequently signed a book deal, *The Huffington Post* published the article "Pantsuit Nation Is a Sham." *The Huffington Post* positioned Chamberlain as purposefully aiming to capitalize on the group and also to share posters' stories without consent (Lewis 2016). Additionally, the group was accused of promoting "white feminism" by repeatedly silencing the critiques of women of color (Lewis 2016). In a Facebook post on the group's page, Chamberlin clarified that members involved in the book would have to give consent for the use of their stories and images. Further, in response to the *Huffington Post* article, Heather Dockray took to *Mashable* and suggested, "instead of calling a group that four million people belong to a 'sham,'… why not work together to make it better? Instead of shaming our allies, we should be holding them accountable as we build them up. There's not as many as we need, and they're easier to lose than we think" (Dockray 2016).

Dockray raises an interesting point here when suggesting we [feminists] should simultaneously hold our allies accountable while also building them up. For perhaps, when dealing with such a multitude of feminist voices and stories, we don't need, and nor should we ever expect, consensus. Rather, we should look at activist spaces such as Pantsuit Nation as a space where we can engage in such a dialogue with each other. In this way, Pantsuit Nation has become a touchstone for critical feminist dialogue and debate. The group has become marketable due to its mass popularity, but turning stories into a book will only freeze specific aspects of the posts and not stop the flow of dialogue between users. What is most significant to our argument is how social media provides communicative platforms to discuss and trouble the notion of easy or simple feminist activism surrounding the voicing of sexual violence. Thus, while consensus was never expected nor the goal of Pantsuit Nation, what it does evidence is an incredible example of feminist dialogue around how to tackle misogyny and sexually violent rhetoric evidenced by Trump pedagogy.

Conclusion: Cyber Survival

The emerging importance of social media for purposes of feminist and social activism has become clear in recent years (Harris 2008; Herring et al. 2002; Keller et al. 2016). We positioned social media as essential platforms for individuals to report or fight back against sexual and gendered violence, a topic also historically defined by men (Brownmiller 1975), and, more recently, a topic that is embodied by the current U.S. president. However, when encouraging women to voice personal narratives of assault and report sexual violence, the emotional and physical well-being of survivors must be accounted for. Never before have women been so visible and accessible to – often anonymous – abusers (Jane 2017) in a space seemingly detached from the social, moral, and legal structures of the offline world. Further, as can be seen from Ringrose's Twitter experiences, the aggressive emotional contagion (De Gelder et al. 2004) that is transmitted through the digital sphere was likely exacerbated in the immediate weeks after the election. Through these means, McRobbie's argument of more aggressive anti-feminism holds true. By way of the Manosphere, toxic masculinity politics are mobilized through fear and hate to identify winners and losers within the heteropatriarchal logic championed by Trump and "has found a home on the Internet" (McRobbie 2016). In stating this, we also are aware that an online/offline binary is no longer tenable as a position for thinking about mediated life (Kember and Zylinska 2012), as gender and sexual violence bleeds across space/time onto social media and back out through the post delivered to our offices. However, through these same porous pathways, social media allows for different feminist positions to operate in dialogue and further enables critical consciousness raising, as users fight back against the escalation of rape culture in the Trump era.

Following the lead of many of the participants on the Pantsuit Nation Facebook group, we the authors, the "celebrity victim" and the "wimpy snowflake," have taken a personal storytelling approach here to unpack discourses of attention seeking and overly sensitive femininity used to disarm and disqualify the feminist challenge to misogyny. What we take heart in is the manifold ways that feminist resistance has taken hold and root in online, and subsequently offline, through manifold narrative formations made possible through social media affordances (Ringrose and Lawrence 2018), such as the personal accounts shared on Facebook Pantsuit Nation. However fleeting and transitory the particularity of these social media examples may seem, they serve a critical purpose for their lifespan in nurturing responders and enabling new connectivities and collectivities of storytelling, enabling new truth claims that can shift the dominant paradigms of real/fake that underpin the critique of the celebrity victim. Collectively, these diverse forms of passionate storytelling may provide a means of shifting the discourse of sexual violence from invisible victims to documented cybersurvivors and thrivers. For less we forget, when snowflakes – each unique and one-of-a-kind – commune, they can take over mountains.

References

Bachman, R. (2000). A comparison of annual incidence rates and contextual characteristics of intimate-partner violence against women from the National Crime Victimization Survey (NCVS) and the National Violence Against Women Survey (NVAWS). *Violence Against Women, 6*(8), 839–867.

boyd, d. (2014). *It's complicated: The social lives of networked teens.* New Haven: Yale University Press.

boyd, d. m., Golder, S., & Lotan, G. (2010, January 5–8). *Tweet, tweet, retweet: Conversational aspects of retweeting on Twitter.* Proceedings of HICSS-42, Persistent Conversation Track. Kauai: IEEE Computer Society.

Brownmiller, S. (1975). *Against our will: Men, women and rape.* New York: Simon and Schuster.

De Gelder, B., et al. (2004). Fear fosters flight: A mechanism for fear contagion when perceiving emotion expressed by a whole body. *Proceedings of the National Academy of Sciences of the United States of America, 101*(47), 16701–16706.

Dockray, H. (2016, December 22). The Pantsuit Nation backlash is liberal elitism at its worst. *Mashable.com.* Retrieved from http://mashable.com/2016/12/22/liberal-backlash-pantsuit-nation-ridiculous/#7Qk2s.1xuOqL

Eranti, V., & Lonkila, M. (2015, May). The social significance of the Facebook like button. First Monday, [S.l.]. ISSN 13960466. http://firstmonday.org/ojs/index.php/fm/article/view/5505/4581, https://doi.org/10.5210/fm.v20i6.5505. Accessed 4 July 2017.

Fisher, B., et al. (2003). Reporting sexual victimization to the police and others: Results from a national-level study of college women. *Criminal Justice and Behavior, 31*(1), 6–38.

Gerbaudo, P. (2012). *Tweets and the streets: Social media and contemporary activism.* London: Pluto Press.

Gerlitz, C., & Helmond, A. (2013). The like economy: Social buttons and the data-intensive web. *New Media & Society, 15*(8), 1348–1365.

Gill, C. (2015, October 21). Kaitlyn Regehr and the rise of the celebrity victim. *Spiked Online.* Retrieved from http://www.spiked-online.com/newsite/article/kaitlyn-regehr-and-the-rise-of-the-victim-celebrity/17559#.WDXEhHeca1N

Ging, D. (2009). All-consuming images: New gender formations in post-Celtic-Tiger Ireland. In D. Ging, M. Cronin, & P. Kirby (Eds.), *Transforming Ireland: Challenges, critiques and resources.* Manchester: Manchester University Press.

Ging, D. (2016, May 6). The Manosphere's 'toxic technocultures': Social media and the new communicative politics of men's rights [Invited Lecture]. Mediated feminisms: Activism and resistance to gender and sexual violence in the digital age, UCL Institute of Education.

Harris, A. (2008). *Next wave cultures: Feminism, subcultures, activism.* New York: Routledge.

Herring, S., et al. (2002). Searching for safety online: Managing "trolling" in a feminist forum. *The Information Society: An International Journal, 18*(5), 371–384.

Jane, E. (2017). *Misogyny online: A short (and brutish) history.* Los Angeles: Sage.

Keller, J., Mendes, K., & Ringrose, J. (2016). Speaking 'unspeakable things': Documenting digital feminist responses to rape culture. *Journal of Gender Studies, 27*(1), 22--36

Kember, S., & Zylinska, E. (2012). *Life after new media: Mediation as a vital process.* Cambridge: MIT Press.

Krol, C. (2017, January 23). Women's March: The numbers behind the global rallies. *Telegraph.co.uk*. Retrieved from http://www.telegraph.co.uk/news/2017/01/23/womens-march-numbers-behind-global-rallies/

Lewis, H (2016, December 20). Pantsuit nation is a Sham. *Huffington Post.com*.

Massumi, B. (2015). *Politics of affect*. Cambridge: Polity Press.

McRobbie, A. (2016, November 28). Anti-feminism, then and now. *Opendemocracy.net*. Retrieved from https://www.opendemocracy.net/transformation/angela-mcrobbie/anti-feminism-then-and-now?utm_source=Daily+Newsletter&utm_campaign=96b4c91414-DAILY_NEWS LETTER_MAILCHIMP&utm_medium=email&utm_term=0_717bc5d86d-96b4c91414-407363651

Mishna, F. (2013). Promoting women's rights in a cyber world: New opportunities, new challenges. International Women's Day, Factor-Inwentash Faculty of Social Work.

Nicholson, R. (2016, November 28). 'Poor little snowflake' – The defining insult of 2016. *The Guardian*. Retrieved from https://www.theguardian.com/science/2016/nov/28/snowflake-insult-disdain-young-people

Papacharissi, Z. (2015). *Affective publics: Sentiment, technology, and politics*. Oxford: Oxford University Press.

Perks, R., & Thomson, A. (1998). *The oral history reader*. New York: Routledge.

Phipps, A., Ringrose, J., Renold, E., & Jackson, C. (2017). Rape culture, lad culture and everyday sexism: Researching, conceptualizing and politicizing new mediations of gender and sexual violence. *Journal of Gender Studies*. https://doi.org/10.1080/09589236.2016.1266792

Pinnegar, S., & Daynes, G. (2007). Locating narrative inquiry historically. In J. Clandinin (Ed.), *Handbook of narrative inquiry: Mapping a methodology*. Thousand Oaks: Sage.

Raleigh Yow, V. (2005). *Recording oral history: A practical guide for social scientists*. Walnut Creek: AltaMira Press.

Regehr, C., & Alaggia, R. (2006). Perspectives on justice for victims of sexual violence. *Victims and Offenders: A Journal of Evidence-Based Practice, 1*(1), 33–46.

Renner, K., & Park, L. (2002, June 28–30). Legal disparities and adult sexual assault. *Society for the Psychological Study of Social Issues*, Toronto.

Rennison, C. (2002). Rape and sexual assault: Reporting to police and medical attention, 1992–2000. Washington, DC. Retrieved from https://www.bjs.gov/content/pub/pdf/rsarp00.pdf

Rentschler, C. (2015). #Safetytipsforladies: Feminist Twitter takedowns of victim blaming. *Feminist Media Studies, 15*(2), 353–356.

Ringrose, J., & Lawrence, E. 2018 "@NoToFeminism, #FeministsAreUgly and Misandry Memes: How Social Media Feminist Humor is Calling out Antifeminism" in Jessalynn Keller, Maureen E. Ryan (eds.) Emergent Feminisms: Complicating a Postfeminist Media Culture, New York: Routledge.

Ringrose, J., & Showunmi, V. (2016, November 10). *Calling out Trump pedagogy: Turning the 2016 USA election into a teachable moment*, GEA – Gender and Education Association, UCL Institute of Education.

Sinha, M. (2013). *Measuring violence against women: Statistical trends: Juristat 85-002-X*. Ottawa: Statistics Canada.

Thrift, S. (2014). #YesAllWomen as feminist meme event. *Feminist Media Studies, 14*(6), 1090–1092.

Tjaden, P., & Thoennes, N. (2000). Full report of the prevalence, incidence, and consequences of violence against women: Findings from the National Violence Against Women survey (NCJ183781), Washington, DC.

Ullman, S., & Filipias, H. (2001). Correlates of formal and informal support seeking in sexual assault victims. *Journal of Interpersonal Violence, 16*(10), 1028–1047.

Wilkinson, A. (2016, November 15). We need to talk about the online radicalization of young, white men. *The Guardian*. Retrieved from https://www.theguardian.com/commentisfree/2016/nov/15/alt-right-manosphere-mainstream-politics-breitbart

www.pantsuitnation.org

www.report-it-blog.tumblr.com

19

#NastyWomen: Reclaiming the Twitterverse from Misogyny

Gina Masullo Chen, Paromita Pain, and Jinglun Zhang

It was a stunning moment in United States presidential politics. Presidential candidate Hillary Clinton was answering a question about Social Security during the third and final debate of the 2016 presidential campaign. Suddenly, her opponent, Donald Trump, interrupted her, as he had many times before. "Such a nasty woman," he said, pointing his finger to highlight his words. Clinton, unperturbed, went on to make her case on how to fund Social Security. Trump shook his head and smirked, as a television audience of 71.6 million – one of the largest debate audiences in U.S. history – watched (The Associated Press 2016). For a beat, much of America paused, aghast that a presidential contender would utter such a disparaging remark during an official event like a debate. In a campaign season that stood out in American politics for its vitriol, the misogynistic statement marked a new low in political discourse. But her female supporters – largely women of color – did not pause for long.

G. Masullo Chen (✉) • P. Pain
School of Journalism, University of Texas at Austin, Austin, TX, USA

J. Zhang
Tsinghua University, Beijing, China

© The Author(s) 2018
J. R. Vickery, T. Everbach (eds.), *Mediating Misogyny*,
https://doi.org/10.1007/978-3-319-72917-6_19

These supporters got busy, reclaiming the term meant to hurt and harm Clinton and turned it into a triumph of female empowerment. #NastyWoman and #NastyWomen hashtags trended across social media, with thousands upon thousands of references on Twitter, Instagram, and Facebook (Prakash 2016). Women used the hashtags to assert their support of Clinton and to denounce men like Trump. They showed up on T-shirts, mugs, and stickers. They morphed into Internet memes and became a rallying cry for Clinton's core supporters, inviting feminist discussions online. The hashtags played a galvanizing role, as Facebook groups formed to gather women who shared their support of Clinton as well as a belief that Trump's sexism, coupled with his inexperience and volatile temperament, rendered him an illegitimate choice for president. Of course, it is impossible to know exactly who embraced the terms "nasty woman" and "nasty women" and tried to reclaim them. However, exit polls after the November 8, 2016, election showed that 53% of white female voters cast their ballots for Trump, but Clinton garnered only 43% of the white female vote (Malone 2016). In contrast, black women, followed by Latinas, were Clinton's most fervent supporters (Williams 2016). This suggested quite strongly that those who were reclaiming "nasty woman" and "nasty women" were predominantly women of color. (For an analysis of cultural misogyny and Hillary Clinton in the 2016 election, please see Chap. 10.)

This chapter examines the "nasty woman" phenomenon by qualitatively analyzing more than 1,390 tweets that used the hashtags after the debate until one week after Trump's election. These hashtags offered a vivid example of the paradox of the Twitterverse as a spot of empowerment for women as well as a place that reinforces misogynistic norms. The goal of this chapter was not to make a political point. Rather, we intended to use our analysis to show that the digital sphere can be a combative place for women – even for women in power like Hillary Clinton. Yet, it also can be a place where women can regain their own sense of power – or agency – through actions that start online and can lead to societal changes. We believe Hillary Clinton's experience with these terms offer a microcosm of what many women endure online, as they face digital misogyny and assert their own power through reclaiming this digital sphere through "hashtag feminism." Hashtag feminism creates a "virtual space where victims of inequality can co-exist together in a space that acknowledges their pain, narrative, and isolation" (Dixon 2014, p. 34).

The primary questions this chapter answers are: How did #NastyWoman and #NastyWomen operate on Twitter? To what extent did these hashtags help women reclaim their agency in the wake of Donald Trump's use of the term to harm Hillary Clinton? What does this mean for how hashtags can be used as a tool of women's digital empowerment?

We begin by reviewing prior studies related to digital female empowerment, specifically as it relates to the use of hashtags. We use Lauren Berlant's concept of "intimate publics" (2011, p. 324) to explain the sense of "we-ness" (Cooks et al. 2002, p. 148) women may feel as they rally around hashtags. Then we explain how we conducted our analysis and reviewed themes that surfaced in our reading of the 1,390 tweets using the #NastyWoman or #NastyWomen hashtags. We conclude by explaining what our analysis means and how it answers our specific questions.

The Twitterverse

Twitter launched in 2006 as a place to share what people were doing right now, but it evolved into a platform to disseminate news and information with the potential for people to form connections with each other through a digital form of camaraderie (Chen 2011). Today, 24% of Americans who are online use Twitter, and women are slightly more likely to use the platform than men (Greenwood et al. 2016). Like many forms of digital communication, Twitter at first was a lauded as an egalitarian space where voices that were silenced in traditional media, including women's voices, could be heard. Many hoped Twitter would "redefine dominant relationship patterns that are culturally instigated" (Ebo 1998, p. 3) and provide an outlet for the marginalized. To some extent, that happened. African-American women, low-income families, sexual minorities, mothers, and many others used digital platforms to express their views, without having to persuade traditional media outlets, such as newspapers, magazines, or television news, to spread their messages (Chen 2013, 2017; Hera et al. 2004). Yet the same inequities offline are apparent online. In the same way that the Internet empowers marginalized voices, it also invigorates hateful speech. The speed and immediacy of digital media have made it easier for trolls to incite discord (Buckels et al. 2014), anti-feminists to attack female gamers (Braithwaite 2016; Chess and Shaw 2015), and bullies to spread abuse that singles out people with less power in society (Cole 2015; Ohlheiser 2016), including women and people of color.

Hashtag Feminism

Hashtags – keywords marked with a hash, or pound, sign – have become a particularly potent tool to both hurt and help women online. Hashtags started on Twitter a year after the platform began (Gannes 2010), as a means to organize tweets. Since then, they have become a method to provide context in 140-character tweets, as well as imbue them with the emotion that is communicated through tone of voice or facial expressions in offline conversations. People use hashtags to highlight what they think is news, draw attention to topics, and connect with others who share their views (Brock 2012). Social activists worldwide have used Twitter hashtags to push for political change, give voice to the voiceless, and organize revolutions. These efforts have been as diverse as fighting crimes against women in Turkey (Alitnay 2014), supporting democratic uprisings in Arab countries (Eltantawny and West 2011), and buttressing the Black Lives Matter movement for African Americans' rights in the United States (Jackson 2016). Specifically, in relation to feminism, hashtags have emerged as a formidable tool to help move women's issues to the forefront. Hashtags have spotlighted public consciousness on topics such as sex abuse, as women used the hashtag #IAmNotAfraidToSayIt to document their own experiences of abuse or fight back against the normalization of misogyny by calling attention to it with the #EverydaySexism hashtag. For feminists, hashtags have emerged as an effective way to share information and impel action about and around issues surrounding women that get little support from mainstream society. They can combat the way the traditional media ignore or symbolically annihilate women by failing to portray or misrepresenting them (Liebler 2010; Strinati 2004). For example, #SafetyTipsForWomen became a way for women to challenge the notion that women bear responsibility for avoiding rape (Harlot Overdrive 2013), rather than placing blame on rapists. For black women in particular, hashtag feminism has been a useful tool to help communities recognize and respond to injustice (Williams 2015). For instance, black feminists started #StandWithJada to flout a destructive hashtag called #JadaPose that mocked the rape of an African-American 16-year-old (Williams 2015). Such hashtag conversations are not only restricted to the developed world, but also have global audiences in countries, such as India, where the #HappytoBleed hashtag was used to fight taboos against menstruating women ("Why Are Indian Women," 2015). Feminists successfully used the #BringBackOurGirls hashtag to pressure the U.S. and Nigerian governments to take action in 2014 after 300 schoolgirls were kidnapped because they wanted an education (Khoja-Moolji 2015).

Hashtag feminism is not without critics. Certainly, hashtags may raise awareness and provide a sense of power, but unless they translate to political action they may do little to solve problems. In addition, efforts to unify women through a hashtag can be circumvented by opponents of the message. For example, a politically conservative radio host started the #HowToSpotAFeminist hashtag in early 2015 to perpetuate negative feminist stereotypes, but feminists co-opted the hashtag and reclaimed it (Bahadur 2015; Romano 2015). However, the hashtag continues to be used to repudiate feminism.

Yet we argue the value of feminist hashtags lies in changing the conversation from an anti-woman narrative to one that supports women and gives them a sense they are not alone. Thus, hashtags can shift the digital space of Twitter from dangerous to empowering for women, at least in a small way. For example, when video game creator Ubisoft declared that female characters were too difficult to create, the hashtag #WomenAreTooHardToDominate protested this idea (Huntemann 2015). Hashtags can offer a "symbolic rerouting" (Yuriko 2013, p. 156) of a conversation by changing the direction of the dialogue. They can shift efforts to damage women and reimagine them as tools to save them. That is the focus of this chapter – how Trump's uncivil comment, calling Clinton a "nasty woman," undoubtedly was aimed at decreasing her political and personal value. However, the reclamation of this term transformed the conversation about what it means to be a "nasty woman." Hashtag feminism can foster connections between people by allowing people who use them to agree on the meaning of topics. Even though the people do not know each other offline – and likely never will – their shared sense of being political together (Berlant 2011) cements them. This helps feminist advocates feel more powerful as a group than they would feel individually.

Gender and Politics

Understanding how hashtag feminism operates in politics is particularly important because gender bias against women political candidates is rampant (Heldman et al. 2005; Lawrence and Rose 2010). At the same time, social media's role for female political candidates is particularly important. For example, a network analysis of 773,038 tweets about candidates for statewide offices in 2014 found that Twitter conversations were more focused on female candidates than male candidates (McGregor and Mourão 2016). The 2016 presidential match-up between Trump and Clinton illustrates the importance of studying female candidates. Clinton, the first female presidential nominee from a major party, "provoked a wave of misogyny" (Beinart 2016, n.p.). At the Republican National Convention, for example, pins that read "Trump that Bitch" or "Life's a Bitch: Don't Vote for One" were on sale (Beinart 2016). Trump credited Clinton's success to playing the "woman's card," not her own hard work, and he claimed she was shouting when she was merely speaking pointedly (Chozick and Parker 2016), tapping into a gender norm that requires women to speak softly. Trump's misanthropic comments about women during the campaign added fuel to this fire. Then a 2005 recording surfaced depicting Trump bragging about grabbing women by the vagina – which he called a "pussy" – without their consent (Burns et al. 2016a). The video sparked heated debate online and led some Republicans to temporarily disavow him (Burns et al. 2016b). Overall, however, it fit an ongoing narrative of Trump's misogyny that seemed part of his appeal to his followers. For example, when Megyn Kelly, a Fox News anchor at the time, questioned his history of negative comments about women, he shot back with a vulgar reference to her menstrual cycle (Khomami 2016). After Clinton revealed that Trump had mocked former Miss Universe winner Alicia Machado about her weight and ethnicity, Trump waged a vicious Twitter war against Machado, claiming falsely that she had been featured in a sex tape (Horsley 2016). Soon afterward, Trump called Clinton a nasty woman, launching the focus of this chapter.

Analysis

For our analysis, we collected tweets in English with the #NastyWoman or #NastyWomen hashtags by accessing Twitter's application program interface (API) repeatedly over the data collection period, which began October 30, 2014, and concluded November 14, 2016. The date, time, Twitter handle, and tweet were collected. We conducted a qualitative discourse and textual analysis of the 1,390 tweets by reading them multiple times, until commonalities among them emerged. This type of analysis focuses on the "underlying ideological and cultural assumption of the text" (Fürsich 2009, p. 240) rather than merely seeking facts or literal meaning. In other words, we looked for context in the tweets in an effort to understand a larger narrative about how people were using the #NastyWoman and #NastyWomen hashtags through their own words. Our aim is to understand the discourse in which these tweets operate, to reveal implied meaning and make broader inferences (Lindkvist 1981; McTavish and Pirro 1990) about how people can reclaim the Twitterverse from misogyny. Overall, three major themes emerged in our data. Each is discussed below. In the interest of accuracy, all tweets that are quoted retain grammar or spelling errors from the original.

Symbolic Rerouting

One strong theme that surfaced was people using the hashtags to talk generally about the power of voting, rather than simply supporting Clinton. These tweets aimed to reconstruct the conversation about "nasty women" into something productive, rather than dwell on the hateful words. For example, a tweet from October 30, 2016, reads: "it's absurd bs. Frustrating too. It will NOT stop us from voting @HillaryClinton As next POTUS #imwithher #nastywoman" (Alicia 2016). Another similar tweet reads: "I'm a Nasty Woman And I Vote" (JohnnyDany 2016). In this way, people reclaimed the term and made being a "nasty woman" synonymous with being a voting woman. The Twitter users symbolically rerouted the discourse about the term "nasty woman" and changed the nature and intent of the dialogue (Yuriko 2013). Some used wit or sarcasm to enact this rerouting in order to deflate the power of the hurtful words. In one tweet, a woman[1] recounted her children wanting to show their cat to friends. "NO, YOU CANNOT GRAB THE PUSSY! #nastywoman" (MacNeal 2016) the woman tweeted, humorously connecting Trump's inappropriate use of the word "pussy" with the "nasty woman" hashtag. Thus, she shifted the power of the term and instead used it to mock Trump. Another woman used the hashtag to challenge views about feminism asserted by Steve Bannon, a Trump strategist and former head of *Breitbart News,* a platform for the alt-right movement – which embraces sexism and white supremacy (Posner 2016). "Steven Bannon's catchphrase is 'feminism is cancer,'" the tweet reads. "He's right and we're coming for ya! Lol. #FeminismisCancer #nastywomen" (Schreindl 2016).

Another aspect of this theme showed people used the hashtags to transform the patriarchal space of Twitter and reclaim it as a space where women are treated equally (Daly 1973; D'Enbeau 2009). "I am POISED," read a tweet from November 14, 2016. "I will SLAY your deplorable flies with my sweet sweet honey. That's what #nastywomen do" (Rose 2016). Another woman used the hashtag to proclaim her donation to Planned Parenthood in the name of Trump's running mate, Mike Pence, a staunch opponent of abortion rights. "@Mike_Pence A donation in your name has been made to Planned Parenthood… Happy Monday! #PlannedParenthood #NastyWomen" (Kaufman 2016), thereby transforming the negative term into a positive. One woman's tweet exemplified this theme, as she demonstrated her goal of organizing her friends to vote – translating hashtag feminism into action: "Just made a plan to vote and organized my friend & family to do the same! #ImWithHer #nastywomen #Election2016 #GoHillary #ThatMexican Thing" (Rodriguez 2016). Another example of this theme comes from the tweet

"#NastyWomen get shit done!" (Vooda 2016). It suggested that Trump's effort to paint Clinton in a negative light with the term had backfired.

Site of Resistance

Our second major theme depicted Twitter as a sphere where women can challenge patriarchal ideas, bolstered by the intimate publics that form through the site. This resistance is sometimes quite simple. "No my first name ain't 'Baby'; it's JANET" (VS 2016). While brief, the tweet confronted Trump's use of the term "nasty woman" as a tool to rob women of agency, by comparing it to another agency-robbing term, "baby." It also referred to the lyrics of Janet Jackson's female-empowering 1986 song, "Nasty." Another tweet offered a more concrete sense of women bonding together over the term, forging a temporary intimate public – a collective digital space (Khoja-Moolji 2015) of solidarity with like-minded people through shared language, emotion, and meaning (Dixon 2014). This tweet depicted this sense of a shared public, particularly with its use of the word "us": "NO; Us #NastyWomen #AngryWomen say ENOUGH IS ENOUGH! #WeVoted4HER" (Howie-Edwards 2016). Another tweet seemed to be a call to action for those who shared similar views: "#ImNeverPreparedForDoing nothing in response to an evil event, or person, #Trump is both! #nastywoman #nastywomen" (Crush Trump 2016). Another tweet referenced FBI Director James Comey's announcement 11 days before the election that the FBI would re-start its investigation of Clinton's use of a private email server (Phillips 2016) – an action many blame in part for Clinton's defeat. It drew on the #NastyWoman hashtag and juxtaposed it with Clinton's "stronger together" slogan, to unite supporters online. "Comey, what made you do it? Really. Uh huh. Sure. #StrongerTogether #Hillary #ImWithHer #nastywoman #NeverTrump" (Just Chez So 2016). One tweet aimed toward resistance by calling on Clinton to lead the effort: "#GoHillary fight for all the woman before you & the ones you are leading Fight for the men who believe in you" (Hope 2016). Thus, the hashtag united people in solidarity with others, based on their shared belief that Trump's insult of Clinton was wrong. It provided a space for people to help each other feel empowered (Carstensen 2013). Hashtags can be a public performance of racial identity (Brock 2012), and they also can help people display their gendered identities. In essence, the technology of Twitter provides a wider collective audience than any one person could capture alone (Chen 2017). This forms *counter-publics* that extend feminist frames by connecting communities in inclusive discussions (Jackson and Banaszczyk 2016).

Reaffirming the Violence

Our final theme focused on use of the hashtags to thwart women's positive efforts. Much like other hashtags before it – such as #HowToSpotAFeminist – #NastyWoman and #NastyWomen are terms reclaimed by feminists. Yet others used them to re-perpetuate violence against women. One tweet bearing the hashtag read: "@CNN If you know anyone voting for Hillary Clinton, have them committed to a psych ward! #nastywomen #IamWithHer #NeverHillary" (SmallBizGroup 2016). In that tweet, even the use of the #IamWithHer hashtag despite the anti-Clinton content of the tweet suggests the writer intended Clinton supporters to see and perhaps be insulted by the tweet. This theme also was illustrated by a tweet that said: "Hillary is a total war hawk #GoHillary Hope all those #NastyWomen don't mind their sons going to war" (Badger 2016). The tweet suggested that so-called "nasty women" do not really know their candidate and would oppose her if they were more informed. Thus, it attempted to disrupt the positive discourse that developed around the #NastyWoman and #NastyWomen hashtags. In a similar vein, a tweet by Santa Baby (2016) used the hashtag to suggest Clinton's supporters were misguided in failing to see her use of a private email server as a violation of public trust: "Been reading #nastywomen posts afraid of losing the Republic but don't give a f**ck about Clinton emails the prove she's sold out Americans." Another tweet was even more pointed in its disparagement of Clinton and used the #NastyWoman hashtag as an affront: "What is Hillary doing to America? #HillaryEmails #payforplay #nastywoman #hillarybullies" (Trump for President 2016). These tweets and others like them suggest that even though feminists aimed to reclaim the term "nasty woman," they encountered formidable pushback on social media. The effort to reclaim the term seemed to anger some people. One user suggested that Clinton would end up in jail, and see her supporters there, indicating quite strongly a very literal reading of the term "nasty woman": "I'm sure she'll meet a few #NastyWomen in jail" (Dillon 2016).

Conclusion

Overall, our findings suggested that people used the #NastyWoman or #NastyWomen hashtags in the weeks just before the 2016 election to shift the conversation about Hillary Clinton into a positive discourse and wrest from Trump the misogynistic power he attempted to use against her by calling her a "nasty woman." Answering our three research questions, these findings clearly showed that #NastyWoman and #NastyWomen operated in a powerful place on Twitter that attempted to reclaim a negative term and use it to gain agency for women through hashtag feminism. As one Twitter user wrote after the election: "I've decided to combat their hatred with kindness. We'll get through this! #NastyWomen Don't give up!" (Kathryn 2016). This suggested at least some people had reframed the insult as a tool of digital empowerment, answering our third research question. Much like other hashtags, this one became a site of resistance where the dominant discourse is contested as a space to promote digital agency, much as the #BlackLivesMatter hashtag disrupts racist speech (Bonilla and Rosa 2015). The hashtags allowed women who felt oppressed and harmed by Trump's words to reclaim them and use them in a different way. As a result, the hashtags connected people in intimate publics (Berlant 2011), where they felt political together, emboldened by their visible show of solidarity. These hashtags allowed people to form counter-publics that offer a "critique of cultural values from the standpoint of women as a marginalized group within society" (Felski 1989). The hashtags united people publicly, so others could see their collectivism in a process called "signifyin'" (Brock 2012, p. 539) that has been used in reference to racial identity on Twitter:

The signifyin' hashtag invites an audience, even more so than the publication of a Tweet to one's followers, by setting the parameters of the discourse
to follow. It's also a signal that the Twitterer is part of a larger community
and displays her knowledge of the practice, the discourse, and the group's
worldview. (Brock 2012, p. 539)

Yet, the question remains: Does reclaiming the hashtags thwart the original violence against Clinton and women that Trump perpetuated when
he called Clinton a "nasty woman"? Our analysis suggested the answer is
complicated. While the hashtag resisted Trump's misogyny and reclaimed
a space for female empowerment within the Twitterverse, some still used
the hashtag to harm women. That does not mean efforts to reconstitute
#NastyWoman and #NastyWomen failed. Women were energized and
united as they used the repurposed term. Though Clinton lost the election, women gained a seminal unifying moment that demonstrated their
power. For some, this power may wane as the Trump presidency pro-
gresses. But our hope is that at least for some the term "nasty woman" will
live on as a beacon of hope that hashtag feminism can unite people and
call them to action. Without giving too much power to Twitter, we suggest the reclaiming of #NastyWoman and #NastyWomen sounds a warning that resistance and reclamation will occur online when women
candidates are attacked as Clinton was. Perhaps it will invigorate others
to raise their voices. As one hashtag user put it: "A woman's place is in the
Revolution!" (Bedard 2016).

Note

1. Twitter users who are quoted were assumed to be women if they had a
   stereotypically female American name.

References

Alicia. (2016, October 30). Alicia, @MtdMD @samsteinhp it's aburd bs. Frustrating too. It will NOT stop us from voting @HillaryClinton As next POTUS #imwithher #nastywoman. [Twitter post].

Alitnay, R. E. (2014). There's a massacre of women: Violence against women, feminist activism, and hashtags in Turkey. *Feminist Media Studies, 14*(6), 1102–1103.

Badger, L. H. (2016, October 30). Hillary is a total war hawk #GoHillary Hope all those #NastyWomen don't mind their sons going to war. [Twitter post].

Bahadur, N. (2015, May 6). Feminists have taken over #howtospotafeminist, and it is glorious. *Huffington Post*. Retrieved from http://www.huffingtonpost.com/2015/05/06/how-to-spot-a-feminist-is-now-a-feminist-hashtag_n_7221894.html

Bedard, P. (2016, November 12). A woman's place is in the revolution! #nastywomen #pussygrabsback @ Trump Tower, 725 5 Ave, New York. [Twitter post].

Beinart, P. (2016, October). Fear of female president, *The Atlantic*. Retrieved from http://www.theatlantic.com/magazine/archive/2016/10/fear-of-a-female-president/497564/

Berlant, L. (2011). *Cruel optimism*. Durham: Duke University Press.

Bonilla, Y., & Rosa, J. (2015). #Ferguson: Digital protest, hashtag ethnography, and the racial politics of social media in the United States. *American Ethnologist, 42*(1), 4–17.

Braithwaite, A. (2016). It's about ethics in games journalism? Gamergaters and geek masculinity. *Social Media + Society, 2*(4), 1–10.

Brock, A. (2012). From the blackhand side: Twitter as a cultural conversation. *Journal of Broadcasting & Electronic Media, 54*(4), 529–549.

Buckels, E. E., Trapnell, P. D., & Paulhus, D. L. (2014). Trolls just want to have fun. *Personality and Individual Differences, 62*, 97–102.

Burns, A., Haberman, M., & Martin, J. (2016a, October 7). Donald Trump apology caps day of outrage over lewd tape. *The New York Times*. Retrieved from http://www.nytimes.com/2016/10/08/us/politics/donald-trump-women.html

Burns, A., Martin, J., & Haberman, M. (2016b, October 9). Donald Trump vows retaliation as Republicans abandon him. *The New York Times*. Retrieved from https://www.nytimes.com/2016/10/10/us/politics/republicans-trump.html?_r=0

Carstensen, T. (2013). Gender and social media: Sexism, empowerment, or the irrelevance of gender? In C. Carter, L. Steiner, & L. McLaughlin (Eds.), *The Routledge companion to media and gender* (pp. 483–492). New York: Routledge.

Chen, G. M. (2011). Tweet this: A uses and gratifications perspective on how active Twitter use gratifies a need to connect with others. *Computer in Human Behavior, 27*, 755–762.

Chen, G. M. (2013). Don't call me that: A techno-feminist critique of the term mommy blogger. *Mass Communication and Society, 16*(4), 510–532.

Chen, G. M. (2017). Social media: From digital divide to empowerment. In C. P. Campbell (Ed.), *The Routledge companion to media and race* (pp. 117–125). New York: Routledge.

Chess, S., & Shaw, A. (2015). A conspiracy of fishes, or, how we learned to stop worrying about #gamergate and embrace hegemonic masculinity. *Journal of Broadcasting & Electronic Media, 59*(1), 208–220.

Chozick, A., & Parker, A. (2016, April 28). Donald Trump's gender-based attacks on Hillary Clinton have calculated risk. *The New York Times*. Retrieved from https://www.nytimes.com/2016/04/29/us/politics/hillary-clinton-donald-trump-women.html

Cole, K. K. (2015). "It's like she's eager to be verbally abused": Twitter, trolls, and (en)gendering disciplinary rhetoric. *Feminist Media Studies, 15*(2), 356–358.

Cooks, L., Paredes, M. C., & Scharrer, E. (2002). There's 'o place' like home: Searching for community on Oprah.com. In M. Consalvo & S. Paasonen (Eds.), *Women & everyday uses of the internet* (pp. 139–167). New York: Peter Lang.

Crush Trump. (2016, October 30). #ImNeverPreparedFor doing nothing in response to an evil event, or person, #trump is both! #nastywoman #nastywomen. [Twitter post].

D'Enbeau, S. (2009). Feminist and feminist transformation in popular culture. *Feminist Media Studies, 9*(1), 17–36.

Daly, M. (1973). *Beyond God the father: Through a philosophy of women's liberation*. Boston: Beacon Press.

Dillon, J. (2016, October 30). #GoHillary this GIF sums up corrupt Hillary Clinton's entire campaign. I'm sure she'll meet a few #NastyWoman in jail. [Twitter post].

Dixon, K. (2014). Feminist online identity: Analyzing the presence of hashtag feminism. *Journal of Arts and Humanities, 3*(7), 34–40.

Ebo, B. (1998). *Cyberghetto or cybertopia? Race, class, and gender on the internet in perspective.* Westport: Greenwood Publishing Group.

Eltantawny, N., & West, J. B. (2011). Social media in the Egyptian revolution: Reconsidering resource mobilization theory. *International Journal of Communication, 5,* 1207–1224.

Felski, R. (1989). *Beyond feminist aesthetics: Feminist literature and social change.* Cambridge, MA: Harvard University Press.

Fürsich, E. (2009). In defense of textual analysis. *Journalism Studies, 10,* 238–252.

Gannes, L. (2010, April 30). The short and illustrious history of Twitter #hashtags. *Gigaom.* Retrieved from https://gigaom.com/2010/04/30/the-short-and-illustrious-history-of-twitter-hashtags/

Greenwood, S., Perrin, A., & Duggan, M. (2016, November 11). Social media update 2016. *Pew Research Center.* Retrieved from http://www.pewinternet.org/2016/11/11/social-media-update-2016/

Harlot Overdrive. (2013, March 20). #SafetyTipsForLadies (or why I want you to stop telling me how I can prevent being sexually assaulted) [Web log message]. Retrieved from http://harlotoverdrive.wordpress.com/2013/03/20/safetytipsforladies/

Heldman, C., Carroll, S. J., & Olson, S. (2005). "She brought only a skirt": Print media coverage of Elizabeth Dole's bid for the Republican presidential nomination. *Political Communication, 22,* 315–335.

Hera, B., Merkel, C., & Bishop, A. P. (2004). The internet for empowerment of minority and marginalized users. *New Media & Society, 6*(6), 781–802.

Hope. (2016, October 30). #GoHillary fight for all the woman before you & The ones you are leading fight for the men who believe in you. [Twitter post].

Horsley, S. (2016, September 30). Trump again attacks former Miss Universe. *National Public Radio.* Retrieved from http://www.npr.org/2016/09/30/496050913/trump-again-attacks-miss-universe-contestant

Howie-Edwards, K. (2016, October 30). No; US #NastyWomen #Angry Women say ENOUGH IS ENOUGH! #WeVoted4HER #VoteBlueDEMSUpDownBallot. [Twitter post].

Huntemann, H. (2015). No more excuses: Using Twitter to challenge the symbolic annihilation of women in games. *Feminist Media Studies, 15*(1), 164–167.

Jackson, S. J. (2016). (Re)imagining intersectional democracy from black feminism to hashtag activism. *Women's Studies in Communication, 29*(4), 375–379.

Jackson, S. J., & Banaszczyk, S. (2016). Digital standpoints debating gendered violence and racial exclusions in the feminist counterpublic. *Journal of Communication Inquiry, 40*(4), 391–407.

JohnnyDany. (2016, October 30). I'm a nasty woman and I vote. [Twitter post].

Just Chez So. (2016, October 30). Comey, what made you do it? Really. Uh huh. Sure. #StrongerTogether #Hillary #ImWithHer #nastywoman #NeverTrump. [Twitter post].

Kathryn. (2016, November 11). @StephLovesKaos I've decided to combat their hatred with kindness. We'll get through this!! #NastyWomen don't give up! [Twitter post].

Kaufman, D. (2016, November 14). @mike_pence A donation in you name has been made to Planned Parenthood….Happy Monday! #PlannedParenthood #nastywoman. [Twitter post].

Khoja-Moolji, S. (2015). Becoming an "intimate publics": Exploring the affective intensities of hashtag feminism. *Feminist Media Studies, 15*(2), 347–350.

Khomami, N. (2016, October 8). Donald's misogyny problem: How Trump has repeatedly targeted women. *The Guardian*. Retrieved from https://www.theguardian.com/us-news/2016/oct/08/trumps-misogyny-problem-how-donald-has-repeatedly-targeted-women

Lawrence, R. G., & Rose, M. (2010). *Hillary Clinton's race for the White House: Gender politics & the media on the campaign trail*. Boulder: Lynne Rienner Publishers.

Liebler, C. (2010). Me(dia) culpa: The "missing white woman syndrome" and media self-critique. *Communication, Culture, & Critique, 3*(4), 549–565.

Lindkvist, K. (1981). Approaches to textual analysis. In K. E. Rosengren (Ed.), *Advances in content analysis* (pp. 23–41). Beverly Hills: Sage.

MacNeal, S. E. (2016, October 30). Kiddo wanted to show cat to his friends. She was scared and trying to hide. Cut to me, yelling: 'NO, YOU CANNOT GRAB THE PUSSY!' #nastywoman. [Twitter post].

Malone, C. (2016, November 9). Clinton couldn't win over white women. *FiveThirtyEight.com*. Retrieved from https://fivethirtyeight.com/features/clinton-couldnt-win-over-white-women/

McGregor, S. C., & Mourão, R. R. (2016, July/September). Talking politics on Twitter: Gender, elections, and social networks. *Society Media + Society, 2*, 10–14.

McTavish, D. G., & Pirro, E. B. (1990). Contextual content analysis. *Quality & Quantity, 24*, 245–265.

Ohlheiser, A. (2016, July 21). Just how offensive did Milo Yiannopoulos have to be to get banned from Twitter? *The Washington Post*. Retrieved from https://

www.washingtonpost.com/news/the-intersect/wp/2016/07/21/
what-it-takes-to-get-banned-from-twitter/?utm_term=.27ca27d651fa

Phillips, A. (2016, October 31). FBI director James Comey's Republican critics
are growing by the hour. *The Washington Post*. Retrieved from https://www.
washingtonpost.com/news/the-fix/wp/2016/10/31/meet-the-republicans-
defending-hillary-clinton-from-fbi-chief-james-comey/?utm_term=.
cbde23500cba

Posner, S. (2016, August 22). How Donald Trump's new campaign chief created
an online haven for white nationalists. *Mother Jones*. Retrieved from http://
www.motherjones.com/politics/2016/08/stephen-bannon-donald-trump-
alt-right-breitbart-news#

Prakash, N. (2016, October 19). Twitter reclaims Donald Trump's "nasty
woman" debate comment with badass messages of feminism. *Glamour*.
Retrieved from http://www.glamour.com/story/donald-trump-nasty-woman-
feminism

Rodriguez, N. (2016, October 30). Just made a plan to vote and organized my
friend & Family to do the same! #ImWithHer #nastywomen #Election2016
#GoHillary #ThatMexican Thing. [Twitter post].

Romano, A. (2015, May 5). Sexist #howtospotafeminist hashtag is reclaimed by
feminists on Twitter. *Mashable*. Retrieved from http://mashable.
com/2015/05/05/how-to-spot-a-feminist/#ajoLM5t3xaq

Rose, D. (2016, November 14). I am POISED. I will SLAY your deplorable flies
with my sweet sweet honey. That's what #nastywomen do. [Twitter post].

Santa Baby. (2016, October 30). Been reading #nastywomen posts afraid of losing the Republic but don't give a f**ck about Clinton emails the prove she's
sold out Americans. [Twitter post].

Schreindl, J. (2016, November 14). Steven Bannon's catchphrase is 'feminism is
cancer'. He's right and we're coming for ya! Lol. #FeminismisCancer #nasty-
women. [Twitter post].

SmallBizGuy. (2016, October 30). @CNN If you know anyone voting for
Hillary Clinton, have them committed to a psych ward! #nastywomen
#IamWithHer #NeverHillary. [Twitter post].

Strinati, D. (2004). *An introduction to theories in popular culture*. New York:
Routledge.

The Associated Press. (2016, October 20). Final presidential debate is third
most-watched presidential match ever. *Fox News*. Retrieved from http://
www.foxnews.com/entertainment/2016/10/20/final-debate-is-third-most-
watched-presidential-match-ever.html

Trump for President. (2016, October 30). What is Hillary doing to America? #HillaryEmails #payforplay #nastywoman #hillarybullies. [Twitter post].

Vooda. (2016, October 30). #NastyWomen get shit done! #Vote4Hillary. [Twitter post].

VS. (2016, October 30). No my first name ain't 'Baby'; it's JANET. [Twitter post].

Why are Indian Women "Happy to Bleed"? (2015, November 23). *BBC.com*. Retrieved from http://www.bbc.com/news/world-asia-india-34900825

Williams, S. (2015). Digital defense: Black feminists resist violence and hashtag activism. *Feminist Media Studies, 15*(2), 341–344.

Williams, V. (2016, November 12). Black women – Hillary Clinton's most reliable voting bloc – look beyond defeat. *The Washington Post*. Retrieved from https://www.washingtonpost.com/politics/black-women--hillary-clintons-most-reliable-voting-bloc--look-beyond-defeat/2016/11/12/86d9182a-a845-11e6-ba59-a7d93165c6d4_story.html?utm_term=.6d07cb92484a

Yuriko, F. (2013). *Cinema of actuality: Japanese avant-garde filmmaking in the season of image politics*. Durham: Duke University Press.

20

Conclusion: What Can We Do About Mediated Misogyny?

Jacqueline Ryan Vickery, Tracy Everbach,
Lindsay Blackwell, Mary Anne Franks,
Barbara Friedman, Sheila Gibbons, Tarleton Gillespie,
and Adrienne Massanari

The chapters in this book make a strong case for the severity and pervasiveness of online harassment. Several chapters critique the systems and ideologies that perpetuate misogyny and several examine how activists, journalists, and scholars can respond to and fight back against harassment. However, real change cannot take place at only the individual or

J. R. Vickery (✉)
Department of Media Arts, University of North Texas, Texas, TX, USA

T. Everbach
Mayborn School of Journalism, Digital/Print Journalism, University of North Texas, Texas, TX, USA

L. Blackwell
School of Information, University of Michigan, Ann Arbor, MI, USA

M. A. Franks
University of Miami School of Law, Coral Gables, FL, USA

B. Friedman
School of Media and Journalism, University of North Carolina-Chapel Hill, Chapel Hill, NC, USA

© The Author(s) 2018
J. R. Vickery, T. Everbach (eds.), *Mediating Misogyny*,
https://doi.org/10.1007/978-3-319-72917-6_20

even collective levels, but rather change must be holistic, structural, and systemic. As the book has established, the problem is not simply the technology, but rather a white supremacist patriarchal culture.

In conclusion, we consider four stakeholders who have an investment in (and profit from) shaping cultural ideologies: digital platforms, journalism, the law, and universities. None of these organizations or institutions alone can solve misogyny; however, each has the power to influence practices and contribute to cultural change at structural levels.

Digital platforms shape online experiences through code, policies, algorithms, and business models. Decisions about the visibility of our interactions, who is allowed to participate, what is allowed to be said, how inappropriate behavior is reported, to whom, and to what effect, and how platforms generate profit, all shape the ways we interact in digital spaces and with each other.

News media play a powerful role in shaping social discourse and cultural attitudes. The ways journalists report about online harassment and the language they use can either draw needed attention to a problem or amplify the problem, even intensifying the attacks. Journalists must carefully consider the ethics of reporting about harassment in ways that do not contribute to greater harassment or blame victims, but instead contribute to solutions.

By nature, *laws* are usually retroactive in that they typically respond to a problem after it has occurred. The widespread adoption of the Internet is relatively young; thus, legal systems are still trying to catch up to new social problems. We are seeing changes to the ways laws can hold perpetrators responsible for harassment, but progress is slow and varies among

S. Gibbons
Media Report to Women, Carmel, CA, USA

T. Gillespie
Microsoft Research, Cambridge, MA, USA

A. Massanari
Department of Communication, University of Illinois-Chicago,
Chicago, IL, USA

cities, states, and nations. It's debatable whether the law can really prevent harassment, but it undoubtedly plays a role in shaping attitudes and behaviors, as well as holding citizens accountable.

Finally, as we addressed in the introduction, scholars must pay more attention to who is safe and empowered to conduct research about misogyny. *Universities* have a responsibility to protect researchers and facilitate inclusive scholarship. Likewise, as universities continue to incorporate the Internet into classroom curricula and assignments, educators must carefully consider how to protect students online.

We do not contend that it is only the responsibility of these four stakeholders, but each plays an integral role in shaping and responding to online cultures, and in supporting research about harassment. We have structured the conclusion as a series of questions and answers with experts trained in and knowledgeable about digital media, journalism, law, gender, and harassment. We asked each contributor to respond briefly to one of the following questions:

1. What can digital platforms do to help combat online harassment?
2. How should journalists and media organizations ethically report about online harassment?
3. How can the law respond to online harassment?
4. How should universities respond to and protect researchers and students from online abuse?

Taking the answers into consideration collectively, we end the book on a positive note that can propel the conversation forward toward a more equitable, ethical, and inclusive digital world. Additionally, we have included a list of resources for scholars, journalists, and students to use to protect themselves online and to combat mediated misogyny.

Question: What Can Digital Platforms Do to Help Combat Online Harassment?

Answers from Dr. Adrienne Massanari and Dr. Tarleton Gillespie. Massanari is an assistant professor of communication at the University of Illinois, Chicago, and former director of the Center for Digital Ethics and Policy at Loyola

University. Gillespie is a principal researcher at Microsoft Research, New England, and an associate professor of communication at Cornell University.

Adrienne Massanari We know that online harassment does not occur in a vacuum; rather, it reflects culture at large. But we also know that online platforms provide a unique environment that can both amplify and legitimize toxicity. This means that platform administrators, community managers, and designers have an ethical responsibility to think how they can minimize harassment. Here are a few suggestions as to how platforms can become safer and more welcoming environments:

1. Platform designers must design for harassment. Creating positive user experiences in which platforms can be used to connect often-diverse populations is the fun part of the job; thinking hard about how those same individuals might harass others isn't. But the current approach that platforms like Twitter have taken – basically dragging their heels in the face of harassment and pushing the work of combating that harassment onto users – isn't working.

2. Designing for harassment means creating community rules and policies early on in the development process, rather than trying to retroactively address these issues. While it's not possible to foresee every possible way that someone might harass another individual, it's much easier to cultivate communities where harassment is not normalized in the first place rather than try to address these issues as they occur. Community norms take time to develop, but they can be difficult to shift once established. Reddit, for example, has long had problems with its platform being a hostile space for women and people of color. Despite having changed the community's rules and banning some subreddits notorious for harassing individuals, it still remains a toxic environment.

3. Community moderators and designers should work together to create tools that allow harassment to be reported easily and with minimal effort. It's especially important that designers create tools that do not require those who are harassed to do the heavy lifting when it comes to reporting harassment. Expecting victims of online abuse to fill out lengthy reports that require them to detail their abuse, for example,

suggests that they should be able to clinically detach from their harassment. Or, assuming that individuals will create the tools that the platforms themselves should have created in the first place to mitigate harassment, devalues their labor and contributions to the community. It tacitly suggests that harassment is an individual problem that will be fixed with one-off, individual tools, rather than reflecting a systemic issue that requires (and deserves) large-scale solutions.

4. Likewise, platform administrators should not expect users to do all of the hard work of moderating and reporting harassment. It's important that they do not rely solely on the free labor of their users to protect other users from toxicity. This isn't fair, nor is it effective in the long term.

5. Platform managers should be wary of easy algorithmic fixes for harassment. Like all technologies, algorithms have politics. Often bots and scripts are created in such a way that they unintentionally suppress certain speech and images shared by marginalized communities. Or they may be gamed by harassers to target individuals in an effort to intimidate them off the platform. For example, those affiliated with #Gamergate have abused YouTube's flagging function in an attempt to prevent Anita Sarkeesian's *Feminist Frequency* videos from remaining visible to other viewers.

6. Platform creators should not always assume that enabling more communication on their site is better for all individuals. Designers often unintentionally center cisgendered, white, straight men in their design choices. For example, designers might think more communication in a social network site will strengthen community ties. However, even seemingly benign information about user activity – about when messages are read, profiles are visited, or posts are made, for example – can become tools for harassment. Therefore, is critical that platform designers consider the ways that features they create impact diverse audiences.

As Tarleton Gillespie mentions in his response, the approaches platforms take when dealing with harassment are embedded in complex sociotechnical systems that are resistant to change. But creating communities that remain committed to reducing harassment and minimizing its harm is imperative – not just for the victims, but for all of us.

Tarleton Gillespie It feels a bit futile to hypothesize about what social media platforms should do about misogyny and harassment, or what more they should do. Facebook, Twitter, and the like have each developed a massive sociotechnical apparatus for content moderation, massive logistical arrangements that involve employees setting rules at the platform, contract workers doing piecemeal policing all over the globe, users enlisted to flag violations, and software systems trained to identify violations automatically. Lashed together, these Rube Goldberg moderation machines chug along, turning complaints into data into decisions. Chug, chug, chug. Some instances of harassment get identified and addressed, others are overlooked or misapprehended. Lots of conflict on these platforms pass right through this system, and plenty never finds its way into it. A one percent error rate is considered the gold standard – meaning even a near perfect system fails millions of users. A user being harassed can either submit to this impersonal megasystem and hope for some relief to pop out the other end, or skip it and fend for themselves.

And it's hard for platforms to do things much differently. This apparatus is now fully installed and established. Even as is, it can barely keep up with the complaints from users and the innovations of harassers – evasion, veiled threats, images, dog whistles, brigading, doxxing, swatting, bots. The demands of their moderation machines are always about to drown them, a stone around their necks. And, the platforms are always hard at work on something new, always on the cusp of the solution. Today, platforms dream of electric shepherds: the perennial hope that AI machine learning systems will eventually replace the messiness of human moderation, surgically slicing out the harassment the moment it happens; and/or the quieter hope that they can introduce enough grit in the interaction that the harassers and trolls lose interest – saving the platform from the tough work of policing, and the tougher work of asserting affirmative values, beyond "being connected."

There are many things platforms could do, right now, that would likely help. Adrienne Massanari's comment is full of good ideas, the right ideas.

But if we continue to look for improvements on the same fundamental arrangement, we may forget to wonder whether the fundamental arrangement itself is flawed. As Massanari also noted, harassment is not simply a social media problem, it's endemic to a culture in which the powerful maintain their position over the less powerful through tactics of intimidation, marginalization, and cruelty. But Silicon Valley engineers and entrepreneurs are largely unaware or ignorant of this – they're a privileged lot, who tend to think that society is fair and meritocratic, that communication just needs to be more open, and information more free – and they tend to build tools "for all" that continue, extend, and reify those inequities.

So instead, I want to make two proposals that are both politically untenable and economically outlandish.

1. Platforms need a new business model

It has become clear that harassment is not an aberration, but a condition, of social media. This is in part because it takes the same shape as the best kinds of participation. In the fever dreams of their founders, these platforms were intended to allow everyone to speak their minds, to connect with others around issues that matter to them, to be findable on the network, to present themselves as they choose, and to form bonds through conversation untrammeled by status or location. Harassment is all of those things, at least for the harasser. Harassment is not a perversion of that dream; it is one logical version of that participation – just not the one designers had in mind.

And from a business perspective, at least in the short term, harassment and trolling are just as valuable to the platform as other forms of participation. If it's advertising they seek, these are eyeballs to be sold like any other. If it's data, these are traces to be sold like any other. Would Reddit make more money if it cleaned up its act, or has it dragged its feet because all those trolls and men's rights harassers and alt-right blowhards and pornographers bring an awful lot of activity and energy to the platform? Don't mess with success, as they say. Under business models hinged on popularity as the proxy for engagement, platforms will err on the side of encouraging as many people to stay as possible, imposing rules with the least consequences, keeping users if they can, and bringing them back quickly if they can't.

Platforms also hold popularity to be a fundamental value, the core value that serves as proxy to every other value: relevance, merit, newsworthiness. It is their core metric for engagement, and they perform it back to users as recommendations, cued-up videos, trends, and feeds. Harassment and hate take advantage of this by doing things that accumulate popularity: cruel insults that classmates will pass around, insults aimed at women that fellow misogynists will applaud, nonconsensual porn that appeals to the prurient interests. These are not just attacks, they're generators of likes, views, comments, retweets, making it very hard for platforms to discern or pass up.

Under a different business model, platforms might be more willing to uphold a real expectation for compassionate and just participation, and drop those users unwilling to consent to the new rules of the game. Where is the platform that not only prioritizes the longer-term goal of encouraging people to stay and helping them thrive, and sells that to us for a fee? Where are the platforms that gain value when fewer users produce a richer collaboration? Until then, general use platforms are unlikely to pursue an affirmative aspiration – what are we there to accomplish – only a negative one – what shouldn't we do while we're there.

2. Platforms need a fundamentally more diverse workforce

In the end, it will continue to be difficult for platforms to address the truly acidic effects of harassment on the victims and on the public at large – because these platforms are run by a very narrow population of people with a specific and limited perspective on the world. As a straight, white man myself, I am not suggesting that we are incapable of compassion, unwilling to make progressive changes that largely benefit others, or might not come up with an ingenious solution. But the straight, white men of Silicon Valley have proven, convincingly and repeatedly, that they cannot do so alone. There's a reason why social media not only seems to make room for abuse and hatred per se, but for the very same abuse and hatred that have plagued society long before social media: against women, against racial and ethnic minorities, against gay, queer, and transgender people.

It turns out that what the straight, white men of Silicon Valley are good at is building communication spaces designed like brutalist economic markets, where it is necessary and even celebrated that users must shout each other down to compete for voice; where users feel entitled to toy with others as an end in itself, rather than feel complicit in accomplishing something together; where the notion of structural inequity is alien, and silencing tactics take cover behind a false faith in meritocracy. They cannot see what the world, or even their platforms, look like from the perspective of someone who has endured structural inequity or blatant hatred.

Slight improvements in workplace diversity aren't going to make the difference. We've seen what corrosive environments some of these companies are for those who do show up. Social media platforms should commit that for the next decade, *all* of their new hires, 100 percent, be women, queer people, and people of color. Sound like an outrageous exercise in affirmative action and social engineering? It is not for the benefit of the new employees, but for the benefit of the platform. And it is no more outrageous that platforms can't seem to lift even just the number of women past 20 percent, and that's when they're trying.

It is not that women and queer people and people of color know how to solve the problem of harassment, necessarily. Or that the job of solving these problems should fall on their shoulders. But the social media platforms need teams that are *so* diverse that the landscape just looks different, the problems just surface differently, the goals just sound different. With diversity behind the scenes – not token diversity but radical, worldly diversity – these companies would have a dramatically better shot at imagining their way out of the current conditions. Teams that diverse might be able to better stand for their diverse users, might recognize harassment as truly antithetical to the aims and spirit of the platform, and might have the political nerve to intervene.

These are certain never to happen.

Question: How Should Journalists and News Media Organizations Ethically Report About Online Harassment?

Answers from Barbara Friedman and Sheila Gibbons. Dr. Barbara Friedman is a former journalist and an associate professor of media and journalism at the University of North Carolina, Chapel Hill. Gibbons is the editor of Media Report to Women, *a quarterly journal about how all types of media depict women and issues of interest to women.*

Barbara Friedman   Journalism has a vital role in fostering social recognition of online abuse, and, in doing so, creating possibilities for changes in attitudes, behavior, policies, and law. A good deal of coverage has helped to raise awareness of the issue, and to draw attention to specific facets, such as the responsibility of influential companies to mitigate the abuse that occurs on their platforms. Based on current understandings about the forms of online abuse, its targets and impacts, what follows are recommended practices (not intended to be exhaustive) for reporting about online abuse:

The Sources

Targets   Like other forms of violence, harassment can be traumatic to the targets of abuse. If you have no experience interviewing survivors, consult a trained sexual assault counselor or professional organization such as the Dart Center for Journalism and Trauma *before* you proceed. Then, to build trust, journalists might need to cede some control over the newsgathering process to victim-sources. Reporters should be candid about their intentions. If they plan to also interview the perpetrator, the victim must be given the opportunity to withdraw from a story or decline further participation. Victims who request it should be granted anonymity to avoid further abuse, and news organizations should consider permitting these sources to read their quotes or the entire article before publication. Journalists should notify victims when stories are about to be published, as they may need to prepare themselves for reader response. Additional caveats:

- Although online abuse is easily witnessed on social media, journalists should never reprint examples without first contacting the victim-source for permission. To do so can retraumatize individuals and trigger additional abuse.
- Repeating claims that online threats aren't serious, or that harassment is the cost of participating in the digital sphere is a form of victim-blaming that normalizes violence, discourages reporting, and minimizes the harmful impact of online abuse on individuals, groups, and society.
- Journalists should work with editors to decide whether they will allow comments on a story about online abuse. If commenting is permitted, consider moderating it and/or requiring commenters to identify themselves.

Perpetrators Interesting and productive reporting has emerged from interviews with perpetrators of online hate, but this kind of coverage works best when it explains, rather than excuses, online abuse. It is indefensible to give a perpetrator a platform to heap additional abuse upon victims. Preferable is to consult scholars and others who have studied online abuse for insight into what motivates abusers. As news sources, violence-prevention specialists can speak to the ways that online abuse is connected to other forms of violence.

Official Sources For stories involving suspected criminal behavior, police are valuable sources, but individual officers may not be attuned to the dynamics of online abuse or the uses of social media. Legal experts studying and/or working in the field of cyber law and policy can help audiences understand how and why particular measures are effective/ineffective in fighting online abuse.

Newsroom Sources As addressed in this book, journalists have been frequent targets of online abuse; their analyses offer valuable perspectives and mitigate the need to publicize private figures' experiences with abuse. Similarly, stories that analyze a news site's user comments can illuminate patterns of abuse. In one such project, staff at the *Guardian* discovered that articles written by women attracted more disruptive or abusive comments than articles by men. Ethnic and religious minorities, and LGBT authors also experienced high levels of abuse (Gardiner et al. 2016).

The Story

Connect the Dots "Online abuse" refers to a wide range of malicious behavior intended to embarrass, frighten, malign, silence, and even extort individuals. It is a symptom of social inequality. Its many forms must be made visible and their connection established to the widespread and patterned abuses that groups experience on- and offline in order to identify remedies.

Go Beyond the Individual and the Unusual The tendency of news to focus on singular and often extreme cases of online abuse, or abuse waged within a narrow category of Internet users, has done much to raise the alarm about the ways that Internet users are targeted. Sustained coverage of this nature, however, obscures the problem of everyday abusive encounters. Further, limiting coverage to individual narratives might inadvertently neglect the social problems that animate online abuse generally, such as racism and misogyny.

Avoid False Equivalence That "men are targets of online abuse, too" is fact, but coverage is misleading when it suggests they are attacked in the same ways and to the same effect as other groups. As this book and other research have repeatedly shown, online harassment of men tends toward name-calling and embarrassment, whereas women and minority groups are subjected to discrimination, physical threats, and stalking that may be sustained over time.

Cite Evidence, and Warn When Appropriate Online abuse often contains profanity, obscenity and/or graphic threats of violence. Publishing the content verbatim brings home the reality of online abuse to an audience ("the sender threatened to cut Smith's throat"), but in some settings it may be preferable to characterize the message ("the sender threatened to harm Smith"). When the former approach is taken, reporters, in consultation with editors, should decide whether a warning should be added to the story.

Stories Unexplored or Underexplored There are many angles journalists can take to report about online abuse. As just a few examples, reporters could examine: how school resource officers are being trained to identify and investigate online abuse; the role of Title IX laws (or similar gender equity laws in other countries) in addressing online abuse; the success or failure of anti-abuse technology and campaigns; the experience of media companies that have eliminated online comments; the connection between "fake news" and online abuse; and how online abuse affects the exercise of free speech.

As an issue that affects more than half of Internet users, online abuse has significant news worth. Moreover, the institutions implicated in and charged with responding to online abuse are the purview of journalism: government, economy, and education, for example. Yet, as Chemaly (2016) points out, "There is no one organization or institution responsible for solving the problem of online harassment." Rather, "this is a social problem that requires social responses" (para. 21). Journalism, as a primary means by which the public learns about issues such as online abuse, comprises a vital part of that response.

Sheila Gibbons It was an arresting four minutes of video: men reading to female sports journalists the ugly tweets the journalists had received following publication of their work. The purpose: expose online harassers in a public service announcement called #MoreThanMean, produced by Just Not Sports in 2016.

The men squirmed, distressed about the sentiments they were being asked to read. The messages, sent to Chicago sports journalists Julie DiCaro and ESPN's Sarah Spain, ranged from put-downs of their work, to sneering personal mockery laced with c-words and f-words, to threats of sexual violence. DiCaro and Spain had seen the tweets before, but the men recruited to read them had not. The men were stunned, but they should not have been.

Social media tools have made it possible for hostile users to hide behind aliases for the express purpose of expressing deep-seated misogyny toward women. Journalists' employers have encouraged more multiplatform involvement for their reporting, thereby increasing journalists' visibility to the public and making them more reachable targets for trolls. Studies show that male or disguised usernames dominate the comments sections of major media websites, and that female journalists represent a disproportionate number of those harassed by trolls and stalkers.

Journalists can no longer avoid being part of the story, as they have long been trained to do. They have been thrust into an ugly subversion of technology that has veered from annoying to frightening to dangerous.

In December 2016 Dallas-based reporter Kurt Eichenwald opened a tweet with a message, "You deserve a seizure for your posts." The tweet erupted into a flashing strobe light. Eichenwald, an epileptic, immediately had a seizure, followed by weeks-long physical effects. His lawyer compared the tweet to throwing a bomb.

Journalists' efforts to parry and discourage online threats have often been met with frustration. Twitter and Facebook were slow to respond to escalating vitriol on their platforms, and local law enforcement was ill-equipped to investigate Internet threats. Twitter and Facebook eventually improved their policies, expanding their ability to receive and act on complaints, and punishing some offenders by locking or suspending their accounts. Eichenwald's lawyer went to court to press Twitter to assist in identifying the sender of the strobe tweet. A man was subsequently arrested, but it's rare that people are held accountable for online behavior.

"Consider the cases of the journalist Amberin Zaman, who reported on the Gezi Park protests in Istanbul in 2013 [and who said tweets she subsequently received were 'abusive, violent and sexual'], or the American journalist Amanda Hess, who documented the issues of online abuse of women in her pioneering *Pacific Standard* piece 'Why Women Aren't Welcome on the Internet' (Hess 2014). These are not isolated stories, but rather snapshots of a clear global trend of online abuse faced by women raising their voices," writes Sejal Parmar. "Indeed, initial surveys of this phenomenon show that female journalists and television news presenters receive about three times as much abuse as their male counterparts, that more than a quarter of instances of intimidation against female journalists takes place online, and that female journalists covering technology are subjected to heightened levels of abuse" (Parmar 2016).

News organizations are uniquely equipped to expose online harassment and the forces that drive it. Asking victims to talk on the record about their experiences can expose them to more of the same, but news organizations can shield victims' identities if necessary to illuminate the scope of the problem. As to reporting approaches, here are suggestions about how to discuss cyber harassment:

- As emblematic of a widespread cultural shift with psychological and social origins and ramifications.
- As a crime when criminal intent is explicitly threatened or implied.
- As a business story with multiple angles, including reputation management and protection of employees who are victims.
- As the underbelly of technological prowess, where whiz-bang electronic communication tools are used for nefarious purposes.
- As inspiring creative counter-measures that push back against online attacks.

With regard to the last item: highlighting the work of groups such as TrollBusters, led by Ohio University professor Michelle Ferrier, would show that the journalists are not just passively receiving and deleting ugly emails and tweets. As she discusses in Chap. 8, Ferrier was herself the victim of a stalker during her career as a newspaper columnist. TrollBusters facilitates counter-attacks on trolls and supportive endorsements of reporters under attack. Calling attention to efforts such as these, and revealing news organizations' own actions to neutralize trolls, makes a powerful statement that attempted intimidation of reporters will be fought with the vigor it deserves.

Question: How Can the Law Respond to Online Harassment?

Answer from Dr. Mary Anne Franks, professor of law at the University of Miami School of Law and the Vice President and Legislative & Tech Policy Director of the Cyber Civil Rights Initiative, a nonprofit organization dedicated to combating online abuse and discrimination.

Mary Anne Franks The first thing the law must do to respond to online harassment is to take it seriously. That requires, as an initial matter, acknowledging that online harassment is a form of abuse marked by gender and race. It is a phenomenon that predominantly involves white men using technology to terrorize women and minorities with near-impunity. U.S. law has for a very long time tolerated and even encouraged harms that are disproportionately directed at women and minorities, from domestic violence to racial profiling. Our society has been reluctant to recognize these forms of abuse as abuse, characterizing them as inevitable, trivial, or somehow deserved, and law enforcement has a history of treating victims with disrespect and disbelief. Abusive expression, in particular, has often been defended in the U.S. as a form of free speech protected by the First Amendment, a conception that both mischaracterizes free speech doctrine and ignores the silencing effect of harassment on victims.

The technical nature of online harassment complicates things further, as the level of technological literacy of legislators, law enforcement, and judges varies considerably. Accordingly, the law must ensure that legal actors have the knowledge and training they need to tackle technology-facilitated harassment. The most effectively crafted legislation will be of little use if law enforcement and courts do not understand it or have the resources to apply it.

There are many laws already in existence that can and should be used to fight online harassment. Federal and state laws prohibiting stalking, harassment, extortion, computer fraud, identity theft, and threats can be very effective against online harassment, but they are rarely used because law enforcement either does not know, does not care, or does not have the training and resources to use them. In addition, the fact that many existing offenses are classified as misdemeanors makes it a practical impossibility for prosecutors to obtain warrants and conduct thorough investigations. Both the general public and law enforcement should be made aware of the extensive range of existing laws to fight online harassment and be encouraged to make use of them.

Existing law must also be updated to address the innovative and constantly evolving nature of online harassment. Many stalking and harassment laws require direct communication between perpetrators and victims as well as a repeated pattern of conduct. These requirements do not reflect the dynamics of social media mobs and targeted online harassment campaigns. One of the most pernicious forms of online harassment, the unauthorized distribution of private, sexually explicit images (often referred to as "revenge porn"), was not even recognized as a crime in the U.S. by the majority of states until very recently. A recent study found that 1 in 8 social media users has been the victim of this abuse and that 1 in 20 has been a perpetrator of it; however, as late as 2013 only three states had passed laws prohibiting it. Due in large part to the efforts of advocacy organizations, that number was 38 as of 2017, and a federal bill addressing the issue is set to be reintroduced.

In many U.S. cases, legislators, courts, and law enforcement are reluctant to challenge online harassment because of concerns about Section 230 of the Communications Decency Act, the federal law that provides broad immunity to online intermediaries for content provided by users. The provision is not absolute by any means, however, and courts should be wary of expanding its protections beyond what the statute actually provides. The policy goals of §230 include the promotion and protection of free speech principles, but such principles are presumably meant to apply across the population. When online harassment silences women and minorities and pushes them out of public spaces and conversations, then the principles of free speech have not been upheld. The goals of §230 are moreover not limited to free speech; the law is also intended to promote the "vigorous enforcement of Federal criminal laws to deter and punish trafficking in obscenity, stalking and harassment by means of computer."

Question: How Should Universities Respond to and Protect Researchers and Students from Online Abuse?

Answer from Lindsay Blackwell, a PhD candidate at the University of Michigan School of Information and a former fellow of the Institute for Research on Women and Gender. Blackwell's research focuses on the motivations of users who engage in online harassment.

Lindsay Blackwell In June 2017, an assistant professor of classics at the University of Iowa named Sarah Bond published an article in *Hyperallergic* (an online arts publication) about research proving that human figures depicted in ancient Western artifacts were painted in different colors, a practice known as polychromy. Over time, these artifacts have faded, exposing the light color of their marble base and creating the false impression that white skin was the classical ideal – which Bond argues has historically underpinned white supremacist ideology in the modern Western world.

Bond's essay was subsequently circulated in conservative media circles, prompting online threats, anti-Semitic harassment (Bond is of Jewish descent), and calls for her termination (Flaherty 2017). Following a similar article she authored for *Forbes* in April, Bond published a blog post about the harassment she had experienced as a result of her public scholarship: "I had thought that I was prepared for the internet trolls," Bond writes. "After all, I have crossed many proverbial bridges on Twitter—where they usually lurk. However, the hatred and invective I received from this post was more than anything I have ever received to date."

Fortunately, the University of Iowa stood by Bond; department chair John F. Finamore, who worked with the dean's office and the university's threat assessment team to support and protect her, called the attacks "shocking" and "an unjustified assault against freedom of expression." Bond is certainly not the first scholar to face threats of violence online – Keeanga-Yamahtta Taylor, an assistant professor of African-American studies at Princeton University, canceled public talks after facing severe online threats in the wake of her criticism of then-presidential candidate Donald Trump. Similarly, Tommy Curry, an associate professor of philosophy at Texas A&M University, faced racist harassment when a years-old podcast resurfaced out of context.

The American Association of University Professors (AAUP) has raised concerns about increasing harassment and intimidation of scholars, urging "administrations, governing boards and faculties, individually and collectively, to speak out clearly and forcefully to defend academic freedom and to condemn targeted harassment and intimidation of faculty members." Tressie McMillan Cottom, an assistant professor of sociology at Virginia Commonwealth University, recommends six proactive measures institutions should employ to prepare for the possibility that a student or faculty member could be targeted:

1. Have a "first line of defense" for a possible rush of emails and phone calls.
2. Develop a formal protocol for threats against scholars.
3. Develop a formal policy for publicly representing faculty against attacks.
4. Educate faculty governance about the implications of social media on public scholarship.
5. Have unions develop policies for academic freedom that account for the blurring of professional and personal selves online.
6. Provide resources to scholars who experience online harassment, including legal support and mental health resources.

Marwick et al. (2016) make several additional recommendations specific to universities and institutions seeking to better protect scholars from online harassment, including: involving university and department public relations and social media personnel in communications planning; appointing a point of contact who is knowledgeable about cybersecurity, social media, and harassment whom scholars can rely on for support; and allowing community members to opt in to university directories that publish contact information and office locations.

Students and faculty members are uniquely at risk for online harassment, particularly given mounting pressure – especially for younger scholars – to engage in public scholarship, whether by authoring articles like Bond's, designing talks or workshops, or interacting with other scholars and with the public on social media platforms. The potential negative effects of online harassment are myriad: beyond emotional impacts and the potential for physical danger, the propagation of false, misrepresented, or private information may negatively impact a scholar's reputation and career.

While the harassment levied against scholars online certainly risks chilling speech and the productive exchange of ideas, there is perhaps an even more insidious outcome: that women, people of color, LGBT people, and other marginalized persons – who are already vulnerable to the most severe forms of online abuse (Duggan 2014) – may be deterred from pursuing research on sensitive or controversial topics, or perhaps dissuaded from engaging in public scholarship at all. If marginalized persons are discouraged from pursuing research into sensitive or controversial topics, or even pursuing research careers, the entire landscape of our academy risks changing.

Above all, institutions are responsible for ensuring that their employees enjoy safe and secure working environments – which includes Internet and social media use. Marginalized scholars should never have to choose between sharing their expertise and their own comfort or safety, and it is the responsibility of universities, departments, deans, and faculty mentors to ensure that all in the academy – undergraduate and graduate students, postdocs, faculty, and staff – are educated about and protected from the potential consequences of engaging in public discourse.

As McMillan Cottom wrote in 2015: "In this moment, we should call for institutions to state explicitly what they owe those who venture into public waters." Universities must swiftly and unreservedly demonstrate their public support for scholars who do fall under attack for the unusual crime of intellectual expression – lest the very foundation on which our academy is built should crumble.

* * *

The following is an excerpt from the Data & Society Research Institute's "Best Practices for Conducting Risky Research and Protecting Yourself from Online Harassment" (Marwick et al. 2016) that Lindsay Blackwell mentioned and co-authored. It provides practical steps universities and researchers can take to protect faculty and students from online abuse. This is just an excerpt (reprinted with permission under Creative Commons License Attribution 3.0). You can access the full report online. It also includes a two-page guide that researchers can pass along to their administrators (e.g. chairs, deans, IRBs) to educate them about online harassment and what they can do about it.

We believe the academy needs to recognize that researchers conducting sensitive or risky research – particularly research about controversial topics – may be susceptible to online harassment and related threats. We also believe that institutions are responsible for ensuring that their employees, whether graduate students, postdocs, faculty, or staff, enjoy safe and secure working environments – which includes internet and social media use.

Recommendations for Departments and Institutions – for institutional leadership, department chairs, and other administrators:

- Have a proactive communications plan for dealing with online harassment, involving university and department public relations and social media personnel.
- Appoint a point person(s) who is knowledgeable about cybersecurity, social media, and harassment whom researchers or students can rely on for support.
- Educate department and university personnel about these issues.
- Create a one-sheet guide that can be easily disseminated across campus. Include definitions of online harassment, links and contact information for security, counseling services, IT, and relevant resources. – Example: Rutgers University guide to offline harassment (https://uhr.rutgers.edu/sites/default/files/userfiles/HarassmentBrochureStudent.pdf)
- Harness university resources (e.g., IT, campus police) to protect the researcher; filter email accounts, secure websites, provide additional security (if necessary), etc.

- Do not give out any additional information about the researcher(s) without their explicit consent and communicate suspicious activity to them if requested.
- Investigate the merit of claims or threats and discuss them with the researcher for further context and clarification before acting.
- Acknowledge that online harassment is a real and significant problem, and that it cannot be solved by simply "staying off the internet." (A helpful analogy: if a student were being stalked, would you suggest they never go outside?)
- Recognize the psychological harm that can result from online harassment and make emergency counseling services available, should harassment occur. Recommendations to Advisors and

Senior Faculty – for those with a student in their department who wishes to undertake potentially risky research:

- Have a frank discussion with the student about the possible risks of such research.
- Be aware of available university resources, such as counseling services, campus police, information technology experts, and policies to protect students from harassment and harm, and share them with your student.
- Help the student connect with other researchers doing similar work, using your personal network, relevant mailing lists, professional organizations, etc.
- Support the student if they are harassed; if others in the department are dismissive of their experiences, advocate for their needs and the validity of their work.
- Give the student opportunities to discuss their experiences with you, should they choose.

Recommendations to Supervisors – for those conducting risky research that requires research assistants, postdocs, etc.:

- Consider removing student names from public websites and documents about the project.
- NOTE: it is also important that all project participants are recognized for their work. Ask the student what they prefer. Consider restricting student names to published papers.

- Give students opportunities to participate in other projects. Do not penalize them for choosing not to work on controversial topics.
- Give students opportunities to discuss their experiences with you, should they choose. Let students debrief after any research experience that may be difficult.
- Serve as a point person for all media inquiries and public discussion of your research.

Recommendations to Researchers:

- Before beginning your research, notify your institution that you are engaging in research that may be susceptible to online backlash, and that your advisor, PI, department, university marketing team, etc., may receive negative messages or false information about you.
  - Use our information sheet to educate your institution about online harassment.
  - Talk to campus security about the options available in case you experience harassment.
  - Instruct colleagues and department administrators not to reveal any personal information about you over the phone or via email.
- Explain online harassment to your friends and family, and warn them about the possibility of your research making you vulnerable to online attacks. If you live with a roommate or partner, make sure they are aware that your research activities may make them vulnerable as well, particularly if your home address is compromised.
- Follow the steps in a cybersecurity guide such as the Speak Up and Stay Safe project or Crash Override's interactive guide C.O.A.C.H. to remove personal information (such as your phone number or address) from the internet, protect cloud storage, secure passwords, and so forth.
- Reach out to people doing similar research. Be proactive about building community and having conversations with people who understand your experiences. Invest time and attention into building offline friendships and relationships.
- Take breaks. Switch to less taxing projects. Recharge yourself by enjoying life outside of work.

Access the full report by Alice E. Marwick, Lindsasy Blackwell, and Katherine Lo (2016) here: https://datasociety.net/output/best-practices-for-conducting-risky-research/

References

Chemaly, S. (2016, April 15). Online harassment is a social problem that requires a social response. *Huffington Post.* http://www.huffingtonpost.com/soraya-chemaly/online-harassment-is-abou_b_9702696.html

Duggan, M. (2014). *Online harassment.* Washington, DC: Pew Research Center.

Flaherty, C. (2017, June 19). Threats for what she didn't say. *Inside Higher Ed.* https://www.insidehighered.com/news/2017/06/19/classicist-findsherself-target-online-threats-after-article-ancient-statues

Gardiner, B., Mansfield, M., Anderson, I., Holder, J., Louter, D., & Ulmanu, M. (2016, April 12). The dark side of Guardian comments. *The Guardian.* Retrieved from https://www.theguardian.com/technology/2016/apr/12/the-dark-side-of-guardian-comments

Hess, A. (2014, January 6). Why women aren't welcome on the internet. https://psmag.com/why-women-aren-t-welcome-on-the-internet-aa21fdbc8d6

Marwick, A., Blackwell, L., & Lo, K. (2016). *Best practices for conducting risky research and protecting yourself from online harassment (Data & Society Guide).* New York: Data & Society Research Institute. https://datasociety.net/pubs/res/Best_Practices_for_Conducting_Risky_Research-Oct-2016.pdf

McMillan Cottom, T. (2015). Everything but The Burden: Publics, public scholarship, and institutions. Personal blog.

Parmar, S. (2016). Protecting female journalists online: An international human rights perspective in *Countering Online Abuse of Female Journalists,* Office of the Representative on Freedom of the Media Organization for Security and Co-operation in Europe (OSCE). http://www.osce.org/fom/220411?download=true

Appendix

Resources and Guides for Protecting Yourself and Responding to Harassment

This list is intended to help you protect yourself online as a citizen, journalist, student, and researcher. Although the resources and guides will continue to evolve alongside changes in technology and culture, we hope this list provides you with a starting point for protecting yourself from harassment and finding support if you are the target of harassment. We have included technical guides for protecting your privacy, identity, devices, and data; a limited list of resources and guides to your legal rights; and a list of organizations that provide real-time support, tools, research, and advocacy to fight abuse. The brief descriptions come from the websites for each respective source.

Remember, abuse of any kind is *never* your fault. Help is available and you are not alone.

© The Author(s) 2018
J. R. Vickery, T. Everbach (eds.), *Mediating Misogyny*,
https://doi.org/10.1007/978-3-319-72917-6

Technical Guides to Internet Security & Social Media Safety

- *A Feminist's Guide to Digital Security*

  http://communityred.tumblr.com/post/100186015819/9-ways-to-dodge-trolls-a-feminists-guide-to
  Building a digital safety net for citizen journalists and activists around the world.

- *Best Practices for Conducting Risky Research and Protecting Yourself from Online Harassment*

  https://datasociety.net/pubs/res/Best_Practices_for_Conducting_Risky_Research-Oct-2016.pdf
  The fear of harassment may have a chilling effect on the type of research that is conducted and the capabilities of individual researchers. This document is a set of best practices for researchers—especially junior researchers—who wish to engage in research that may make the researcher susceptible to online harassment.

- *Fight Cyberstalking Social Network Safety Toolkit*

  https://www.fightcyberstalking.org/online-safety-tips/
  Safety and privacy tips for social media, blogs, and Internet business owners.

- *HeartMob Social Media Safety Guides*

  https://iheartmob.org/resources/safety_guides
  User-friendly guides provide information on how to use different platforms' reporting and privacy tools.

- *HeartMob Technical Safety Guide*

  https://iheartmob.org/resources/tech
  This guide will walk you through the immediate steps you need to take
  to feel safe and give you the information you need to make informed
  decisions about creating strong passwords, two-step verification processes, and other privacy and safety tips for sharing information and
  personally identifiable data online.

- *How to Remove Yourself from People Search Websites*

  http://www.zdnet.com/article/how-to-remove-yourself-from-people-
  search-websites/
  People search services provide the general public with a dangerous
  amount of personal information about you. Here's how to opt-out of
  most—for now.

- *Online Safety Guide from Feminist Frequency*

  https://onlinesafety.feministfrequency.com/en/
  Guides to removing potential doxxing information, setting up gaming
  security, password and login security, website security, physical mail
  protections, and more.

- *StaySafeOnline.org*

  https://staysafeonline.org/stay-safe-online/
  Powered by the National Cyber Security Alliance, the resource offers
  practical guides to protect your devices, passwords, data privacy, and
  accounts from hacking, viruses, spyware, and other cyber attacks.

- *Take Back the Tech!*

  https://www.takebackthetech.net/
  Take Back The Tech! is a call to everyone, especially women and girls,
  to take control of technology to end violence against women. It's a

global, collaborative campaign project that highlights the problem of tech-related violence against women, together with research and solutions from different parts of the world. The guides address topics such as privacy and anonymity and safely storing personal data.

Guides to Legal Rights and Protections

* *FBI Internet Crime Complaint Center* (IC3) (U.S.)

  https://www.ic3.gov/default.aspx
  The IC3 accepts online Internet crime complaints either from the actual target or from a third party.

* *HeartMob Guide to Your Rights*

  https://iheartmob.org/resources/rights
  This guide walks you through some key definitions you might need when talking to a lawyer and/or law enforcement, what federal and state laws are there to keep you safe, as well as what to expect if you go to the police. They also include a comparative policy report for how governments across the U.S., Australia, Canada, and the U.K. address online abuse.

* *Responding to Revenge Porn (U.K.)*

  http://www.stoponlineabuse.org.uk/revengepornguide
  Resources for responding to the nonconsensual sharing of your image online.

* *Stop Online Abuse (U.K.)*

  http://www.stoponlineabuse.org.uk/using-the-law
  Guide to legal rights, advice, and action for reporting and responding to online abuse in the U.K.

- U.S. students should contact the *Title IX office* at their local universities if they are being harassed by other students or faculty, either online or offline. Title IX is a federal civil rights law that prohibits discrimination on the basis of sex in educational programs and activities.

Advocacy & Self-Care

- *Committee to Protect Journalists (CPJ)*

  https://cpj.org/2016/04/attacks-on-the-press-responding-to-internet-abuse.php
  CPJ promotes press freedom worldwide and defends the right of journalists to report the news without fear of reprisal. CPJ ensures the free flow of news and commentary by taking action wherever journalists are attacked, imprisoned, killed, kidnapped, threatened, censored, or harassed.

- *Crash Override*

  http://www.crashoverridenetwork.com/
  Crash Override is a crisis helpline, advocacy group, and resource center for people who are experiencing online abuse. It is a network of experts and survivors who work directly with victims, tech companies, lawmakers, media, security experts, and law enforcement to educate and provide direct assistance working to eliminate the causes of online abuse.

- *Cyber Civil Rights Initiative (CCRI)*

  https://www.cybercivilrights.org/
  CCRI fights nonconsensual pornography and other forms of online abuse via victim support and referral services, advocating for legislation, collaborating with the tech industry, and educating the court, lawmakers, and enforcement about the nature and prevalence of online abuse.

- *The Cybersmile Foundation*

  https://www.cybersmile.org/
  Through education and the promotion of positive digital citizenship, the Cybersmile Foundation aims to reduce incidents of cyberbullying. Through professional help and support services, it enables victims and their families to regain control of their lives.

- *Digital Rights Foundation (Pakistan)*

  https://digitalrightsfoundation.pk/
  DRF envisions a place where all people, and especially women, are able to exercise their right of expression without being threatened. Its organizers believe that free Internet with access to information and impeccable privacy policies can encourage such a healthy and productive environment that would eventually help not only women, but the world at large.

- *Fight Cyberstalking*

  https://www.fightcyberstalking.org/
  Resources for reporting a cyberstalker, getting emotional support, and keeping your personal information private.

- *Global Fund for Women*

  https://www.globalfundforwomen.org/
  Global Fund for Women is one of the world's leading foundations for gender equality, standing up for the human rights of women and girls. It campaigns for zero violence, economic and political empowerment, and sexual and reproductive health and rights. Its vision is that every woman and girl is strong, safe, powerful, and heard. No exceptions. It funds and partners with women-led groups who are courageously fighting for justice in their own communities. This rights-based approach gets to the root of gender inequality and is the most effective way to create permanent social change.

- *HeartMob*

  https://iheartmob.org/
  HeartMob is a project of Hollaback!, a nonprofit organization powered by a global network of local activists who are dedicated to ending
  harassment in public spaces. It's a platform that provides real-time
  support to individuals experiencing online harassment and empowers
  bystanders to act.

- *List of International Domestic Abuse Hotlines*

  https://www.7cups.com/forum/DomesticAbuseSupport
  Community_121/DomesticAbuseResourcesandMedia_1045/
  ListofInternationalDomesticAbuseHotlinesContribute_65972/
  A growing list of international domestic abuse hotlines, sorted by con-
  tinent and country. You can help by adding numbers to the list.

- *TrollBusters*

  http://www.troll-busters.com/
  TrollBusters provides just-in-time rescue services to support women
  journalists, bloggers and publishers who are targets of cyberharass-
  ment. It uses its virtual S.O.S. team to send positive memes, endorsements and testimonials into online feeds at the point of attack. It
  dilutes the stings of cyberbullies, trolls and other online pests to support you, your voice, your website, your business and your
  reputation.

- *Women's Media Center Speech Project*

  http://wmcspeechproject.com/online-abuse-101/
  Guide to understanding online abuse, including tactics, defamation,
  doxxing, flaming, hate speech, and more.

Index[1]

---

[1]Note: Page numbers followed by 'n' refer to notes.

© The Author(s) 2018
J. R. Vickery, T. Everbach (eds.), *Mediating Misogyny*,
https://doi.org/10.1007/978-3-319-72917-6

421

Printed by Printforce, the Netherlands